Biopolitics, Materiality and Meaning in Modern European Drama

New Materialisms
Series editors: Iris van der Tuin and Rosi Braidotti

New Materialisms asks how materiality permits representation, actualises ethical subjectivities and innovates the political. The series will provide a discursive hub and an institutional home to this vibrant emerging field and open it up to a wider readership.

Editorial Advisory board
Marie-Luise Angerer, Karen Barad, Corinna Bath, Barbara Bolt, Felicity Colman, Manuel DeLanda, Richard Grusin, Vicki Kirby, Gregg Lambert, Nina Lykke, Brian Massumi, Henk Oosterling, Arun Saldanha

Books available
What If Culture Was Nature All Along?
Edited by Vicki Kirby
Critical and Clinical Cartographies: Architecture, Robotics, Medicine, Philosophy
Edited by Andrej Radman and Heidi Sohn
Architectural Materialisms: Non-Human Creativity
Edited by Maria Voyatzaki
Placemaking: A New Materialist Theory of Pedagogy
Tara Page
Queer Defamiliarisation: Writing, Mattering, Making Strange
Helen Palmer
Biopolitics, Materiality and Meaning in Modern European Drama
Hedwig Fraunhofer

Books forthcoming
How Literature Comes to Matter: Post-Anthropocentric Approaches to Fiction
Edited by Sten Pultz Moslund, Marlene Karlsson Marcussen and Martin Karlsson Pedersen
Visit the series web page at: edinburghuniversitypress.com/series/nmat

Biopolitics, Materiality and Meaning in Modern European Drama

Hedwig Fraunhofer

EDINBURGH
University Press

Edinburgh University Press is one of the leading university presses in the UK. We publish academic books and journals in our selected subject areas across the humanities and social sciences, combining cutting-edge scholarship with high editorial and production values to produce academic works of lasting importance. For more information visit our website: edinburghuniversitypress.com

Edinburgh University Press Ltd
The Tun – Holyrood Road
12(2f) Jackson's Entry
Edinburgh EH8 8PJ

First published in hardback by Edinburgh University Press 2020

Typeset in 11/13 Adobe Sabon by
IDSUK (DataConnection) Ltd

A CIP record for this book is available from the British Library

ISBN 978 1 4744 6743 8 (hardback)
ISBN 978 1 4744 6744 5 (paperback)
ISBN 978 1 4744 6745 2 (webready PDF)
ISBN 978 1 4744 6746 9 (epub)

Contents

Acknowledgements

Materialist philosophy in the neo-Spinozist tradition is about unexpected encounters and about networks of relations. 'It is through relation that we derive greater potential, intensify our powers of existence', Brian Massumi writes. It is thus time for me to thank the people that have helped make this book become a reality. Ken Calhoon, Wolfgang Sohlich, Linda Kintz and Forest (Tres) Pyle first inspired my love of philosophy and drama many years ago. I owe Eric Santner and the participants of his 2013 DAAD seminar, 'Economies of Desire: Political Economy and Libidinal Economy in German Culture and Thought', one of the main ideas of this book: the argument that an often one-sided analysis focused on meaning *or* materiality has failed to capture the complexities of European modernity and modern theatre. The 2014 SLSA in Turin, Italy organised by Cristina Iuli introduced me to Roberto Esposito's work, and I thank the crowded public transportation system in Turin for giving me the opportunity to stand next to and chat with Tim Campbell, Esposito's English translator and among other things the co-editor, with Adam Sitze, of *Biopolitics: A Reader*. David Levin's 2017 DAAD faculty seminar at the University of Chicago taught me much about Performance Theory and Performance Practice and helped me bridge the disciplinary gap between drama studies and theatre or performance studies. Branka Arsič taught me to think of the flesh as a material concept that travels between the realms of nature and culture – or better, throughout the natureculture continuum. Over the years, Dagmar Herzog, Julie Johnson, Mariatte Denman, Gray Kochhar-Lindgren, Mark Freed (especially), Susan Cumings, Dwight Call, Myron Avila, Ana Baginski, Katja Herges, Mark Causey and others read and provided valuable feedback on my work. Muriel Cormican and Monika Fischer wrote letters of support. I thank Oliver Aas for his thoughts on old and new materialism and Sarah Bezan for her book tips and modelling how to 'slay the dragon' in her own, inspiring work. During a time when my writing confidence was at a low point, Miriam Piilonen invited me for coffee and simply said: 'I like it.' The prize for Best Review of Recent Publications at an Academic Book Exhibit goes to Daniel

Gilfillan at the 2017 SLSA conference at Arizona State. I thank my home institution, Georgia College, for the faculty development funds supporting my travel to conferences as well as my participation in the 2016 School of Criticism and Theory at Cornell University. Kirsty Woods at Edinburgh University Press, Bruce Gentry and Jennifer Townes shared their knowledge of book contracts and copyright issues with me. Carol Macdonald, Senior Commissioning Editor at EUP, was the most professional and encouraging editor any author could hope for. I thank James Dale and Peter Williams, my copy editors, for their prompt responses and thoroughness. The rigorous review process at EUP and the Readers' expert suggestions taught me much and helped make this book what it is. I thank Iris van der Tuin for her unflagging support of this project. Iris, Rosi Braidotti and the people they work with have indeed put the new materialist ethics of generosity and care into real-life practice. I thank *gender forum* (University of Cologne, Germany), where an earlier and shorter version of my Sartre chapter was published, and Östlings Bokförlag Symposion in Stockholm, which published my earlier work on Strindberg, for their permission to reproduce these materials. I am grateful to my friends and my students for their love and cheer. Finally, I thank Roy Cordell for his infectious enthusiasm; he already called this project my 'book' when I was still afraid he was going to jinx it. I am thankful to Alycia Cordell for her emotional intelligence and listening skills. The irrepressible Isabella Jones is the joy of my life. I dedicate this book to them.

Introduction: Anxious Flesh

... Bruno Latour ... argues that one of the originary impulses of modernity is the project of 'partitioning,' or deepening the imaginary gulf between Nature and Culture ... Yet ... the project of partitioning has always been contested, and never more so than at the inception, and nowhere more vigorously than in places that were in the vanguard of modernity. (Ghosh 2016: 68–9)

Matter and meaning are not separate elements ... Mattering is simultaneously a matter of substance and significance ... Meaning is neither intralinguistically conferred nor simply extralinguistically referenced. Meaning is made possible through specific material practices ... There is a need to understand the laws of nature as well as the law of the father. But understanding and reworking different disciplinary apparatuses in isolation won't suffice. Intra-actions matter. 'Not simply intervene, enact the between.' (Barad 2007: 3, 148, 222, 359; citation marks in original)

You start with the in-betweenness ... If there is one key term, that's it: relation. When you start in-between, what you're in the middle of is a region of relation ... we're in affect, affect is not in us. It's not the subjective content of our human lives. It's the felt quality of a relational field that is always 'more than' ... and always more-than human. (Massumi 2015b: 48, 124)

The time is coming when it will hardly be possible to write a book of philosophy as it has been done for so long ... The search for new means of philosophical expression was begun by Nietzsche and must be pursued today in relation to the renewal of certain other arts, such as the theatre or the cinema. (Deleuze 1994: xxi)

A human body convulsing in a lethal epileptic fit. A protagonist who dies crawling on all fours while protesting 'I am not a rat'. Black fleshy flies that infest a city. Spectators shaking with hysterical laughter. What do these bodies have in common? Literal and emblematic, these corporeal and material manifestations – these 'marks on bodies'[1] – express the anxiety pervading modern Europe. Linked to fear, one of the forty-eight affects identified by the seventeenth-century Dutch philosopher Baruch Spinoza, anxiety diminishes the body's ability to act. Yet this anxiety is performed, with differing theatrical means and by different kinds of bodies, in plays by August Strindberg, Bertolt Brecht, Jean-Paul Sartre and Antonin Artaud. The concept of affect – the affective intensities, the constantly changing tonality in a connected network that can include its sedimentation as human emotions, but cannot be reduced to them[2] – this concept of affect is central to posthumanist, new materialist philosophy.[3] The enactment of affect is also central to the plays presented here.

Yet another concept central to this study is the concept of the flesh. Like anxiety – an affect as well as a psychosomatic condition – the flesh is corporeal or physical, but it is also more than that. It is what Jacques Derrida called 'the becoming-body' (Derrida 1994: 6). As Diana Coole and Samantha Frost have argued in their edited anthology, *New Materialisms*, 'materiality is always something more than "mere" matter: an excess, force, vitality, relationality, or difference that renders matter active, self-creative, productive, unpredictable' (Coole and Frost 2010: 9).[4] The feminist and posthumanist scholar Rosi Braidotti underlines this liveliness of materiality in her conceptualisation of *zōē* – the pre-individual or impersonal self-organising and affirmative life force exceeding the limits of human consciousness and hegemony (Braidotti 2012: 22).[5] In new materialist philosophy, materiality is continuous processual excess. Affect is excess.[6] Life is excess.[7]

The ontological indeterminacy or 'threatening' dynamic unpredictability of this excess – of a materiality that collapses the dualistic oppositions of the rationalist western philosophical tradition and especially the conceptual bifurcation between nature and culture – is at the heart of this book. In theatre, this excessive flesh expresses itself on and through the bodies of human and nonhuman actors and spectators and in the materiality and tonality of the theatrical space. In the bodies of actors and spectators and in the elements and conditions of theatrical production, the aesthetic and quotidian intra-act[8] in a common affect (or common, entangled affects).

A Story, a Cartography, a Tour

Co-constituted by the enmeshed, onto-epistemological realms of materiality and meaning, the flesh is also a concept with a long philosophical and theological heritage. Following Donna Haraway's concept of *naturecultures*, Celia Roberts writes: 'there can be no reference to biology . . . that is not a story, connected to other stories' (Roberts 2007: 105). In my view, this statement applies not only to biology, but also to the more-than-biological.

The flesh is what marks the convergence of the material and the semiotic worlds. In Eric Santner's words, the flesh is located at the 'jointure of the somatic and the normative dimensions of human life' (Santner 2016: 238), demonstrating the inability to keep these two realms – the body and the discursive – apart. In her essay on Gilles Deleuze, 'Teratologies', Braidotti describes the 'enfleshed' Deleuzian subject in similar, but (in contrast to Santner) post-anthropocentric terms, as 'rather an "in-between"', as 'a folding-in of external influences and a simultaneous unfolding outwards of affects' (Braidotti 2000: 159). The (human or nonhuman) subject is not given in advance, but materialises at this threshold, 'in the spaces that flow and connect the binaries' (Braidotti 2013: 164). The flesh examined in my study is thus not ontologically stable, but is produced by and dynamically intra-acts with the many non-linear, polycentred material and affective shifts that mark modern Europe and the modern stage.

The flesh that is my focus is the product of a story and itself contributes to this story. In democratic modernity, the king's sublime body loses its transcendence and is replaced by the people's body and an immanence that leaves a remainder, a surplus: the flesh. During the structural shift from premodern Europe to modernity and the anxieties that accompany this transition, this surplus energy manifests on modern bodies as extreme restlessness, as a restless search for new forms of community and affective affiliations. The stresses once absorbed by the ruler's body now press on and express themselves on or as the flesh of every subject (Santner 2016). In 1947, W. H. Auden published his hundred-page-long poem 'The Age of Anxiety'. For our contemporary times, in the 2017 *New York Times* article, 'Prozac Nation Is Now the United States of Xanax', Alex Williams refers to the wave of recent 'anxiety memoirs'. Pointing to the imbrication of medicine and culture in anxiety as a condition, Williams writes: 'Anxiety has become our everyday argot, our thrumming lifeblood' (Williams 2017: 1–2). From 2004 to 2019, the suicide rate in the United States has increased 30 per cent.[9] Using the medical language of contagion, the media are speaking of an 'epidemic'. My study as well goes beyond anxiety as an exclusively interior condition. Its focus is the theatre, one of the biopolitical spaces of modernity that create 'a kind of experimental space in which bodies are subject to mostly invisible torments and the viewer is variously interpellated as scientist, tormentor, complicit bystander, voyeur' (Santner 2011: 139–40). The stage, in other words, is a microcosm of modernity, a biopolitical space that co-produces and manages bodies, a space that – in Michel Foucault's words – fosters life or disavows it to the point of death.[10] Like

Auden's poem, the plays in this study show us that anxiety is not a new phenomenon brought on by our contemporary media consumption, by helicopter parents, terrorism, wars, economic or political upheavals (and agitation) or the climate crisis (all good enough reasons in themselves to feel anxious). Instead, our most recent iteration of what the US National Institute of Mental Health (NIH) calls Generalized Anxiety Disorder (GAD) is – like the anxieties enacted by the plays presented here – part of the ever-fluid quotidian experience of modernity.

This book is thus a project about materiality, about what can be perceived through the senses; but it is also a project about de-materialisation, about the invisible or imperceptible. As my focus on the flesh already indicates, what interests me is indeed the very tension between materiality and abstraction. What all of the plays selected enact is not just mechanistic 'matter'; it is instead a materiality that is alive. But some of the plays presented also enact the threat posed by a crisis of symbolic representation or meaning that expresses itself materially, in the flesh.

Based on the conceptualisation of both materiality and social identities as enmeshed, never pre-given, stable or static, but always vital, becoming, mobile and multiple, this project unpacks connections: it unpacks the diffractive connections among (1) the larger material-discursive transformations in post-eighteenth century transnational European modernity, (2) their historically and geographically specific/ localised material, scientific and discursive environments or conditions, and (3) their iterative expressions in dramatic texts and theatrical performances, that is in aesthetic objects or signposts that are very much part of and – as *dispositifs* or apparatuses – themselves co-constitute, enable and sustain the intra-active immanent relations that brought them about. The descriptive, decelerated readings in this study take seriously the agentive processual materiality of the dramatic texts and theatrical visions selected. They present Strindberg's naturalist dramatic work, with a special focus on *Fordringsägare (Creditors)* (1889), Brecht's *Baal* (1920), Artaud's *Les Cenci (The Cenci)* (1935) and Sartre's *Les Mouches (The Flies)* (1943). My reading of Artaud's *Les Cenci* in particular follows the aims of post-critique by 'restor[ing] the temporality to the analytic axis', as Stephen Best (following Paul Ricœur) calls it, following how the play ' "discloses itself" aesthetically' (Best 2017: 342). For the purposes of this project, the plays described act as entry points into or as nonhuman actors/actants in a dynamic network or topology of four spatiotemporal locations or assemblages that map the movement of complex and entangled materialities, ideas and affects across modern Europe. In this endeavour I take my inspiration from

Deleuze and Guattari's description, in *A Thousand Plateaus*, of what a map does:

> A rhizome is . . . a map and not a tracing . . . What distinguishes the map from the tracing is that it is entirely oriented toward an experimentation in contact with the real . . . It fosters connections between fields . . . The map is open and connectable in all its dimensions; it is detachable, reversible, susceptible to constant modification. It can be torn, reversed, adapted to any kind of mounting, reworked by an individual, group or social formation . . . A map has multiple entryways, as opposed to the tracing, which always comes back 'to the same.' The map has to do with performance, whereas the tracing always involves an alleged 'competence'. (Quoted by Groot Nibbelink 2019: 88)

Rather than mirroring a fixed, already existing reality, my practice aims to co-create heterogeneous processes, providing an open-ended reworking of European modernity and its moveable parts, an always provisional staging and reshaping of what Liesbeth Groot Nibbelink calls 'a complex and dynamic set of interrelationships of natural processes, histories, local stories, and economic or political forces' (2019: 88).

Engaging with the scientific theories and popular concerns of the late nineteenth century, Strindberg's naturalistic dramas enact the anxiety related to the renegotiation of the status of the human following the publication of Charles Darwin's theory of evolution. At the *fin de siècle*, the loss of human exceptionalism in the natural sciences intra-acts with the socio-political crisis of symbolic male authority in modernity. An emerging posthumanism and the crisis of gender, that is ontological and socio-political questions, converge. Sartre's early existentialist work exemplified by *Les Mouches*, on the other hand, posits a fetishised and phobic notion of human consciousness that wins out over the border-crossing threat posed by a pre-existing gendered, but ultimately nonhuman materiality (the flies). Sartre's philosophical, novelistic and dramatic work frames the question of human existential freedom in the context of threatening matter. By contrast, Brecht's lesser-known early theatrical work, and notably his first full-length play, *Baal*, enacts a transgressive unity with material-natural life. Finally, my last chapters propose a reading of Artaud's theoretical and theatrical work of the 1930s, specifically his most famous play, *Les Cenci*, through the lens of new materialism. Artaud's work provides a dynamic affective network, a performative assemblage[11] of human and nonhuman actors or actants, (human) spectators and organic (organism-based) and inorganic forces and energies that transverses the binary distinction between materiality and mind, aesthetic perception and meaning.[12]

In performance, as theatre scholar Hans-Thies Lehmann reminds us, dramatic texts serve as one of the elements – as the 'material' – of scenic production, but they do not, or not necessarily, play the dominant role (Lehmann 1999: 13).[13] Lehmann emphasises (what others would call) the materialsemiotic intra-connectedness not only of the written text and the aesthetic performance, but also of the theatre and society. This intra-connectedness includes the social nature of production involving an audience, public financing, the community's and critics' reception, and the play's relationality with social norms of perception and behaviour (Lehmann 1999: 16). The latter is an aspect I will also emphasise in my study. I agree with Christian J. Emden, who calls for a new materialist account of norms, pointing out that, in John Protevi's words, 'we are owed an account of the emergence of normativity in material conditions and [. . .] that account should show how the political and ethical world engage with the material' (Protevi 2017, referencing Emden 2017: 273). In contrast to Lehmann's work, my readings will therefore ultimately move towards an assertion of sociality as a human *and* more-than-human network and sociality.

All of the plays assembled here enact the threshold of the flesh, the human and the more-than-human, and the role of material-social life in modernity. Located at the border, the flesh transcends dualisms. What constitutes such a threat in the plays presented – what contributes to the characters', actors' and spectators' anxiety – is the growing indistinction in modernity of the dualistic categories that had marked western society since antiquity. Public and private, human and more-than-human, materiality and meaning collapse in a common life.

Nomadic Transpositions, or How I Learned to Love New Materialism

My project about the modern collapse of binary dichotomies is first of all inspired by Rosi Braidotti's concept of nomadic subjectivity. According to Braidotti, nomadic subjectivity is, in contradistinction to classical philosophy, 'a nonbinary way of positing the relationship between same and other, between different categories of living beings, and ultimately between life and death' (Braidotti 2010: 209). Braidotti's posthumanist project based on a Nietzschean and Spinozist ethics of affirmation proposes to move away from advanced capitalism's 'logic of claims and compensations' (Braidotti 2010: 212) and with it from the academic critique of the negative, for instance in gender and critical race studies. But while Braidotti is correct that certain historical wrongs are beyond repair and meaning, I am also wondering if an ethics of affirmation that posits a posthuman depersonalisation of the event as the ultimate ethical challenge (Braidotti 2010: 213) is completely feasible for my project. As we seek to move beyond the poststructuralist 'cultural' or 'linguistic turn' through a renewed engagement with materiality, does such depersonalisation, by de-emphasising humans' embodied, material experience, run the risk of leading to further abstraction? On the other hand, is the search for material tangibles ultimately a renewed search for immediacy, for access to the real?

There are no easy answers to these questions. Braidottti's assessment that the cultural turn's focus on identity has ultimately just been another idealism seems at least partially accurate. But is it necessarily accurate? While Rick Dolphijn and Iris van der Tuin are correct in pointing out that identity politics involve dualism (Dolphijn and van der Tuin 2012: 87), is this true for *all* identity politics?[14] In other words, does it matter *how* we conduct identity studies? Does a critical focus on difference as social otherness (gender, sexuality, class, race and so on) necessarily stand in opposition to the new conceptualisation of difference as a 'process of becoming' in new materialism (Braidotti 2012: 16)? Does such a focus on social alterity necessarily repeat and reinforce the dualist, anthropocentric focus on human, ego-indexed notions of subjectivity? Or can we link a critique of humans' problematic relationship to certain human others to an exploration of the role traditionally ascribed to the nonhuman? Is it possible to apply a transversal of the identity dichotomies in western thought to our relationships with nonhumans – to nonhuman animals, plants, bio-systems and inorganic matter? Put differently, can an investigation of the nonhuman extend – rather than oppose – our analysis of human subjectivity without necessarily giving primacy to the latter? Braidotti suggests as much when she points to the 'transversal connections between sexual, social, racial, and species inequalities' and 'the interdependent nature of structural inequalities' (2011: 91), or when she proposes relocating sexual difference from being a boundary marker to becoming 'a threshold for the elaboration and the expression of multiple differences, which extend beyond gender but also beyond the human' (2011: 80). If what is in question in our rejection of identity is the *fixity*, the pre-existing, ontologically inherent and independent boundedness of identity or subjectivity, such an anti-essentialist critique has already been central to poststructuralist analyses, for instance to gender and sexuality studies, critical race studies, or theories of the subject-in-process (Kristeva) or gender as performance (Butler).[15] If identity or subjectivity is in process, it is so because it is in interaction (or even in mutually constitutive intra-action) with some sort of environment. In fact, have not the important humanist theories of the nineteenth century from Marx to Darwin and Freud already to a certain extent been theories of the interconnectedness of the world? Leibniz, who is considered one of the 'forefathers' of today's posthumanist philosophies and who sees the world as an entangled mesh, also laid the groundwork for psychoanalytic theories of the unconscious (Kissler 2016: 20, 28), thus collapsing a view of new materialist philosophies and Freud as incompatible.[16] Rather than treating them as pre-existing identity categories, my own study maps the emergence and flux of concepts of gender and sexuality within multiple heterogeneous (socio-political, economic and material) assemblages traversing (and transversing) the human AND nonhuman realm in the theatrical practices of the end of the nineteenth and the beginning of the twentieth century.

In addition to 'identity', it is equally important not to essentialise 'matter' or materiality in a unitary way. In the introduction to her edited collection on *Mattering: Feminism, Science, and Materialism*, Victoria Pitts-Taylor expresses her interest in 'mattering's differential distributions' (2016: 16), that is in the ways in which matter is 'involved in, or shot through with sex/gender, class, race, nation, citizenship, and other stratifications'. How, Pitts-Taylor asks, do power relations 'materialize in bodies, corporeal processes, and environments?' (2016: 2). In other words, can we 'think power and ontology together?' (Pitts-Taylor 2016: 12).

Rather than abandoning critique altogether, I suggest that there is a link – a continuity, intersectionality or transversality – between the anti-speciesism and nature/culture debates of recent posthumanism or the recent 'new' or 'object-oriented' emphases on materialism (the critique, really, of human exceptionalism) on the one hand and critical race studies or gender and sexuality studies on the other hand. Barad puts it succinctly: '[I]sn't the undoing of the very idea of an inherent nature-culture boundary a useful tool, if not a prerequisite, for destabilizing sexism, racism, and homophobia and other social ills that are propped up by this dualism and its derivatives?' (Barad 2007: 368–9) In his groundbreaking article 'Thing Theory' (the introduction to the 2001 special issue of *Critical Theory* on 'Things'), Bill Brown also comments on Adorno already: 'Most simply put, his point is that accepting the otherness of things is the condition for accepting otherness as such' (cited by Jacoby 2015). Moreover, the argument that there can be a relationality between the cultural critique of (initially postmodernist) queer studies and contemporary work in new materialism and ecocriticism is corroborated by the emergence in recent years of the field of queer ecology and performativity (such as the work of Timothy Morton, Karen Barad, Wendy Arons and Theresa May, and others).[17] As this book will show, my own work shares with queer ecology the provenance from gender and sexuality studies and the critique of biopower informed by Foucault.[18] It shares with queer ecology a focus on contingent co-constitutive relations between beings and phenomena; the transversal of pre-existing, stable identity concepts, dualistic boundaries and normativity; and an understanding of the imminent threat of ecological disaster. While I continue to use some of poststructuralist feminism's terms such as 'alterity' in this study in order to reconfigure nineteenth- and early twentieth-century worldviews to whom biopolitical identity categories such as gender, race and nature were central, I ultimately see sexuality not only in terms of individuated libidinal desire or as a biopolitical category in Foucault's sense. In addition, sexuality is also a more-than-human vital force or deterritorialising surplus that includes the individual ego, but also decentres and exceeds it.[19]

In new materialist thinking, 'otherness' or alterity is thus ultimately replaced by the concept of entanglement.[20] In other words, while NM does not stop talking about race or gender for instance, social inequalities are addressed as 'physical arrangements embodied in and through the apparatuses that produce, frame, and give them meaning' (Davis 2017: 116, paraphrasing Barad 2007: 128–9). Theatre is such an apparatus physically embodying social-material encounters. As we will see, the stories of gender and sexuality, the stories of material forces, the human and the nonhuman are deeply enmeshed. The contemporary Italian philosopher Roberto Esposito has recognised the central role of race in biopolitics. In my project, I establish the relationship between biopolitics, the story of species and the story of gender and sexuality. To cite Morton, 'the lineage that brought us slavery and racism is also the lineage that brought us the anthropocentric boundary between human and nonhuman' (2012b: 167). My study will demonstrate that the lineage that brought us gender and heteronormativity is part of this very same problematic as well. As I will show for the period examined in my study – the time leading up to early twentieth-century European fascisms – gender, sexuality, race and human exceptionalism are all linked.

Put differently, do Bruno Latour's, Rita Felski's or Braidotti's warnings against negativity,[21] in spite of the promise of their affirmative visions, not just establish another binary logic – between affirmative or reparative work and negative, 'paranoid' or 'suspicious' critique (including readings influenced by Marx and Freud)?[22] And is there a way to transverse yet another dualism: the perceived *analytical* divide between identity/subjectivity and matter, that is the very same dichotomy of which some new materialists accuse postmodernism (with its alleged privileging of language), but that we can arguably also find (with the reverse privileging of materiality) in some (though not all) more recent work? Is this analytical divide between materiality and meaning not just another replay of the rationalist tradition's division of matter and mind? Is meaning necessarily normative and equivocal/exclusionary? I submit that meaning is not necessarily anthropocentric, that it is a term that can also apply to nonhuman entities, in terms of meanings that these diverse subjects effect or relationally contribute to effecting, rather than a meaning that is imposed by the human subject on the nonhuman object in order to give order to the world.

I continue to wonder, however, if a complete abandonment of critique would not fail to give a voice to the actual, material suffering of human and nonhuman bodies and to the material damage done to the environment. I am concerned that the posthumanist attempt to move beyond the philosophical hegemony of the human may run the risk of overlooking the fact that not all humans enjoy such hegemonic status. Is the embodied, material suffering of these deprivileged humans not itself a product of this hegemony? My concern is that we might also leave these humans behind – marginalised humans that themselves have been treated as objects – if we choose to move towards a purely post-human focus. As Pitts-Taylor confirms, 'the turn to matter/ing raises a host of new questions for feminists and others concerned with politics, or power, inequality, and suffering' (2016: 7).[23]

Demonstrating the variety of current work in new materialisms and related fields, Claire Colebrook, for instance, asks rhetorically: 'Should we really be asking about normativity, values, identity and self-maintenance in an era of climate change, when this very *self*-furtherance and myopia threatens not only human existence but life in general?' (2015: 48, emphasis in original). Anthropocentric instrumentalisation has certainly got humans and the planet into the pickle that we are in today. I question, however, if we are really ready to – and if we should – completely move beyond Enlightenment notions of human accountability in spite of our more qualified contemporary understanding of notions of autonomy and agency. Does the abandonment of negativity – including a critical reassessment of what has gone wrong in the past, conceptually and materially – not run the risk of ahistoricity or 'historical amnesia' (Braidotti 2011: 176)? I do believe that we should not abandon the attempt to reconceptualise historically contingent entanglements through reconfigurations that undo 'the static authority of the past' (Braidotti 2011: 2). If we realise that human timelines are only part of and dependent upon other, non-teleological and non-linear, zigzagging and open-ended timelines or rhythms of becoming on a variety of scales, I trust that historical genealogy does not necessarily place humans in a position of active mastery, as Colebrook (2014: 129) suggests. Rather than seeing memory or remembrance in purely human terms, I suggest conceptualising them instead as an affective force or a collective process of becoming that goes beyond the individual.[24]

While I agree with Vicky Kirby's warning against 'the Cartesian reflex of thinking "about" (subject versus object)' (2017: 22), it seems to me that academic writing or philosophy might no longer be feasible if we forgo any attempt to know or understand, if we view our endeavours as purely ontological rather than epistemological. As Pitts-Taylor reminds us, both Haraway and Barad refuse to 'demarcate epistemology and ontology' (2016: 9).[25] On the one hand I agree with Graham Harman that, in Steven Shaviro's words, 'an object can never be equated with, or reduced to, our knowledge of it' (Shaviro 2015: 38). But I also side with Shaviro when he argues that '[t]here is no reason why overcoming what [Quentin] Meillassoux calls "the correlation between thinking and being" should require the extirpation of thought (or knowledge or experience) altogether' (Shaviro 2015: 24).[26] I argue that such a limitation of the concept of 'knowledge' to human forms of knowledge is in itself a problematic case of anthropocentrism.[27] In *The Posthuman*, Braidotti refers to Latour's epistemological work exploring 'how knowledge is produced by networks of human and non-human actors, things and objects' (2013: 5).[28] Resonant with new materialism's focus on embodied processes and practices, theatre scholar Una Chaudhuri similarly reminds us that knowledge does not always have to be purely cognitive.[29] As Barad puts it, '[b]rain cells are not the only ones that hold memories, respond to stimuli, or think thoughts' (2007: 379). Chaudhuri speaks of 'a kind of somatic knowledge', 'a way of understanding the other by going beyond rationalizations and abstractions to embodiment and physicalization' – an embodied empathy that performance and theatre allow us to share (2017a: 161).[30] In her reading of the play *War Horse*, Chaudhuri establishes the value of such an endeavour for theatre: 'This is a story about how hard it is to know the other animals, and yet how vital, how rewarding, how *literally unspeakable* and therefore how *theatrically necessary* it is to try' (2017a: 192, emphasis in original).

Somewhat paradoxically, given object-ontology's assumption of objects' withdrawn status, Harman 'argues that things think when they interact, or enter into relations, with other things' (Shaviro 2015: 40–1). I wonder, tongue-in-cheek, how Harman knows that, given objects' inaccessibility[31] (except through aesthetic experience), that is I wonder if object-oriented ontology's (OOO's) assumption of matter's unmediated transparency is not itself ultimately only a new essentialism (as fellow object-oriented ontologist Morton himself acknowledges; see 2016: 72). But I also take this statement as a starting point to ask why we humans should be excluded from being considered as things in this sense. We humans also think when we interact (or intra-act) with other things. OOO in fact agrees.[32] We are part of what we seek to understand. In the move from realist-naturalist theatre to the 'historical avant-garde' of the early nineteenth century, modern theatre as well increasingly overcomes the division between the spectators and the stage, between subject and object.

Dramatic and Post-Dramatic Theatre

The questions discussed so far concern both philosophy and aesthetics, in a study focused on theatre. In this context, it is then also fair to ask if the current disciplinary gap can be breached between (philosophically inflected) drama studies on the one hand and theatre or performance studies on the other hand, a field focused on aesthetic experience. Given the preference for aesthetic perception over anthropocentric representation, of diffraction over reflection/mimesis, in new materialism and its related fields, should we forgo a focus on language and philosophy, that is should we de-emphasise the verbal or textual side of theatre, its traditional western foundation in (human) dialogue and semantic reference? Should we do so in favour of the primary focus on aesthetic perception and non-mimetic theatrical performance that characterises for instance what Lehmann has called the 'post-dramatic' theatre of the last third of the twentieth century? As Elinor Fuchs has argued (2011: 66), however, a return to narrative marks recent theatre and even some postdramatic work itself, destabilising the opposition established by Lehmann between the 'dramatic', humanist-realist/naturalist tradition and the historical and new avant-gardes of the early twentieth century and post-1960s 'post-dramatic' theatre.[33]

My own study presents plays from both traditions, that is from the realist-naturalist tradition on the one hand, represented by Strindberg and Sartre, and from the 'historical avant-garde', exemplified by Brecht and Artaud. Here, I again posit that in terms of methodology, a focus on materiality/the performance on the one side and attention to meaning/ signification on the other side are not mutually exclusive. My project aims to productively utilise tensions between this and other seemingly contradictory paradigms, an objective or practice again also shared by some new materialists, such as Hanna Meißner (2016: 46). As *philosophies* about *aesthetic perception*, new materialism and other posthumanist philosophies are, I argue, in an advantaged position to traverse the described gap between philosophy and performance studies. Given that, as Harman reminds us (2009: 47–51), Latour has advised us to think of objects not in terms of substances but rather as performances, theatre is in a prime position to benefit from the philosophical insights of the material turn – and the material turn from theatre.

What is ultimately at stake here – another way of framing the dichotomies discussed – is the relation between (linguistic) signifier and (aesthetic) sign. While Colebrook, following Deleuze, opposes what she sees as postmodernism's transcendental privileging of the signifier, she is not against what she calls 'various regimes of signs, with formal language being one of them. A sign, for Deleuze and Guattari, is not other than life, not an order imposed on life, but a relation within, or of, life' (2014: 234). How does this distinction relate to theatre? According to Colebrook, 'all perception is (a) sexual or desiring, (b) a sign, because the difference encountered must be read'. But when she gets to '[all perception is] (c) anti-interpretative, because this reading or perceiving does not posit a meaning behind what it perceives but creates a body and relation, a territory of assemblage, and (d) expressive, because these signs, perceptions and strivings are not signs of a life that lies outside them, for life is just this striving, perceiving whole' (2014: 234–5), things get a bit confusing. Apparently, 'meaning' or 'interpretation' are, for Colebrook, tantamount to an anthropocentric imposition of hierarchical order onto the nonhuman world (2014: 237). Colebrook sees a referential use of language, the link between (privileged) signifier and the (deprivileged) 'outside' signified, as fraught with the same problems – a reading that is compatible with the view, in theatre studies, of the realist-mimetic, 'dramatic' tradition as anthropocentric. Colebrook's understanding of signs on the other hand does resonate with Artaud's theory of a material theatre presented in this book. But what do we mean then by 'reading' in 'the difference encountered must be read'?

What Colebrook has in mind is 'a mode of thinking that operates without a normative image of thought' (2014: 236), that is a conception of thought that is not necessarily human. As Elizabeth A. Wilson writes in 'Organic Empathy: Feminism, Psychopharmaceuticals, and the Embodiment of Depression', '[b]iology too can decipher, parse, and appraise' (2008: 387). While maintaining a distinction between the semiotic and the nonsemiotic, Ian Bogost (paraphrasing Levi Bryant) rules out neither narrative nor discourse, suggesting that 'our work need not exclude signs, narrative, and discourse', but that 'we ought also to approach the nonsemiotic world on its own terms as best we can' (Bogost 2015: 86). As my study of modernist theatre will show, a play on the stage is always more than just written text or spoken language. My goal in this project is to provide a network of dramatic/theatrical texts as 'special bodies' in Jane Bennett's sense, open textual and aesthetic bodies that help connect humans and matter; such texts or performances 'help us feel more of the liveliness hidden in [a variety of bodies] and reveal more of the threads of connection binding our fate to theirs' (Bennett 2010a: 234–5).

Concepts and Approaches: The Rift

Aware of the pitfalls, this book then aims to cut across binary methodologies – mind and matter, identity and materiality, epistemology (knowledge/how 'we' know, with 'we' traditionally read as 'we humans') and ontology (being/what exists or is becoming), critique and affirmative writing, dramatic and post-dramatic theatre. The book specifically applies this transversal approach to a rewriting – a reworking or reconfiguring – of modernity, passing through and beyond the very dualisms and hierarchies that are so central to modern thought itself. While there is certainly no shortage of valuable and valid theories explaining modernity, I first suggest that existing modernisation theories have nevertheless been unnecessarily one-sided. Having exclusively focused on questions of (human) identity, representation and meaning on the one hand, or on material factors (such as capitalism, the sciences and technology) on the other, these theories have had difficulty fully capturing the complex material-discursive forces that have shaped modernity. These forces also include the multifaceted pressures that co-produced *fin-de-siècle* and early twentieth-century European theatre and society leading up to modernity's crisis point, totalitarianism. While Braidotti affirms one of the Greek terms for life, *zōē* – which she defines as the productive energy that flows across all species and across cosmic life – as the basis of a new, post-anthropocentric worldview, my book surveys the problematic relationship of western modernity to this human and more-than-human alterity, establishing a dialogue between Braidotti's ontology and Agamben's work on biopolitics, and ultimately moving beyond difference as pejoration towards affirming difference.[34]

The problematic, biopolitical human relationship to difference as pejoration reached its phobic extreme under modern European fascisms. In her essay 'Postmodernism Is a Humanism: Deleuze and Equivocity', Colebrook cites totalitarianisms as an example of equivocal ontologies, where 'signifiers imprison and order a life that in itself remains radically other or phantasmatic'. Although not politically fascist, this is what *some* of the plays in this study do: they attempt to fend off a phantasmatic zoological life that presents the perceived threat constituted by radical, nonhuman alterity. Colebrook speaks of a 'gap' that 'opens a symbolic order that both produces and precludes its mourned outside' (2014: 214). My study problematises this gap in greater detail, exploring how it relates to modernity and in particular to modern theatre practices.

Colebrook reads this ontology as not only postmodern, but also equivocal (that is in its extreme, totalitarian). Rather than doing away with the concept of symbolic worlds altogether, however, I view what we used to call 'the' symbolic (that is human culture) as part of the material-social cosmic environment. I see no reason why the human naturaldiscursive sphere, including human language, cannot be seen as part of human-and-more-than-human materialsocial relations and sign systems. The concept of the 'flesh' and its permutations that interest me in this project mark this imbrication of the material and signification or meaning, and (again) the impossibilty of keeping these two spheres apart. My project explores among other things the relationships between theatre, fascism and what Colebrook calls 'equivocity' – 'grounding the truth of the world on some higher logic of what really and truly is' and the subjection to this truth (such as, in Colebrook's view following Deleuze and Guattari in *A Thousand Plateaus*, the signifier for the postmodern, linguistic turn) (Colebrook 2014: 214). In contrast to Colebrook, however, I see postmodernism itself as a critique of transcendental signifiers rather than as an equivocal ontology.

While not using the term 'the symbolic', Timothy Morton also speaks of 'an intrinsic and irreducible gap within a thing between what it is and how it appears', a gap he calls 'the Rift' (Morton 2016: 67). For object-oriented ontologists, it is this gap that constitutes objects' 'withdrawn' status (2016: 74). What is at stake in the terminological move from 'the symbolic' to 'the Rift'? What seems to be at issue is that the postmodern dividing line between the real and the symbolic is traditionally the opposition between the nonhuman and the human. Morton's Rift on the other hand runs through things themselves, in a posthuman ontology that is no longer primarily interested in the human. At the same time, in a reference to Kant's distinction between *noumena* and phenomena, Morton explains that the Rift is the difference between the appearance of a thing – that is, how a thing appears *not only to humans, but to other entities and itself* (Morton 2016: 67, 69, 78). The human, in other words, is not categorically excluded. In fact, object-oriented ontology's assumption of objects' withdrawn status seems to be able to accommodate, as a specific instance of the Rift, what we used to call the sphere of human culture, as well as the postmodern (and Barad's)[45] assumption that humans have no direct access to the real, that is no access outside human conceptual frameworks and sensory perception. At the same time, Morton's post-Kantian Rift assumes objects to pre-exist their ontological engagements and thus seems to be indebted to a classical (Newtonian) view of separate objects rather than quantum physics' (and Barad's) view of relata that do not pre-exist their entangled relations.

While I will continue to use the term 'symbolic' in this study, my own understanding of this concept nevertheless has a certain affinity with Morton's Rift. As was the case with our discussion of 'thought', 'narrative' or 'discourse' above, I see no need to restrict the term 'symbolic' to the human. If humans are part of the things that constitute the real (and Morton's reference to the possibility that a thing might be able to speak[36] confirms that assumption), we can then understand the flesh as the Rift that *also* (but not exclusively) applies to humans. In other words, we can see the Rift as the ontological difference between the reality of the thing (human or more-than-human) and 'symbolic' (human or nonhuman) investiture. While my study explores the decline or loss of human symbolic, androcentric investiture in European modernity, '[w]hat object-oriented ontology does', Morton states, 'is simply apply this thought to any object whatsoever' (2016: 73).[37] So far so good. In fact, we can argue that the loss of human symbolic investiture, the loss of anthropocentric and androcentric authority that I map in this study, allows us to perceive the equality of material, human and more-than-human, objects. The loss mapped thus leads us to posthumanism.

There is a point, however, on which I differ from Morton. In traditional, postmodern usage, the symbolic is of course the term employed for the realm of human language, history and culture. Morton goes on to specify that the gap he calls the Rift 'cannot be located anywhere in what I am calling ontically given space-time. That is, I can travel all around the surfaces and depths of a thing, study its history, think about how it is used, interview it – if it can speak – and I will never be able to locate the Rift' (2016: 67). Harman (2011:10–12) criticises the 'overmining' of objects through historical contextualisation, a criticism which is itself consistent with their assumption of objects' withdrawn status. In contrast to Harmann, I suggest that reconfiguring the complex and contingent historical processes and the changing topologies that define modernity, for instance, can help us avoid an understanding of material culture or matter itself as unitary and stable rather than as dynamic and indeterminate.[38] Rather than 'remov[ing] the social out of the world', as Kimberly DeFazio (2014) puts it, I propose that a historically and socially inflected ontology or an awareness of the ultimately social, intra-connected nature of the cosmos can help us understand what is at stake in the contemporary moment, a moment that has reached a new, though different crisis point – politically, economically and ecologically. Such a conceptualisation of historicity, in other words, while going beyond simple causation, establishes a relationship between the past, the present and the future, demonstrating that all phenomena are ontologically connected and open rather than separate or enclosed.

Colebrook's project in *Sex After Life* is to explore 'sexual time', since 'historical genealogy will in turn place us once again in an active position of mastery and meaning' (2015: 129). My project, by contrast, is not ready to give up completely on the concept of meaning. I want to understand how we – not only as humans, but as a planetary system – got to where we are today. I want to put forward a conceptualisation of meaning and historicity that does not see these concepts in exclusively human terms. In short, following Harmann's suggestion that objects of thought, ideational objects, are objects too (Bennett 2010a: 230), I want to ask: what is this 'thing' – or maybe better, this 'phenomenon' – called modernity? How can we understand modernity as a living system co-constituted by human and nonhuman, biological and more-than-biological components? How can we specifically materialise the concept of modernity by exploring its theatrical practices? As some of the plays presented show, what modernity is mourning is not only a lost real (given modernity's increasing abstraction), but the loss of premodern sublime transcendence, including human exceptionalism. Given this loss, modernity perceives 'disorderly', unruly matter as threatening to come back and engulf humans in the death that – in a humanist view – marks nonhuman animals and matter.

My goal is not so much transhumanism, that is the enhancement of the human species based on eighteenth-century ideas of perfectibility, reason and agency, as the related goal of problematising the contemporary and future suffering of human and nonhuman life forms. If this latter goal is still based on rationalist humanist notions of progress and emancipation (as Haraway has, correctly, argued),[39] so be it. I understand well enough that western, androcentric and anthropocentric notions of human mastery have contributed to the ecological situation we are in and have helped produce the experience of suffering that is my concern. In fact, this book takes it as its task to reconnect to these very problematic itineraries. But without wanting to engage in a determinism that sees the world again as passive matter, I also share historical materialism's belief that 'human activity can be 'a positive force in the constitution of reality' (Meißner 2016: 47). I believe, in other words, in what Barad calls 'reworking the material effects of the past and the future' as part of an 'ethics of entanglement' (Barad 2011:150).[40]

A unitary understanding of all humans as occupying positions of unchallenged hegemony is in my view just as misplaced as an understanding of the multiplicity of animal species as 'the animal', a homogeneity famously criticised by Derrida in *The Animal That Therefore I Am* (2004: 23). My study will explore, among other things, the role of humans who are suffering because they perceive their status as lethally threatened by modernity. The theatre is the meeting-point of their anxious bodies. And it is also more than that.

Old and New Materialism

Finally, but importantly, when I speak of overcoming the perceived binary divide between (human) identity/subjectivity and materiality, what exactly do I mean by materiality? On the one hand, as a project on biopolitics, my study is centrally focused on sovereignty and issues of socio-political representation. It shows these issues to be intimately connected to questions of credit and credibility, including financial credit. Summarising the stakes of this very interaction in his book *Der Souveränitätseffekt* (2015), Joseph Vogl (following Richard Wernham's argument) posits that it is the aggressive coupling of state authorities and private finance that has led not only to a capitalist 'regime of accumulation' (*Akkumulationsregime*), but to one of the most brutal and most bigoted periods in the history of modern Europe (2015: 118, 126). But by 'materiality', I also mean more than a recourse to classic Marxism's focus on the state and more than an identification of materialism with economic (base) structures. By 'materiality', I ultimately mean even more than an identification of matter with human embodiment – although both an economic analysis and the sacrifice of human (and, by extension, more-than-human) bodies are central to my project.

Some excellent work has been done recently on the convergences between 'old', that is historical, materialism and the ontologically oriented new materialism.[41] In her talk on 'Old Materialism', Amanda Jo Goldstein (2014), for instance, breaks down the opposition between 'old' and 'new' materialism by pointing out that Karl Marx wrote his doctoral dissertation on the natural philosophy of Epicurus. As Sonia Kruks notes, the 'early' Marx's vision 'radically historicises nature and naturalises history' (2010: 260). Goldstein points out that Louis Althusser, whose aleatory materialism is again popular with new materialists, also shared Marx's interest in ancient philosophies of nature. Jane Bennett as well questions whether the 'new' materialism is indeed so very new:

> It is misleading to call it a 'new' materialism or even a 'post'-humanism, for the philosophical perspective and the sensibility it advocates sit alongside a strong and lively tradition of (human) body feminisms, Marxist ecophilosophies, Merleau-Ponty's phenomenology, New Left experimentations with eros and an under-explored tradition of indigenous thinking and seeing. (Bennett 2018: 448)

My own work as well is influenced not only by new materialism, but also by earlier feminisms (the French feminisms on which I cut my intellectual teeth), by Merleau-Ponty (I am applying his conceptualisation of the body as the primary site of knowing the world to the theatre), and in particular by the Freudo-Marxism of the first generation of the Frankfurt School, as the beginning of the next section of this Introduction explains. Christopher Breu argues that 'to reach its full political potential, the account of materiality in NM [new materialism] and SR [speculative realism] needs to be put into dialogue with Marxist materialism' (2016: 21). When it comes to 'old' materialism's emphasis on history, I have already argued (in this Introduction) that new materialism's greater ontological emphasis also needs to be complemented with a focus on history.

What is ultimately at stake with our recent renewed focus on materialism, however, is a view of production that differs from historical materialism. This new view of production goes beyond the narrow focus on the formal sector of the economy and human economic structures (production, distribution, consumption), separability (the separation of individual entities and their pre-given attributes), and stable boundaries between the human and the non-human, describing instead the ontological co-production or becoming of heterogeneous, human and more-than-human relations. As Barad points out, '[p]roduction should not be thought of as the repetition of some fixed set of processes' (2007: 238). On the one hand, as Massumi points out, the *co-constitutive relation* between worker and capitalist already lies at the heart of Marx's work (2015b: 88). At the same time, however, as Barad notes, the flow of capital is in fact 'but one stream in a turbulent river of agencies' (2007: 238–9, 240). The move from an analysis primarily based on socio-political categories (historical materialism), including the flow of capital, to a larger engagement with ontological matters is exactly the process mapped by my study. Nevertheless, rather than showing a linear progression, the socio-political and the ontological are often deeply entwined in the plays presented and old and new materialism can be diffractively read through one another. My study replaces Marxist determinism, in which separate individuals either do or do not have agency, with an open-ended process philosophy that views agency as co-produced by heterogeneous, human and more-than-human contingent phenomena.

The arc mapped by my project is also the arc from a conceptualisation of sexuality and desire in a Freudian (or Freudo-Marxist) and Foucauldian sense in Strindberg and Sartre to sexuality and desire as *transindividual* life energy or excessive materiality (as *zōē* in Braidotti's sense or Spinoza's *conatus*) in my engagement with the early Brecht and with Artaud. Similarly, in lieu of the rationalist Marxist tradition's critique of false consciousness[42] what is ultimately at stake in 'new', posthumanist materialism – and what is brilliantly enacted in Artaud's theatre – is the reconceptualisation of consciousness altogether. What the western rationalist tradition used to call consciousness entailed an *anthropocentric* privileging of mental abstraction over the material conditions of human and nonhuman lives – conditions that were seen as pre-existing 'dead matter' to be dominated by hegemonic human agency. This problematic is at work in Sartre's *oeuvre*. But this hegemonic domination of mind over matter ultimately fails in the Marxist Sartre's later work (for space reasons not discussed here). Even 'old' materialism is arguably already anti-Cartesian in this sense, exploring the excessive dynamic agency of matter (Marx's description in *Das Kapital* of the aliveness and 'transcendent nature' of a table comes to mind, for instance).

In spite of its understanding of history as a force that goes beyond the individual subject or body, however, historical materialism is arguably still anthropocentric in its subtending concern with *difference* (in particular class) as it relates to human society, as a dialectical pejoration and as a pre-existing attribute (that could, however, be changed).[43] We can also find this view of difference as pejoration (think gender) in what Lehmann calls the 'anthropocentric' 'dramatic' tradition encompassing Strindberg and Sartre, and my reading re-enacts among other things the dialogue between Strindberg, Freud and Marx at the end of the nineteenth century. But my argument also establishes a non-dialectical continuum transversing the opposition between social difference and ontological difference (and thus again methodologically between old and new materialism), as well as between race, class and gender and the status of the nonhuman, viewing them as mutually constitutive parts of intra-active phenomena (rather than as pre-given identity attributes). In the immunitarian, biopolitical discourses of the *fin de siècle* and the first half of the twentieth century (here Strindberg and Sartre), identity categories – pre-existing stabilities that refuse to remain stable – are still all seen in the pejorative, threatening terms that lend themselves to ideology critique (the kind of critique that typified old materialism). To overcome this negative view of difference, historical materialism's utopian vision – its aspiration to economic or social equality and the discourse of rights to which it is linked – is linear or teleological and, like the 'anthropocentric' dramatic tradition (Strindberg, Sartre), limited by human time scales. In contrast to Freudo-Marxism specifically, new materialism on the other hand views difference, sexuality and desire (Spinoza's *conatus*) as agentive more-than-human, cosmic components that unify rather then divide heterogeneous bodies in aleatory ways and that only come about through these contingent relations. This latter view finds its expression in Brecht's early, pre-Marxist work and in Artaud.

In spite of the differences between old and new materialism, the material flows of capitalism (and the abstraction brought on by capitalism) are nevertheless an interest shared by both approaches (as well as by my own study). While traditional materialism critiqued the reification of humans and their relationships, more recent studies, such as Jeffrey Nealon's 2016 *Plant Theory* (which also features an excellent chapter on Deleuze and Guattari, among other 'giants' of theory), problematise the current and future private ownership and commodification, patenting and financialising of human and more-than-human life-forms in the services of neoliberalism or (what we optimistically call) 'late capitalism' (Nealon 2016: 112–13). But Nealon argues that we need more flexible weapons, 'a series of ways to adapt and respond to rapidly shifting unknowns, accelerating threats, new opportunities', than historical materialism's defining focus on class can provide (Nealon 2016: 114–15). While my own project is inspired by Marxist analyses of the material and ideological changes taking place in modernity, class or the classic Marxist understanding of production are no longer central focus points in my work. While the readings of exponents of 'dramatic' theatre in this study (Strindberg, Sartre) can still function within a dialectical framework that includes difference (gender instead of class) as pejoration, my investigation is nevertheless ultimately indebted to Deleuzian rhizomatic flows and multiplicities instead of dialectical three-steps.

In spite of 'old' materialism's anthropocentrism, when Marx's critique of Hegel's idealism introduced history into dialectics, it was also the history of humans' interactions with material objects and structures. It is true that historical Marxism, or ideology critique in general, is typically more concerned with larger, macropolitical *structures* and contradictions than with micropolitical *practices or processes*, the focus of Deleuzian, 'new' materialism. (My own project is interested in larger movements or shifts as well as in specific theatrical and cultural practices.) Unlike new materialism, however, historical materialism does not view objects (commodities) as self-producing, but rather as products of human labour and exchange. In addition, the fact that capitalism also turned humans and human relationships into objects was of course a central point of Marx's critique. While reification thus made the boundary line between humans and objects porous, 'object' nevertheless remained the secondary, inferior category. Whether historical materialism sees objects as endowed with a live energy independent of human agency is therefore at the very least open to debate. As this book will show, however, historical materialism can bring important tools to a project also inspired by newer approaches to materialism. Historical materialism's sophisticated understanding of issues of authority/power, of capitalism and of lived, quotidian material practices that produce interconnected materialdiscursive relations resonates particularly well with a new materialist approach. Historical materialism conceptualises authority as negative (as does Agamben, though in contrast to historical materialism not as part of a dialectical three-step), located in the state or in capitalist ownership, and (in contrast to Foucault) as acting on a pre-existing subject. New materialist scholars, on the other hand, generally follow Foucault's analysis of the multivalence and ubiquity of power as co-constitutive of the subject, while also distinguishing (as Braidotti does, for instance) between (negative) *potestas* and (affirmative) *potentia* (and also going beyond Foucault's humanist perspective).[44] My study puts into conversation discussions about the role of authority, the state and economics in modernity and 'new' materialist views of ontology and performance (as mapped most prominently in my Artaud chapter). In contrast to the ideology critique that would mark Brecht's later Marxist work in more pronounced ways than it does his *Baal*, Artaud *performs* resistance by enacting what Massumi calls 'participatory immersion' or 'techniques of relation aimed at immanent field-modulation' (2015b: 107).

In this context, it also bears mentioning that in clear contrast to historical materialism and its goal of ideological unmasking and class struggle, the 'post-critical' approach of new materialism has sometimes been accused of being apolitical. In my view, just as this accusation was inaccurate for poststructuralism (including deconstruction), so it is also for new materialism. At the same time, however, I also agree with Breu, who argues that '[f]or contemporary materialist discourse to reach its fullest potential, it needs to embrace the political more fully'. Breu adds: 'Fortunately there is much recent work that links issues of race, gender, and sexuality to theories of materiality' (2016: 22). Again, my own study aims to contribute to this scholarly conversation. In his recent work, however, Nealon (who is also well known for his earlier work inspired by historical materialism) suggests that we should be engaged in 'examining how the mesh of life is altered by x or y practice, rather than securing the best theoretical or epistemological ground for our political actions' (2017: 114). For Nealon, contemporary materialist political work is diagnostic. While I believe in thinking through the conceptual implications of our work (and Nealon's book is indeed a book on theory), I would also like to think of my own work as diagnostic. I am, however, interested in the diagnostic mapping of conditions that are anything but fixed. I am interested in an open-ended mapping of the materialdiscursive theatrical practices of European modernity and a 'situated cartography' (Dolphijn and Van der Tuin 2012: 14) or a tour[45] of the mesh of forces affecting situations, experiences and events, a mesh of which we (I as writer and you as reader) are very much an embodied, situated and entangled part. I would like to think of my work as an exploratory bricolage breaking down subject-object divisions rather than as an attempt at theoretical mastery.[46]

Central to any kind of political work is of course also the question of agency or purposivity at the heart of our contemporary paradigm change from humanist philosophies based on consciousness to posthumanism. What is the relation between consciousness and socio-political activism? Can there be activism without rational consciousness? If so, what does such activism look like? What is 'the political and ethical action of matter', as Braidotti (2012: 22) calls it? I agree with Breu that this is a question that new materialist philosophy has so far not yet fully answered. Nevertheless, adding to Massumi's important work on affect, Ben Highmore has made a helpful contribution to this discussion with his call for 'a politics of the gut' (2010: 135–6). Lone Bertelsen and Andrew Murphie as well write of 'a pluralism that might escape an increasingly conservative "Politics," in favor of the infinity of little affective powers available to every day life' (2010: 139). A potential answer, in other words, seems to have to do with a politics based on affect. Bertelsen and Murphie note: 'Affect always carries subjectivities elsewhere, to new territories and a dismantling of the old, ever toward the infinite possibilities and powers contained within our bodies, our friends (and our foes?), and their ecological contexts' (2010: 153). *Potentia*, in short, the power that resides in the productive life force of *zōē* (in Braidotti's sense), is based – but then goes beyond – the individual body. It ultimately finds its expression in the entanglement and solidarity of human and more-than-human bodies, in the affect that links these bodies based on affirmative, joyful difference and on an ethics of generosity and care (rather than an ultimately still oedipal resistance against the 'Master').[47] This power again lies in the quotidian material practices (a focus based on Deleuze's work) that democratically connect rather than separate heterogeneous communities. In new materialist philosophy, difference is political in a sense that can include and also affirm the human. But as the basis of a true post-anthropocentrism, it no longer privileges 'us'. While theatre has received its share of accusations of anthropocentrism (see below), this is also the perspective employed in my study.

Going beyond but also extending the work of historical materialism, a new materialist view of the human as *part* of the dynamic materiality of the *more-than-human* cosmos then unambiguously differs from the rationalist philosophical tradition by clearly establishing meaning-making as processes going in both directions.[48] (My project thus differs from object-oriented ontology, which opposes the idea of matter's dynamic fluctuations or intra-actions.) The plays assembled in this project enact the threat of the flesh, a threat located at the threshold between materiality and semiotic flows, in other words the threat posed by the inability of keeping the discursive realm separate from materiality – an inability already recognised by 'old' materialism.[49]

For me personally, what will always keep Marxist materialism close to my heart is its focus on human suffering, a focus that I want to expand as 'damage' or 'harm' to all modalities of life. *Rather than considering them in isolation, my cross-materialist[50] project thus explores the confluences among different forms of materiality – economic, embodied and inorganic.* It would in fact be impossible, for instance, to separate different non-biological and biological materialities and bodies from their interactions with capitalism. As I have argued, what makes a methodology, including my own, posthumanist is not the rejection of historicist approaches or an abandonment of human concerns. What makes a discourse posthumanist is instead the altered role it ascribes to the human. It is my goal to write an account of the material-historical contingencies co-constituting modernity without falling into the trap of human exceptionalism.

The Politicisation of Biological Life

Expanding the transdisciplinarity of recent work on materialism to critical methodologies as well, this book thus establishes a generative dialogue between the different vocabularies of generations of modes of inquiry that have often been seen dualistically, as incompatible – modes of inquiry or analytical frameworks that cut across what Dolphijn and van der Tuin have called 'the linear spatiotemporalities conventionally assigned to epistemic trends' (2012: 100). As Ashley Barnwell correctly notes , '[t]o the reader of posthuman theory, exciting questions about context, ecology, and agency are clearly opened up, but sometimes it seems that this explosion of provocative and unforeseen possibilities may be won at the expense of existing methods and concerns' (2017: 29). Kirby similarly suggests that 'the progressivism in new materialism – the hope that we can separate ourselves from earlier errors – is something that we might want to reconfigure if the need to narrativise tends to denigrate and devalue what came before' (2017: 14). Resisting this urge to discount earlier work in cultural criticism, my study performs readings across the divide between the discursive and the material turns. Inspired by critical traditions from Freud and Marx (and their homologies) via Foucault and Agamben to non-dialectical (Deleuzian) new materialism and queer ecology, this project creates a diffractive assemblage of methods and components.

Many decades ago, the Freudo-Marxism of the first generation of the Frankfurt School – the work of Max Horkheimer and Theodor Adorno in particular – already provided an early integration of identity/

representation and (economic) materiality, linking symbolic authority structures to material, social and economic practices. As a more recent concept that links difference/s to the materiality of the (biological/ species or more-than-biological, human or more-than-human) body, the concept of *life* can additionally help trouble the analytical divide between identity and matter. As Massumi puts it: 'There is no life substance. Life is not a thing. Life is the way in which the mental and physical poles of events come together – differently every time. . . . Whitehead says that life is in the interval between things – in the way things relate, in the way they come together in events . . . towards the generation of new forms' (2015b: 183).

In what is considered his first use of the term 'biopolitics' at a 1974 conference in Rio and in several courses he taught in the 1970s at the Collège de France,[51] Foucault emphasised the central importance of the modern, post-eighteenth century *politicisation of biological life* for capitalist society (Esposito 2008: 27). Yet Freudo-Marxism and the Foucauldian tradition have sometimes been seen as irreconcilable. In spite of this perceived incompatibility, my project reads the theoretical work on biopolitics first inspired by Foucault's *oeuvre* (and in particular his most famous text, *La Volonté de savoir*, the first volume of *The History of Sexuality*, published in 1976) within the horizon of a focus on materialism, including the governance of bodies and material space and the materialist critique of capitalism. In capitalist modernity, the Italian Marxist philosopher Paolo Virno (2013: 272) reminds us, bodies and life are managed and controlled because they provide commodified labour-power. But following Foucault, the economy, finance and wealth also constitute one of the areas that modern power is forced to address in order to optimise the welfare of the population that it aims to regulate (Esposito 2008: 36–7). As Dolphijn and van der Tuin have pointed out in an interview with Meillassoux, Foucault's 'idea of discourse did not start with language, but with material forms', for instance the material form of the prison (2012: 76–7). As Barad also notes, 'Foucault's analytics of power links discursive practices to the materiality of the body' (2007: 63).

Additionally inspired by both the Freudo-Marxist tradition and by more recent work on affect, my 'bio-psycho-social'[52] project also explores the drives/instincts, psychic tensions, desires, affects, intensities and impasses that unite human and nonhuman life at the end of the nineteenth and the first half of the twentieth centuries. Ignoring the 'historical avant-garde' and 'post-dramatic' theatre of the early and later twentieth century and associating theatre exclusively with what

Lehmann calls 'dramatic theatre' – that is with the western realist-mimetic dramatic tradition (here exemplified by Strindberg and Sartre), a theatre that verbalises or externalises human psychic conflicts – and also ignoring that humans are part of nature, Arons and May's work on performance and ecology posits that 'theatre in its present form – with its emphasis on human conflict in the context of human institutions' – occupies a space at the far end of the human–nature spectrum, away from 'nature' (2012: 1). It is true that the tradition of 'dramatic', realist-naturalist theatre is indeed anthropocentric in its focus on what Santner calls 'the conflict-ridden space of normativity' (Arons and May 2016: 238). As I will argue, however, even this humanist, anthropocentric theatrical tradition intra-acts in a material context. In fact, 'dramatic' theatre may even be in a privileged position to enact the way human social stratifications, sexual differing and desires are not pre-existing, but are performatively *materialised* as entangled practices. Even in the 'anthropocentric' tradition, in other words, conflicts are by definition located at materialdiscursive relational contact zones. While humans seek to claim agency to ease their corporeal and psychic suffering both on and off the stage, these affects are not subject to exclusive individual, rational control and thus put in doubt the dualistic separation of subjectivity and materiality.[53] From Greek tragedy's condemnation of human hubris to the biopolitical theatre presented in this book that attempts, *in vain*, to defend against the perceived threats posed by 'matter' against the characters' autonomy or immunity, the diverse theatrical work in the western tradition in fact ultimately *puts in question* any claims to humans' status as autonomous, sovereign subjects.

Rather than viewing performance as 'always already a cultural interpretation of an overlay onto the 'natural' world' (Arons and May 2012: 1–2), an interpretation that ultimately keeps intact the binary division between nature and culture, my work therefore aims to explore the *performativity* of theatre in its double sense: as theatrical production and as the intra-activity or *enactment* of a live, open and dynamic system of multiple relations between co-constitutive human and more-than-human actors/actants, energies and affects. Artaud's work indeed realises this potential of theatre to a greater degree than the tradition of western psychological theatre that he opposes. In his well-known dispute with György Lukács, Brecht also argued that art should be seen as a field of production rather than as a container of content. But it can also be argued that *any* theatrical performance enacts such an open becoming, and that any play and author are themselves produced by and co-constitutive of entangled historical-material systems of moving local and transcultural parts, flexible networks whose relationality also includes the diffractive readings of dramatic texts through diverse onto-epistemological paradigms, as performed in this project.

Biopolitical thinking – the heightened human need for psychic and material security in a post-metaphysical, modern age – is ultimately phobic, neurotic or even psychotic thinking. The generalised, object-less fear of the changes wrought by modernity is displaced onto more concrete others, furnishing the subject with an – illusory – sense of agency and mastery or sovereignty. With a reconfiguration of related historic moments of acute material and psychic pressure, my project aims to contribute not only to academic engagements with biopolitics, but specifically to the engagement with *biohistory* at the European turn from the nineteenth to the twentieth century. As Timothy Campbell and Adam Sitze pointed out in 2013, '"biohistory" is a term just as neglected today as "biopolitics" used to be ten years ago'. With the term 'biohistory', they explain, 'Foucault proposes to mark those moments of pressure 'in which the movement and processes of history interfere with one another', and which, in turn, parallel an intensification of biopower (Campbell and Sitze 2013: 9). The decades leading up to early twentieth-century European totalitarianism were marked by exactly such an intensification of biopower.

In this way, my project's focus on historical and geographic specificity and materiality then aims to address the concern voiced by some crit-ics (and practitioners) of 'the biopolitical turn' over the field's lack of historical contextualisation.[54] Combining a reconfiguration of European modernity (as an ongoing contingent project that spans several centuries) with historical contextualisation, this book specifically seeks to answer a central question posed by one of the leading thinkers in biopolitics. Concerning totalitarianism, Esposito asks: 'What was twentieth-century totalitarianism with respect to the society that preceded it? Was it a limit point, a tear, a surplus in which the mechanism of biopower broke free, got out of hand, or, on the contrary, was it society's sole and natural outcome' (2013b: 380)? How do we account for the mass production of death in twentieth-century Europe? Was twentieth-century totalitarian-ism the result of a crisis, a breakdown of modern rationality? Or was it a result inherent in this same political rationality, and is it therefore a polit-ical and material threat that still exists today? Foucault never answered this question unambiguously himself.

Esposito analyses totalitarianism as the paroxysm of the mod-ern, post-eighteenth century biopolitical paradigm of 'immunity'[55] – a concept that links the biomedical with the political-juridical sphere

(2008: 45) and, according to Esposito, 'the explicative key of the entire modern paradigm' (2010: 12). While, as Johannes Türk has shown, immunity as a literary theme has a history that dates back as far as the Greek writer Thucydides' work, immunology as a medical field has its origins in the eighteenth century and is thus a modern science. Bringing with it an acceleration of global travel, migration and exchange, modernity is a time in which the possibility of biological and political conflicts has grown exponentially (Türk 2011: 298). Our current time is consequently obsessed with risk and defence. The immune system reacts to changes from the outside or to the disturbance of the body's internal balance. Given that it deals with identity and difference, with 'the recognition and misrecognition of self and other' (Haraway 2013: 275), the immune system is thus indeed a fitting figure to ground an engagement with dramatic enactments of difference in modern times. In the twentieth century, biopolitics intensifies and transforms into thanato-politics, into a politics that chooses death in its defence against perceived external and internal threats to the integrity of the body politic and the population's biological survival. Death becomes a constitutive trait of biopolitics.

Ironically, thanks to the scientific advances of the time, modernity also sees death for the first time as avoidable or at least deferrable. The medical advances that helped articulate the knowledge and practice of immunology and immunisation – starting in the eighteenth and nineteenth centuries with the inoculation against smallpox – are part of these scientific advances. In modernity, medicine is increasingly able to prevent illness and death, progressively allowing humans to plan their future. At the same time, however, modern European society is also a society that has lost faith in traditional symbolic authority – in the king's and the father's authority, in religion and life after death – and that thus experiences itself as at risk. Starting with Johann Wolfgang von Goethe's bildungsroman *Wilhelm Meisters Lehrjahre* (1795/96), the medical term 'crisis', the point of acute danger where the body intensively fights unassimilated elements, begins to assume a cultural dimension: it now also starts to apply to the psychological experience of life transitions, to the loss and regaining of a material and psychological balance. The perception of illness itself changes from the passive suffering bestowed by Providence to an active experience, a fight (Türk 2011: 110).

The fights enacted on the modern stage are indeed fights for biological survival. In modern society, the attempt to protect life and postpone death becomes the highest good, which consequently requires developing a defensive strategy that heightens immunity. According to Esposito, the change to an immunitarian logic starts to occur in the second half of the sixteenth century (Esposito 2013a: 319, 329–30). Only in modernity does immunisation thus become society's most intimate core, leading – paradoxically – to an intensification of death in the material experience and rhetoric of life, to a thanato-politics. The 'biopolitical' plays presented enact exactly this immunitarian concern with defending against death. The view of death is one of the greatest differences between the immunitarian tradition here exemplified by Strindberg and Sartre and the historical avant-garde encompassing Brecht and Artaud, which sees death as only a point of transition in a larger process of life. These different views of death are also one of the main distinctions between the epistemological philosophical tradition that includes Agamben's work on biopolitics on the one hand and, on the other hand, new materialism and the posthumanist ontological tradition exemplified for instance by Braidotti's work.

As we have seen, in modernity, which is marked by the declining belief in life after death, the modern sense of risk is linked to the crisis of traditional symbolic authority. Modernity itself is of course the result of the crisis of sovereignty, the result of revolutions that deposed absolute monarchs and reformed the Catholic Church. As early as in his *Discipline and Punish* (*Surveiller et punir*, 1975), Foucault linked the crisis of sovereignty to the birth of biopolitics. Slavoj Žižek also connects the crisis of male symbolic authority – what Santner has called 'the crisis of investiture' (Santner 1996: for instance 26) – to the politicisation of biological life in modernity. Žižek writes: 'The key point here is that the expert rule of "biopolitics" is grounded in and conditioned by the crisis of investiture; this crisis generated the "postmetaphysical" survivalist stance' (Žižek 2004a: 396). The plays studied enact this crisis of sovereignty in a variety of ways.

Tracing the rise of the immunitarian, 'postmetaphysical' logic of biopolitics in modernity, this book presents plays by key writers of European modernism as contingent relational events in the differential materialisation of a crisis of representation. This crisis is the crisis of symbolic authority that has unfolded from the political challenge to royal authority in seventeenth-century England to an ever-expanding 'crisis' of the sign and representation in general in the twentieth century and beyond. In the twentieth century, the crisis of representation and the sign finds its expression in fascist closure.

Fascist Immunitarianism

To examine the relationship between fascism and the modern European transnational political 'mainstream' (that is culturally dominant movements and processes), I have chosen to write this book as encounters between plays by well-known, canonical authors not usually associated with totalitarianism on the one hand and National Socialism itself on the other. It is true that these encounters are unexpected. The Nazis burned Strindberg's work. As a communist, Brecht fled the Third Reich in February 1933, immediately after the National Socialists' advent to power. And critics have long celebrated Sartre as an antifascist writer. Although some critics have accused Brecht and Artaud of fascist tendencies, my readings refute these accusations. I argue instead that by enacting the modern crisis of the sign, Brecht's avant-garde play *Baal* already announces the theatre of the absurd. Brecht's play enacts a post-anthropocentric sense of unity with natural life that transverses the psychic blockages inherent in the mind-matter duality of modern western thinking – blockages that arguably reached their apex under European totalitarianism. On the other hand, my reading suggests that Sartre's early work presents a phobic immunitarian logic that can serve as an example of the implication even of antifascist philosophy and art in fascist thinking. The 'moment of impasse where everything seems to be locked and gridded', as Massumi puts it, referencing Georges Simondon, 'that's the moment of anxiety and death'. As Massumi points out, 'Simondon's concept of anxiety is clearly in dialogue with existentialist and existential phenomenological thinking. It's a response to the anxiety attached to . . . Sartre's prescription for absolute subjective freedom of decision in the face of anxiety' (Massumi 2015b: 159–60). In contrast to the anxious interiority of the human subject in Sartre, Artaud's theatre centrally enacts the open-ended relationality of heterogeneous human and more-than-human components. But Artaud's theatre is nevertheless also a 'cruel' theatre; it is a theatre that creates a tonality of anxiety without, however, necessarily individualising it.

Based on the non-relational philosophy of individual merit, success and survival that anxiously views the other as a threat, modernity set in motion what Esposito calls an immunitarian response – a defensive stance designed to protect life – that ultimately led to death on a large scale under totalitarianism. By creating a 'new caesura internal to species-being' (Campbell and Sitze 2013: 19), that is, a quasi-biological division between insiders and dehumanised outsiders, National Socialism tried to avert the threat of death by deferring death to racialised outsiders. It tried to preserve life through the sacrifice of the living. National Socialism combined the modern power aiming to manage and optimise life (the life of members of the Aryan population) with the historic reversion to premodern sovereignty (the king's right to kill).

While Nazism was thus a product of the immunitarian logic of modernity, the modern scientific achievement of medical immunisation is in fact no longer based on exclusion, however, but on controlled infection. Immunisation benefits from the threshold where nature and culture (medical research and practices) intra-act, where the illness itself becomes a cure. In politics as well as in biology, the French philosopher Michel Serres explains in the terms of systems theory, 'systems have been immunised by becoming more complex. They became stronger by becoming more tolerant. They were acclimated to the revolutionary, the madman, the deviant, the dissident: an organism lives very well with its microbes; it lives better and is hardened by them' (Serres 2007: 68). Nazism on the other hand tried to keep the dualistic boundary between the socio-political body and the threatening other intact – an ultimately illusory move.

Nazism established this borderline between insiders and outsiders through modern normativity, through the demands imposed by norms. Since what is at stake in modernity is the – biological as well as political – life of the individual and the species, these norms were centred around concepts pertaining to health. As Campbell and Sitze observe, '[t]he modern concept of life refers less to a single, stable essence, than to a set of continuously shifting norms (pertaining to health and welfare, safety and security) that measure out a set of intrinsically limitless demands' (Campbell and Sitze 2013: 23). My project focuses on the structural relationality between the way social norms were established in terms of gender or sexual difference at the turn from the nineteenth to the twentieth century – as is evident in Strindberg's work, for instance – and in racial terms under National Socialism. Mapping this very link between *sexuality and race*, Foucault – in his discussion of the modern regime of sexuality in *HS* I – speaks of the modern management 'of life and survival, of bodies and the race' (Foucault 1980a: 137).

In the end, however, my work reads the totalitarian 'crises' of modernity as inherent in – and co-extensive with – modernity itself, and the plays presented highlight this connection. Ironically, the immunitarian logic that is itself a product of 'democratic' modernity – the result of a society that perceives itself at risk following the loss of absolutist and transcendental authority – again finds its expression in the sovereign totalitarian leader. Sovereignty reiterates in modernity – both in the abstracted and delegated sovereignty of the people in democracy, and in the embodied sovereignty of the totalitarian leader. The sovereign leader claims the right to protect or 'immunise' the qualified political or cultural life of the members of the national population (Aristotle's *bíos*) against the perceived threat of contagion or death inherent in community. The sovereign thus 'preserve[s] individuals *through the annihilation of their relation*' (Esposito 2010: 29, my emphasis). I will explore the problematic of immunity and community in greatest depth in Strindberg. *What is at stake in all of the plays presented, however, is exactly the relation between heterogeneous elements, and most importantly the relation between the human and the more-than-human worlds.*

All of the plays examined in this study thus centrally enact the relation to difference. In eighteenth-century medicine, vitalism was the first theory that conceived of the body as an organism or force of life that individually reacts to stimuli or invasion and is thus separate (though not completely) from its environment/community (Türk 2011: 162). Nazism combined such Enlightenment vitalism with the racialised theory of biological heritage or morbid predisposition. The late nineteenth century's theories of race and inheritance conflicted, however, with discoveries between 1870 and 1900 in the new field of *bacteriology*. In addition to advances in bacteriology, the second half of the nineteenth century and the turn to the twentieth century also saw a heightened phase in the development of *experimental immunology*. Starting in the 1880s, laboratory medicine discovered microorganisms as the cause of infectious diseases and internal biological conflicts that had earlier been invisible. Today, we have learned that humans are made up of trillions of nonhuman microorganisms, of what Nealon calls 'a swarm of tangled and connected life-forms, with much of the life-activity taking place at a level unseen by the naked eye' (Nealon 2016: 59).

In the period that led to the birth of bacteriology and microbiology, Freud also formulated his theory of the unconscious, arguing that human decisions are not made exclusively at the conscious level. In his early text *Die Abwehr-Neuropsychosen* (*The Neuro-Psychoses of Defense*) (1894), Freud described the psychic material that cannot be integrated and thus leads to psychosis as *parasites* (Türk 2011: 280–1), a term that we will encounter again in Strindberg's work, as well as of course in the rhetoric of early twentieth-century fascism. Like potentially contagious microorganisms or like the unconscious, the declared internal enemies of Nazi Germany – such as Jews, homosexuals and socialists – were often externally indistinguishable from 'Aryans', to the point where a visibly worn yellow star (and in the camps stars of different colours) had to remedy this invisibility. Whereas immunological preventive therapies aim to raise the body's ability to integrate any future infectious matter (through immunisation or desensibilisation), National Socialism's goal was the complete extinction of marked outsiders.

In political theory, sovereign power claims the right to 'immunise' the population against any perceived external threats. According to the early twentieth-century conservative German jurist Carl Schmitt's definition of sovereignty, however, the sovereign leader also has the right to declare a state of exception from the norm (which can itself become the norm). In other words, the sovereign leader can declare internal threats as external, that is exclude certain parts of the population, and reduce their life to the natural-zoological – to what the Greeks called *zōē*, what Agamben calls bare life and what Santner calls creaturely life. The sovereign can even end this bare life in the interest of saving or improving the (qualified) life of the species or race. In this way, the distinction between war and peace ultimately falls away. War and the state of exception become part of the new normal. In spite of modernity's foundation in legal equality, the exercise of sovereignty entails 'the enactment of differential rights to differing categories of people for different purposes within the same space', as well as the division of space into separate compartments (Mbembe 2013: 173–4) (think ghettos or racial segregation). Modernity links sovereign power to both communal self-preservation and self-destruction (Campbell 2008: xii).

The threat is thus not always an external threat. The community itself also poses an expropriating threat to individual identity – a threat enacted in Strindberg and in Sartre's work, for instance. The plays attended to in this project express the modern perception of threat in a variety of different ways. Since modernity perceives the threat level as lethal, the reaction as well must be lethal and must thus ultimately end in thanato-politics (or necropolitics, to use Achille Mbembe's term). For Georges Bataille, death reduces the human subject to animality (1988: 336) – in other words, to *zōē*. *This animality – the loss of human hegemony replaced by the post-anthropocentrism of zōē – is exactly the primary way in which some of the plays assembled enact the threat of modernity.* New materialist philosophy (such as again Braidotti's work), on the other hand, sees *zōē* as a productive life force that also includes death as part of the process of becoming.[56]

The plays studied in this project show that twentieth-century totalitarianism was not an isolated phenomenon brought about by a few irrational madmen on the fringe that happened to usurp political power (as György Lukács, for instance, had argued in *Destruction of Reason*, or George Mosse in *Masses and Men*). With Horkheimer and Adorno, I argue instead that European fascism was indeed a 'logical' (though not inevitable) outcome of a longer, mainstream tradition, of the dark side of the Enlightenment and its problematic relationship to its intersecting others, of what we can call – in Foucauldian terms – its regulatory system of exclusion. 'Europe' is thus more than a geopolitical region. Associated with the Enlightenment project, it is paradigmatic for western democratic modernity as well as for the western rationalist philosophical tradition and its privileging of human consciousness. But with the Shoah, which has become synonymous with evil, Europe also stands for the worst excesses of this tradition.

Mbembe additionally discusses colonialism and slavery as 'the first syntheses between massacre and bureaucracy, that incarnation of western rationality'. Similar to explorations of colonial systems and slavery, research on German National Socialism has typically – and for obvious reasons – focused on issues of racialised subjugation and persecution: 'What one witnesses in World War II is the extension to the "civilized" people of Europe of the methods previously reserved for the "savages"' (Mbembe 2013: 171). Without in any way trying to minimise the central importance of the Shoah or the extraordinary suffering of the Jewish people, my exploration adds enactments of gender and sexuality at the European *fin de siècle* to the reconfiguration of this time period, surveying the enmeshed relationship between, on the one hand, the multifaceted immunitarian responses against sexual difference that reach an apex in the late nineteenth century and, on the other hand, the biological racism of twentieth-century fascism. I am interested, in other words, in the link between the thanato-political state racism of European fascism and its complete normativisation of life – establishing norms for all aspects of life – and the normative logic related to gender and sexuality that already marks the last decades of the nineteenth century (and is enacted in Strindberg's work). Similar to colonialism, early twentieth century state racism would then take the power of normalisation a step further, to the resumption and generalisation of the old sovereign right to kill (Foucault 2013: 75, 78).

'Domestic' Drama, or the Politicisation of the Private

It was of course the Frankfurt School that first explored the 'dark' side of the Enlightenment and its link to National Socialism, while also providing an early integration of Freud and Marx. Although the influence of their work on subsequent theorists of modernity such as Foucault has now been recognised, some of the issues first brought up by this critical tradition also deserve to be thought anew in their own right. Calling Foucault 'a scholar from whom I have learned a great deal in recent years' (Agamben 2009a: 7), Agamben in turn has contributed to the contemporary rethinking of Foucault's work. Agamben and Esposito specifically link Foucault's work on biopolitics more explicitly to totalitarianism.[52]

Putting this problematic in conversation with plays, the chapters that follow seek to make sense of the apparent discontinuities between well-known understandings of the power or authority structures at work in modernity. As we have seen, it was changes in authority structures that brought about the modern sense of risk or crisis that in turn called forth immunitarian thinking. In this context, my work strives first of all to resolve the apparent theoretical paradox of the *decline* of paternal – or, by extension, male symbolic – authority in modernity on the one hand (which the Frankfurt School saw as ultimately leading to fascism) and, on the other hand, the *central role* of the father and the family as both targets and instruments of disciplinary power in Foucault's theory of modernity. In *La Volonté de savoir* (*HS* I), Foucault asserts that the deployment of sexuality 'first developed on the fringes of familial institutions' (in the direction of conscience and pedagogy for instance) and then 'gradually became focused on the family'. The family is ultimately the 'crystal' in Foucault's theory of the deployment of sexuality (1980a: 110–11). The plays in my study in fact lend themselves with ease to both readings. Although they represent paternal authority as threatened or obsolete (that is in decline), they ultimately all belong to the larger tradition of modern (post-seventeenth century) 'domestic' drama, of a tradition that makes the family its central focus.

The emphasis on the omnipresence of 'paternal' control is where Foucault's panoptical society of surveillance also meets Žižek. Both Foucault's well-known argument against repression as the all-encompassing explanation of modernity and Žižek's work diminish the traditional role of the father who overtly issues prohibitions. Žižek follows Jacques Lacan in analysing modern society as a society of enjoyment rather than a society of prohibition. At the same time, however, the enjoyment offered in consumer society is an enjoyment commanded by what Žižek calls 'the anal father of enjoyment'. This anal father does not respect any private space; he spies into and controls everything. In fact, instead of speaking of a 'decline' of paternal authority, Žižek attributes increased power to the less overt authority of the ever-present anal father (Žižek 2008: 145). Here it is also worth remembering that short of leading us into anarchy, a society of enjoyment does not necessarily forgo all prohibitions.

One of the things that interest me most in these discussions of the changing role of paternal authority and the family is that both Foucault and Žižek posit some structure at work in modernity that blurs the boundary between *public and private*.[58] While the split between the public sphere and the domestic sphere is at the core of bourgeois, post-eighteenth-century ideology, bourgeois, 'domestic' drama (in a sense of the term not limited to the drama of the eighteenth century) also enacts the very collapse of this distinction by subjecting the intimacy sphere to public scrutiny. While conflicts within families have indeed been the topic of theatre dating as far back as ancient Greece, the conflicts of modern dramas often no longer play out in the agora, but in private, interior spaces. The ancient Greeks located the realm of the *oikos* – that is the domestic realm of the household and the family – on the side of *zōē* (natural life), not *bíos* (qualified life). In modernity, however, private interests for the first time gain public significance (Arendt 2013a: 120). *When all instances of male symbolic authority – from God the Father to the king to the father in the family – become increasingly open to question in the modern age, the 'distinctions between public and private, state and society, local and global' collapse* (Esposito 2008: 15). In modernity, these territories fold into each other.

In the human rights declarations of the eighteenth century, natural life is for the first time the basis for inalienable political rights (Agamben 2013a: 152–4). Anonymous physical life – *zōē*, in other words, not *bíos* – was at the basis of the principle of equality and modern European democracy. Foucault summed up this groundbreaking transition in his famous observation: 'For millennia, man remained what he was for Aristotle: a living animal with the additional capacity for a political existence; modern man is an animal whose politics place his existence as a living being into question' (Foucault 1980a: 143). Under National Socialism, being born racially 'pure' or Aryan was the requirement for membership in the German nation – a term that derives from the Latin *nascere*, to be born. Race/biology and political identity thus become synonymous. A biological given – blood – determines the juridical status of the person

(Esposito 2008: 183). The difference between *zōē* (biological life) and *bíos* (qualified life) thus collapses – at least for qualified members of the body politic – not only under National Socialism, but in western modernity in general. The care of the natural life of its members becomes the central task of the modern state. Life itself becomes central to politics; politics becomes biopolitics.

Paradoxically, the constant redefinition of the relationship between 'man' (*zōē*) and 'citizen' (*bíos*) – the question of who is a citizen and who is not – then becomes the incessant political task of modern nation states. This redefinition started with the French Revolution, but did not end with National Socialism: 'One of the essential characteristics of modern biopolitics (which will increase in our century) is its constant need to redefine the threshold in life that distinguishes and separates what is inside from what is outside' (Agamben 2013a: 155–6). *The modern plays presented here centrally problematise – some obsessively – the question of inside and outside, of belonging and alterity, and of limit states.* 'The fundamental categorical pair of western politics', Agamben notes in his *Homo Sacer*, 'is not that of friend/enemy but that of bare life/political existence, *zōē/bíos*, exclusion/inclusion' (Agamben 1995: 8). Braidotti also speaks of 'the power relations around bios/zoe' as 'the defining feature of our historicity' (Braidotti 2011: 121).[59]

It is this problematic of inclusion and exclusion that lends itself most readily to an exploration of the relationships in European modernity between culturally dominant concerns (as enacted in the theatre) and fascism's problematic relationship to difference. The totalitarian state takes the modern collapse of the distinction between public and private to its extreme. As Ernst Cassirer observes in *The Myth of the State*, '[i]n the totalitarian state, there is no private sphere, independent of political life; the whole life of man is suddenly inundated by the high tide of new rituals' (Cassirer 1946: 284). It is now also time for me to come clean: while I am interested in exploring the transnational cultural dynamic of European modernity (with the help of plays from different national contexts and with the aim of going beyond what Braidotti calls 'methodological nationalism'[60]) and while this historic dynamic led to fascist regimes in several European countries, I will focus on (German) National Socialism. The relationship between National Socialism and other totalitarian systems is a question that has been asked elsewhere (in the *Sonderweg* discussion, for instance) and will not concern me here. Foucault's, Agamben's and Esposito's work on biopolitics also focus primarily on Nazi Germany. These writers agree that what is at stake in modern politics is life, and they see totalitarianism as a result of the politicisation of the life biology of humans, as a result of the modern transformation of politics into biopolitics.[61] Even the life that had previously been considered private (that is part of the domestic sphere) is politicised in modernity. Agamben calls the entry of bare life into the political sphere 'the decisive event of modernity' (Agamben 1995: 4).

Since the politicisation of life (and death) affects *the body*, the theatre – the genre that puts bodies on the stage and affects spectators' bodies – especially lends itself to an investigation of this modern problematic. While the relationship between state and body was seen as an analogy or metaphor in classical times, with the collapse of *zōē* and *bíos*, body and state coincide in modernity: 'no politics exists other than that *of* bodies, conducted *on* bodies, *through* bodies' (Esposito 2008: 84). The body is located – Haraway would say 'is produced' – at the threshold of indistinction where *zōē* and *bíos* meet (Esposito 2008: 58). The lines of defence in the immunitarian paradigm are located at the confines of the body: 'The body is both the instrument and the terrain of this battle', of the battle between life and death (Esposito 2013a: 318).

Here finally, *zōē* – as bare or creaturely life – is again linked to the modern crisis of male symbolic authority in a variety of ways. Bare life is what Santner calls 'the wretchedness of the human animal stripped of his or her social insignia' (Santner 2011: 58). It is the kind of life that is refused or denied representation. Bare life extinguishes human kinship structures and symbolic entitlements, creating instead creaturely monstrosity – difference as such, representing nothing but its own perceived frightening uniqueness. The plays assembled enact the heightened threat posed by this feminised creaturely monstrosity at a time when traditional male symbolic and anthropocentric entitlements are being questioned. But if the invasion of/by *zōē* into the polis is perceived as threatening, this abject, border-crossing threat, this collapse of *zōē* and *bíos* is ultimately the threat of modernity itself. Beyond this collapse of the political into the biological in modernity, the final symbolic entitlement threatened will be – not only in postmodernist or decolonial theory, but also in posthumanism – Europe's or the western world's self-consciousness as the ideal, normative site of universalist humanist reason and progress.[62]

Sexuality between Biology and Culture

The modern plays presented are all centrally focused on what lies at the *vanishing* border line between *zōē* and *bíos*, and between the private and the public. In addition, the central tension enacted in Strindberg's naturalistic dramas results from the plays' position at yet another point of transition: the transition from a premodern, paternalistic society to a modern, democratic society of equals. As Foucault has argued, the question of life – its protection, development and normative management – gains central importance in modernity, exploiting and intensifying the body as an object of power and knowledge. As Santner has observed in *My Private Germany*, the case of Daniel Paul Schreber (the presiding judge at the Dresden Higher Regional Court who suffered a severe mental breakdown and became the subject of Freud's famous case history) 'no doubt owes much of its fascination to the fact that it brings into such sharp relief a moment of crisis in this history of tension between different forms and systems of power and authority' (Santner 1996: 89). As I will show, Strindberg's work enacts the same tension.

In contrast to the functions it had exercised in premodern times, the family was reorganised and intensified in the modern regime of sexuality. As we can see most prominently in Strindberg, where the family was concerned, the modern incitement to discourses on sexuality meant an incessant broadcasting of the sexual difficulties experienced in the bourgeois family. In the modern regime of sexuality, the embattled nature of the premodern system was encoded as the psychologised or psychiatrised symptoms or figures of an 'abnormal' sexuality, such as the impotent husband, hysteria or the homosexual (Foucault 1980a: 110) – all featured in Strindberg's work. The behaviour of these scientific 'cases', as enacted on the stage, had to be analysed so it could subsequently be normalised in society. Whereas in premodern drama and society the central issue is adherence to the law, that is the question of guilt or innocence, the relevant categories in modern society and drama are typically normalcy and deviancy, health and pathology.

Premodern plays such as classical Greek tragedies represent the family as the model of the government of the state. Sophocles' Antigone, for instance, challenges her uncle, King Kreon. Similarly, as Hannah Arendt points out, in the context of premodern Christianity, 'Thomas Aquinas compares the nature of household rule with political rule; the head of the household, he finds, has some similarity to the head of the kingdom' (Arendt 2013a: 116). The modern plays in this project, on the other hand, were written and first staged at a time when the family as model had already been replaced by the regulation of the *population* as the primary theme. The enactment of the family in these plays no longer thematises the analogy between the government of the family and that of the state, but explores instead the sexual behaviour, consumption and demographics of certain parts of the population as observed in the changing family unit. Among the plays assembled in this project, the sexual behaviour of the changing family unit is again most prominently enacted in Strindberg.

Since gendered, sexual, racial and national identity norms would become inextricably linked by the beginning of the twentieth century, these plays ultimately point to the cultural relationality between historic conceptions of gender or sexual difference at the *fin de siècle* and the National Socialist rhetoric concerning racialised and sexual minorities, all defined in terms of a stable, quasi-biological, naturalised identity. Modern immunitarian thinking – the thinking that establishes the boundaries of life and death within the population, between normal and abnormal, fit and unfit life – has its beginnings in early modernity. At the end of the nineteenth and the beginning of the twentieth centuries, it is at the level of biological life – of the bodily health of the species or population – that questions of sexual difference and sexuality intersect implicitly with similar discussions about racial health or 'hygiene'. Foucault links the establishment of a biological caesura, the 'separating out of groups that exist within a group' to modern state racism, where this caesura ultimately becomes a radical split between the living and the dead (Foucault 2013: 74). As the following chapters will show, we can already witness such a separating out, along the norms concerning sexual difference, in the theatre of the late nineteenth century.

As we will see, the theatre can act as a discursive field furnishing certain experts' legitimating truth, including the truth of supposed core gender, sexual, racial and national identities. As Foucault has shown, the imposition of disciplinary and regulatory identity norms – affecting and reiterated by both the individual body and the population as a whole – is a phenomenon of modern western society, replacing the power of physical force of the premodern regime.[63] Whereas pre-liberal states exercised control through overt violence and coercion, liberal capitalist societies exert control through the collection and production of information and through the implementation of scientifically legitimated norms, such as those established by psychoanalysis or psychiatry. Closely linked to the body, sexuality helps establish the disciplinary controls that both subject and create the subject. But sexuality is also the point where the individual body meets the regulation of the population that also typifies modern society. The work of normalisation of behaviour is done not only in prisons, the confessional or psychoanalysts' offices, as analysed by Foucault, but also in literature and on the stage.[64] At the same time, the plays presented also enact these norms as very much in flux.

Although sexuality at first glance seems to belong to the domestic or intimacy sphere, both intimacy and sexuality are politicised in bio-political modernity. Sexuality thus defined, as an inevitably political issue, emerges at the point of indifferentiation between biology and culture. Linked to the body, it is also created within the discursive sphere, including by its representations in writing and enactments on the stage. In European modernity, the experts that have intervened in the disciplining of bodies and the control of the population have been not only medical, psychiatric or religious experts, but also aesthetic experts. Literary representations or theatrical enactments can them-selves be acts of power, acts of division and exclusion that present themselves as knowledge.

The 'dramatic' (realist-naturalist) modern European theatrical tra-dition in particular (here represented by Strindberg and Sartre) is, in other words, part of modern knowledge production. Without being 'fascist', it is a discourse that participates in the problematisation of identity categories and of the immunitarian border between insid-ers and outsiders – the difference between bíos and bare life – that early twentieth-century totalitarianism would then take to its violent extreme. As the attraction of totalitarian regimes proved, knowledge can again provide a sense of certainty, a renewed feeling of social and cultural belonging, in a world that has started to question traditional symbolic-discursive identities. But as we will see, the theatre can also shatter any such reassurances.

Put differently, I will argue that plays can be *dispositifs* constituted by and themselves co-constituting knowledge discourses. Following Foucault's work, Agamben has further explored the 'apparatus' (Italian *dispositivo*; Foucault's *dispositif*), which he understands as 'anything that has in some way the capacity to capture, orient, determine, inter-cept, model, control, or secure the gestures, behaviors, opinions, or discourses of living beings' (Agamben 2009b: 14). Barad (inspired by Niels Bohr) refers to the apparatus as a 'device for making and remaking boundaries' (Barad 2007: 201–2). Taking advantage of the reverberations among these different writers' theorisations of the term 'apparatus', my own reading of modernist theatre is most importantly informed by Barad's understanding of apparatuses as 'dynamic (re)configurings of the world, the specific practices/intra-actions/perfor-mances through which specific exclusionary boundaries are enacted' (Barad 2008: 134). As 'boundary work' (Una Chaudhuri's term), the-atre is in a prime position for the – literal and figurative – enactment of boundaries. Linking concerns that critiques of biopolitics (*potestas*) from Foucault to Agamben share with the affirmative transversal of ontological boundaries (*potentia*) proposed by new materialist philosophy (including Barad's work) in spite of their differences, my project reconfigures the materialdiscursive (ontological and socio-political/ epistemological) practices and processes through which the immunitarian identity boundaries of modernity have been co-produced.[65]

Theatre and the Family

As Stefanie von Schnurbein has demonstrated in Scandinavian novels of the late nineteenth century, questions of identity and gender are centrally linked to images of the family (Schnurbein 2001: 315). Like the novel, drama has traditionally lent itself to an engagement with concepts of family, sexual difference and authority structures. In the western tradition, families and questions of authority have furnished the subjects of drama since the times of Greek drama. Aristotle, drawing his examples from the great tragedies of Attic Greece, urges writers of tragedy to dramatise stories involving family violence if they wish most fully to arouse pity and fear (Aristotle 1961: XIV: 8–9). As the twentieth-century French writer Jean Giraudoux declares, '[l] a plupart des pièces que nous considérons comme les chefs-d'oeuvre tragiques ne sont que des débats et des querelles de famille' ('the majority of the plays that we consider to be tragic masterworks are nothing but family discussions and family fights'; Giraudoux 1942: 293, my trans.).

Domestic or bourgeois drama in particular, whose origins in the eighteenth century coincide with the re-conceptualisation of the theatre as an interior space glimpsed voyeuristically through a fourth wall, represents a point of un-differentiation between the theatre and the family. In European modernity, the theatre becomes what Jürgen Habermas, in his classic work *Strukturwandel der Öffentlichkeit* (*The Structural Transformation of the Public Sphere*), refers to as the platform ('das Podium') of the bourgeois public sphere (Habermas 1987). In the bourgeois public sphere, the debates on marriage, family, gender roles and child-rearing took place predominantly in the medium of literature. Drama enjoyed great prestige as the social centre of 'good society', as the site of the bourgeoisie's self-expression and as an influential didactic genre. In Germany and France respectively, Gotthold Ephraim Lessing and Denis Diderot turned the stage into a public forum propagating bourgeois ideology and the central role of the bourgeois or nuclear family in it.

In nineteenth-century Europe, contemporary political discussions indicate a growing public interest in the sexual life of the family. In the second half of the nineteenth century and in particular the first decades of the twentieth century, the discussions on sexual life initiated by natural and social scientists, politicians, clerics and 'pressure groups' were increasingly taken up by a larger public and debated as the 'sexual question' in urgent need of solutions. The regulation of prostitution, the fight against venereal diseases, the 'treatment' of homosexuals and birth control became the central themes of this debate (Eder 2002: 188). In Scandinavia more than in other European countries, major works by both male and female authors contributed to the public debate about marriage, sex and morality. The scientific, economic and political developments unfolding in northern and central Europe strongly influenced Scandinavian authors of the 1870s and 1880s. With *Pillars of Society* (1877), Henrik Ibsen managed to transform the stage into a forum on which the bourgeois public debated prominent issues of the day.

At this point, about a hundred years after the heyday of domestic drama in the eighteenth century, however, the stress fractures of bourgeois ideology started to show in literature and on the stage. Ibsen's work specifically revealed the hypocrisy on which the bourgeois family was based, driving 'his protagonists so far beyond the world of bourgeois conduct that the self-destructive excess of the tragic shone forth in them' (Lehmann 2016: 390). Strindberg's naturalistic dramatic works – plays such as his well-known *The Father* (1887), a 'naturalistic tragedy', and his generally lesser-known drama *Fordringsägare* (*Creditors*) (1888), labelled a 'naturalistic tragicomedy' – similarly enact a crisis of male symbolic authority and bourgeois ideology that also actualises – in different ways – in Brecht and Sartre.

Brecht, who defines himself quite explicitly in opposition to (Ibsen's) bourgeois/naturalistic drama, reaches beyond the scope of domestic drama, focusing his analysis of the family on class struggle and the critique of capitalism.[66] While Brecht's first play, *Baal*, was written before Brecht's conversion to Marxism and the primary focus on class struggle in his subsequent plays, it is clearly an affront to bourgeois morality. In 'Beyond Bourgeois Theatre', Sartre as well, although for different reasons, criticises bourgeois theatre and seeks ways to move beyond it (Sartre 2000). In spite of its thematic innovativeness, however, Sartre's existentialist drama remains formally or dramaturgically in the tradition of bourgeois, naturalist drama. Most importantly, as we will see, the repudiation of difference in Sartre's early work is itself reminiscent of the denigration of the other characteristic of bourgeois thinking (as theorised by Mosse) and of the fear of feminised difference that Klaus Theweleit, in his classic work on German fascism, *Männerfantasien* (*Male Fantasies*), has analysed as one of the central traits of the fascist psychic constitution. Sartre's work enacts a biopolitical, immunitarian thinking that tries to shelter life from the expropriating features of the other, of community, from an intolerable excess. Sartre's early work aims to reinforce the boundaries threatened by the common with a humanist (bourgeois) philosophy of the heroic, outstanding, autonomous individual.

While bourgeois modernity gives birth to the ideology of individual autonomy, it is, paradoxically, exactly this individualistic model that is threatened by the blurring of the boundary between the private and the public in modern society. As Arendt puts it, 'man had hardly appeared as a completely emancipated, completely isolated being who carried his dignity within himself without reference to some larger encompassing order, when he disappeared again into a member of a people (Arendt 2013b: 83). The plays in this study all enact such ego dissolution in one way or another: as a negative threat to the paranoid, narcissistic ego (Strindberg, Sartre) or as an affirmative possibility resonant with new materialist philosophies (Brecht, Artaud). The immunitarian thinking that is supposed to fend off this merging, however, in Sartre (and arguably in Strindberg) paradoxically reaches its paroxysm in totalitarianism, an ideology and practice that again forces individuals to merge with the totality of the nation or racial group. What is ultimately at stake (that is what is enacted as threatening or as desirable) is the merging of the human ego with a more-than-human world, the death of the individual human ego.

Why Theatre? Or, between Molar Structures and Molecular Practices

Far from being 'private' and inaccessible to the public eye as posited by the bourgeois ideology of the separation of spheres, sexuality is not only grounded in the materiality of the body but, according to Foucault, it is also to a large extent produced by a panoptical societal control the focus of which is the body and its sensations. As a disciplinary apparatus of modern society that literally embodies – that is co-produces bodies that enact – psychic, social and material tensions, the theatre can contribute to establishing this material control. But as Foucault has taught us, power is never unidirectional. It is, in Braidotti's terms, both *potestas* and *potentia*. Theatre as well can therefore also be ambiguous, depending on the situation – the author, the play, the specific performance. Following new materialism and queer ecology, my project explores theatre as part of a dynamic network of intra-active environmental and internal relations. In spite of the transitory and contingent nature of each production or iteration, not only dramatic texts but also theatrical performances function as archives recording (and participating in) the complex material and psychic pressures and forces co-producing human and more-than-human bodies, as well as these active, agentive bodies' reactions. Whether of the 'dramatic' tradition of the nineteenth century or of the historical avantgarde after 1900, the plays of the modern European stage intra-act with the crisis of modernity readily and materially, as affect folding in and out.

What is thus ultimately at stake in all of the plays presented are *object relations*. As we will see, the modern stage is a site where modern citizen-subjects – whether as characters or spectators – no longer act out conflicts with a divine, royal or paternal sovereign, but with what Santner calls 'the last bastion of human sovereignty, the individual ego' (Santner 2016: 241). All plays presented in this project enact in one way or another a problematic of ego invasion and ego dissolution. Lest we see this problematic in exclusively humanist-anthropocentric terms, it is worth remembering that according to Freud's theory of primary narcissism, 'the ego is the original reservoir of libido from which object-cathexes are sent out' (Santner 2016: 244). The interest in this problematic, in the meeting of libidinal drives and objects, is not limited to human objects, in other words, and does continue in posthumanist scholarship. Adam Zaretsky, for instance, notes in 'OOPS: Object-Oriented Psychopathia Sexualis', that the drives are the threshold, the life force, the excess where objects meet: 'The problem of object relations is pressing. This psychic trail to the world is driven by drives' (Zaretsky 2016:163).[67] As we will see in this project, the 'flesh' – the location where the soma and culture intra-act and collapse in the libidinal drives – becomes the battleground of modernity. While the Deleuzian tradition, in contrast to psychoanalytic theory, speaks of (impersonal) fluxes of energy rather than (human) libido, my work sees both views of energy as related rather than as opposed. Although psychoanalysis is commonly considered part of the epistemological (rather than ontological-materialist) tradition, psychoanalysis has always paid close attention to the body and biology and we can thus put it in productive conversation with Deleuzian philosophy in a variety of ways.

The term 'desire', for instance, specifically the desire to endure, is central to both traditions and can thus help us reconcile any perceived incompatibilities between them. For the ontological/Deleuzian tradition, Braidotti defines desire as an assemblage of forces, 'as an ontological layer of affinity and sympathy between different enfleshed subjects' (Braidotti 2011: 154). I argue that this definition – mutual attraction – is not too far from more conventionally humanist, including psychoanalytical, usages of the term 'desire'. Both the psychoanalytic tradition (as we will show) and Braidotti (2011: 158) define desire as surplus and as a relation. What the ontological tradition teaches us, however, is that desire cannot be restricted to the human or even animal realm. At the same time, in contrast to the posthumanist tradition, I again do not see a need to completely exclude the (human) self from our conversations, as long as we see this self as intra-connected with internal and external forces rather than as unitary, and as long as we move beyond the hierarchical thinking of anthropocentrism. The theatre can produce and shape what Santner calls 'the glorious flesh of the social bond', the *libidinal economic base* of sociality (Santner 2016: 99). But as my project will show, the theatre ultimately goes beyond a sociality and beyond an energy or desire defined as purely human, linking human bodies to an intra-active materiality that both includes and goes beyond them.

For my exploration, finally, I have chosen texts by canonical writers, that is plays by writers initially viewed as avant-garde and controversial, but now long considered central to the European theatrical tradition. For my purpose, plays by canonical writers are particularly productive components of analysis because both the controversy these playwrights initially caused and their long-time success in the canon rest at least partly on their ability to give material expression to hotly disputed issues of their time that subsequently became culturally hegemonic or dominant assumptions. For an analysis of the work of normalisation done in modern society by the theatre, canonical texts thus offer a relative advantage. At the same time, however, the plays presented here are not these writers' most celebrated and most frequently produced plays. Brecht, for instance, is much better-known for his later, overtly didactic plays than for his early work. And while Artaud is well known for his theoretical writings on the theatre, his best-known play, *Les Cenci*, is hardly ever staged. While Sartre's *Les Mouches* is indeed, together with *Huis Clos* (*No Exit*), his most celebrated play, my reading differs markedly from traditional interpretations. The new readings offered here thus help expand the critical canon. The 'minor', lesser-known or less frequently performed works of canonical writers in particular can be the very places where alternatives to hegemonic, molar structures actualise.[68] These works and performances can indeed be the very sites where molecular experimental practices occur.

Notes

1. Barad (2007), for instance p. 140.
2. Cf. Massumi (2015b: x): 'affect's openness is unconfinable in the interiority of a subject'. However, Massumi adds, 'it is at the same time formative of subjects'.
3. Cf. Massumi (2015b: 124).
4. Meißner on the other hand, following Derrida, claims 'matter' itself as this kind of excess: 'the notion of matter as non-presence points to the excess of an opposition presence/absence; matter is that which exceeds material-semiotic phenomena'. She quotes from Derrida's *Positions*: '*matter* in this general economy designates . . . radical alterity', before explaining: 'significantly, he adds the specification that this radical alterity relates to philosophical oppositions' (Meißner 2016: 49).
5. Cf. also Braidotti (2006: 147; 2013: e.g. 2, 115; 2010: 208).
6. Cf. Massumi (2015b: 8, 124).
7. Cf. Massumi (2015b: 183–4).
8. With the term 'intra-act' I am following new materialist work in the tradition of Karen Barad, which underlines that things co-constitute each other through their entangled relations. 'Interact' on the other hand could presume the existence of pre-given singular entities.
9. See Jacobson (n.d.).
10. Cf. Foucault (1980a: 138): 'one might say that the ancient right to *take* life or *let* live was replaced by a power to *foster* life or *disallow* it to the point of death'.
11. As we will see, Artaud uses the term 'agencement' (translated into English as 'assemblage') in his theoretical statements. The term is also readily associated with Gilles Deleuze and Félix Guattari's work inspired by Artaud: 'An assemblage, in its multiplicity necessarily acts on semiotic flows, material flows, and social flows simultaneously' (Deleuze 1987: 71).
12. As Massumi explains (2015b: x), in Deleuze and Guattari's understanding, '"transversal" . . . means that it cuts across the usual categories. Prime among these are the categories of the subjective and the objective.'
13. Cf., however, also Lehmann's discussion of the dominance of the text in the modern realist-mimetic 'dramatic' tradition (Lehmann 1999: 21–2), as discussed later.
14. Justifiedly using the words 'pathfinding' and 'pioneering' for van der Tuin's work in new materialism, Vicky Kirby correctly points to van der Tuin's own 'sustained insistence that ontological questions already reside with/in the accepted and apparently circumscribed identity of epistemology' (Kirby 2017: 21 n. 6).
15. Cf. Barad (2011: 144):

    > I have argued [in *Meeting the Universe Halfway*] that in diffractively reading insights from physics and poststructuralist theory through one another it is possible to 'extend' the ideas of Butler's performativity theory

beyond the realm of the human (that indeed one *must* do so in taking account even of the human in its materiality), if certain key notions like materiality, discursivity, agency, and causality are suitably revised in light of the radical revision of classical understandings of matter and meaning-making suggested by these findings.

16. Cf. also Massumi's work on mental processes that function independently or precede conscious calculation (for instance 2015b: 139, 177–8). In 2014, the first complete (mesoscopic) detailed mapping of the brain structure of a mammal allowed us, for the first time, to chart the activity of our brains when we are conscious and when we are unconscious. Referencing Spinoza, the physicist Carlo Rovelli describes our subjectivity ('an individual') as 'a process' (Rovelli 2016: 71–3).

17. See Chaudhuri (2017a: 168) for a summary of the shared interests of queer theory and ecocriticism.

18. See Barad's convincing reading of Foucault's anthropocentric notion of biopower as inadequate for an analysis of contemporary technoscientific practices (Barad 2007: 200–4).

19. Cf. Braidotti (2011: 148–9).

20. Cf. for instance Kirby (2011: x).

21. Cf. Latour (2010), Felski (2008), Braidotti (2013: (for instance 35, 215), Dolphijn and van der Tuin (2012: 126–32).

22. In all fairness, Braidotti's affirmative philosophy does include both critique and creativity as becoming (2013: 165). Cf. also Braidotti (2011: 32): 'the pain and negativity that structure the oppositional consciousness of the "minorities" are a crucial concern for nomadic political theory and practice'. Cf. also Felski (2017: 386): 'In this context, it's worth pointing out that *postcritical* can hardly be taken to mean that we are no longer influenced by the ideas of Marx or Foucault.'

23. Cf. also Braidotti (2011: 232): 'Remembering the wound, the pain, the injustice – bearing witness to the missing people – to those who never managed to gain powers of discursive representation is central to the radical ethics and politics of philosophical nomadism.'

24. Cf. Braidotti (2011: 153).

25. Barad instead speaks of 'the intertwined practices of knowing and becoming'. A quantum physicist herself, she opposes, following the physicist and Nobel Prize winner Niels Bohr, the Cartesian 'representationalist triadic structure of words, knowers, and things' (Barad 2008: 130, 131). Cf. also Barad (2008: 147):

> The separation of epistemology from ontology is a reverberation of a metaphysics that assumes an inherent difference between human and nonhuman, subject and object, mind and body, matter and discourse. Onto-epistem-ology – the study of practices of knowing in being – is probably a better way to think about the kind of understandings that are needed to come to terms with how specific intra-actions matter.

26. Harman, Shaviro and Meillassoux are all considered speculative realists. Object-oriented ontology is a specific branch of SR. For the propositions shared by most speculative realisms see Breu 2016: 19–20.
27. Cf. Shaviro (2015: 25).
28. Cf. also Barad (2007: 185).
29. Cf. also Barad (2007: 379): 'Knowing is direct material engagement.'
30. Cf. also Davis summarising Merleau-Ponty: 'Merleau-Ponty inists that knowledge comes from our sensory life experiences as we are immersed with/in the dynamic energies that circulate through the world: in short, we have an embodied relationship with our surroundings that gives meaning to our experience' (Davis 2017: 41).
31. Morton says that an object is a 'weird entity withdrawn from access, yet somehow manifest' (Morton 2012a: 208).
32. Cf. Behar (2016: 126): 'Object-oriented ontology correctly states that humans are a kind of object.' Barad on the other hand prefers the term 'phenomena' (emerging through co-constitutive, entangled relations) to the 'metaphysics of things' (a metaphysics positing individual elements with pre-given properties) (Barad 2007: 33). But she also agrees that human practices as well are parts of phenomena:

> Notice that the . . . idea that the rightful place of the human is that of an exterior observer, a spectator, removed from the scene of the action, is ironically no less wedded to the humanist conception of man than its anthropocentric counterpart . . . By contrast, a posthumanist stance does not presume that man occupies a special position inside or outside the realm of natural phenomena or the theory that accounts for them . . . In a sense, Bohr shares this posthumanist stance when he remarks that we are part of the nature we seek to understand. (Barad 2007: 323; cf. also 206)

In this study, I will also put the role of the spectator in theatre in conversation with posthumanist discussions.
33. In his more recent *Tragödie und dramatisches Theater*, Lehmann himself states that dramatic theatre continues together with post-dramatic theatre in contemporary times (2013: 19). Transcending the strict border line between both genres, Lehmann points out correctly that every aesthetic experience worth its name also takes part in reflection (Lehmann 2013: 20).
34. My project in fact investigates the connections between the varied orientations in the field of new materialisms as described in Coole and Frost's anthology (2010: 1–43), not only between work focused on Ontology/Agency (for instance van der Tuin and Braidotti) and Bioethics/Biopolitics (for instance Foucault and Agamben), but also engaging with the third sub-field mentioned by Coole and Frost, namely Critical Materialism, which continues the conversations started earlier by historical materialism. Finally, my work is also in conversation with affect studies.

35. Cf. Barad (2007: 30–1).
36. See below.
37. In his essay 'All Objects Are Deviant' (2016), Morton basically applies Kant's and Lacan's theories to nonhumans.
38. Morton himself also argues that '[m]ovement is part of being a thing, period, such that a thing deviates from itself, just to exist' (2016: 78).
39. Cf. Meißner 2016: 53.
40. Meißner puts this sentiment elegantly in Marxian terms: 'Marx's social theory is a project of critique that applies the "visualizing 'power of theory'" . . . in order to make conceivable that certain structures of our historical reality are effects of human practices and can thus be transformed by cooperative human agency' (Meißner 2016: 47).
41. Cf. for instance the work of Jeffrey Nealon (presentation at the pre-conference session on 'Networking around Materialist Concepts' organised by Iris van der Tuin at the 2017 meeting of the American Comparative Literature Association in Utrecht, Netherlands), Hanna Meißner (2016), Sigrid Vertommen (2016), Susanne Lettow (2017), or Diana Coole (2013). According to Breu (2016: 20), the field known as 'material culture studies' in particular 'draws on the engagement with materiality and materialism in older traditions such as Marxist theory, phenomenology, and semiotics as well as with more recent attempts to push beyond the linguistic turn'.
42. As Massumi points out, rather than as false consciousness, Deleuze and Guattari read 1930s fascism as *affective* ressentiment: 'the "masses", Deleuze and Guattari say, were not ideologically duped into submitting to fascism. They positively desired it. They actively affirmed it. Fascism emerged from the bare-active stirrings of a mode of collective affective attunement tending towards ressentiment' (2015b: 104).
43. Massumi does give a more positive, process-oriented reading of class as 'continually produced by the capitalist process' (2015b: 88).
44. Massumi refers to the affirmative 'process that augments powers of existence' as Ontopower (2015b: 110).
45. Cf. Groot Nibbelink 2019: 105, paraphrasing Michel de Certeau's *The Practice of Everyday Life*: 'The map presents places as situated next to each other . . . whereas the tour describes spatiotemporal operations . . . The map colonizes and territorializes space, whereas the spatial operations of the tour subvert the power relations inscribed in the map.'
46. Cf. Jagoda (2017: 361).
47. Cf. also Massumi (2015b: 106): 'Resistance comes of immanence. It cannot be led.'
48. Cf. Dolphijn and van der Tuin (2012: 110).
49. Historical materialism is also a key interlocutor for the Marxist Sartre.
50. Sigrid Vertommen also calls work engaging both old (historical or feminist) and new (posthumanist) materialism – work that would also include my own – 'trans-materialist' (Vertommen 2016: 216).

51. According to Lebovic (following Esposito), 'the term biopolitics . . . was coined by Rudolf Kjellén in the context of the German discourse of *Lebensformen* (life-forms) in his 1920 *Outline for a Political System*' (Lebovic 2013: 183). My book will address this period in my chapter on Brecht's early work.

52. I am borrowing this term from Rebecca Oxley (2017: 90).

53. In Derridean or Heideggerian terms, I argue that humans are *weltarm* (poor in world, the category that Heidegger assigns to animals); we humans as well are creatures who are part of, but cannot exercise sovereign agency over, our environments (cf. also Nealon 2016: 53–4). While Breu establishes a contrast between speculative realism's proposition that there are 'aspects of objects that exceed human control or access' and 'the move in new materialism to collapse subjects and objects, discourse and matter into each other' (Breu 2016: 20), I do not see the difficulty of access (the fact that sometimes access can only be speculative) and the deep imbrication of materiality and the semiotic as a contradiction.

54. Cf. for instance Campbell (2008: 5); Lebovic (2013: 3, 11).

55. Immunity is a paradigm that several theorists, including Jacques Derrida, have explored since Niklas Luhmann's systems theory in *Soziale Systeme* (1984) and Haraway's and Jean Baudrillard's work. In his 'Translator's Introduction' to Esposito's *Bíos*, Campbell analyses 'where Esposito's use of the immunity paradigm converges and diverges with Derrida and others' (Campbell 2008: vii–viii).

56. Cf. for instance Braidotti (2013: 232).

57. Establishing a link between Foucault's work and the analysis of totalitarianism, Agamben registers his astonishment that Foucault's analysis of modern institutions such as the mental asylum or the prison never included the concentration camp: Foucault 'never dwelt on the exemplary places of modern biopolitics: the concentration camp and the structure of the great totalitarian states of the twentieth century' (Agamben 1995: 4; see also 119). Nevertheless, it seems to me that the entangled interaction of modern biopolitics and twentieth century totalitarianism comes out clearly in Foucault (1980a: see for instance 149). Nazism is indeed, in Geoff Eloy's words, 'an intensification of modernist governmentality'. The biopolitics of social engineering, the naturalisation of gender and race, and the techniques and apparatuses of knowledge production mark early twentieth-century fascism as a modernism, as a product of the modern age (Eloy 2010).

58. See also already Mosse (1966: xx).

59. Cf. also Braidotti (2011: 99): 'That these two competing notions of "life" coincide on the human body turns the issue of embodiment into a contested space and a political arena.'

60. Braidotti (2011: 215, 217).

61. Agamben sees modern totalitarian states as products of biopolitics and Nazism as 'the first radically biopolitical state' (Agamben 1995: 143). He adds that 'the dimension in which the extermination took place is . . . biopolitics' (Agamben 1995: 114).
62. Cf. Braidotti (2011: 210).
63. In *The Parasite*, Michel Serres writes of modern bureaucratic power based on knowledge and information (Serres 2007: 37).
64. Cf. also Serres (2007: 149):

> It is true that *agere*, Latin for 'to act,' has as its first concrete and physical meaning, 'expulsion.' It is not uninteresting to take note of what action was for our immediate ancestors. It was purging, banishment, eviction, rejection, elimination. It is not at all astonishing that the word *action* is now used in the theatre. The tragedy with goat's feet expels the scape-goat, the victim that Girard talks about. Tragic action is a more or less sufficient expression. But we, too, know this well: satire, fables, and comedy, around the parasite, speak essentially of exclusion. In the beginning is the action, that is to say, the crime.

65. As Barad says: 'Boundaries do not sit still' (Barad 2008: 135).
66. 'Die Konflikte ausschließlich in den Schoß der Familie oder in die Parteizelle eines einzigen Betriebs zu verlegen, heißt nur, ein spätbürgerliches Schema, das des naturalistischen Stücks, nachahmen. Der Klassenkampf, in dem die Arbeiter und Bauern die neue Gesellschaft aufbauen, ist weder eine reine Familien- noch eine reine Betriebsangelegenheit' (Brecht 1967: 937). ('To situate conflicts exclusively in the bosom of the family or in the party cell of a single company means only to imitate a late bourgeois pattern, that of the naturalistic drama. The class struggle, in which the workers and peasants build the new society, is neither a mere family nor a mere business affair' (my translation).)
67. Jacoby (2015) also quotes Karla Scherer: 'for Lacan, the Thing proves to be the center around which the drive achieves its ethical force.'
68. While *Creditors* is not part of the rather small sampling of Strindberg plays that are frequently performed outside of Sweden, Anna Stenport mentions Alan Rickman's 2008 production in London with guest performances at the Brooklyn Academy of Music in New York City as successful recent international productions (Stenport 2012: 9).

PART I

COPENHAGEN AND PARIS, circa 1889:
ECONOMIES OF EXCESS

Apparatuses are not merely about us. And they are not merely assemblages that include nonhumans as well as humans. Rather, apparatuses are specific material reconfigurations of the world that do not merely emerge in time but iteratively reconfigure spacetimematter as part of the ongoing dynamism of becoming. (Barad 2007: 142)

CHAPTER 1

Posthumanism and Gender, or the Fall Back into Nature

Anxiety is sticky; rather like Velcro, it tends to pick up whatever comes near. (Ahmed 2010: 36)

In her much discussed 2015 book, *The Limits of Critique*, Rita Felski sees literature, in Susan Stanford Friedman's words, 'as a nonhuman actor existing in *a fluid and ever-changing network* across the globe and through time' (Friedman 2017: 345, my emphasis). In the introduction to his by now classic text, *Cultural Mobility* (2009: 7), Stephen Greenblatt already encouraged scholars to 'recognize and to track the *movements* that provoke both intense pleasure and intense anxiety' (my emphasis). In their *Communist Manifesto* of 1848, Karl Marx and Friedrich Engels famously proclaimed that 'a spectre' was haunting Europe. While Marx and Engels were of course speaking of the communist movement, I will argue that after the Darwinian turn the spectre haunting modern Europe, the movement provoking intense anxiety, was a spectral materiality at the threshold or imbrication of the human and the nonhuman. Co-produced historically by the rapid material and socio-political changes in European modernity and by ground-shifting scientific discoveries, this spectrality induced intense ontological anxieties about the status of the human. My project seeks to conceptualise this anxiety in a way that goes beyond its psychologisation as an interior, personal quality and instead maps anxiety as what Lawrence Grossberg (2010: 327) calls a 'structure of feeling' within a conjuncture. I am interested, in other words, not only in the exhilarating, pleasure-producing modern belief in scientific and cultural progress, but also in the relationality constituted by anxiety as a 'sticky' affect within the materialdiscursive ecology of the heterogeneous bodies and lived practices of modernity.

I would like to begin this exploration with one of the best-known theorists on the topic of affect, the Canadian philosopher Brian Massumi, who points out that 'the affective reality of threat is contagious' (2010: 58).

Anna Gibbs also observes that feelings or affects – such as anxiety – are infectious: 'Bodies can catch feelings as easily as catch fire; affect leaps from one body to another, evoking tenderness, inciting shame, igniting rage, exciting fear – in short, communicable affect can inflame nerves and muscles in a conflagration of every conceivable kind of passion' (Gibbs 2001: 1). This phenomenon, called 'affect contagion', is 'the bioneurological means by which particular affects are transmitted from body to body' (Gibbs 2010: 191). Contagion, affects and bodies are central to my project – both thematically and as material processes in performance. In an age of increasing abstraction, a spectral materiality and this contingent contagion – both human, conscious and unconscious emotion affecting nerves, skin, glands and muscles, as well as affect in excess of the individual body – find their expression on the modern stage, linking (for my project) past, present and future.[1]

In his 1936 Nobel prize speech, the American playwright Eugene O'Neill called the Swedish playwright, novelist, poet, essayist and painter August Strindberg (1849–1912) 'the most modern of the moderns'. At the end of the nineteenth and the beginning of the twentieth centuries, Scandinavia could rightfully claim its place in Europe as the leader of avant-garde naturalist playwrights. Strindberg himself lived in Germany and France for significant periods of time. The German book market was dominated by translations of Ibsen and Strindberg (Robertson 2004: 2), and as we will see, Strindberg entertained close professional and personal relations with contemporary French writers. While Strindberg's naturalist dramatic *oeuvre* is usually associated with the gender crisis of the late nineteenth century, I suggest that what is ultimately at stake in his work is the most anxiety-provoking border of all: the border between the human and the nonhuman, between two kinds of bodies, and ultimately between life and death. In 'Knots: Notes for a Daemonic Naturalism', Levi R. Bryant has correctly pointed to 'the core insight of naturalism: that we are embedded in material being, and that there is no domain of the transcendent' (2016: 27). Strindberg's naturalist plays enact exactly this loss of the transcendent and the *fin de siècle*'s desperate 'struggle against nature', as Strindberg himself called it (Preface to *Miss Julie*, Strindberg 1970: 78). Whereas Strindberg is often cited as a modernist for his formal departure from classical playwriting in his work after his 'inferno' crisis in the mid-1890s, I argue that his earlier, naturalistic dramatic work is equally modern in that it engages with emerging bioscientific theories concerning the etiology of disease and the ontological status of the human. Strindberg's work thus carries out what the theatre scholar Una Chaudhuri calls the historical task of performance, namely 'boundary work' (Chaudhuri 2017a: 82).

Let me start the conversation about human and more-than-human bodies with the encounter of two defining documents of modernity that speak about biological bodies – one political and one biological text, although these spheres are deeply entangled in both works. Strindberg's *oeuvre*, I submit, is the site where both these foundational events, and with them politics and biology, meet.

In 1679, during the reign of King Charles II, the Parliament of England passed a legislative act, the Habeas Corpus Act (literally 'you have the body'). Initially intended to assure the presence of the accused at trial, this legislation obliged the courts to explore the lawfulness of a detainee's imprisonment and prevent arbitrary confinement. In the habeus corpus writ, now generally considered a founding document of modern democracy, the central term is *corpus*, 'body'. Giorgio Agamben, in *Homo Sacer*, points to the privileged position of this term, 'corpus', in the philosophical and scientific texts of the Baroque age, 'from Descartes to Newton, from Leibniz to Spinoza', calling it 'the central metaphor of the political community'. In Hobbes, Agamben writes, 'the body's capacity to be killed ... founds ... the natural equality of men' and thus 'the new political body of the West' (Agamben 2013b: 149–51).

Providing the basis of the principle of equality, anonymous physical life was thus at the centre of European democracy's fight against absolutism. In the human rights declarations of the eighteenth century – such as the French Declaration of the Rights of Man and Citizen of 1789 – natural life, the simple fact of being alive, is then for the first time the basis for inalienable political rights (Agamben 2013a: 152–4). Paradoxically, the constant redefinition of the relationship between 'man' and 'citizen' – the question of who is a citizen and who is not – then becomes the incessant political task of modern nation states. Strindberg's naturalist work enacts the debate over social and political inclusion and exclusion through the woman question of the late nineteenth century.

The second decisive event involving the status of biological life followed eighty years after the Habeas Corpus Act: the publication on 24 November 1859 of Charles Darwin's *Origin of Species*. In it, Darwin presented the scientific theory that populations of (human and non-human) animals evolve over time through reproduction, random variation and natural selection. Seventeen years before Darwin, however, the French novelist Honoré de Balzac, influenced by the contemporary natural sciences (in particular Georges Cuvier and Geoffrey Saint-Hilaire), had in his famous 1842 'Préface' to *La Comédie Humaine* already established a continuity between animals and humans. For Balzac, both human and nonhuman animals are products of and continuous with their environment:

> The Animal . . . takes its external form, or, to be accurate, the differences in its form, from the environment in which it is obliged to develop. Zoological species are the result of these differences . . . I . . . perceived that in this respect society resembled nature. (Balzac 1968)

The human types that appear and reappear throughout Balzac's novels are embedded in their social milieux. Balzac's realist work exemplifies a constitutive trait of modernist literature: its new perception of humans as part of the animal kingdom. Starting in the 1860s, naturalist writers such as Emile Zola would continue and expand the scientifically inspired work of their realist predecessors. Zola also entertained a correspondence with his Swedish contemporary, Strindberg, who himself (from 1883 to 1889) spent a significant amount of time in France and whose influence (including that on Sartre and Artaud) would continue in the French context (Stenport 2012: 14). As part of a wave of Scandinavian avant-garde plays, three of Strindberg's plays – *Miss Julie*, *The Father* and *Creditors* – were performed in Paris in the early 1890s. In 1888, Strindberg's play *The Father* had been published in France with a preface by Zola.

Reminiscent of Zola's view of the novel or theatre as a laboratory experiment and a product of his passionate engagement with the sciences of his day,[2] Strindberg's naturalist work follows the doctrine that knowledge can be derived from experiment and observation of the natural world, a doctrine based on the assumption that the biological-material realm has agency. This approach then ultimately sees the theatre as a scientific apparatus or 'agency of observation', in the physicist-philosopher Karen Barad's terms.[3] But in contrast to Barad's (and the early twentieth-century Nobel prize-winning physicist Niels Bohr's) view of the apparatus as part of the nature that it seeks to observe, Strindberg's naturalist theatre, together with nineteenth-century realist-naturalist theatre in general, is an example of representationalism and its 'geometrical optics of externality' (Barad 2007: 381), establishing an *inherent*, fixed – one could say Cartesian – agential cut between 'subject' and 'object', that is between the spectator and the stage and between the stage as mirror on the one hand and society or nature as the 'original' on the other. In contrast to Bohr's argument that apparatuses produce the phenomena they measure, realist-naturalist theatre, a theatre predominantly based on human dialogue and a 'tropology of sameness', sees language as referential and transparent, providing an objective copy of nature or society from a certain distance. As we will see, the theatre of the twentieth century on the other hand will increasingly complete 'the shift from linguistic practices to discursive practices (which are specific material practices)', as Barad argues (2007: 334, 382), enacting active entangled engagements.

The 'experiment' in Strindberg's 1889 play *Creditors* involves only three characters: Tekla, her first husband Gustav and Adolf, her second and present husband. While Tekla is away, Gustav arrives incognito at Tekla and Adolf's vacation hotel to settle old 'debts' and to rid Adolf of any illusions he has about his wife, in particular about her faithfulness. Gustav takes the part of the outside 'expert', of the 'psychoanalyst' who intervenes in the domestic organisation of the bourgeois family.[4] Spectators of modern plays, themselves seduced into a voyeuristic relationship witnessing the 'privacy' of this space and the characters' interactions, have had frequent opportunities to observe 'outside experts' like Gustav on the stage. Within the larger framework of Michel Foucault's theory of the modern deployment of sexuality, his student and colleague Jacques Donzelot has pointed to the increasingly important role played by doctors during the eighteenth and nineteenth centuries in family counselling. While medical intervention in sexuality had at first been restricted to private hygiene, this restriction slowly came undone during the nineteenth century, leading to the inclusion of sexual behaviour in medical counselling and to the appropriation by physicians of the role of sex expert (Donzelot 1997: 172). Given the medicalisation of sex in modern culture, it does not really come as a surprise that nineteenth-century family doctors should have diagnosed sexual malfunctions in growing numbers of men. While the National Socialist biocracy would later take the modern politicisation of biological life and medicine to its extreme, Strindberg's play also enacts male sexual pathology as a central medical and cultural concern. In the panoptical environment of the stage, Gustav listens and helps Adolf and Tekla openly examine their sexual suffering and establish the 'truth' about their marriage.

When Strindberg's characters and spectators have acquired sufficient knowledge about the sexual dynamics of bourgeois marriage and above all about a supposed quasi-biological core identity of 'woman' – which is clearly negativised and held responsible for the misfortunes of sex befalling the bourgeois family – and when Adolf's suspicions concerning his wife are corroborated, Strindberg's male protagonist has an epileptic seizure and dies. His death in turn enacts the annexation in the nineteenth century of sexual irregularity to mental illness[5] and illustrates the lethal danger posed by aberrations from established gender norms. The play specifically alerts the public to the dangers of a man manifesting feminine traits. In a time preoccupied with defining, within the bourgeoisie, a strict gender dichotomy with a clearly defined and static gender role distribution, such a feminisation of masculinity or blurring of gender lines was perceived as especially threatening and dangerous, as what Strindberg in the Preface to his play *Miss Julie* (1888) called a 'desperate struggle against nature' (Strindberg 1970: 78). Strindberg thus frames the 'war of the sexes' of the late nineteenth century as an immunitarian struggle for survival grounded in biology. The threat posed is the fall back into nature, what Michel Serres calls 'a certain horror of falling into the beastly' (Serres 2007: 140). Given the patriarchal association of man and human, it is an often feminised threat against human exceptionalism, against the privileged status of the human in the natural world.

The reconfiguration of humankind's relationship to biological life and the natural and material world at large is a trait of modernist literature and drama. Responding to the enormous influence of the sciences in the nineteenth century, Strindberg from 1886 to 1890 adopted Naturalism as the credo of literature as science. Given women's perceived closeness to animals, the question of the relationship between the human and the more-than-human (or more accurately, the question of the animal nature of humans) was displaced onto gender in the scientific and social debates of the *fin de siècle*. Both women and men became the targets of the new contemporary sciences and their taxonomic passion for classifying and measuring life and hierarchising bodies and behaviours – a taxonomic passion that contradicted, or reacted to, the universalising impulses of the foundational documents of democratic modernity. While scholars (including myself) have often read Strindberg primarily as an exponent of the gender crisis of the *fin de siècle*, what is at stake in Strindberg, however, is ultimately not only male authority or gender, but the status of the human in the natural world. While Strindberg's work is part of the naturalist 'dramatic' theatrical tradition (as opposed to the anti-mimetic, 'post-dramatic' theatrical tradition explored by Hans-Thies Lehmann), a tradition generally considered 'anthropocentric', I argue that Strindberg's work implicitly marks the intersection of gender and a beginning (thematic) posthumanism.[6]

Already about a century removed from the heyday of domestic or bourgeois drama in the eighteenth century, Strindberg's dramas – similar to Ibsen's work – enact the perceived crisis of bourgeois modernity. In theatre this crisis would soon find its expression in the shift from the naturalist 'dramatic' tradition represented by Strindberg (before his Inferno crisis) and, in this study, Sartre to what Lehmann calls the 'historical theatrical avant-garde' of the early twentieth century, as explored in my chapters on Brecht and Artaud. The theatre of the historical avant-garde would increasingly leave the bourgeois world behind and (as I argue) further move towards posthumanism. Strindberg enacts the crisis of bourgeois ideology and drama as the feminised threat posed by natural-zoological life to anthropocentric and androcentric hegemony and to the family patriarch's role in the bourgeois domestic sanctuary. This sanctuary is the space of bourgeois domestic drama, a space whose borders have become porous, although this porousness does not yet find its scenic expression in a new vision of theatre and a more active role of the spectator, as it will in Brecht and Artaud. The ontological threat posed by natural life, however, is ultimately the threat of modernity itself; it is the socio-political and metaphysical threat posed by the excess of immanence following the loss of transcendent – divine and royal – authority in European modernity. What is at stake in Strindberg are thus the boundaries between the human and the nonhuman worlds. While the Nazis would later racialise perceived threats to these boundaries, the late nineteenth century draws the immunitarian line of separation in terms of sexual difference, along a binary gender distribution.

Medical science clearly played a central role in the creation of the stricter gender dichotomy that marks modernity. In early modern Europe, medical models of reproduction had been based on the belief that women and men shared a similar reproductive anatomy and sexual psychology. Only from around 1800 onwards did physicians begin to differentiate radically between what would hence be called the 'opposite sexes'. In other words, after 1800 scientific discourses helped shore up the bourgeois ideology of split (domestic vs. public) spheres and its rigid gender role distribution. Darwin's theory of evolution, for instance, while generally opposed to dualistic oppositions, nevertheless posited that higher civilisations feature more distinct and refined attributes of masculinity and femininity. Following this argument, contemporary eugenicists then claimed that the perceived threat of national decline facing many of the European nations of the late nineteenth century could only be halted or reversed by virile men and 'feminine' women. This claim in turn led to pervasive anxieties about the 'masculinisation' of modern women and the 'effeminacy' of the men with whom they would produce children (Tickner 1992: 7). To alleviate such anxieties, clothing styles started sharpening the distinctions between the sexes while at the same time blurring class lines (Solomon-Godeau 1997: 215–19). The new focus on gender dimorphism also led to the exclusion of non-reproductive sexualities, of cases of ambiguous sexuality and of homosexuals.

In the years from the 1870s to the Second World War, however, the women's movement and the increasing visibility of homosexuals, avant-garde artists and intellectuals threatened the patriarchal system and the sexual divisions so important to the construction of modern masculinity. In the 1870s and 1880s, the confrontation with the so-called woman problem was of special importance to the Scandinavian authors of the movement called the Modern Breakthrough (*det moderna genombrottet*) and its call for a new era. At the time, Swedish women did not have the right to vote, and only in 1874 did Sweden pass a law that enabled married women to have control of their earnings and inheritance. Georg Brandes, the intellectual leader of the Breakthrough, translated John Stuart Mill's book *The Subjection of Women* into Danish in 1869 and in 1872 advocated that literature address gender relations. It was Brandes, an early proponent of what we today call comparative literature, who encouraged his compatriots to pay attention to influences from abroad, for instance to French writers (Brandes 2017: 696). It was Brandes as well who made Friedrich Nietzsche known to a European audience and who, like Nietzsche, attacked the notion of God and challenged patriarchalism. Brandes's most immediate disciples were Ibsen, Strindberg and other Scandinavian writers of the Breakthrough period. Strindberg's naturalist dramas follow Brandes's call to represent gender relations in literature and problematise patriarchal authority. In spite of having left Sweden for Central Europe from 1877 to 1897, Strindberg is therefore considered part of the Modern Breakthrough and one of the innovators on the Scandinavian literary scene. Reflecting his status as an avant-garde writer and demonstrating the relation between discussions of gender or male authority and the position of the human in the modern world (which threatened the position of established religion), he was put on trial for heresy in the 1880s.[7]

Formally, Strindberg's naturalist plays are not avant-garde, that is anti-Aristotelian or 'epic' in Brecht's sense. In the Preface to *Miss Julie*, Strindberg explains that he has abolished the division into acts 'because it has seemed to me that our increasingly weak capacity for illusion possibly would be disturbed by intermissions, during which the spectator has time to think and thereby escapes the dramatist-hypnotist's suggestive influence' (Strindberg 1970: 81–2). Strindberg thus aims for what Aristotelian theatre called identification and what Maaike Bleeker (2008: 21) analyses as the 'absorption' that characterises dramatic theatre – in contrast to the 'theatricality' (Barbara Freedman's term in *Staging the Gaze*, 1991) of a theatre such as Brecht's or Artaud's that draws attention to the spectatorial process (Groot Nibbelink 2019: 51). In the same Preface, incidentally, Strindberg expresses quite negative views of his title character and women in general. But as Matthew Wilson Smith argues in *The Nervous Stage*, Strindberg's plays – his enactment of hysteria and hypnotism – participate in a shift from the theatre of sentiment of the eighteenth century to a theatre of sensation in dialogue with the neuroscientific discoveries of the nineteenth century and already announcing Artaud's theatre of cruelty (Smith 2018: 11). The fact that Strindberg calls his own role as a playwright that of a hypnotist (hypnotising, impacting the senses of the audience) establishes a link between himself and his two central characters, Gustav and Tekla, to whose hypnotic eyes the weakened male protagonist, Adolf, ultimately succumbs in *Creditors* (Strindberg 1960a: 22). Strindberg, in other words, does not make it his mission as a writer to rescue the victim of this hypnotic influence, his embattled male protagonist. Strindberg's naturalistic dramas thus clearly problematise a binary gender division in a time that both stipulated gender dimorphism with renewed pseudoscientific vigor *and* increasingly put these static societal norms in question.

Strindberg's naturalist plays diagnose the perceived dangers for men in particular of not abiding by the immunitarian defence line and not asserting their core gender identity, their masculinity. While the changes in gendered authority structures were the result of the socio-economic, material changes brought on by capitalism, Strindberg's plays convey the sense prevalent at the end of the nineteenth century that the crisis of masculinity was primarily due to women's transgression of traditional gender boundaries and their usurpation of masculine power. The perceived threat to the population's immunity is accordingly feminised. Tekla is the New Woman who challenges male supremacy in art, the professions and in her marriage. At the same time, the crisis that Strindberg's male characters undergo is not only a crisis of personal health/ immunity or even only the crisis of male supremacy. It is the crisis of the status of the human.

Degeneration

Discourses on human and nonhuman animals, as well as on sexual difference, race and the body, intersect in late nineteenth- and early twentieth-century discussions of degeneration. After the Darwinian turn, the *fin de siècle* associated the perceived threat brought on by the Industrial Revolution, modern technology and urbanisation with the term coined by Max Nordau in *Degeneration* (published in 1892 in German, 1893 in French and 1895 in English), in adaptation of the ideas of Bénédict-Augustin Morel (*Traité des dégénérences physiques, intellectuelles et morales de l'espèce humaine*; Paris 1857) and the Comte de Gobineau (*Essai sur l'inégalité des races humaines*; 1855). The theory of degeneration, a term first used in psychiatry, also proved highly influential in 'nineteenth-century criminology, the public hygiene movement, general social theory, and a wide range of racial and eugenical movements' (Nye 1982: 20). Here we can then witness not only the enormous influence of the sciences on nineteenth-century life and culture, but also the links between the cultural crisis of the *fin de siècle* and the racism and eugenics of the early twentieth century. Criminality, madness and various abnormalities were conceptualised in racial terms. Because society perceived itself as a biopolitical organic unit, individual weakness constituted a social crisis.

According to Nordau, modern Europeans, and in particular the upper classes, were suffering from degeneration, neurasthenia and nervous exhaustion. The disease 'abulia' – defined as 'exhaustion more or less general of the cerebral faculties' – had been discovered in the early 1840s (Smith 1989: 104, 107). In 1888 Camillo Golgi succeeded for the first time in visualising nerve cell processes in their entirety, revealing the brain as an extraordinarily complex organ consisting of millions of cells. Neurasthenia became the bourgeois illness of the time and the prevalent disease afflicting male intellectual workers (such as the artist Adolf in Strindberg's play) in particular.[8] A constitutive trait of modern masculinity, will power – as opposed to feminised acquiescence or passivity, as theorised by Sigmund Freud for instance – assumed a central role in the definition of manliness toward the end of the nineteenth century. The period's cult of masculine will in Germany and other European nations was derived from Nietzsche. Nietzsche himself, however, characterised the age as one of fatigue and exhaustion (Nietzsche 1967: 48, 134). Nordau and many others warned that exhaustion and the enervation of the will would lead to the evolutionary decline of European and North American society. In 1918, Oswald Spengler's history, *The Decline of the West*, became a popular best-seller. It argued that human cultures periodically renew themselves, moving through the stages of 'youth, growth, maturity, decay' (Spengler 1926: 16). In *Creditors*, written in August and September 1888, the vampiric, animal-like Tekla, herself lacking cognitive control and thus a pawn of sexual instincts, has sucked any masculine will out of her husband Adolf, ultimately reducing him to an epileptic body wrecked by involuntary convulsions. This thematic of the will enacts a central problematic of the rationalist, Cartesian western philosophical tradition based on a sovereign human 'I' and on a consciousness defined as essentially male.

In Foucauldian terms, modernity involves a transition to a new medical rationality based on internalised, immanent norms targeting individual bodies as well as populations and distinguishing between health and illness. Strindberg's male protagonists' illness consists in the lack of will power. The Nazis, on the other hand, would stage their own rise as a resurgence, as what the title of Leni Riefenstahl's 1935 Nazi propaganda film would call a *Triumph of the Will*. Will, the human imposition of order onto the cosmos, is of course a humanist thematic. Strindberg enacts this human dominance as threatened.

Degeneration – as a lessened ability of the body to defend itself against dangers to its immunity, contamination or in short 'evil' – intersected with the projected fears of difference of the *fin de siècle* and with the immunitarian anxieties that would also form the basis of the National Socialist biocracy. As the works of French naturalism show, in France the notion of decline found its literary representation primarily in terms of race or heritage, as a threat to white masculinity and ultimately the (white) nation. The view of racial degeneration as a threat to national survival would later also resurface in Germany, where the Nazis made the regeneration of the racialised body politic to originary Germanic purity and greatness their primary political programme. The Nazis applied the term 'degenerate' to racial outsiders as well as to ideologically suspect art. Nazi propaganda presented Jews and Sinti and Roma ('Gypsies') as embodying the feminised threat of the nervous degeneration and decline of races and nations.

As Strindberg's dramatic work demonstrates, *fin de siècle* culture frequently interpreted the perceived threat of social decline in terms of sexual difference, viewing any deviation from a normative gender ideal as a threat to the stability of society. Throughout late nineteenth-century Europe, there was an unprecedented preoccupation with crime statistics, with the number and forms of insanity, and with the appearance of apparently novel forms of sexual behaviour. Together with

degeneration and decadence, the weakness of (heterosexual and homosexual) men – effeminacy – which brought with it the threat of steril-
ity and national extinction, was a central concern of the *fin de siècle*
and its medical experts. In France, where (as we have seen) Strindberg
had lived during his naturalist period, the problem of the falling birthrate ensured that impotence became the master metaphor for national
decline (Nye 1994: 68).[9] On the other side of the spectrum, the ideal of
robust manhood, a return to idealised 'natural' and non-decadent manhood, would later reach a climax and become a national symbol under
National Socialism.

In *Creditors*, Adolf's acceptance of the 'feminine' part in his interaction with Gustav points to the role distribution in his marriage
with Tekla and is an example of decadent manhood. Since Nordau
associated modern art with degeneration, it makes sense that the role
of a degenerate man is played by Adolf, an artist. Emphasising the
intersections of sexual difference and race, Gustav, using a racially
charged metaphor, also calls Adolf a 'slave' (to Tekla) (Strindberg
1960a: 22). Adolf says to Gustav: 'Do what you will with me. I'll
obey.' When Gustav orders him to get up, Adolf cannot do so. He
says: 'My bones are as weak as a baby's. And my mind is all at
sea' (Strindberg 1960a: 24). Adolf plays the role of an infant who
is dependent on either Tekla or Gustav and cannot yet distinguish
between himself and the world around him. Adolf does not have a
will, but accepts Gustav's opinions as his own. Tekla and Gustav
have the same eyes that seem to hypnotise Adolf (Strindberg 1960a:
22). There is one big difference between the two relationships, however – between Gustav and Adolf's relationship on the one hand and
Tekla and Adolf's on the other hand. Although, as I will explore in
more depth in the next chapter, both Gustav and Tekla are vampire
or cannibal figures[10] who deplete Adolf's resources, Gustav has a
socially valid motive (revenge) and his strength is a positive character trait. As Angus McLaren's analysis of nineteenth-century court
records shows, contemporary judges and juries backed up a man's
right to use violence against those who threatened his honor or violated his home (as Adolf had done to Gustav by seducing and marrying his wife).[11] The power exerted by Tekla, however, is clearly
demonised within the play. The fact that her second husband dies
from epilepsy at the end of the play, an illness formerly assigned to
possession by demons, enacts both Tekla's demonic nature[12] and,
as we will see, the nineteenth century's interest in the neurological
causes of illnesses.

The Biopolitics of Gender

Strindberg's naturalist dramas enact the dualistic logic of modernity, a defensive logic aiming to protect or immunise the biological life of the population. In the Scandinavian drama of the late nineteenth century, the immunitarian crisis of modernity manifests itself as an especially intense renegotiation of concepts of sexual difference. Strindberg's work enacts the feminised and queer threats to bourgeois ideology and the bourgeois patriarchal family, problematising the perceived threat posed by a femininity increasingly identified with modernity. While fixed identity concepts such as gender are – not only in modernity or modernism, but always, intrinsically – in crisis from the start and ultimately a failure, European modernity constitutes an especially intense juncture in the debate over difference – a juncture that is itself the result of changing material conditions. What is of particular interest in this context is the historical proximity of the *fin de siècle* crisis of gender and sexuality to one of the most massive short-circuits of western modernity, namely early twentieth-century totalitarianism. What makes the often-discussed 'crisis of masculinity' that occurs at the turn towards the twentieth century so fascinating is that it can function as an entry point to an understanding of western modernity – of its basic tensions as well as its paroxysms.

As the short remarks above already show, 'crisis' itself – as used in this project, as a moment of cultural shifts and redefinition – is not necessarily a negative term. What makes such moments of cultural renegotiation or transformation dangerous in socio-political terms, however, is the attempt to short-circuit them with simplistic answers. As extreme examples of such short circuits, totalitarian regimes fought the crisis of modernity with attempts to implement a would-be, artificial and violent 'final solution'. Although German National Socialism in particular defined itself in opposition to modernist art, we can see both National Socialism and modernist art – including Strindberg's dramas – as different reactions to the same cultural situation, as reactions, that is, to the material changes that occurred in modernity. We can read the modern cultural debate about identity categories – from gender and sexuality to race and nation –as a dualistic sorting out and hierarchising of populations according to quasi-biological criteria. This hierarchisation of insiders and outsiders has helped modern biopolitical apparatuses establish a security system that is designed to negate any random threats inherent in biological life and defend against threats to the population's health or immunity. Literature and the theatre can act as apparatuses that participate in this sorting out and hierarchising.

The rise of immunitarian thinking in modernity is the result of a society that increasingly perceives itself at risk due to the decline of traditional symbolic authority – from religious authority to the authority of the king and the father in the family. The immunity strategies of modern biopolitics reach their extreme under totalitarianism.

Although current research into the modern politicisation of biological life (or biopolitics) sees itself as primarily indebted to Foucault (as discussed in my Introduction), the argument of a link between the crisis of symbolic authority and fascism was first initiated by one of the most influential and also most controversial theories of fascism. It was the Frankfurt School theory of the fatherless society, that is the Critical Theory of the first generation of the Frankfurt School that, quite problematically in its gender blindness, posited a causal connection between the post-eighteenth-century decline of paternal and paternalistic authority and the rise of European fascism. In the 1930s, Max Horkheimer, Theodor Adorno and Herbert Marcuse (along with several other scholars at the Institute for Social Research in Frankfurt am Main, Germany) collaborated on a project entitled *Studies on Authority and the Family* (1936). Their Freudo-Marxist analysis explored the socio-critical potential of psychoanalytical concepts and the relation between the rise of National Socialism and anti-Semitism in Germany during the 1920s and 1930s on the one hand and the decline of the European patriarchal family on the other.

In their analysis of modern family dynamics, the members of the Frankfurt School tracked the increasing loss of male authority back to the material conditions of post-eighteenth-century Europe. They saw the growing helplessness of the individual under monopoly capitalism and the loss of entrepreneurial freedom, responsibility and decision-making as the cause of the father's declining moral authority. According to the Frankfurt School, in modernity the father has lost his economic power and independence; he is no longer the mainstay, the ideal public representative of the family. In both *The Father* (1887) and *Creditors* (1889), Strindberg's protagonist suffers from a debilitating and ultimately fatal illness that is symptomatic of the larger, societal crisis of male symbolic authority in western modernity.

The theories of the Frankfurt School also influenced the work done several decades later by Alexander Mitscherlich in *Auf dem Weg zur vaterlosen Gesellschaft* (1963) (*Society Without the Father*). Mitscherlich, a German psychoanalyst writing in the tradition of the Freudian left, again applied psychoanalytic concepts to social history. Mitscherlich as well attributed the breakdown of paternal authority to the change in material/economic conditions since the eighteenth century. In modernity, work separated from the domestic site and became associated with mechanical mass production and with a complex administration of the masses. It became increasingly fragmented: the independent producers of premodern times became workers and employees who earned wages and consumed goods. The father was thus no longer the model of work and social interaction for his children. As a consequence, paternal and paternalistic authority decreased both within the family and in modern society at large. Strindberg's plays enact the cultural consequences of these material changes brought on by capitalism.

As we can already see, the term 'fatherlessness' ultimately transcends the domestic sphere and also refers on a larger, societal scale to the end, in modern times, of the predominance of paternalistic structures of authority – domestic (the father), political (the monarch) and religious/divine (God the Father). Up to the eighteenth century, the histories of European countries are the history of monarchy – a paternalist system based on the central role of the symbolic father within the Judeo-Christian tradition. European modernity, however, with its programmatic birth in the French Revolution, spells death to the father in all his various forms and functions.

In France, the Marquis de Sade (1740–1814) was one of the first modern critics of divine authority. In Germany, traditional Christian belief was powerfully challenged by a philosophical tradition that included G. W. F. Hegel (1770–1831), Ludwig Feuerbach (1804–72), David Friedrich Strauss (1808–74), Karl Marx (1818–83) and Friedrich Nietzsche (1844–1900). French authors such as Ernest Renan (1832–92) and Hippolyte-Adolphe Taine (1828–93) were clearly influenced by Hegel, and Feuerbach's and Strauss's work challenged traditional Christian doctrine throughout Europe.[13] The modern is thus the 'post-deist, post-paternal, post-monarchic self' (MacCannell 1991: 19). In modern democracy, the abstract sovereignty of the people replaces the embodied authority of the king, and the authority of the physically present pater familias increasingly vanishes under modern, capitalist work conditions.

In modern Europe, authority thus becomes increasingly abstract and increasingly interiorises. Even hell – the punishment for not leading a god-fearing life – transforms from an exterior to an interior space and secularises. In many of Strindberg's plays, the problematic relationship to the Other/alterity and others finds its expression in a private hell set in a bourgeois interior that very much foreshadows Sartre's notion of 'l'enfer c'est les autres' ('hell is other people'). Heightening the intensity of this close intimacy, any contact with the feminised Other is seen as potentially deadly.

Managing Bodies

In the long preface to *Miss Julie*, written right before *Creditors*, Strindberg lays out his revolutionary aesthetic programme, speaking of his era as an age of transition: 'I have depicted my characters as modern characters, living in an age of transition, more hysterically in a hurry than during the preceding period at least. I have presented them as vacillating, tattered mixtures of old and new' (Strindberg 1955a: 65). His protagonists' ultimately lethal hysterical illness is the psychosomatic symptom of the tension between two competing systems of power. It delineates a crisis of the premodern system of kinship and blood at the transition point to the modern system of sexuality. Like Strindberg's other naturalist dramatic work, including most prominently *The Father*, *Creditors* enacts the perceived threat of the feminine to patriarchal kinship structures and seeks to restrict sexuality within the terms of such normative kinship. Related to the crisis of patriarchal authority, 'woman' is clearly the primary object of knowledge and social control not only in Strindberg's plays, but (according to Foucault) in practically all discursive and social (legal, political, aesthetic, medical, philosophical and so on) fields of the period examined. In *Creditors*, Tekla, the erotic woman, is the target of the play's obsessive examination of sexuality. It is she who questions the system of kinship represented by the two male protagonists: patriarchal law, the legal authority of the husband and the institution of marriage. The embattled nature of the premodern system of patriarchal authority is encoded as the figure of Adolf's 'abnormal' (feminised) sexuality.

Marked by the politicisation of biological life, modernity manages individual and social bodies through a politics and technology of biological normalcy/deviancy and health/pathology. In the 1890s, certain male forms of sexual behaviour – the homosexual, the sadist, the exhibitionist, the transvestite – became medicalised and pathologised in the scientific (legal, medical, biological, psychiatric) literature, which much expanded and modernised the terminology devoted to descriptions of the unmanly. As Robert Nye noted, this scientific discourse on social deviance gradually gained widespread influence beyond the professional community and helped shape the language of day-to-day political and popular culture (Nye 1984: 330). In the nineteenth century, as Foucault pointed out, sexuality thus became the foundation of the modern

subject's 'identity', a quasi-biological identity open to the immunitarian intervention of experts. Coinciding with the *fin de siècle*'s creation
of the masculine 'other' or outsider, Adolf's 'scientific' or medical case
is, arguably, enacted on the stage so it can subsequently be 'cured' or
normalised in society. With *Creditors* and many of his other naturalist
plays, Strindberg seems to call for the re-establishment of a normative
masculinity. At the same time, however, his plays enact this normative
masculinity as irretrievably damaged and in flux. In *Creditors*, Adolf's
deviancy from a fixed (male) gender identity norm is shown to have
disastrous physiological consequences.

The stereotyping and homogenising of gender identities found in
many of Strindberg's naturalist plays is a cultural product of an age that
witnessed the creation of new, more rigid dualistic gender divisions that
increasingly classified and disciplined the human body and also used
these classifications to hierarchically differentiate between bodies. The
increasing focus of the contemporary sciences on individual and group
differences can be seen as part of the European turn away from the
Enlightenment doctrine of natural, universal human rights. While the
Enlightenment had collapsed natural-zoological life and political life –
at least in the legal theory of universal human equality – we can here
witness the biopolitical move to the splitting off of natural life and the
qualified, political life available to members of privileged groups.

Given the immunitarian exclusion of 'outsiders' as the founding principle of the modern nation, the post-eighteenth-century crisis of modernity is linked to a new focus in modern western society on normative
identity concepts and the abjection or exclusion of difference. The modern disciplines 'characterize, classify, specialize; they distribute along a
scale, around a norm, hierarchize individuals in relation to one another
and, if necessary, disqualify and invalidate' (Foucault 1977: 222–3).
While, in its extreme form, this disqualifying and invalidating would
take the form of thanato-politics, the slide of biopolitics into a politics
of death under totalitarianism, this problematic relationship of western
modernity to difference is also enacted in Strindberg's work. What is
at stake in Strindberg are the boundaries between self and other that
constitute the biopolitical, immunitarian dualism of the modern West.
Strindberg's work draws this immunitarian line of separation along a
dualistic but unstable gender distribution.

Together with the embattled norm of masculinity, what Strindberg
foregrounds in *Creditors* is the question of Tekla's – and by implication
'woman's' – identity, her quasi-biological 'true nature'. Here again, I argue
that this pseudoscientific immunitarian and equivocal stereotyping and

essentialising of gender identity already foreshadows the racist, homophobic and misogynous rhetoric and praxis of National Socialism. Only
a few decades later, the primacy of masculine virility was most dramati-
cally emphasised in Adolf Hitler's *Mein Kampf* (1923). The rhetoric of
the National Socialist movement feminised racialised outsiders, and the
pathologisation of sexual outsiders in the nineteenth century would find
its iteration in National Socialist laws mandating the castration of homosexuals and other male 'sex criminals' diagnosed as 'sick'. Together with
the immunitarian separations of modern biopolitics, the discourse of rights
that the premodern sovereign had been able to grant or take away for
specific parts of the population as tools of his domination would return in
force under totalitarianism.

Threats to Bourgeois Ideology

The primary means Strindberg's women characters use to challenge
the authority of the paterfamilias is infidelity. The first thing Tekla
expropriated from her second husband was his friends. In this context, although Adolf admits his jealousy, he affirms to Gustav that
he was never afraid of Tekla being unfaithful. When Gustav answers
that '[a] married man never is afraid of that' (Strindberg 1960a: 10),
this assertion already sounds greatly ironic to spectators or readers
familiar with other plays of Strindberg's. In fact, one of the recurrent
themes in Strindberg's plays is exactly the male characters' monomanic
obsession with the question of paternity and, thus, the wives' faithfulness. In *Creditors*, Tekla does not meet bourgeois society's ideological
demands for a subordinate and sexless, faithful and chaste wife. She
refuses to assume the place reserved for her in the sexual and social
codes and spends entire nights away from the home. Adolf's 'acceptance' of his wife's behaviour is an indication of his weak position in
their marriage. In Tekla and Adolf's marriage, not Adolf but Tekla is
the dominant figure. Adolf, in Gustav's words, 'lowered [his] voice and
bowed to the apron strings' (Strindberg 1960a: 12).

The topic of the wife's infidelity and the related issue of paternity
addressed in Strindberg's plays are deeply rooted in bourgeois ideology
and are among the traits that anchor Strindberg's plays within the tradition of bourgeois drama. The new code of morals, which emphasised
morality and sexual 'purity', in particular for women, originally served
the rising class of the bourgeoisie to distinguish itself from the excesses
and dissipation of the aristocracy. Moreover, given the rise of the middle class in economic status and its accumulation of wealth, the wife's

faithfulness had to ensure the legitimacy of the heir(s). As Friedrich Engels has shown, the uncertainty of paternity – the fact that, as Freud wrote in 'Der Familienroman der Neurotiker', 'pater semper incertus est', while the mother is 'certissima'[14] – is the basis of the double standard that dictates monogamy for the wife, but not for the husband, in order 'to make the man supreme in the family and to propagate, as the future heirs to his wealth, children indisputably his own' (Engels 1972: 128). Finally, in bourgeois ideology, the virginal purity of the woman was to guarantee the establishment of a site of morality in the family – a refuge that was to provide a source of spiritual replenishment for the male, who was exposed daily to the merciless world of commerce and its corrupting influence. As a result of these considerations, however, bourgeois women's libidinal desires often had to be constrained.[15]

The focus on fidelity and paternity in Strindberg's play again demonstrates the tension at the point of transition from a premodern regime to modernity. On the one hand, paternity is clearly linked to kinship ties and the transmission of names and possessions based on the principle of birth/blood (all linked to the dominant role of the nobility in pre-revolutionary Europe). On the other hand, the themes of infidelity and paternity allow for an exploration of issues of population. As we have seen, Foucault theorises the regulatory control of populations as one of the primary techniques of power in western modernity: 'the sexual conduct of the population was taken as an object of analysis and as a target of intervention' (Foucault 1980a: 26). The theatre, as exemplified by Strindberg's work, participated in this analysis and intervention. Before the constitutional crisis in England and the French and American Revolutions, royal – and with it paternal – authority had been able to claim transcendental justification. By the twentieth century, scientific testing would be able to establish biological paternity. The nineteenth century, however, was a period in which fatherhood and paternal authority were uncertain assumptions.

In Strindberg's naturalist work, it thus becomes clear that the modern crisis of male symbolic authority calls into question the basic premises of bourgeois ideology: When, in *Creditors*, Tekla explicitly denies Adolf's authority as her husband, Adolf tries to assert his male authority by commanding her to go home with him by the next boat. Whereas Tekla sends Adolf away ('I don't want a husband'), Adolf insists on his authority as her husband: 'But now, as I mayn't be your lover, I am going to be your husband, whether you want it or not' (Strindberg 1960a: 35–6). This power struggle between Tekla and Adolf not only enacts Tekla's questioning of patriarchal authority, it also brings to the foreground key concepts of bourgeois ideology. According to Hegel, love is the basis of the sentimental family (as opposed to the rationality of the state). The argument between Tekla and Adolf exposes the bourgeois ideology of marriage that holds up love and marital happiness as signs of a new society free of domination. The opposition between love and marriage established in their dialogue contradicts the tenets of this ideology, which posits the family as a safe haven exempt from the rationality of the economic sphere, as a haven in a heartless world that transcends the fungibility of goods and relations in the sphere of commerce. The ideology of a spiritual bond between husband and wife distinguished the bourgeois family from the traditional family forms of the other – both lower and upper – social classes. The new ideal of marriage and family life was part of the new focus on internal values used by the bourgeoisie to distinguish itself both from the aristocracy and its emphasis on external appearance, and from the petty bourgeoisie and lower classes, which lacked this moral perfection. Although generally considered prototypes of bourgeois drama, Strindberg's plays, however, depict the ideal of marital happiness as illusory. Instead, many of Strindberg's plays enact marriage as hell.

In short, although initially at least in part brought on by the bourgeoisie's challenge to royal authority, the growing modern crisis of male symbolic authority in Europe ultimately became a crisis of bourgeois ideology itself, including the ideology of the bourgeois paterfamilias and the family. In the revolutions of European modernity, the bourgeoisie had asserted its claim to political power based on its enormous economic power as the merchant class, whose rise had begun in the Middle Ages. While capitalism had enriched the bourgeoisie, it would finally not only lead to the overthrow of premodern authority structures (the *ancien régime*), but also to a general loss of male symbolic authority that would in turn entail the decline of bourgeois ideology.

Libidinal Economies

In contrast to bourgeois ideology, which theorises the family as a realm of ethical love and solidarity within a society ruled by exchange and competition, the title of Strindberg's play, *Creditors*, already establishes a link between the play's domestic setting and an economic problematic. In this context it is important to remember that Foucault locates the modes of sexual conduct in European modernity 'at the boundary line of the biological and the economic domains' (Foucault 1980a: 26). *Creditors* presents the relationship between the sexes in the language of capitalist commodity exchange. The play couches the contemporary fear of cultural decline in terms of economic decline and enacts the crisis of male symbolic authority as the threat of bankruptcy. In an age that produced both Karl Marx's work on capital and Sigmund Freud's work on libidinal structures, Strindberg's play enacts the growing contemporary interest in both domains as well as their intersection. At the end of the nineteenth century, social scientists used sexual metaphors to describe economic phenomena.[16] Conversely, Freud described the dynamic struggles of the elements of psychic structure – libidinal investments, drive substitutions and excess – in a way homologous to Marx's work on exchange values and surplus capital. The medical establishment described the bourgeois illness of the time, neurasthenic collapse, as physical and medical bankruptcy. The imprudent neurasthenic had overdrawn his account of nerve force, provoking 'what always happens if great expenses are met by small incomes; first the savings are consumed, then comes bankruptcy.'[17]

'Economic' concerns regarding the conservation or exhaustion of energy, forces and power – concerns that are also present in Freud's work – are themselves a thoroughly modern problematic linked to the scientific discoveries of the age and ultimately the larger shift from what Jane Bennett calls 'a matter-based physics to an energy-based physics' (Bennett 2010b: 64 n.2). According to Foucault, in the seventeenth century modern power starts to exert itself over the body as a machine to be optimised and integrated into 'systems of efficient and economic controls' (Foucault 1980a:139). In the nineteenth century, the newly discovered laws of mechanics – specifically the law of energy conservation, that is the discoveries by the German physician and physicist Hermann von Hermholtz that the supply of natural energy is irreducible – were also applicable to the human body. Breaking down the boundary line between machines and humans, the new image of the body was as a field of forces and motion. The question, however, was not only one of personal, individual optimisation, but also of the optimisation of a population or society in an age of intense competition between industrialising and militarising nations (Rabinbach 1982: 46–8). Gustav Freytag's best-selling epic novel *Debit and Credit* (1855) also explored this economic thematic in terms of national characteristics.

The sciences of the nineteenth century saw sexual activity in particular as posing the risk of physical exhaustion and decline. In *Creditors*, Gustav (the 'outside expert') recommends sexual abstinence for Adolf, who recovers once his wife Tekla has left for a while. The contemporary scientific literature viewed an active sex life as detrimental to one's health:

> The frequent exercise of the act of copulation leads directly to anemia, malnutrition, asthenia of the muscles and nerves, and mental exhaustion. Immoderate persons are pale and have long, flabby or sometimes tense features. They are melancholic and not fit for any difficult and continued corporeal or mental work.[18]

In his book *Science of a New Life* (1869), the American physician John Cowan made it clear that, in this context, men ran the greater risk. Equating semen with vital essence, he argued that '*any* loss of semen was a significant loss of vital essence to a man'.[19] An earlier, eighteenth-century Swiss medical text, S.-A.-D. Tissot's *De l'onanisme* (Lausanne, 1760), had referred to semen as that 'essential oil' whose loss produces weakness and the illnesses of the time. Tissot links the old medical theory of body fluids to the modern focus on nerve function. According to Tissot, an excessive loss of semen causes a dramatic disturbance in the male individual's physical and mental 'economy', influencing the brain and threatening the loss of free will (Mehlmann 1998: 107). Given that Adolf's death is caused by epilepsy in Strindberg's play, Tissot's equation of coitus and epilepsy is especially interesting. The fact that epileptic seizures can be one of the clinical manifestations of syphilis,[20] the 'exemplary neuropathological contagion' (Casper 2016: 182), reinforces Tekla's role as a contaminant or (literal) parasite. In the early 1880s the American neurologist George Beard also introduced the term neurasthenia to denote 'all forms and types of nervous exhaustion', including male sexual exhaustion, which he posits as tantamount to feminisation (Beard 1884: 176). Freud was the first scientist who stood this theory on its head by claiming that sexual repression was in fact the main cause of nervous illness.

In *Creditors*, Tekla, the erotic, vampiric woman has depleted Adolf of his vital essence, semen, and has turned him into a feminised and mentally and physically exhausted invalid. His death, an epileptic seizure, makes it clear that Adolf dies of semen depletion, as a result of sexual excess, of the violation of the bourgeois ideal of moderation in all things. The play's focus on 'excess', together with Gustav's figurative role as a psychoanalyst or psychiatrist, is an enactment of psychiatry's focus in the nineteenth century on 'excess' as the cause of mental illnesses.[21] Since capitalism is, by definition, based on the excess of capital, of profit, over the mere exchange of equivalent goods, we can at the same time read this preoccupation with excess as a product of the economic changes marking modernity.

The importance accorded semen also finds expression in the seminal-nutrition theory that reached its height in the first two decades of the twentieth century. On the basis of this 'scientific' theory, which views semen as a beneficial form of nutrition, it becomes clear why Tekla – in contrast to her depleted husband – is doing so well in Strindberg's play. In his *Pure Sociology*, first published in 1903, the American sociologist Lester Ward asserts that coitus constitutes a special kind of nutrition that renews the organism. Ward's argument echoes Rémy de Gourmont's *The Natural Philosophy of Love*, published the same year, which argues that fecundation is a phenomenon of nutrition. While the seminal-nutrition theory gives men quasi-reproductive functions, it also implies a proportional virilisation of women. Many eighteenth- and nineteenth-century texts conjure up the nightmare of dominant women and exhausted males and lead to the conclusion that any man who does not prudently manage his finite sexual resources runs the risk of gradually losing his virility. This neurasthenic collapse and bankruptcy is exactly what happens to Adolf in the play.[22]

The Economy of Exchange/The Parasite

Enacting the collapse of the public/private distinction in modernity, Strindberg's characters use the economic language of capitalist commodity exchange to describe their domestic relationships. Whereas bourgeois theory posits a separation of the domestic sphere and the sphere of commerce, the relations of exchange of the sphere of the market deeply influence the interpersonal relationships within the family. While bourgeois ideology seeks to anchor marriage in love, the marriage contract of bourgeois society establishes marriage as a relation of exchange. In *Creditors*, Strindberg links specifically the husband's authority to the capitalist economy of commodity exchange – through Tekla, who questions Adolf's authority by discrediting the language of business transactions: 'Are you giving me the bills for your gifts now?' Adolf, however, insists on his authority as Tekla's husband, and he insists on resuming an economic language:

> . . . I've tried to remind you of your debt. Then at once I became the unwelcome creditor whom one only wants to get rid of. You wanted to repudiate your notes of hand, and so as not to increase your debt to me, you stopped pillaging my treasure chest and started on other people's. (Strindberg 1960a: 36)

The two male protagonists are the creditors who give the play its name. Described as a material, alien or nonhuman element, a vampire and an invasive parasite, Tekla is indebted to her husband Adolf. Both Adolf and Tekla are in turn debtors to Gustav, whom Tekla left for Adolf. Gustav tells Tekla that he came to recover what she had stolen, not what she had received as a gift. He argues that she stole his honour and that he could only regain it by taking hers. Gustav speaks of Tekla making good his losses and concludes his argument with her by stating: 'So, I have cancelled my note of hand. Now go and settle your account with the other one' (Strindberg 1960a: 51). This theme of debt is linked to the authority structures in the text: Tekla 'owes' Adolf respect because he is her husband. Adolf and Tekla, described as 'brother' and 'sister' figures, both owe respect to Gustav, who is depicted as a paternal figure or an older brother. In this sense, the economic language of the play is linked to male authority. Tekla rejects both.

By rejecting the exchange of gifts or the notion of indebtedness Tekla rejects not only participating in paternalistic kinship structures, but in community in general – specifically again in the community dominated by men. Claiming a dispensation from reciprocal gift-giving (what the Roman Republic called *munus*) is, according to Roberto Esposito's work, a claim for immunity: 'He who has been freed from communal obligations or who enjoys an originary autonomy or successive freeing from a previously contracted debt enjoys the condition of *immunitas*' (Campbell 2008: xi). Since Tekla is a woman, however, and thus without access to such privilege, her claim to difference from the community only questions and negates the rules of this very community, making her an outside threat.

At the same time, however, the relationships in Strindberg's play also enact what Michel Serres describes as parasitic relations. In *The Parasite*, Serres writes: '. . . a human group is organised with one-way relations, where one eats the other and where the second cannot benefit at all from the first . . . The flow goes one way, never the other. I call this semiconduction, this valve, this single arrow, this relation without a reversal of direction, "parasitic"' (2007: 5). For Serres, this scenario is, in Cary Wolfe's words, 'the ur-dynamic of social and cultural relations' (Wolfe 2007: xv). As Serres puts it, 'parasitism is the heart of relation' (Serres 2007: 52). Humans parasitise each other and they parasitise the world around themselves (Serres 2007: 24) Serres reads this dynamic as a deviation from equilibrium: 'the introduction of a parasite in the system provokes a difference, a disequilibrium' (Serres 2007: 182). Strindberg's Tekla is this parasite, this difference and this deviation from a perceived prior (premodern) balance. She unilaterally feeds on the men she marries, but gives nothing in return. In a word play on Marx's concepts of use value and exchange value, Serres here speaks of 'abuse value': 'a relation without exchange, an abusive relation' (Serres 2007: 80).

Adolf himself, the now-husband who had inserted himself in Tekla and Gustav's marriage as a lover, is himself initially a parasite ('someone who places himself in the middle of a relation of desire to parasite it'; Serres 2017: 115). In addition, as the 'new arrival' who intercepts the current relationship between Adolf and Tekla, Gustav also assumes the role of parasite. This arrival of the third in the form of Gustav gives Strindberg's play its impetus. Serres notes the importance of the third for our traditional logic: 'In order to succeed, the dialogue needs an excluded third' (2007: 57). He notes that the parasite's role is 'to animate the event. His role is a social role and thus, theatrical' (2007: 190). Serres analyses Molière's Tartuffe, who is, like Strindberg's Gustav, 'the third between husband and wife', 'attack[ing] relations more than beings'. Of interest for this book on biopolitics and immunitarian thinking is also Serres's description of parasitism as 'the logic of epidemics: the virus multiplies; it goes everywhere. The action of the parasite is to go to the relation. It instinctively goes to the mediations, occupying them all' (2007: 206). Moreover, Serres writes: 'The animal-host offers a meal from the larder or from his own flesh; as a hotel or a hostel, he provides a place to sleep, quite graciously, of course' (6). In Strindberg's naturalist plays, this hostel is provided by the bourgeois patriarchal family. With the arrival of the parasite (Gustav), the domestic sphere of bourgeois marriage opens itself up to contamination. What is at stake is *communitas*; we are spectators to what Serres calls 'the game of the collective and its metamorphoses' (2007: 210). In Artaud's work, as we will see, this collective will become not only thematically, but formally central. Like a parasite (in one of its French meanings, as the signal that disturbs the communication), the collective makes noise.[23] Sound, noise, immerses and disorients the spectator in Artaud.

In the constantly changing game of the collective, Strindberg's Gustav, like Molière's Tartuffe (discussed by Serres), ultimately assumes all roles: 'Name all the characters – he has substituted himself for every one'. Gustav, as interceptor, plays the role that Adolf as lover had initially played in the three characters' relationship. As Serres writes about Tartuffe, 'suddenly the cuckold cuckolds the cuckolder.' As I will show, Gustav not only plays the role of the oedipal father in the triangle with Tekla and Adolf, but also participates in a brotherly, homoerotic rivalry of peers over Tekla. Finally, Gustav is also Tekla, whom he, as the first husband, had shaped in her initial role as female *tabula rasa*.

In Serres's terms, '[h]e is the joker, placed everywhere at once' (Serres 2007: 207). While theatre traditionally enacts antagonisms, Serres proposes moving beyond binary thinking: 'Inside or outside? Between yes and no, between zero and one, an infinite number of values appear, and thus an infinite number of answers. Mathematicians call this new rigor "fuzzy" . . . They should be thanked: we have needed this fuzziness for centuries' (Serres 2007: 57). While Strindberg's *Creditors* centrally thematises a problematic of border invasion and thus of inclusion and exclusion, the play's shifting roles also enact these borders as constantly changing, complexifying the system or network of flows and relations that constitute the play.

As Wolfe notes, '[t]he arrival of the "third," the "joker," provokes what may be viewed in Serres as a primordial act of exclusion or "sacrifice" . . . whereby society constitutes itself in a founding countermove against the endlessly complexifying and disrupting parasitic chain' (Wolfe 2007: xv–xvi). As Wolfe remarks, for Serres, following the work of René Girard and Jacques Derrida, 'sacrifice, expulsion, and scapegoating are rudimentary forms of achieving social cohesion'. Does the scapegoat/sacrifice enacted in theatre constitute a countermove against parasitic chains, as Wolfe's first statement seems to suggest, or does theatre enhance social cohesion and the social norm through scapegoating and exclusion? In either case, scapegoating the Other does not address the fundamental, ontological problem, the fact that, as Serres puts it, 'the system itself is never stable. Its equilibrium is ideal, abstract, and never reached . . . That is what existence is: facing death, being in perpetual difference from equilibrium . . . As soon as the world came into being, its transformation began. The system in itself is a space of transformation' (2007: 72). Strindberg's naturalist plays nevertheless equate parasitic and vampiric women with death and with the changes or threats posed to the patriarchal kinship system in modernity.

In addition to problematising a parasitic chain, the language of the characters of Strindberg's *Creditors* is not only an economic language indicative of a (malfunctioning) economy of exchange (in Serres's terms, the arrow of the parasitic relation is only going one way), but it also enacts an instrumental rationality. What Serres calls 'the growing objectification of our intersubjective relations' (2007: 650) – in Marxist terms, the commodification of non-commodities in Strindberg's play and the instrumental rationality to which it attests – fit Horkheimer's thesis of a transition in modernity from substantive reason (a rationality that judges moral values and goals) to instrumentalised, depersonalised relationships and a rationality based on the calculation of self-interest, efficiency and necessity (Horkheimer 1974). In spite of her explicit rejection of the economic language used by the two male characters, Tekla is portrayed as instrumentalising – and thus turning into an object – first Gustav and then Adolf. While the male protagonists' indictment of Tekla's vampirism could at first glance be read as a critique of instrumental reason, the more sympathetically depicted male characters also, however, use economic terms to characterise the interpersonal relationships in the play and to (re)assert their authority. Horkheimer sees the shift to instrumental reason as a result of the loss of paternal authority, and Strindberg's play enacts this connection. Whereas Adolf tries to rely on an economic, instrumental rationality to assert his authority, this rationality is itself already a result of the loss of male authority. Adolf, therefore, will not be able to assert his dominant position in the marriage. Finally and most importantly, however, what a vampire or a parasite does is not exactly characteristic of the subject-object relationship that the term 'instrumentalisation' suggests. What parasites/viruses and vampires do instead is blur the borderline between two organisms, entering the host's body and making it create and spread more copies of themselves. This blurring of species boundaries is the threat posed by posthumanist modernity.[24]

Castration, or the Modern Gap

In the play, Adolf's impotence, his failure to establish his male authority in his marriage becomes clear when he touches Tekla's most vulnerable point – her age – and she brings out the ultimate weapon against him. It is the weapon that kills the title character in Strindberg's *The Father*: the fact that the husband can never be certain of his wife's fidelity, and the question of his honour (or ridiculousness) already addressed by Gustav (Strindberg 1960a: 37).[25] Adolf's loss of honour is a form of castration, as Strindberg makes explicit in *The Father*, where the title character says to his wife: 'And now – now when I should be stretching out my hand to gather the fruit, you chop off my arm. I'm robbed of my laurels; I'm finished. A man cannot live without repute.'[26] This passage makes clear why Adolf has to die at the end of *Creditors*. Enacting the modern crisis of masculinity, Tekla has taken away his repute, his honour – a historically changing and yet central and normative attribute of masculinity – and a man cannot live without his honour. Strindberg's *Creditors* and *The Father* enact the nineteenth-century sexualisation of honour and, conversely, the moralisation of sex. The relation between the loss of honour and castration finds its expression in the male protagonists' impotence. The conflation of life and honour also pervades National Socialism and appears, for instance, in a poem titled 'Youth', which appeared in the 1940 edition of one of the most popular readers for German schools, *Hirts Deutsches Lesebuch*. The poem reads: 'Be hard against yourself, / Chaste in the glow of your strength and the passion of your sexuality, / Love and lust must be kept separate from one another / Just as life and death are opposites / *Life and honor are one*' (Eilemann 1940: 243, my emphasis).[27] The 1935 Nuremberg laws on citizenship were the 'Law for the Protection of German Blood and the Honor of the German People'. As Eric Santner puts it, referencing David Graeber (2011: 170):

> The degradation of the vanquished gets converted into . . . the *surplus dignity* – honor, magnificence, greatness, splendor – of the victor: 'this ability to strip others of their dignity becomes, for the master, the foundation of his honor.' (Santner 2016: 121 n. 8; emphasis in original)

Given the decline of male authority in modernity, however, Adolf can no longer play the role of victor based on the inferior status or degradation of his wife.

The loss of honour, in other words, reduces qualified life to biological-material life. In Strindberg's plays, this reduction to natural life defines the threat posed by the female protagonists. What the English translation of Strindberg's most famous play calls 'repute' is the relation that connects (a) what his male protagonists are immediately, immanently (that is natural life) with (b) their symbolic/socio-political mandate (qualified, human life) as husbands and heads of the patriarchal family. Without this connection, a gap opens up that symbolically castrates these men. Slavoj Žižek writes: 'Castration is the very gap between what I immediately am and the symbolic mandate that confers on me its "authority"' (Žižek 2004b: 87). In *Creditors*, Tekla's infidelity opens up this gap between the body and symbolic identity, undermining Adolf's honour, authority and his male (bodily as well as symbolic) potency. Adolf's impotence is an impotence on all levels: 'GUSTAV. Is he prudish? TEKLA. Well – in speech he is. GUSTAV. But not in – other ways? TEKLA. He's not well just now' (Strindberg 1960a: 45).

Given the contemporary shifts in authority structures, it is then not surprising that castration is a master trope of nineteenth-century literature. Following Ernst Kantorowicz's influential theory of the king's two bodies (the natural body and the sublime body), Santner suggests that 'the very topic of castration and the emergence of psychoanalysis as its master theory' (Santner 2011: 78) in the nineteenth century need to be understood against the background of a shift of sovereign power from the king's 'two bodies' to the people. In other words, in modernity the king's authority is no longer seen as both immediate/natural *and* transcendent/sublime. The loss of the symbolic dimension, the loss of human transcendence or exceptionalism – the castration addressed by Žižek – ensues.

Santner furthermore links the gap described – the gap that opens up between human beings and their (surplus) entitlements – to yet another gap: to the sexual, libidinal yearning that results from the gap between the human body and the surplus of enjoyment. The term castration denotes both of these gaps and both of these surpluses or excesses:

> For psychoanalysis, then, symbolic castration is the ordeal whereby the joint between the body and the order of language (and human institutions more generally) comes to be established as the very 'site' at which we acquire a 'too much' of psychic reality, one that Freud characterized as libido, the substance of human sexuality . . . As Zupančič puts it, 'It is because this paradoxical joint between the biological body and the Symbolic is inherently sexual (in the sense that it constitutes the generative source of human sexuality) that its effect is called castration. (Santner 2011: 80)

Human sexuality, libido, is the surplus that emerges at the intersection of the biological body and the sphere of human culture. In Strindberg's *Creditors*, this libidinal surplus is located at the threshold between the male protagonist's excarnated symbolic impotence and the threat posed by the female protagonist's erotic embodiedness.

Although psychoanalysis is of course a humanism based on the distinction (but also the ultimate inseparability) of the somatic and the symbolic/semiotic realms, I argue that there is a certain structural resemblance between a materiality that is constitutively excessive (see the beginning of my Introduction) and Jacques Lacan's dialectic of desire – as long as we do not limit our understanding of desire or signification to humans alone. Lacan posits a gap between speech and signification, between what we are able to articulate and what we want. The difference between the two, the surplus that goes beyond materiality, creates desire. In his book, *What Money Wants: An Economy of Desire*, for instance, Noam Yuran links this dialectic of desire to the gap between material objects and monetary symbols (Yuran 2014: 144–5). Similar to Massumi's focus on animal instinct in 'The Supernormal Animal' (2015a), certain scholars (such as Žižek or Santner), on the other hand, locate this excess 'not in desire but in what is often considered its biological counterpart, namely in drive' (Yuran 2014: 261). Pointing to the link between the flesh (as excess) and the problematic of symbolic investiture, Santner writes: 'every call to order addressed to a human subject – and a symbolic investiture is such a call – secretes a 'surplus value' of psychic excitation that, as it were, bears the burden, holds the place of the missing foundation of the institutional authority that issued the call' (Santner 2001: 50–1). In other words, although male symbolic authority has lost its transcendental foundation in the immanence that is modernity, it has left behind an unsettledness or restlessness: anxious flesh. The dramas presented in this project enact the drive energy of this anxious flesh. What is important to note here, however, is that this drive energy or flesh is not limited to humans only. It does in fact not even have to be biological. This drive energy or flesh is instead the affect that unites humans and agentive matter, a materiality that is anything but dead.

The threat enacted in Strindberg is exactly the threat posed by a (nonhuman and feminised) materiality that is no longer held in check by the (human, male) social or symbolic system. In modernity abstraction increasingly reaches a point where any discursive grounding in materiality threatens to be lost. Whether for money or for the structure of political authority, the difference between material reality and signification opens wide in modernity. The perceived threat is an encroachment by nonhuman matter, by a materiality that has 'cut itself loose'. In spite of – or because of – the primacy of the abstract in modernity, sublime signification, the premodern co-extensiveness of embodiment and transcendental, sublime authority (the co-extensiveness of the king's physical and symbolic bodies), though ultimately unreachable, remains highly desirable. In *Creditors*, Adolf yearns to replace his lost faith in God with the worship of his wife. As he finds out in the course of the play, however, this yearning for the embodied sublime is based on illusion. What remains at the modern juncture of the 'king's two bodies' is a horrible, monstrous excess, a surplus that Santner calls 'the rotting flesh of the sublime body' (Santner 2011: 44). What starts as 'the "stuff" of the king's glorious body . . . is, in modernity, dispersed into the body politic of the People as a "spectral materiality"' (Santner 2016: 23).

In *The Weight of all Flesh*, Santner (building on Derrida's work in *Specters of Marx*) establishes a link between this spectral materiality of the king's deposed body (or his two – physical and sublime – bodies) and Marx's theory of the *gespenstische Gegenständlichkeit* (spectral materiality) of the commodity. Derrida writes: 'The specter is a paradoxical incorporation, the becoming-body, a certain phenomenal and carnal form of the spirit. It becomes, rather, some "thing" that remains difficult to name: neither soul nor body, and both one and the other. For it is flesh and phenomenality that give to the spirit its spectral apparition' (Derrida 1994: 6). This excessive spectral materiality is the position that the female protagonist (as a commodity to be exchanged between men) and the feminised male protagonist occupy in Strindberg's *Creditors*, a play with an economic title. As Santner's reference to Marx's commodity shows, this spectral materiality is ultimately not limited to organic bodies.

The Flesh

Following Edmund Husserl and Maurice Merleau-Ponty, Esposito distinguishes between two different kinds of materality: the physical body (German *Körper*, French *corps*) and the flesh (German *Leib*, French *chair*), although both are closely linked. The flesh is a concept associated with the work of Simone de Beauvoir, Georges Bataille, Antonin Artaud and Merleau-Ponty. Similar to Derrida, Santner (2011: 28) characterises it as 'something in the body that is more than a body yet is not simply spirit'. Defined as a surplus that exceeds corporeality, 'it is a fantasy construct, charged with human desires, fears, and values, a virtual reality that has often gathered around bodies ... yet remains abstracted from them' (Goodman 2016: 7). Given that this description is almost a description of the theatre (which is also a fantasy product gathered around bodies or actors, creating a virtual reality), the theatre lends itself to the enactment of this liminal space. The dramas explored in this study enact the historic 'displacements of a spectral substance that no amount of conjuration, necromancy, and exorcism manages to fully elaborate and master' (Santner 2016: 66).

As already noted, there is a difference between the flesh – the pressure exerted by affect, 'desire' or drive – and bodies, however. Esposito explains: 'There is something about the flesh, like a hiatus or an original break, which resists incorporation' (2013a: 323). While Derrida speaks of 'becoming-body', flesh in fact *resists* becoming body. It is, in Esposito's words, 'nothing but the unitary weave of the difference between bodies'. Both unitary and marking difference, the flesh bridges a gap, even between immunity and community. According to Esposito, it is 'simply the way of being in common of that which seeks to be immune' (Esposito 2013a: 325). As I have argued, there a link between this spectral materiality and the excess that ontologically marks agentive matter in posthumanist discussions. Bridging the gap between discursivity and materiality, a gap that is narrowed but still remains in Foucault's theory,[28] is the prime achievement of new materialist philosophy.

For this flesh, Cary Wolfe explains, 'the distinction between "human" and "animal" is no longer an adequate lexicon, as even Nietzsche realised. "Flesh" thus becomes the communal substrate shared by humans with other forms of life in and through which "the body" is both sustained and threatened' (Wolfe 2014: 166). As I have argued, what Wolfe calls 'other forms of life' does not even have to be limited to animal (that is organic or individuated) bodies.

The threat enacted in the dramas presented here is the threat marked by the flesh – the threat of losing not only androcentric, but anthropocentric hegemonic status, the threat of losing cognitive control over a material world. Given the restricted definition of life in traditional western philosophy as human life only, it is the threat of death. At the same time, in Strindberg the flesh goes beyond the enactment of threat; it is also already the result of this very loss. Strindberg already enacts the loss of embodied male authority – the gap between men's actual bodies and sublime authority, and with it the loss of anthropocentric hegemony – as a fait accompli.

The ambivalent excess or remainder of the flesh calls forth the apparatuses of modern biopolitical administration (Santner 2011: 81), including – as this project shows – plays that enact exactly this surplus. In his analysis of Jean-Louis David's painting, *The Death of Marat* – and particularly of the 'empty' upper left corner of the painting – Santner points out that the spectral materiality of the flesh becomes the 'subject-matter' of modernist art (Santner 2016: 29). I will also explore this spectral materiality – the materiality of abject flesh reminiscent of the empty space in David's painting with its 'lack of any ultimate reference' (Santner 2016: 29) – in my reading of (what I argue is) Brecht's move towards absurd theatre, or in what Lehmann calls the non-mimetic tradition of the 'historical avant-garde' of the early 1900s .

In addition to modernist theatre or art, another apparatus of modern biopolitical administration, namely psychoanalysis, is of course the master theory of this modern problematic of fleshy excess.[29] Like psychoanalysis, the theatre is not only a normative venture that – in the mainstream western tradition – restores patients to 'normality', but also a fundamentally anti-authoritarian endeavour pointing to the contingency of authority in modernity – a tendency exemplified by all plays examined in this study, and again by Brecht and Artaud in particular. Strindberg's work – with its ambivalent enactment of patriarchal authority and the flesh – is a prime example of this duality.

Santner refers to the fleshy surplus created in modernity by the loss of transcendent power as 'the *entsetzlich* [horrible] body of the creature' (2011: 50). This surplus is thus associated with animality – with a 'creatureliness' that goes beyond mere animal life, however. (Santner 2006: xix) Strindberg's work as well enacts the perceived threat posed by this creaturely 'flesh' as femininity and animality. The Nazis would later feminise racial(ised) and sexual outsiders and use animal tropes (for instance rats) in relation to these persecuted others. Since the western philosophical tradition defines animals (and matter in general) as excluded from life (*bíos*), death – rotting flesh – is the threat that Strindberg's male protagonists succumb to in the end.

Notes

1. As Massumi points out, threat (and thus fear or anxiety) is 'from the future' (Massumi 2010: 53); it links present and future.
2. Cf. M. Wilson Smith (2018: 164–5).
3. Cf. Barad (2007).
4. Anna Stenport correctly points out that 'in *Creditors*, characters are dislodged from a domestic setting and located in the transient space of a contemporary resort hotel, a pensionat' (Stenport 2012: 149). Bourgeois domesticity is really no longer available in this play.
5. Cf. Foucault (1980a: 36).
6. Presumably speaking of Strindberg's post-Inferno, post-naturalist dramatic work, Matthew Wilson Smith also argues that Strindberg's theatre, as part of the 'theatres of sensation' emerging in the nineteenth century, uses 'nonrepresentational and sensorial means' to materially impact the audience's nervous systems, thus anticipating Artaud's theatre of sensorial immersion (Smith 2018: 11).
7. *Creditors*, for instance, does not present religion as a viable option anymore.
8. Cf. Bederman (1995: 130).
9. On the fears related to the declining German birthrate during the Weimar Republic, see Peukert (1989: 8–9, 102). Cf. Eder (2002: 196): 'Demographen stellten um die Jahrhundertwende fest, dass die Fertilität auch in Mitteleuropa–und nicht nur in angeblich dekadenten und degenerierten Staaten wie Frankreich–deutlich zurückging.' ('Demographers determined around the turn of the century that fertility was decreasing in Central Europe as well – and not only in the supposedly decadent and degenerate states like France', my trans.) For the situation in Britain, see Tickner (1992: 7) and Andrew Smith (2004: 16–17).
10. Adolf tells Gustav:

> As long as I kept my secrets to myself I still had my vitals, but now I am empty. There's a picture by some Italian master – of a torture – a saint whose intestines are being wound out on a winch. The martyr is lying

there watching himself growing thinner and thinner, as the roll on the winch gets thicker . . . Well, it seems to me as if you had swelled since you emptied me out, and when you go you'll take my vitals with you and leave an empty shell. (Strindberg 1960a: 23)

11. McLaren analyses several hundred court cases involving homicide in the early 1900s, showing 'that, if it was a question of defending one's "manhood," society might even permit an individual the right to kill . . . a murderer had few better defenses than to claim that his victim was a homosexual or the seducer of his wife' (1997: 8).

12. Serres writes of 'the game of the third' that it 'works at exclusion and inclusion'. Serres quotes Plato's *Symposium*: 'If it includes, it is the symbol. If it excludes, it is the dia-bol. The appearance of the Devil, in person' (Serres 2007: 249). Tekla's position is that of the Devil.

13. Cf. also the important contributions made by Jean-Baptiste Lamarck, Georges Cuvier and Auguste Comte.

14. Cf. also Freud (1974: 114): 'Maternity is proved by evidence of the senses while paternity is a hypothesis, based on an inference and a premiss.'

15. It is important to note that in his discussion of the role of repression in European modernity (the 'anti-repressive hypothesis'), Foucault neglects to discuss the effect on women of the new ideological demands for women's sexlessness.

16. Cf. for instance Laqueur (1992: 187) and Pocock (1985: 99).

17. Quoted by Russett (1989: 116). For further examples, see Corning (1884: 47), Stewart (1881: 226) and Nordau (1895: 39–40).

18. Bernard Talmey, *Woman*, quoted by Dijkstra (1986: 170).

19. Quoted in Dijkstra (1996: 55).

20. Seizures can also be a physical symptom of hysteria (now termed 'conversion disorder'), a possible instinctual response to threat (Kinetz 2006: 5).

21. Cf. Foucault (1980a: I: 29).

22. An article in the *New York Times* of 14 April 2011 reported that the president-elect of the American College of Surgeons, an emeritus professor of surgery at the University of Michigan's School of Medicine, resigned after a prolonged controversy caused by an editorial he had written arguing for 'the mood-enhancing effects of semen on women during sex', anti-depressive effects that could not be achieved when condoms were used. Many women in the medical profession had reacted with outrage to the editorial. Apparently, even today the seminal-nutrition theory still has not been completely laid to rest (Harris 2011: A16).

23. Cf. Serres (2007: 210).

24. Claire Hooker, Chris Degeling and Paul Mason point to the occurrence of influenza pandemics and viral mutation when great genetic shifts (that is interspecies genetic mixing) occur/s (Hooker et al. 2016: 271–2). The sense of biological threat enacted in Strindberg manifests itself at a time of a perceived species mixing (Darwin).

25. The fear of becoming ridiculous is a trait that Strindberg's male charac-
    ters share with the proto-fascist men whose texts Theweleit examines in
    his classic text on German fascism, *Männerfantasien* (*Male Fantasies*).
    According to Theweleit, the fear of becoming ridiculous results from the
    frailty of these proto-fascists' 'ego armour', that is from their lack of solid
    ego boundaries (Theweleit 1989: 382). Given that Adolf's relationship
    with Tekla is a symbiotic relationship without clear body boundaries, the
    threat that Tekla poses for Adolf of making him look ridiculous seems to
    corroborate Theweleit's analysis.
26. Strindberg (1955: 42).
27. Quoted by Mosse (1996: 106).
28. Cf. Barad (2007: 64).
29. Freud explored the somatic-sublime surplus located at this threshold in
    'Beyond the Pleasure Principle'.

CHAPTER 2

Death and Community, or Metaphors and Materiality

The parasite is a microbe, an insidious infection that takes without giving and weakens without killing. The parasite is also a guest, who exchanges his talk, praise, and flattery for food. (Wolfe 2007: x)

The position of the parasite is to be between. (Serres 2007: 230)

As Johannes Türk recounts in his book *Die Immunität der Literatur* (2012), briefly after the start of the last plague epidemic in Europe in 1720, a new epidemic, smallpox, crystallised the contemporary population's fears. Unlike the 'black death', this highly infectious disease found its victims not only among the poorest, but among all socio-economic classes. The successful debates surrounding effective prevention that constituted the beginnings of modern medicine were thus by necessity debates about the nature of community. The individual had to be considered as part of an infectious and infected collective (Türk 2012: 48–9), as the etymology of the word 'contagion' (from Latin *con*, together, and *tangere*, to touch) already makes clear. Up to the nineteenth century, that is before the advent of bacteriology, however, illness was mainly seen as the result of an inherited disposition or – in the 'miasma' theory of the immune or unhealthy location – as the product of one's geographical environment. The racial, familial or local community rather than the individual were thus thought to determine vulnerability to illness. Only between the 1860s and the 1880s did medical immunological 'germ' theories (by, most notably, Koch, Pasteur, Semmelweis and Lister) discover the invasion of the individual body by microbacteria as the exact cause of infectious diseases.

In spite of this long dependence on community – or maybe because of the problematic nature of community – bourgeois modernity is ideologically based on the concept of the individual, on a concept of autonomous agency that works in opposition to the social relations of *communitas* and is ultimately based on the fear of alterity or

difference. As Yunjin La-mei Woo points out, in the nineteenth century, 'urban congestion with rapid population growth, pollution, poor
living conditions, and subsequent epidemics', including widespread
and repeated cholera outbreaks in European cities, led to public policing measures based on 'separation and containment of purity from
pollution' (Woo 2016: 193). If community can potentially infect us, it
needs to be avoided – even at the cost of isolation and loneliness. Since
the ideology and practice of modern individualism, however, cannot
satisfy the human longing for community, the fundamental ontological (human and more-than-human) desire for relation, connection and
bonding with others, it ultimately produces totalitarianism (Esposito
2013a: 324). Due to this totalitarian reaction, modern individuals are
then again ready to submit to an all-powerful state that (1) proposes to
protect them against the threatening other by enforcing an immunitarian line of defence and (2) provides social bonding.

In legal theory, natural life and political life intra-actively converge
in modernity's declarations of universal human rights; in practice, however, the modern immunitarian sense of threat will require repeatedly
dividing the population or community by slicing off ultimately inter-
changeable and intersecting groups of others as groups to be excluded
and defended against. The end of the nineteenth century perceives the
threat to individual autonomy as the threat of sexual difference – as
a threat posed by women and feminised men. In gendered images of
engulfment or incorporation, August Strindberg's naturalist dramas
enact a perceived threat that is not only external but also internal,
that is inherent in community itself. The female protagonists in Strindberg's plays expose themselves as such internal threats by not playing by the community's established norms – in the economic language
of Strindberg's 1889 play *Creditors*, by not paying the debt owed. By
not reciprocating in the communal gift exchange, Strindberg's female
protagonist in *Creditors* claims to be exempted or immune from the
obligation imposed by the community. Ultimately, however, Tekla
receives no dispensation and has to repay her debt. Her (second) husband Adolf's death is the sacrifice that constitutes the compensation
required by her first husband and the community. The community
itself is bound together both by this compensation and by the threat
of alterity Tekla represents: 'the common is not characterised by what
is proper but by what is improper, or even more drastically, by the
other' (Esposito 2010: 7). Even when gifts are in fact given, however,
the border transgression associated with the exchange constitutes the
greatest danger: 'That which everyone fears in the *munus* [lt. office,

obligation, gift], which is both "hospitable" and "hostile," according to the troubling lexical proximity of *hospes-hostis*, is the violent loss of borders' (Esposito 2010: 8). The biopolitical sacrifice of life is to defend against this invasion of borders and, paradoxically, to protect life. Adolf's death at the end of *Creditors* is an enactment of this modern immunitarian logic.

Enacting natural life and community as lethal threats, Strindberg's plays are paradigmatic of post-metaphysical European modernity, which equates community and death. As Esposito points out, 'it's only in the modern period ... that this fact [the equation between death and community] begins to appear as a problem, indeed as *the* fundamental problem that political philosophy is obliged to interpret and resolve' (Esposito 2010: 9). The host of animal emblems and tropes of degeneration in Strindberg's work – the loss of anthropocentric hegemony – are linked to this modern lethal threat of community or natural-zoological life.

As Esposito argues, finally, '[t]he "immune" is not simply different from the "common" but is its opposite, what empties it out until it has been completely left bare' (Esposito 2010: 12). This phrasing establishes a link between immunitarian thinking and Giorgio Agamben's concept of bare life (explored in more detail in my chapter on Brecht). The defensive thinking of modernity strips community down to bare life and finds its paroxysm in twentieth century totalitarianism, which produced concentration camps filled with humans reduced to suffering physical-material life.

Parasites, Semen and Blood

In many of Strindberg's naturalist plays, the threat that the female protagonists pose to the immunity or autonomy of patriarchal authority structures is enacted as a bodily threat to the male protagonists' health and life. In contrast to the premodern concepts of sin (a religious term) or guilt and innocence (legal terms), (physical and mental) health and sickness became the decisive criteria in modern society and drama. Framing the economic, political and social decline of the nobility in images of moral and physical decline, the bourgeoisie used a moralised focus on health and hygiene to set itself apart as the newly dominant class. The frequent problematisation of bodily threat and contamination in many modern texts are a product of not only this new focus on health and sickness, but also of the modern decline of embodied male symbolic authority. According to Julia Kristeva's well-known work in

Pouvoirs de l'horreur (*Powers of Horror*), the strength of purification rituals in a society – what, in the modern context, we call 'hygiene' – is linked to the decline or weakness of paternalistic symbolic authority. These purification rituals are designed to protect against abjection, against the contamination or blurring of the binary categories formerly upheld by a strong symbolic system. Given the weakening of symbolic male investiture, the line of separation between these binaries becomes more porous in modernity. But modernity also becomes less willing to tolerate this kind of abject threat, given its increased sense of risk in an immanent world that has increasingly lost faith in a transcendent authority and thus any hope of life after death and eternal salvation.

In Strindberg's *Creditors*, the crisis and instability of male authority is figured from the very beginning of the play. According to the stage directions, the female protagonist's former husband, Gustav, is sitting on the sofa, smoking a cigar, itself an emblem of the power, economic as well as physical, he embodies. Tekla's current husband, Adolf, by contrast, appears with his crutches, which underline his dependency on his wife, who is away on a trip. The relationship between Adolf and Tekla is a symbiotic mother-child dependency. Adolf describes his condition after Tekla's departure as that of a deserted infant who cannot survive on his own: 'For the first days after my wife went on this trip, I just lay on a sofa, unable to do anything but long for her. It was as if she had taken my crutches with her, so I couldn't move at all' (Strindberg 1960a: 9). Adolf displays a frailty of ego boundaries reminiscent of the proto-fascist men analysed by Klaus Theweleit in his classic study, *Männerfantasien* (*Male Fantasies*). Strindberg's male protagonist shares with these men a constant fear of engulfment by the feminine, specifically by the devouring mother.[1] He consequently describes the need he feels for Tekla as a consuming need:

> . . . the moment she leaves me, I am consumed with need for her – as I need my own arms and legs. It's really extraordinary. I sometimes feel she isn't a separate being at all, but an actual part of me . . . an intestine that carries away my will, my will to live. It's as if I'd given into her keeping my very solar plexus that the anatomists talk of. (Strindberg 1960a: 10)

Adolf thus characterises Tekla as a parasite that eats away at his internal organs, at his inner strength and will power. It is therefore consistent for Adolf to continue the beginning of his conversation with Gustav by referring to his revival after Tekla's departure.[2] After recovering from the shock of his wife's departure, Adolf has regained some of the strength of the past, of which Tekla's presence seems to have deprived him. Not only can Adolf start to regain his former strength because his wife is absent, but his recovery is also hastened by male company in the person of Gustav. Adolf, as Gustav points out, 'needed a rest and . . . male company' (Strindberg 1960a: 9). Without even having appeared on stage yet, Tekla – like the female protagonists in other Strindberg plays such as *The Pelican* and *Dance of Death* – is already cast in a role frequently found in Strindberg's plays, namely that of the vampire. In *Creditors*, Tekla starts out as a fallen (divorced) woman. Like a vampire, she becomes stronger as her husband increasingly weakens. Strindberg here posits an economy, a battle of conflicting forces, in which the male protagonist loses.

Individual health and life in nineteenth-century Europe faced such medical threats as parasites, anaemia, syphilis, tuberculosis and hysteria. During this period, it became for the first time possible to attribute to parasitic infection the aetiologies of a number of illnesses that had previously remained unexplained. The nineteenth century was in fact 'the golden age of parasitology' when the life cycles of many parasites were explored for the first time. As Michel Serres points out, most parasites are protozoa, bacteria or viruses (2007: 193). As we have seen, the late nineteenth century also marks the advent of immunology. The trope of vampirism as well is frequently present not only in Strindberg's plays, but also in nineteenth-century art, and in particular in the popular culture of the period after 1870. Consistent with the medicalisation of sex in the nineteenth century (which also continued in the Weimar Republic and under Nazism), the contemporary medical sciences considered specifically anemia a principal cause of the weakness of effeminate males such as Adolf. Due to the high number of anaemia cases, both the general population and the medical establishment started to believe in the existence of vampires, and in particular vampire women (Dijkstra 1986: 338). The contemporary medical literature particularly established the association between vampirism and female sexuality, and by the end of the 1920s, the term 'vampire' had come to denote a medical condition. In Strindberg already, vampirism can thus be seen as more than a metaphor enabling normative-moral categorisations of human behaviour, and instead as the enactment of a physical, medical condition. Contemporary society and theatre displaced the anxieties concerning the women's movement upon the vampiric/parasitic illness of the sexually assertive woman, who depleted men not only in the physical realm (of his semen) but also in the world of intellect and capital gain. Linking medical and economic terms (as well as communication and systems theory), Serres writes of parasites as 'those who destroy the system they feed on, by multiplying. And finally disorder reigns, by infection, by depletion of stocks, and by noise' (2007: 250).

The economic language used by both Gustav and Adolf in Strindberg's play specifically enacts the late nineteenth century's biomedical conflation of semen, vital essence, blood and capital also familiar from Sigmund Freud's famous 'Dora case'.[3] Both men perceive the semen they have given Tekla, or the blood that Tekla the vampire has sucked, as a loss of capital. Exemplifying the popular nineteenth-century association of sex and cannibalism, Gustav (when addressing Adolf) also refers to Tekla and Adolf's relationship as 'pure cannibalism': 'Well, savages eat their enemies so that they'll get their strength for themselves. She has eaten your soul, this woman, your courage, your knowledge' (20).[4] The association of sex and cannibalism found its inspiration in biology and contemporary scientific descriptions of the mating habits of various predatory insects and other animals. In *The Parasite*, Serres establishes an equivalence between parasitisim, vampirism and eating: 'The Greeks were not wrong in showing us the immortals constantly feasting, drinking ambrosia, and laughing endlessly . . . We know that it is enough to break the asymmetric chain, the series of abuses; we know that it is enough not to eat the one who precedes us in the order' (2007: 183). When Serres advocates practising an exchange and equilibrium, this balance includes transforming the 'logicial' (*sic*) into the material (2007: 184), the transversal of the hierarchical differentiation of logic/meaning and matter. As Serres points out, '[t]he parasite is an element of relation' (2007: 184). It is the 'third' that we have called the 'flesh'. Strindberg's naturalist plays enact relations, a system.

In Strindberg's plays, medically or biologically inspired tropes – parasitism, vampirism and cannibalism – enact the perceived threat posed by the feminised libidinal drives to a related boundary: the autonomy or immunity of the body. As we have seen, the surplus exceeding the biological body is sexuality, libido. In *Creditors*, in a passage establishing the relationship between Tekla as maternal figure providing symbiotic union and Tekla as blood-sucking vampire, Adolf says: 'It's extraordinary how that woman is in my body, just as I'm in hers.' In response, Gustav speaks of blood transfusion: 'Well, you seem to have bled yourself' (Strindberg 1960a: 14). Blood establishes a link with women's menstruation and birth and thus, again, with the mother. Fluids, including blood, are an example of abjection, of the transgression of boundaries. The borders between Tekla's and Adolf's bodies and personalities have become blurred. Serres writes: '[The parasite] enters the body and infests it. Its infectious power is measured by its capability to adapt itself to one or several hosts' (Serres 2007: 190). Tekla adapts equally well to both her husbands. Strindberg's play enacts the fear of abjection, the invasion of immunitarian ego boundaries and engulfment by the (m)other with images of fluidity. Emphasising the threat posed by women, Gustav compares the end and climax of his brother's epileptic fits to drowning (Strindberg 1960a: 15). Given the frailty of Adolf's ego boundaries, this ability to transcend boundaries is seen as an extreme, lethal threat to the integrity of the self. In Strindberg, community – the feminised libidinal other – threatens human individuality and autonomy with fusion. In his analysis of the parasite, Serres also speaks of inundation and epidemics: 'when a system admits a parasite, the parasite [like a vampire] multiplies immediately, reproduces, makes a chain, a crowd, a number, an inundation. At the end of a few hours one single bacterium will have provided several million. Epidemic' (Serres 2007: 250; cf. also 253).

Strindberg's female protagonist thus enacts the threat posed by eroticism as theorised by Georges Bataille. In her Introduction to her edited collection, *Object-Oriented Feminism* (2016), Katherine Behar also summarises this threat:

> Forgoing the subject's instinct for self-preservation, eroticism heeds no boundary, neither the boundary between self and other, nor even the boundary between life and nonlife, putting connection and continuity with the world above self-annihilation. 'Eroticism,' Bataille writes,' is assenting to life even in death.' Bataille eschews 'subjecthood through excess, unholy alliances, and nonlife.'

Behar points to the implications for Object-Oriented Feminism of this theory of the erotic, of 'the radical surrender of self in becoming other-than-subject', stating that 'fomenting erotic fusion with an object, as a means of becoming object, is a creative, generative act' (Behar 2016: 16).

Strindberg, on the other hand, enacts exactly the lethal threat posed by such a radical transgression of ontological boundaries, a threat posed not only to the individual body in the form of annihilation, but also to human sovereignty or subject-hood over the 'non-life' of more-than-human objects. What is ultimately at stake in eroticism as defined by Bataille is the 'humanist subject-position of sovereignty', which, as Behar correctly points out, is of course 'doomed, insofar as it is precisely the position eroticism seeks to overcome' (Behar 2016: 16). At stake here are two different conceptions of life. While Bataille as well as theorists working in new materialism or related fields view life as going beyond human life, the anthropocentric philosophical and dramatic tradition opposes human life to the threat of death posed by the nonhuman.

In the 'anthropocentric' theatrical tradition that includes Strindberg, even though (as I argue) 'on his way out' of this tradition, the threat posed by *communitas* is more often expressed in nonhuman metaphors of border-crossing otherness than through nonhuman characters themselves (such as, for instance, Sartre's title 'characters' in *The Flies*, discussed later). At the same time, Strindberg questions the status of his female protagonists as not fully human through their association with nonhuman materiality (parasites, blood, semen and so on). This association then also enlivens this materiality, which can no longer be reduced to passive matter only.

'Die passive Materie'

Demonstrating again the intra-connectedness of ontology and socio-politics, the various (pseudo)scientific discourses of the nineteenth century – not only the natural sciences, sociology and psychoanalysis, but also theatre, literature and art – came up with an image of woman as *tabula rasa*. Contemporary women's demands for access to higher education and public and intellectual life had only reinforced the patriarchal fear of the feminised threats of modernity. This image conceived of woman as quite the opposite of a gynander, as the white, empty space that Serres (2007: 180–1) locates at the beginning of human history and dominance, of a history based on the logic of the eradication of alterity.

In *Creditors*, the appraisal of the female protagonist's artistic work as not up to par with the work of male artists is prototypical of the late nineteenth and early twentieth centuries, which obsessively argued the inferiority of women artists.[5] In *The Descent of Man* (1871), Charles Darwin, with an emphasis on (female) degeneration, established a link between women, the 'lower races' and 'lower' states of civilisation. Women and lower races, he argued, showed greater ability to imitate, but man was said to attain greater excellence in whatever he took up – 'whether requiring deep thought, reason, or imagination, or merely the use of the senses and hands' (Darwin 1898: 576). In 1900, the German psychiatrist Paul Julius Möbius published his book *Über den physiologischen Schwachsinn des Weibes* (*On the Physiological Feeble-Mindedness of Woman*), which maintained that women were by nature weak-minded. As Laurie Marhoefer points out, 'Feebleminded[ness]' (*Schwachsinn*) was a 'term used by both psychiatrists and those outside of psychiatry to designate a supposedly relatively mild intellectual disability that consisted of an impaired moral sense' (Marhoefer 2011: 530). Freud, of course, also argued that only fathers could instill a moral compass or super-ego in their children. The very influential Italian psychiatrist, anthropologist and criminologist Cesare Lombroso claimed that women's perceptual abilities were less acute than men's. As the voluminous antifeminist literature of the day proves, many contemporary cultural critics, artists, philosophers, social thinkers and politicians agreed with Lombroso and Möbius. While by the second half of the nineteenth century women had started claiming their place in literary life and the arts, Strindberg's Tekla is only successful as an artist because Adolf uses his influence on her behalf and because she copies him. Only a few decades later, National Socialist aesthetics would also share the view that only men were capable of artistic achievement (even though it seems to have made exceptions for a few female artists such as Leni Riefenstahl).

It is of course not only possible, but necessary to see the nineteenth century's emphasis on questions of originality and influence as a counter-reaction to the historical crisis of male authority and the ontological crisis of human hegemony. Ideologically, the male fantasy of the woman as *tabula rasa* is related to bourgeois individualism as well as anthropocentrism and the conception of the human individual as shaping the material world around himself. As *tabula rasa*, 'woman' is the ideal, unadulterated reflection back to mankind (men as well as humanity) of its own perceptions and disfiguring projections onto her. Like Freud, Strindberg's contemporary, the Viennese writer Otto Weininger, also defined 'woman' as inherently 'passive matter': 'Die Frau ist die Materie, die passiv jede Form annimmt' (Weininger 1980: 430). ('Woman is the material that passively takes on any shape', my trans.). At the same time, however, this parasitic mimicry or mimetic power[6] is perceived as threatening. The threat posed by Strindberg's female protagonists is the threat of a materiality that does not remain dead, the threat that a post-anthropocentric world poses to the human.

At the turn from the nineteenth to the twentieth century sexual difference, race and the status of the human thus intersect. Weininger's work *Geschlecht und Charakter* (*Sex and Character*), published in 1903, also helps us assess the relationship between Strindberg's enactment of feminised alterity and the National Socialist rhetoric of race a few decades later. Weininger discusses the intersection of femininity and Jewishness, establishing *Geschlecht und Charakter*, in George Mosse's estimation, as 'one of the most influential racial tracts of

the twentieth century, profoundly affecting the views of Adolf Hitler and many other racists' (Mosse 1985: 145).[7] In a note to his
book, Weininger explicitly expresses his admiration for Strindberg's
'extraordinary' and 'powerful' dramatic *oeuvre*. After Weininger's
suicide in 1903, Strindberg paid homage to him in Karl Kraus's journal *Die Fackel* (Robertson 2004: 7). Although today Weininger has
a reputation as an eccentric lunatic, it is important to note that for
several decades after the publication of his book, Weininger remained
one of the most highly respected and frequently quoted 'authorities'
on the subject of sex and race, both in Europe and the United States.
In the German language alone, Weininger's *Geschlecht und Charakter*
was published from 1903 to 1927 in twenty-six editions. Not only
Freud, but also Ludwig Wittgenstein and Georg Trakl were among
Weininger's many admirers. The enduring success of Weininger's
book in the early twentieth century demonstrates that his arguments
expressed the prevailing public opinion concerning race and gender
among his mostly 'Nordic' readers. His arguments concerning sexual
difference also reverberate in Strindberg (specifically in Strindberg's
male characters' assessments of his female characters).

Establishing the intersections between race and sexual difference,
Weininger presents Judaism as the extreme manifestation of the 'feminine
principle' (as opposed to the Aryan 'masculinity principle'). Anticipating National Socialist rhetoric, Weininger describes 'the Jew' as a *parasite* that adjusts or assimilates to any environment, changing its outside
appearance while staying the same (that is still dangerous) inside. Most
importantly, while seemingly submitting to its host, the parasite in reality
subjugates the other (Weininger 1980: 430). As we have seen, in *Creditors* the female protagonist is presented in similar biopolitical, immunitarian terms as just such a parasite that penetrates the biological body. She
adjusts equally well, first to Gustav then to Adolf. The difference between
adaptive parasites and devouring mothers, however, is only one of degree
(or opportunity). Weininger describes the relationship between the parasite and its host as a struggle for domination and subjugation. Unless
exterminated, the parasite is the real winner.

In short, in spite of the view of women as empty vessels enacted
in Strindberg's play, what Weininger alleges to be women's 'surprising
receptivity' (1980: 376) always threatens to revert back to its seeming
opposite, namely feminised engulfment, the invasion of the biological
body by the maternal. Gustav and Adolf's creation ultimately comes
back to haunt and hurt or even destroy them. Tekla devours Adolf
and absorbs his strength. Her assertive sexuality has depleted Adolf

physically, mentally and artistically. By the time the action of Strindberg's play sets in, Adolf has lost all his energy and fallen ill. Adolf says
to Tekla: 'I gave, I gave, I gave – until I had nothing left for myself'
(Strindberg 1960a: 20). In *The Parasite*, Serres writes:

> There is no exchange, nor will there be one . . . this eternal host gives over and
> over, constantly, till he breaks, even till death, drugged, enchanted, fascinated.
> The host is not a prey, for he offers and continues to give. Not a prey, but the
> host. The other one is not a predator but a parasite. (Serres 2007: 7)

Interestingly (and problematically in its one-sidedness), Serres also
applies this term, the parasite, to the mother–child relationship:

> Would you say that the mother's breast is the child's prey? . . . But this relation
> is of the simplest sort; there is none simpler or easier: it always goes in the same
> direction. The same one is the host; the same one takes and eats; there is no
> change of direction. This is true of all beings. Of lice and men. (Serres 2007: 7;
> cf. also 216, 230)

This passage is interesting in at least two ways: First, in Strindberg's
play the (parasitic) relationship between Tekla and Adolf is described
as a mother–child relationship. In addition, Serres's argument also
does away with the ontological dividing line between humans, animals
and material objects (Serres 2007: 64–5), that is between human and
nonhuman parasites.[8] The breaching of this dividing line is exactly the
post-Darwinian threat enacted in Strindberg's play.

For Adolf, in short, the economy of exchange has not worked. There
has not been an exchange; Tekla has not given anything in return, and
Adolf's feminised nurturing is thus negativised. Adolf had not realised
that any form of social sharing, of *communitas*, weakened his position
as an immune individual. Having succumbed to Gustav's and Tekla's
hypnotic eyes, it is now Adolf who does not have any individuality or
opinion of his own left. After Tekla, the devouring mother, has laid the
groundwork, Gustav, the male psychoanalyst, imposes his own personality on the feminised hysteric Adolf.[9]

Of Male Mothers and Quaggas

Modernity politicises biological life and issues such as birth, disease
and death/mortality. In a modern, biopolitical society that prizes life
above all else, authority is necessarily defined as reproductive power.
The etymological (Latin) root of the term 'authority', *auctoritas*, is
augere, to grow. As Agamben explains, an *auctor* is 'the person who

augments, increases or perfects the act – or the legal situation – of someone else' (Agamben 2005: 82). When Tekla tries to invalidate Adolf's
claim to the male authority of a husband by calling him a child, Adolf
acknowledges that he has come to play this part in their relationship,
but he also asserts that he used to nurse and console Tekla 'like a small
baby'. He describes himself as having taken motherly care of Tekla.
Adolf claims to have given life to Tekla, like a mother does to a child.
Without him, Adolf asserts, Tekla's body and her mind were lifeless
and empty.[10] Before Adolf, Gustav had filled the *tabula rasa* and given
Tekla a personality that still reflects his own. Then Adolf raised Tekla
like a mother does her child until she could 'stand on her own feet'
(Strindberg 1960a: 38).

Both Gustav and Adolf's perception of their relationship with Tekla
betrays the male wish to appropriate the generative power of female
reproduction in an attempt to bolster their own authority. When Gustav
suggests that Adolf must have made passionate love to Tekla, Adolf
responds: 'Yes, so passionately that I could not tell if she were I, or I,
she. When she smiles, I smile; when she weeps, I weep. And when she –
can you imagine it? – when she was giving birth to our child, I felt the
pains in my own body' (Strindberg 1960a: 14). On the one hand, this
statement is indicative of the symbiotic nature of Adolf and Tekla's relationship, Adolf's feminisation through Tekla and her own usurpation
of male power. But this passage also gives voice to the male desire of
giving birth, of circumventing the maternal – and ultimately threatening – principle in creation that pervades many centuries of both western
and eastern theatre and literature. When Tekla's 'motherliness' threatens
Adolf's male authority and ultimately his life, he counters this challenge
by referring to tropes of 'male maternity'.

The attempted circumvention of the threatening maternal principle
is also at the basis of the emphasis on paternity in the conception of a
child. In *Creditors*, Adolf and Tekla had a child that Tekla – the bad,
parasitic mother who only takes but does not give[11] – had sent away
because it looked like Tekla's first husband, Gustav. Adolf affirms to
Gustav that he does not have any suspicions about his own paternity. Gustav acknowledges: 'the children of a widow who remarries
are often like the dead husband. It's vexing, of course – that's why they
used to burn the widows in India, you know' (Strindberg 1960a: 16).
Gustav proposes the – even continuing – prevalent importance of the
man in siring a child, a notion reminiscent of similar passages in patriarchal theatre, literature, philosophy and 'science' from Greek antiquity to the nineteenth century.[12] According to Foucault, the nineteenth

century established the control of population as an important technique of power. The issue of paternity links the modern demographics of population to the premodern focus on paternalistic kinship.

A scientific article entitled 'Fécondation' and published in 1885 in *La Grande Encyclopédie* asserts the possibility thematised in Strindberg's play of a child resembling a man who is not the biological father, but with whom the mother has had prior sexual contact (17:102–5; quoted by Olrik 1986–7: 128). To describe this phenomenon, the biologist August Weismann in 1892 coined the term 'telegony'. However, the concept itself dates back even farther, to the seventeenth century physician Jan Baptista Van Helmont (1579–1644). Since Van Helmont, physicians had been convinced that after having had children with one man, a woman later continued to pass on the traits of her first mate to her children with a second man. Darwin as well expressed his firm belief in telegony and summarised the most widely known report of telegony, the case of the quagga also cited in *La Grande Encyclopédie*.

Here are the alleged historical facts. In 1820, the Earl of Morton had reported to the President of the Royal Society of London that he had recently attempted to domesticate the quagga, a zebra-like species native to South Africa that would go extinct in 1883. Having failed to find a female specimen of the species, he had been compelled to cross a male quagga with 'a young chestnut mare of seven-eighths Arabian blood, and which had never been bred from'. Later, he had given the mare away to a fellow peer, who had mated her with an Arabian horse. The progeny of that second union had 'the character of the Arabian breed' but the colour and the hair of their manes bore a 'striking resemblance to the quagga'. Lord Morton's report circulated widely, and the term 'quagga taint' came to be used in the scientific community to refer to the traits in the offspring of the physical characteristics of its mother's earlier sexual partner (Sengoopta 2000: 127).

The same scenario is also – in almost identical terms – addressed by Weininger (1980: 307), showing to what extent such pseudoscientific knowledge was part of the dominant cultural assumptions of the European *fin de siècle*.[13] Going even further, Weininger asserts that another man's *intellectual* influence over the mother (which was clearly given in Gustav and Tekla's case) can be responsible for the child's resemblance to him. In this context Weininger talks about the 'mental impregnation' of the (again inherently passive) woman by the man. The view of the inherent receptiveness of woman also pervades French naturalism. The physician Prosper Lucas used the word *imprégnation* to express the theory that, once exposed to the influence of a strong male personality, a woman will retain that influence for a considerable length of time.[14]

As this term shows, there is an obvious link between the biological theories concerning the enduring role of the father in conception and the theory of the natural intellectual receptiveness of woman. According to Weininger, 'woman' does not possess any individuality of her own. Instead, she is glad to be *forced* to comply with the man's wishes. Many passages in Weininger's book stop short of explicitly advocating rape. More than happy in her passive, receptive role, 'woman' demands of the man that he forces her – physically as well as intellectually – to receive (Weininger 1980: 353, 395). Unable to recognise the other as an external, independent person, the 'scientific' discourses of the *fin de siècle* (as typified by Weininger) wanted to see women as an extension of men. Strindberg's Adolf also cannot distinguish between Tekla's body boundaries and his own.

As the eugenics movement and – a few decades later – the racial laws of the Third Reich would make excessively clear, the telegony argument also has clear racial implications. It enacts the anxieties about the dilution or 'pauperisation' of the 'superior' white race through racial interbreeding that characterised the nineteenth and early twentieth century, a period marked by colonialism, migration and acculturation. The abjection, contamination or ego invasion that threatens the male individual's self is also a threat to the purity of the white race. The anguished rejection of femininity and the shared concern with the contamination of 'pure' blood by prior 'impure' and inferior sexual exposure thus establishes thematic links between Strindberg's work and the racial rhetoric of early twentieth-century totalitarianism. What is maybe most interesting in this entire discussion, finally, is that humans are seen as part of the animal kingdom; inheritance is seen as following the same rules for humans and nonhuman animals.

The theory that only the male contributes to conception dates all the way back to ancient Greece, to the writings of Aristotle. It is a fantasy consistently recurring over the long history of Western patriarchal society and, as we have seen, examples abound. With the discovery in 1827 that the woman must produce an egg that unites with the man's sperm in order to create life, however, men could no longer claim to be the sole creators of life. In 1875 the German zoologist Oscar Hertwig formulated with certainty today's recognised theory of reproduction. Nevertheless, fantasies of male self-generation and 'womb-envy' re-emerged with particular vehemence in the 1880s – a product of and a counter-reaction to the acute crisis of male authority. The theory of impregnation or telegony, which denies the mother's role in conception and gestation, in fact survived far into the twentieth century. At the beginning of the twentieth century, male self-parthenogenesis is again and again central to the proto-fascist texts discussed by Theweleit. In this context, Theweleit refers to the term 'direct filiation', a term taken from structural anthropology. 'Direct filiation' psychologically eliminates the biological parents; the (male) subject construes himself to be the son of God and Mother Nature. For Theweleit's proto-fascists, however, God as an authority had become obsolete and any maternal figure threatened engulfment. Instead, the fascists thought of themselves as 'sons of themselves and of history' (Theweleit 1989: 241). In this context, one can then read *Männerbünde* – the kind of associations of men that were so fundamental to both Wilhelmine and NS social organisation, but also characterised German post-war society – as replacements of the threatening mother (and the bourgeois family). *Männerbünde* take their basis from the phobic exclusion and rejection of biological women. The initiation to fraternal organisations cancels out birth from the biological mother and replaces it with a new abstract, good mother.[15]

Animals

Adolf's death at the end of *Creditors* illustrates the dangers of *not* circumventing the mother. In addition to her 'motherliness', what makes Tekla so dangerous is her sexually assertive nature. Here again, Strindberg's play is prototypical of its time. In spite of the incitement to discourses on sexuality in bourgeois society as described by Foucault, the nineteenth century perceived the expression of libidinal drives and of sexuality in particular as dangerous. Foucault in fact argues that '[t]he limitless dangers that sex carried with it justified the exhaustive character of the inquisition to which it was subjected' (Foucault 1980a: 66). On an age marked by instrumental rationality, any expression of non-instrumental desire or libido was seen as a threat, including the excessive dynamic surplus that constitutively, ontologically marks all materiality. On the trajectory towards ever greater abstraction, modern society perceives any libidinal implication in the sensory as constituting danger. While Strindberg enacts the flesh as passive matter initially awaiting animation by the male human, this feminised materiality then comes alive, posing a lethal threat.

In Strindberg and other enactments of eroticised femmes fatales in *fin-de-siècle* theatre, literature and painting, it was women who came to personify this threat and these blockages. The equation of sexual experience and danger that can again be found in the texts of Theweleit's proto-fascist men also marks late nineteenth-century discourses. Beyond the assumed role of the first husband or sexual partner in the conception of later children, the conflation of female eroticism and aggression – which is also again present in Freud – is yet another argument for the virginity of women before marriage, traditionally a major concern of bourgeois ideology. In *Creditors*, Gustav insinuates to Adolf that Tekla does not love him, because 'one only lets oneself be taken in once'. Gustav equates being in love with being 'taken in', being deceived. He warns Adolf of Tekla: 'You have never been taken in, but you had better beware of those that have. They are dangerous, those' (Strindberg 1960a: 17).[16] In Strindberg's play not only women but animals as well function as expressions of the perceived danger posed by sexuality. In his *Die Traumdeutung* (*The Interpretation of Dreams*), Freud interprets animals as the displacement of unconscious libidinal drives (Freud 1960: 337). As is typical of modernist drama, in *Creditors* animals also stand in 'for the descent into primitive emotionality' (Chaudhuri 2017a: 55), or rather for an uncensored libidinality, a libido that starts to resemble nonhuman material energy. This otherwise threatening animal desire is supposed to be normalised in the bourgeois family.[17]

What interests me most in this context, then, is the question of whether the animal images in Strindberg are in fact that – representational images or metaphorical referents (a 'movement from the sensible to the intelligible'[18]) for human behaviour, norms and values – or whether Strindberg enacts his female protagonists *as animals*. Considering the level of reality his male protagonists attach to their fantasies or projections, and given both women's assumed biological closeness to animals on the evolutionary scale and the fetishisation of 'woman' in terms of her animal nature, the latter assumption is not far-fetched at all. At the height of Adolf and Tekla's central argument in *Creditors*, for instance, Adolf calls Tekla a threatening insect: 'You destroy my brain with your clumsy pincers – you claw my thoughts and tear them to pieces' (Strindberg 1960a: 40). Serres explains that parasites take hold by becoming invisible and that they become invisible through their small size: 'Bacterium, worm, virus, bacillus, phage – seldom if ever larger than the size of an insect . . . Animal parasitism is the work of invertebrates' (Serres 2007: 217). Tekla *is* a parasitic insect.

Importantly, then, Adolf does not say: 'You are *like an animal*.' He says: '*You are* an animal.'[19] Gustav similarly calls Tekla the erotic woman, 'the serpent' (Strindberg 1960a: 28). On the metaphorical level, the figure of the snake evokes the Medusa, the feminised monster of Greek mythology whose hair consists of snakes. Freud established a link between the female genitals, snakes of hair and the Medusa's head, which threatens castration (Freud 1959: 105). Theweleit discusses the fascist men's hallucinations of the genitals of the devouring woman – hallucinations that figure rats, snakes, moles and crabs. The snake is a figure replete with mythological overtones (reminiscent of the Garden of Eden, for instance) that help displace the origin of sin onto the woman, phallicising her in the process and converting man (Adam/Adolf) into the passive victim. It is indeed a fitting metaphor for Tekla. On the literal level, however, the serpent is one of the cannibalistic predatory animals whose mating habits so fascinated contemporary science. Finally, Tekla is not only literally called a snake, but a snake that vomits: 'Now the snake, being full, vomits' (Strindberg 1960a: 20) – suggesting abjection in Kristeva's sense, an overstepping of the boundaries of inside and outside. As an erotic, 'loose' woman overstepping the boundaries of bourgeois gender expectations, Tekla incarnates animal desire. She *is* the sexual threat or parasite that will infect her husband with syphilis, the most infamous venereal disease of the nineteenth century, for which a treatment would only become available in 1909.

What also interests me on these entangled levels, moreover, is that (1) Freud associates animals with the libidinal unconscious and that (2) Freud's psychoanalytic practice sees it as its goal to provide access to the unconscious. Freud's theory in other words views as possible some sort of communication between what had previously been seen as separate domains – human and animal, conscious and unconscious. It is here that the well-documented influence of Darwin on Freud (Rentzou 2016: 31–2) becomes palpable.

While this border crossing has potential medico-therapeutic value in Freud, Strindberg's women characters enact the perceived dangers of this breach of humanist borders. Whereas the consequence of Eve's transgression in Genesis is the (metaphysical) Fall of humankind, Adolf, at the end of *Creditors*, becomes the victim of an attack of epilepsy. 'Falling sickness' (German 'Fallsucht') is the vernacular expression for epilepsy.[20] The disobedience (ultimately Eve's disobedience) leading to the Fall, which creates human law, reduces Adam and Eve and here Adolf to Agamben's *la nuda vita* or bare life after their expulsion from Paradise – to the state of natural-biological, zoological life that also marks Adolf's fate at the end. In Strindberg's play, Adolf loses the protection that his social entitlement as bourgeois family patriarch, his status as part of *bíos politikos*, had afforded him. The convulsions and spasmodic motions characteristic of epilepsy enact what Eric Santner calls the excess of immanence in modernity. In modernity the sovereign's sublime body loses its transcendence and is replaced by the people's body and an immanence that leaves a remainder, a surplus. During this time of structural transition and related anxiety, the surplus energy once absorbed by the king's body manifests itself – in Santner's terms – as 'a convulsive movement of nerve that . . . afflicts the flesh of every subject' (Santner 2011: 139). For Cesare Lombroso, one of the leading medical authorities of Strindberg's day (and Nordau's teacher), the epileptic fit was 'the exemplary physiological display of deviance, for it offers the spectacle of a body convulsed and decomposed by its otherness to itself' (Bernheimer 2002: 151). Epilepsy thus functions as an emblem of difference and bare life.

Like the trope of the Fall, the association of women and animals in Strindberg again brings up the topic of degeneration, one of the scientific discourses of the nineteenth century that would later also prove central to the rhetoric and genocidal politics of National Socialism. Strindberg's work problematises 'woman's' perceived inferior biological status in a manner that already foreshadows the rhetoric concerning the assumed biological inferiority of certain groups of human 'outsiders' under National Socialism. The negative enactment of the threatening feminine as parasitic and vampiric – as well as the portrayal of the feminised outsider, Adolf, as hysterical or neurasthenic – already announce the stereotyped representation of the primary racialised outsiders of the time, namely Jews, in exactly these terms (feminine, parasitic, vampiric, hysterical, neurasthenic), both in nineteenth-century European racial science and under the NS regime.[21] Not incidentally, around the same time that Strindberg's views on women were turning problematic, his views on Jews also became increasingly negative (Banville 2012: 50).

In *The Stage Lives of Animals*, Una Chaudhuri (following Jean Baudrillard) comments on the anthropocentrism of the representation of animals in modern theatre (Chaudhuri 2017a: 50). As we have seen, Strindberg's plays certainly do not seem to constitute an exception to the anthropocentric use of animals as metaphors for human behaviour and conflicts. But I am also wondering if this metaphorical use of animals necessarily refuses 'the animal its radical otherness', as Chaudhuri (2017a: 51) puts it. Is it possible that a metaphorical use of animals does not always reduce the animal to human traits, but instead establishes *the human* thus described or enacted as radically other, *as animal*? As the comparison with National Socialism shows, the use

Strindberg makes of animals does not remain at a comfortably human/ metaphorical level. Nazi rhetoric argued that Jews really *were* some sort of animal, an identification that then allowed the regime to exterminate the Jewish population to fend off the perceived threat of contamination to the health of the human, Aryan population. As Jeffrey Nealon (following David Krell) points out, Heidegger's infamous *Notebooks* in fact describe Jews not only as *weltarm* (poor in world), but as *weltlos* (lacking world) like a lifeless stone. Just as Jews or enemies of the Reich were not *like* animals but instead inhabited the same ontological category as animals (at most) in Nazi thinking (Nealon 2016: 46–7), in Strindberg's naturalist dramas, women are not *like* animals – that is the animal imagery used in these plays is not *purely* metaphorical. Instead, the male characters view women as less-than-fully-human and as close to animals on the evolutionary scale. Women – like the racialised others of Nazi ideology – inhabit the liminal zone where human and nonhuman identity becomes blurred. The imagery used in Strindberg in other words does not make any safer the threat of overproximity posed by animals and women. Instead, Strindberg heightens this threat by showing the insecurity of the border separating the human from the nonhuman. With Strindberg's women characters, this lethal threat has invaded the supposed 'haven' of bourgeois men, the family home. In this way, Strindberg's plays then anticipate (rather than oppose) later plays like Eugene Ionesco's *Le Rhinocéros* (*The Rhinoceros*) or Elizabeth Egloff's 1994 play, *The Swan*, where actual animals physically invade and destroy the stage. While Chaudhuri characterises classic modernist theatre as 'a performance of the superiority of culture over nature' (2017a: 75), in Strindberg this superiority is clearly threatened. His female protagonist's position as a parasite in the word's three senses (in French) – 'physical noise (static), living animal, and human relation' (Serres 2007: 203) – enacts the boundary crossing between the human and the nonhuman. With Strindberg the enactment of difference starts to move in ontological status from a metaphor, that is a primarily representationalist mode of thinking safely controlled by the (human) author, to (in Artaud, for instance) an agentive element of the performance that cannot be readily controlled.

The Struggle for Existence

The enactment of women as both non-threatening *tabulae rasae* and devouring mothers are expressions of an immunitarian struggle for domination. Here the man wins, there the woman. Either scenario eliminates difference. In *Masse und Macht*, the Jewish writer and Nobel laureate Elias Canetti establishes a link between dualistic thinking and what he calls 'Meutenbildung' – the formation of hostile packs and eventually 'Kriegsmeute' ('hostile packs inciting war') (Canetti 1980: 332–3; 1962: 297).

The immunitarian, biopolitical thinking in binarisms that characterises modern society and would mark fascism to an extreme extent a few decades later is already present in Strindberg's plays. Strindberg's characters engage in the most extreme form of dualistic thinking. In *Creditors*, Gustav believes that man has only one choice: to dominate or to be dominated by woman. In contrast to Freud's later assertion in 'Femininity' (1933) that a wife's assumption of the maternal role towards her husband will make their marriage stronger, Gustav argues that 'the woman ... is the man's child, and if she is not, he becomes hers, and that makes a topsy-turvy world' (Strindberg 1960a: 45). Again, Weininger also agrees with Gustav's position: 'Der Mann ist in der Lage, Wert zu spenden, Wert zu übertragen an die Frau, er kann schenken, er will auch schenken; nie kann er seinen Wert, wie das Weib, als Beschenkter finden' (Weininger 1980: 289). ('Man is capable of giving value, of transmitting value onto woman; he can give, he also wants to give; never can he find his value, like woman, in being the recipient' (my translation).) Like Gustav before him,[22] Adolf started out as Tekla's '(good) mother', and when he could not fill this role anymore, the roles reversed and conflict ensued. When the male dream of circumventing the mother in childbirth (by the husband 'creating' the wife) reverts back to the power of the devouring mother, the outcome can only be deadly.[23] *Creditors* thus enacts the war of the sexes and their struggle for domination as rooted in man's and woman's biological dispositions, in their biologically determined, naturalised gender identities. The play enacts 'woman' as a force of degeneration and regression that threatens the spiritual, rational evolution and biological survival of mankind. National Socialism later realised the flight from woman to the strong, godlike *Führer* and put the fantasy of defeminisation into practice against 'effeminate' Jews threatening the survival of the Aryan race. Strindberg's characters' struggle for utter domination of the other is ultimately a struggle for sovereignty and in this sense also foreshadows the sovereignty of the totalitarian leader.

Although *fin-de-siècle* society could use certain problematic elements of Darwin's theories as 'scientific evidence' to support a gender norm that viewed women as biologically inferior and degenerate – as evidence consequently to maintain male social supremacy – we can also link Darwin's displacement of God as Creator to the crisis of male symbolic authority. The focus on competition at the heart of Darwin's theory contributed to an understanding of the relationship between the sexes as based on conflict, as a struggle for existence. Most importantly, however, as a result of Darwin's focus on evolutionary change as well as Freud's theories, it would become possible to see both phylogenetic and ontogenetic development – the development of the species and of the individual – and thus biological and political structures as no longer static or inescapable. Strindberg enacts both contemporary socio-political and ontological structures as in flux.

Family Configurations, or Primordial and Individual Debt

In *Creditors*, Tekla is a sister as well as a mother figure, but she is also an erotic woman. As we find out, the relationship between Adolf and Tekla began when Tekla was still married to Gustav. To disguise the true nature of their passion for each other, Tekla and Adolf 'played brother and sister', as Gustav calls it, and he adds 'and the more physical their emotions became, the more spiritual they declared their relationship to be.' Even as a married couple, they still call each other brother and sister (Strindberg 1960a: for instance 19, 28). In her classic *Speculum of the Other Woman*, Luce Irigaray views the brother–sister relationship as potentially 'a relationship without desire', a relationship where the war of the sexes would not take place. But, as she qualifies immediately, 'this moment is mythical' (1985: 217). In fact, Tekla and Adolf's relationship does include desire and it is very much a war between the sexes. Due to this desire, there seems to exist something like fear of incest. The thematisation of a sister–brother incest in *Creditors* enacts the status of sibling love as the dominant love myth of the nineteenth century and the first half of the twentieth (as later discussed in my reading of Sartre's work).

Tekla is not only a sister figure, however, but also a mother figure to Adolf, who is younger than both Gustav and Tekla. The exploration of the age of husband and wife in Strindberg's play can again be read as an enactment of the modern regulatory interest in demographics and population. The fact that Tekla is older than her second husband goes against the role expectations of bourgeois ideology, which demanded that men provide for the family and that women be fertile, give birth and educate the family's children. As a consequence, at the end of the eighteenth century, bourgeois wives were on average ten years younger than their husbands (Rosenbaum 1982: 288–9). In *Creditors*, Gustav and Tekla's marriage enacts the traditional age hierarchy, whereas Tekla and Adolf's marriage illustrates the supposed dangers of a violation of this hierarchy and enacts the historic changes taking place in the course of the nineteenth century. Whereas the marrying age of men remained more or less the same, the age at which women married rose. There is of course a relation between age difference and authority structure; the difference in age reinforced the authority of the man. Not only was he older and more experienced, he had also seen the world through his studies and professional training, a world which was for the most part inaccessible to the bourgeois wife, whose sphere was limited to the domestic realm. Although this description adequately portrays Tekla's marriage to Gustav, in her marriage to Adolf Tekla does not fit within any of these categories. She is older than her second husband,[24] mundane and experienced (also sexually), and she questions Adolf's male authority. Tekla calls Adolf 'little brother' and talks to him as if he were a baby (Strindberg 1960a: 31, 37). The cause of Adolf and Tekla's fight before she left was that he called her old, too old to flirt. Tekla's age again brings up the theme of incest, this time not as incest between brother and sister, but as incest between mother and son, who takes the mother away from the father (Gustav), the oedipal theme.

Incest, whether brother–sister or mother–son, thus occupies a central place in Strindberg's play, which enacts what Foucault calls 'the affective intensification of the family space' in modernity (1980a: 109). The fact that incest, the love of the same, is represented in negative terms – as problematic – establishes a difference between *Creditors* and such early twentieth-century representations of incest as Thomas Mann's *Der Erwählte*. In the terms of the Frankfurt School tradition, the representation of two structurally different forms of incest – mother–son and sister–brother – enacts the transition from a paternalistic society to a fatherless society, a transition from vertical to horizontal authority structures.

The reading of Tekla and Adolf's relationship as a mother–son relationship casts Gustav in the role of the oedipal father. Gustav and Tekla, the oedipal father and the engulfing mother, symbolically castrate and finally kill Adolf. Gustav is a victorious, admirable father figure who assumes God-like dimensions. At the beginning of Tekla and Adolf's liaison, the absent Gustav, who – as their bad conscience told them – could see everything, watched over a relationship that the lovers themselves perceived as sacrilegious. Gustav retells the beginnings of this relationship:

> And then they took a vow of chastity, and then they played hide-and-seek, till they found one another in a dark corner where they were sure of not being seen . . . But they felt that there was *one* who could see them in the darkness . . . and they grew frightened, and in their terror the figure of this absent one began to

haunt them – to assume gigantic proportions, to be changed, to become a nightmare which disturbed their amorous slumbers, a creditor who knocked at the
doors. (Strindberg 1960a: 18)

Here Strindberg mixes religious and economic language. Gustav is not
only the oedipal father and God-the-Father; he is also one of the creditors that give the play its name. Gustav speaks of 'the debts they [Adolf
and Tekla] left behind' (Strindberg 1980: 18).[25]

In *What Money Wants*, Noam Yuran also speaks of conscience in
an economic context: He writes of the religious conscience inherent
in money. Yuran cites Benjamin Franklin on the relationship between
the creditor's perception of a debtor's actions and habits and argues
that '[b]ecause of the identification of . . . credit and money, money
becomes a special social relation that rests on suspicion' and is associated with 'a hostile, omniscient gaze. In this way a formation of
religious conscience is inherent in money itself.' Conversely, Calvinism
'inserted into the religious dogma a notion of accounting' (Yuran 2014:
190–1), providing 'the *economic articulation of the sublime*' (Yuran
2014: 192, my emphasis). In Strindberg's play, Gustav as creditor per-
sonifies this omniscient, god-like gaze of the other implied in money.
Enacting 'the economic articulation of the sublime', Gustav's role as
a creditor can also be linked to his paternal role. We have already
discussed the enactment of male parthenogenesis in Strindberg's play,
the male protagonists' attempt to circumvent the threatening power of
the maternal. 'Credit' or 'debt' is the paternal, rationalised usurpation
of the procreative role of women. As Freud saw it, the biggest debt is
the debt to one's parents, the debt of life. The maternal body comes
to symbolise eternal indebtedness. The gift of life given by the parents
and the mother in particular constitutes a debt so big that it can never
be repaid and thus contradicts the bourgeois ideology of the autonomous, self-sufficient individual.

In other words, the threat posed by the mother is an immunitarian
threat to individual autonomy, a threat to the primary, most fundamental assumption of bourgeois ideology.[26] As we have seen, Esposito's work establishes a relationship between *communitas*, which is
based on reciprocal gift giving, and a dispensation from such mutu-
ality – *immunitas*. The contagion brought on by community, by 'the
excess of communal gift giving' (Campbell 2008: xi), threatens indistinction, that is the loss of individual identity and autonomy. The
threat posed by the female protagonist's taking of unreciprocated
gifts in Strindberg's *Creditors* is thus the threat of ego dissolution, a

threat to bourgeois individuality or human subjectivity. Conversely, the acceptance of gifts from the mother is just as threatening, posing the same risks. An example of modern immunitarian thinking, Strindberg's preoccupation with questions of individual autonomy – from the host of monstrous mothers in his plays to an explicit thematisation of debt – anchors Strindberg within the tradition of bourgeois drama and marks him as a profoundly modern writer.

Fraternal Oedipus

Since the circulation of goods – giving and receiving – is performative and agonistic in nature, it lends itself to dramatic enactment. In Strindberg, the thematic of debt is linked to the social hierarchies problematised – hierarchies or entitlements that in turn need to undergo investiture in ritual performance. Whereas Adolf, the husband, fails to assert his authority in the dramatic exchanges with his wife, just as Gustav did when he was married to Tekla, Gustav – the oedipal father who comes back to punish the younger generation – succeeds in re-establishing and demonstrating his authority. What is at stake in oedipalisation is hierarchy and thus structural violence, a dialectic of fear and desire, 'the trademark of the Western subject's relation to his "others"' (Braidotti 2011: 223). As is typical of classic bourgeois theatre, in the conflict between two male rivals over the female protagonist in Strindberg's play, nobody asks Tekla, the woman, whom she prefers. Instead, the men solve the conflict between themselves. The fact that in the dispute between the two male protagonists Tekla's opinion does not seem to matter corresponds to Freud's oedipal theory, which reduces women to a passive role, to a contested point on the oedipal triangle. Whereas one can argue that the Hitler regime later provided Germans the opportunity to fulfil their oedipal patricidal fantasies, to take revenge on the old authorities, including their parents, Strindberg's play has not yet reached this point. In *Creditors*, the father (Gustav) survives, takes revenge and kills the son (Adolf). Although the authority of the *paterfamilias* is threatened in Strindberg's play, it seems – however perfunctorily – mended at the end.

At the same time, however, Strindberg's play is also reminiscent of the sons' patricide mythologised by Freud in *Totem and Taboo*. Anticipating Ernst Kantorowicz's theory of the kings' two bodies, Freud distinguishes between the father's (or ruler's) natural body (which no longer exists) and the dead ruler's sublime, abstract body, which still lives on for a while and is – due to the sons' guilt and anxiety about their challenge to paternal power – deified, as Gustav is in Strindberg's play. As we have seen, due to Adolf and Tekla's anxieties about their relationship, Gustav is given some characteristics of an omniscient and omnipresent god. Nonetheless, traditional patriarchal authority – God's as well as the husband's – is shown to be threatened or obsolete in Strindberg.

Both Freud's distinction between the sublime and the embodied father and Kantorowicz' theory are taken up again in the Freudo-Marxist tradition's distinction between abstract and biological father-hood, for instance in Theweleit's *Male Fantasies*. Theweleit argues that while biological fathers had lost credibility after Germany's loss in the First World War, in the Third Reich the idealised Führer could be seen as the link between the power of the 'abstract', sublime father on the one hand and the sons on the other hand (Theweleit 1980: II, 366). Similarly, in addition to a god-like father figure, Strindberg's Gustav is also a brother or son figure – a configuration that Juliet MacCannell calls 'fraternal Oedipus'. In this vein, we can see the conflict between Strindberg's two male protagonists not only as an oedipal conflict, but also as a fight between the older and the younger brother over the father's inheritance in a post-paternalistic age. In the traditional patriarchal system of primogeniture, the older brother is the heir. With Gustav, the older son proves that he is indeed the rightful heir.

Fetishism, or the Autonomy of Objects

Late nineteenth-century culture thus centrally problematises the grow-ing separation between embodied male authority and abstract sub-lime authority. Before Gustav enters the stage and wins the struggle for domination in Strindberg's *Creditors*, Adolf had longed to replace his lost belief in a transcendental authority with the idealisation and quasi-religious, fetishistic worship of his wife. After his disillusionment, Adolf laments that the worst thing of it all is that he has lost Tekla: 'She would be what God was for me before I became an atheist. Some-thing I could reverence' (Strindberg 1960a: 21). For Wilhelm Stekel, the author of a 1923 treatise on fetishism, fetishism is the perverted form of Christianity (Böhme 2012: 416). According to Santner, in the transition from premodern to modern society, the fetishism of persons (the king) is replaced by the fetishism of objects of economic exchange (Santner 2016: 45). Fetishism is thus at the heart of modern European culture. Following Freud, fetishisation is always about overcoming or disavow-ing some sort of loss, death or absence that threatens the disintegration of the self. Fetishes are transitional objects in Donald Winnicott's sense, objects that allow humans to deal with painful separations. The fetishist tries to overcome the absence of the other. The coming-to-terms with the autonomy of objects, with the difference between the self and the other, the fear of difference that is enacted in the plays discussed in this study, is central to fetishism.

The relationship between Adolf and Tekla in Strindberg's *Creditors* is thus an example of the narcissistic fusion between the fetishist and his object. In Strindberg's play, the phallus of transcendental authority lost in European modernity is at first replaced by the female protagonist. According to Richard von Krafft-Ebing's *Psychopathia sexualis* (1912), however, the fixation of libidinal energy on the fetish leads to 'psychic impotence' (Krafft-Ebing 1993: 178), and as we have seen, Strindberg's protagonist suffers from physical as well as socio-political impotence. Moreover, fetishes also carry traits of aggressive sadism, of a secret anger against the dependency they entail. In other words, the fetish is the rediscovery and the extinction of the mother imago in an ambivalent, abject object that is both worshipped and despised (Böhme 2012: 420–1). Consistent with the repulsive and threatening side of this ambivalence, Strindberg enacts the transition to maternal phallic power as not only based on illusions (like a fetish), but as extremely dangerous. When Gustav has destroyed Adolf's feminised 'new religion' by the end of *Creditors*, Adolf dies because he has lost the ego protection provided by the fetish and because the fetish herself (Tekla) is a threat to him. In Strindberg's play, finally, the fetishist Adolf is an artist. Like the fetish, a magical object that is difference, the work of art stabilises the fantasy of the fetishist's independence, integration and exclusive control and possession of the object (Böhme 2012: 444). For Stekel, however, fetishism encompasses both a closure or attempted exclusion of difference/alterity and the fear of disclosure. (Böhme 2012: 414). When the fetishist has to face reality – as Strindberg's male protagonists do – the result can only be deadly.

Given what Hartmut Böhme, in *Fetischismus und Kultur: Eine andere Theorie der Moderne*, calls the 'scenic elements' of the fetish (2012: 401), the theatre again lends itself to an enactment of this problematic. Fetishism is an 'immersion into a fictive world of symbolisms' (Böhme 2012: 415). A fetish is a story, a performance, a cathartic play/playfulness: 'all diese Larvierungen, Vermeidungen, Leidenschaften, Konflikte, Ängste und Widersprüche zwingen den Fetischisten zu Inszenierungen, die nicht ohne bizarre Intelligenz und kreativen Erfindungsreichtum ins Werk gesetzt werden' (Böhme 2012:

414, cf. also 439). ('All of these washes, avoidances, conflicts, fears, and contradictions force the fetishist to create productions that cannot be staged without bizarre intelligence and creative inventiveness' (my translation).) The fetishistic lover has to keep repeating an endless series of fetishistic scenes in order to soothe his narcissistic wound, maintain his desire and perform his phantasms. Fetishism is a performative act that again and again stages ritualistic scenes of omnipotence and powerlessness, of *jouissance* and rage, of fusion (with a symbiotic mother such as Tekla) and abandonment/separation, of primal trust and fear or disappointment, of safety/permanence and death/ego disintegration (Böhme 2012: 440–1).

The fetish is of course a key concept not only in psychoanalysis and the sexology of the late nineteenth century, but also in Marx's theory of commodity fetishism and the theory of labour and value on which it is based. Strindberg's play again links both discourses, discourses based on the relationship between the king's or father's physical and sublime bodies, and between the worker's labour and human labour's abstraction into value. Adolf is initially in denial not only about the erotic charge of his relationship with Gustav's wife, but also about Tekla's 'real value', her 'true nature'. The same oscillation between knowledge/exhibitionist presentation/the sublime on the one hand and denial/secret/materiality on the other – the acting out of 'as if' – marks both the fetishist's relationship to the fetishised object and the illusion of the spectator in the theatre (Böhme 2012: 409). In a way similar to fetishism and the theatre, public stagings of politics, religion and culture enchant consciousness and repress both a more deep-seated knowledge of the actual value of key social signifiers and the fear or panic that these signifiers' real value based on their materiality is going to be uncovered. In Strindberg's play, Adolf's phobias are a symptom of this same dynamic, of the fear that the secret of male symbolic authority – the modern gap between the ruler's or (in the context of the play, the husband's) natural body and his claim to sublime transcendence – will be found out.

On the public political stage of the early twentieth century, the idolisation or fetishisation of totalitarian leaders would help European populations seemingly come to terms with the perceived threats and losses brought on by modernity. Fetishes are closely linked to symbolic orders that establish values to be revered and thus provide meaning, and Hitler's *Tausendjähriges Reich* proposed to do exactly that. In a time threatened with disintegration and change, fetishes artificially and ritually provide permanence (Böhme 2012: 368). The ritual investitures of paternalistic authority had been a constitutive part of premodern transcendence. In modernity – an age that claims to forgo any transcendence – re-fetishisation again provides transcendence and redemption. For this reason, since the twentieth century fetishisation has pervaded all cultural domains (Böhme 2012: 370–1, 383, 418), masking the fundamental fear of difference that marks immunitarian modernity. In *Remembering the Phallic Mother* (1993), Marcia Ian comments on the enduring attraction of fetishism for a culture marked by the fear of alterity: 'Understanding fetishism as an erotic mystification that conceals the fear of difference helps to explain how our culture can be individualistic, democratic, and capitalistic on the one hand, and severely classist, homophobic, misogynist, and racist on the other' (quoted by Böhme 2012: 460).

Homosexuality as a 'Species'

Following the French anthropologist Claude Lévi-Strauss's analysis of kinship structures, Gayle Rubin's well-known essay 'The Traffic in Women' (1975) argued that the essence of kinship is an exchange of women among men and a consequent subordination of women and their desires to the exigencies of this exchange. The fact that there seems to be an incest taboo on Adolf and Tekla's relationship ties in with Lévi-Strauss's and Rubin's accounts, which see the incest taboo as a means of establishing exogamy and regulating the trade of women among men. Rubin also links this trade to the system of obligation and debt, as we have seen another key theme in *Creditors*. The economic language of Strindberg's play fits the idea of the trade of women among men. Adolf has 'usurped' Tekla and violated the incest taboo. This usurpation leaves him with an obligation to Gustav, the 'rightful' owner. Tekla becomes a figure owed, Gustav Adolf's creditor. Gustav, by (indirectly) killing Adolf, stays within the male system of exchange. In exchange for Adolf's violation of this system, Gustav deals him death.

Perhaps most interestingly, in the exchange of women in the patriarchal kinship system as theorised by Lévi-Strauss and Rubin, men use women as conduits of relationships in which the real partners are men. While social relations were based on overt domination and servitude under feudalism and premodern monarchies, the foundation of modernity is legal equality. In reality, however, relations of domination persist in modern capitalism through the mediation of fetishised commodities (Yuran 2014: 59, 245, paraphrasing Žižek). In Strindberg's play, the female protagonist – as commodity/fetish/money that is owed – mediates the male characters' struggle for domination. As Böhme points out, the objects that are fetishised or sacred in a culture are the central symbols of the real relationships between clan members (2012: 295). The exchange of Tekla between the two male protagonists in Strindberg's play is – like any exchange of gifts – a competition where the participants negotiate social identities, rank and hierarchies, that is the power structure that creates the symbolic order of a culture (Böhme 2012: 289).

The dramatic enactment of fetishism marks Strindberg's play as a thoroughly modern text again pointing to the intersections of late nineteenth-century sexology and Marx. As a bourgeois wife, Tekla was supposed to be the 'general' or 'universal equivalent', the privileged signifier exempt from commodification, from the exchange of goods of relative value. As Yuran points out, 'capitalism is . . . involved with the rise of the notion of what money cannot buy' (2014: 218). As a bourgeois wife, Tekla was expected to provide a haven or refuge, a domestic enclave from the male world of business transactions, and provide stability and value. As a mother figure as well, Tekla was supposedly beyond commodification. By leaving her marriage with Gustav, however, Tekla fails as a fetishised, sacred object that only reflects the fetishist's desires – the female *tabula rasa* or mirror – and enters the world of commodity exchange. While the fetishist Adolf ultimately loses his illusions, Tekla loses her magical aura. Instead of guaranteeing permanence as a universal signifier, Tekla brings death to Adolf's narcissistic ego, which cannot survive without a fetish. The Mother ends up engulfing the male ego. The capitalist economy of unfettered exchange as well can only function if certain privileged objects are exempted from circulation. By disturbing this boundary, Tekla disturbs capitalist circulation, the hierarchies associated with it and ultimately (male) cultural identity. As Marx had already pointed out, modern 'secular' society is structurally dominated by elementary religious forms: 'Die moderne Gesellschaft ist eine von elementaren religiösen Symbolen angetriebene Maschinerie' (Böhme 2012: 308). ('Modern society is a machine driven by elementary religious symbols' (my translation).)[27] Tekla's role shows the intimate link between demon and fetish, the double structure of fear and fascination that, according to Kristeva, also characterises the border-crossing abject.

The assessment that Tekla only serves as the conduit of a relationship in which the real partners are men holds true for the relationship between Gustav and Adolf in yet another sense as well. One can read the rivalry between the two men in Strindberg's play as an erotic relationship that both men have only displaced onto the woman.[28] The strong structural parallels that the play establishes between Tekla and Gustav certainly make this erotic attraction a possibility for Adolf. Adolf is in love with Tekla, and Tekla, as female *tabula rasa*, reflects the character traits of her first husband, Gustav. In a heteronormative cultural context, the fact that Adolf is an effeminate male makes him a possible, if not acceptable, love match for Gustav. In *Creditors*, Tekla has taken on masculine traits, while Adolf is represented as a feminised hysteric. In 1908, Freud would establish a link between hysteria – this mimetic, contagious illness[29] – and bisexuality in his *Hysterische Phantasien und ihre Beziehung zur Bisexualität*. In his article 'The Last Word on the *Question* of Women' (1887), written a year before *Creditors*, Strindberg had expressed his growing 'concern that the leveling of difference between the genders could lead to same-sex desire between men – and for the first time – between women' (Aldrich and Wotherspoon 2005: 504). Given the feminisation of homosexuality and of difference in general in modern patriarchal culture, it then becomes possible to read Adolf's effeminacy as homosexuality. In a nineteenth-century medical dictionary, 'sexual inversion', the contemporary term used for homosexuality, is attributed to 'a poorly balanced nervous system marked by infantilism and a lack of masculine energy' (Lacassagne 1886, according to Marhoefer 2011: 531). Adolf is Tekla's 'little brother' (infantilism) and is represented as a neurasthenic or abulic lacking male energy or will power. Finally, nineteenth-century psychiatry also linked homosexuality to degeneration (Marhoefer 2011: 531), as we have seen a key theme of Strindberg's play.

In *Between Men*, Eve Sedgwick establishes a relation between the repression of male homosexuality and the oppression of women through male patriarchal relationships (Sedgwick 1985: 20). If we read Gustav and Adolf's relationship as an erotic bond, we can then also read the ending, Adolf's death, as his punishment for his homosexuality. Tekla is what Serres calls the quasi-object that is being passed, establishing the collective between the two male protagonists. When this game of passing the 'ferret' in the game of Hunt-the Slipper (or Button) stops, however, Adolf is caught, discovered and loses (in French, the one who loses the game is *mort*, dead). Serres explains: 'The member of the offense, the one carrying the ball, is marked as the victim' (Serres 2007: 225).

At the end of the play, Adolf is indeed the one caught carrying the ball and is literally *mort*. He is the one who does not fit the binary gender differentiation of nineteenth-century European society and therefore needs to be abjected, eliminated. The representation of the male protagonist in Strindberg's play illustrates Angus McLaren's observation (1997: 26) that the modern definition of masculinity, which was being worked out in the final decades of the nineteenth century, found its basis not so much in positive assertions as in the repudiation of those men declared to be lacking virility. *Creditors* is a text that helped define contemporary normative gender roles. It reasserts the authority of the father in the oedipal triangle while also enacting the bourgeois family or bourgeois marriage as deeply troubled. Homosexuality clearly jars with modern society's attempt to base the bourgeois gender role distribution on binary fixed gender identities and is therefore refuted or repressed. In this sense as well, Adolf's death is a warning against transgressing prescribed gender assignments.

In this context it is finally of interest to remember Foucault's well-known discussion of the role of homosexual acts in premodern times and, in contrast, the creation of 'the homosexual' as 'a species':

> The nineteenth century homosexual became a personage, a past, a case history, and a childhood, in addition to being a type of life, a life form, and a morphology, with an indiscreet anatomy and possibly a mysterious physiology. Nothing that went into his total composition was unaffected by his sexuality . . . The sodomite had been a temporary aberration: *the homosexual was now a species.* (Foucault 1980a: 43, my emphasis)

With *Creditors*, Strindberg puts the personage or case study that Foucault talks about on the stage. In the play, indeed, nothing is unaffected by the protagonists' (Tekla's female and Adolf's homosexual) sexuality. It is in this unexpected sense that Strindberg's play fits the term that Chauduri creates for posthumanist theatre: the Theatre of Species. We thus have to give Strindberg credit for bringing heatedly debated contemporary issues of sexual difference to the stage. The Swedish penal code of 1865 had listed homosexuality (for both men and women) as a sexual crime *against nature*. Again, what is at stake is thus the relationship between humans and nature. By contrast, France, where Strindberg spent many years of his life, had already abolished its sodomy law during the French Revolution. Germany's infamous Paragraph 175 on the other hand criminalised sexual acts between men (but not women) in 1871. But Germany also gave rise to the new science of sexology, which spread quickly throughout Europe. According to Matthew Roy, Strindberg's work is testimony to his life-long interest in homosexuality as a social phenomenon. As Roy demonstrates, the theme of same-sex desire pervades Strindberg's work, creating an important platform for the contemporary discussion of homosexuality (Roy 2001). With the enactment of controversial issues of sexual difference, Strindberg thus joined a wider European literary and cultural discussion and established his rank as an avant-garde member of the Modern Breakthrough.

Notes

1. Adolf expresses his fear of Tekla coming back: 'I am longing for her to come; yet I am afraid of her. She caresses me; she is tender, but there is something suffocating about her kisses, something weakening and numbing' (Strindberg 1960a: 22).
2. 'Then when I'd slept for a couple of days, I came to and began to pull myself together. My mind, which had been working deliriously, began to calm down. Old thoughts that I had had in the past rose up again; the desire to work, to create, came back, and my eyes regained their old power of looking at things truthfully and boldly. And then you turned up' (Strindberg 1960a: 9).
3. See also Freud's *Fragment of an Analysis of a Case of Hysteria* (1905).
4. Cf. also Strindberg (1960a: 21) (Adolf): 'she ate up my faith'.
5. The classic text arguing the inferiority of women as artists is Karl Scheffler's *Die Frau und die Kunst* (1908). See Strindberg's 'Author's Foreword' to *Miss Julie*: 'their hopes of catching up with men are shattered' (Strindberg 1955a: 65).
6. Cf. Serres (2007: 202 and 214).
7. Weininger was also admired by Mussolini. Cf. Mussolini (1932: 172).
8. Of humans, Serres says: 'we live within the flora as much as we live within the fauna. We are parasites' (2007: 10).
9. There are many examples of the fascination with hypnosis at the end of the nineteenth century. Cf. for instance Weininger (1980: 396): 'Der Wille des Mannes schafft erst die Frau, er gebietet über sie, [comma *sic*] und verändert sie von Grund auf (Hypnose)' ('It is only the will of man that creates woman, he commands her and changes her completely (hypnosis)' (my translation). Cf. also Mosse's discussion of the new scientific interest in male hysteria at the *fin de siècle* (Mosse 1996: 85). Cf. Taylor (2000: 1): 'In 1895, Freud had an explanation of what nineteenth century medicine called "hysteria": He diagnosed it as a traumatic reaction to sexual "seduction" in childhood (what we would call sexual abuse, usually of daughters by their fathers). In 1897, Freud abandoned that hypothesis.' In *Creditors*, written in 1888, the older and more experienced Tekla has seduced the child-like Adolf. Finally, in the late nineteenth century, hysteria was a term usually applied to women, but also

used to describe homosexuals. As I will argue later, the relationship between Gustav and Adolf also has homoerotic undertones.

10. Cf. Strindberg (1960a: 47) (Gustav to Tekla): 'Anyhow, you haven't got a soul. That's just an illusion.' The same view of Woman as lacking a soul can again be found in Weininger (1980: 240, 261).

11. Cf. Serres (2007: 131): 'A parasite never nourishes its children. Otherwise it would be in the position of host. A parasite defends itself from being parasited; the thing is there in all its simplicity.' The refusal of the duties of motherhood is also one of the traits of the New Woman, the virago/gynander, as perceived by the *fin de siècle*. Insects as well do not care for their infants (which are not born prematurely like humans).

12. In Aeschylus' *The Eumenides*, for instance, we read: 'The woman you call the mother of the child is not the parent, just a nurse to the seed, the new-sown seed that grows and swells within her. The *man* is source of life – the one who mounts. She, like a stranger, keeps the shoot alive unless god hurts the roots' (lines 665–70, translator's emphasis).

13. The physical influence of the male over the female is also a central theme in Strindberg's *The Father*, *The Great Highway*, *The Ghost Sonata* and *To Damascus*. Telegony and maternal impressions are strong thematic elements in Ibsen (*The Lady from the Sea*, 1888) and Michelet (*L'amour*, 1858). The theme can be found as early as in Goethe's *Wahlverwandtschaften* (1810). Cf. also Zola's *Madeleine Ferat* and *Le Docteur Pascal* and the title character of Zola's novel *Nana*, who in spite of being the daughter of another man (Coupeau) physically resembles her mother's first lover (Lantier). Cf. also the British writer Arabella Kenealy (1859–1938).

14. Cf. also Freud, 'Das Ich und das Über-Ich (Ichideal)': 'Bei Frauen, die viel [*sic*] Liebeserfahrungen gehabt haben, glaubt man, die Rückstände ihrer Objektbesetzungen in ihren Charakterzügen leicht nachweisen zu können' (Freud 1975a: 297) ('With women who have had much experience in love, one believes to be able to easily prove the remnants of their object cathexes in their character traits', my translation).

15. Fraternal organisations, however, were not only fundamental to modern German society. In *Between Men*, Eve Sedgwick showed homosociality to be a constitutive trait of patriarchal societies and not limited to German or modern society alone.

16. As Adolf will find out, the danger posed by the libidinal drives also includes Gustav. Gustav has more (sexual) experience than Adolf and, together with Tekla, will eventually cause Adolf's death.

17. Cf. Nealon (2016: 65).

18. Nealon (2016: 50).

19. Cf. also Strindberg (1960a: 51), where Gustav says to Tekla: 'Will it satisfy you if I say: Forgive me for your having clawed my heart to pieces.' Cf. also 46 (Gustav about his alleged wife-to-be): '. . . but this time I shall harness the mare better, so she won't bolt.'

20. In *The Dance of Death*, Strindberg also plays with the *leitmotif* of the Fall, this first challenge to paternalistic authority.

21. As Thibault points out, British war propaganda also presented its enemies as parasites and microbes. A contemporary advertisement by a pharmaceutical company represented Hitler as syphilis (Thibault 2016: 85–6).

22. Concerning Gustav and Tekla's former marriage, cf. Strindberg (1960a: 51). Gustav says to Tekla: 'Forgive me for setting you free from the domination of your parents, for releasing you from the tyranny of ignorance and superstition, for setting you over my house, for giving you friends and a position, for making a woman of the mere child you were.'

23. See again the thematic and structural similarities between *Creditors* and *The Father*.

24. Gustav calls Adolf 'my boy' and observes that Tekla always had 'a fancy for innocent youths' (Strindberg 1960a: 26). Tekla herself acknowledges that her infatuation with youth made her fall in love with Adolf (Strindberg 1960a: 31).

25. The economic language is carried on when Gustav accuses Tekla of stealing from Adolf: 'She took when you weren't looking, and that's known as stealing' (Strindberg 1960a: 18). Weininger (1980: 266) argues that since woman does not have an ego, she also does not have any sense of property.

26. Matthew Wilson Smith argues that the bourgeois sense of autonomy was thoroughly shaken by the neurological discoveries of Strindberg's time (Smith 2018: 16). These contemporary scientific discoveries also included Freud's theory of the unconscious.

27. Giorgio Agamben, Joseph Vogl and Eric Santner are also all interested in the iteration of theological or religious elements in modernity.

28. See, for instance, the ambiguity of the last line of *Creditors*, spoken by Gustav after Adolf's death. Gustav says about Tekla: 'She really does love him *too*' (Strindberg 1960a: 52, my emphasis).

29. Cf. Mitchell (2001).

PART II

MUNICH AND PARIS, 1918–1943: ENCOUNTERS WITH FASCISM

CHAPTER 3

Bare Life, or Becoming-Animal

Bertolt Brecht's first full-length play, *Baal* – written in 1918 while Brecht was a university student in Munich, published in 1920, first performed in Leipzig in 1923 and revised five times over the course of Brecht's life (1898–1956)[1] – is in many ways in conversation with the philosophical and political concerns prevalent in Europe in the first half of the twentieth century, and specifically with the period that produced the rise of totalitarianism in Germany. One of the key concepts of this historical moment is the concept of bare life. While today's readers are familiar with the notion of *la nuda vita* from Giorgio Agamben's work on National Socialism, Nitzan Lebovic points out that '[n]aked life, or a naked immediacy, existed in philosophical texts and concepts since the late 1910s' (2013: 185). The notion can be found for instance – as *blosses Leben* – in Georg Simmel's *Lebensanschauung* published in 1918,[2] the year Brecht started writing *Baal*. As the contemporary philosopher Heinrich Rickert noted after Simmel's death that same year, Simmel had turned the concept into the trendiest philosophy of the time, which suggests that Brecht himself was well acquainted with it.

In *The Philosophy of Life and Death: Ludwig Klages and the Rise of a Nazi Biopolitics*, Lebovic reads the Nazi rhetoric on life in the context of the cultural discourses of this period (2013: 185). What National Socialism considered a threat is the liminal zone where certain 'lower' human races were perceived as approaching animality. While Darwin's theory of evolution had established the relationship between non-human and human animals as a continuous spectrum and Nazi rhetoric centrally featured terms from animal husbandry such as 'Züchtung' (breeding) even when referring to the Aryan population, this blurring of the borderline between humans and nonhuman species – degeneration – was, as we have already seen in Strindberg, perceived as the ultimate threat to humanity. Since the late nineteenth and early twentieth century viewed women as situated at a lower rank on the evolutionary scale, this liminal zone and threat were often feminised. The Nazis, moreover, sought to eliminate bare life, this transgressive, purulent flesh, from the *Volkskörper*, the body of the German people, by disposing of non-Aryans, homosexuals and disabled people, among others. The regime considered these 'borderline' humans as devoid of qualified, political life, as 'half-men', 'damaged beings', 'mentally dead', 'leere Menschenhülsen' (empty human husks); or 'Ballastexistenzen' (ballast existences, the kind of superfluous weight that can be jettisoned in perilous situations) (Esposito 2008: 134).

I argue that in spite of his anxiety before his death, an anxiety emphasising his ontological vulnerability, Brecht's protagonist, Baal,[3] generally *embraces* this limit zone between animality and the human realm.

'Fleisch', that is (nonhuman) meat or (human) flesh, is a key emblem in Brecht's *Baal*, enacting the threat of border transgression posed by the title character. As in his play *Im Dickicht der Städte* (*Jungle of Cities*), Brecht turns human beings into food for the male ogre, the parasite at the centre of the play. Baal is a voracious and lazy cannibal who eats flesh ('Fleisch')[4] and reduces his female victims to a nonhuman, 'faceless heap of flesh' ('ein Haufen Fleisch, der kein Gesicht mehr hat') (Brecht 1967: I, 11). Baal eats – this time literally – animal 'corpses' ('Aalleichname') (Brecht 1967: I, 5) ('eel corpses') and metaphorically devours virgins. As in Strindberg, love is domination and the sexual act is an animalistic act of incorporation, 'das Funkeln in den Augen zweier Insekten, die sich fressen wollen' (Brecht 1967: I, 33) ('the sparkle in the eyes of two insects that want to devour each other').[5] Whereas in Strindberg images of incorporation enact the threat to autonomy posed by parasitic women, here the men – and most of all the male protagonist – are 'predatory animals' ('Raubtiere') (Brecht 1967: I, 45) who see women as their prey (Brecht 1967: I, 29). Baal's world is a biological world where the stronger survives, where – like the vultures in the play ('Der Choral vom grossen Baal') (Brecht 1967: I, 4) – you either eat or get eaten.[6] Whereas earlier in the play the animal Baal 'crouches, ready to jump' ('duckt sich zum Sprung') (Brecht 1967: I, 61), at the end of the play he dies crawling on all fours while protesting that he is not a rat: 'Ich bin keine Ratte' (Brecht 1967: I, 66). This latter protest is of course only necessary and ultimately in vain because Baal himself knows that he is in fact an animal (although maybe not a rat). His death is then a return to a natural-biological life. Throughout the play, Baal's cannibalism also leads to the loss of his victims' specifically human identity, reducing them to what he himself embodies, namely creaturely, material life.

Although Baal's outsider status, his relation to natural life and his return to mother earth establish a thematic proximity to Nazism's mystical neo-romanticism, Brecht's early work demonstrates that the psychic trajectory of European modernity to fascism was contingent rather than inevitable.[7] Contrary to fascism's immunitarian rigidity, Brecht's play enacts what Rosi Braidotti, in her call for a 'nomadic subjectivity', refers to as 'a nonbinary way of positing the relationship between same and other' (Braidotti 2010: 209). In contrast to the Cartesian rationalist tradition, Brecht's title character is, to use Braidotti's expression, 'in love with zoē' (2010: 208), in love with material-biological life. Living on the margins of human society, at the threshold of indistinction between nature and culture, between the realm of animals and the law of the city, Baal shares the hybridity of the ancient Germanic myth of the wolf-man – 'the monstrous hybrid of human and animal, divided between the forest and the city – the werewolf – . . . the figure of the man who has been banned from the city' (Santner 2011: 182). Enacting an alterity that transverses dualistic metaphysical boundaries, Brecht's protagonist embodies a unity with nonhuman materiality. Rather than neo-romantic, however, Brecht's ambivalent title figure is instead a modern *homo sacer*. He incarnates the excess – the abjection or horror – of bare life, of what Eric Santner has named creaturely life or, following a long philosophical tradition, the flesh.[8]

A result of the material, political and economic changes wrought by modernity, the excessive liminality enacted in Brecht's play is not only an ontological, but also a thoroughly modern, historical problematic. As Santner has put forth in *The Royal Remains*, the surplus of the flesh – the energy that (I have argued) always exceeds 'matter' in a dynamic, constantly changing universe – is in premodern society and in totalitarianism absorbed by a sovereign master endowed with sublime authority. In democratic, bourgeois modernity, however, a society based on the principle of individual achievement and the people's political power, this excess energy expresses itself as a widespread anxiety or restlessness shared among many bodies. I suggest that there is a productive link between the border-crossing abjection that Brecht's anti-hero Baal celebrates and the state of socio-political authority that comes into play after the abdication of German Emperor Wilhelm II in 1918, the year that Brecht wrote *Baal*. The horrific, monstrous corporeality that Brecht's protagonist embodies is – to follow Santner's description of the flesh – 'not the natural human body left over once all of one's social vestments have been stripped away, but something more like the rotting flesh of the sublime body, what remains when its sublimity has wasted away' (Santner 2011: 44).

While with the body of the fascist sovereign, totalitarianism provided an artificial closure to the increasing de-materialisation of socio-political authority (from the king to the people) and money (to finance capital) in modernity, and while modern theatre sometimes functioned as a bio-political apparatus enacting (and defending against) a sense of biological threat to the immunity of qualified, human life, in the theatre the so-called crisis of representation could also find an alternative expression. Brecht's *Baal* is an example of such an alternate trajectory, a play that embraces biological-material life *and* modern abstraction, in either case moving away from the meaning-making of the discursive sphere towards absurd theatre. Absurd theatre decentres not only meaning, but also the human (in his control of meaning – both the meaning of words/communication and of the universe). While over the years Brecht has repeatedly been accused of totalitarianism, I demonstrate that Brecht's work is qualitatively different from fascist texts, which attempt to re-establish such control.

The 'Totalitarian' Brecht

Indicating the close historical proximity of Brecht's play and the rise of early twentieth-century totalitarianism, it was Theodor Adorno who first criticised the later, Marxist Brecht for his adoption of a socialism that Adorno (mistakenly) held to be totalitarian ('On Commitment' 185).[9] In his controversial Brecht biography, *Brecht and Company* (1994), John Fuegi, referring to Klaus Theweleit's *Männerfantasien* (1977–8) (*Male Fantasies*) and focusing on Brecht's alleged fear of women's engulfing sexuality, compared Brecht to Hitler and Stalin. In his classic work on German fascism, Theweleit analysed autobiographical and fictional texts written by the members of the *Freikorps*, an elite volunteer paramilitary force of around 300,000 men that the German government had used after the First World War (from 1918 to 1923) to put down proletarian revolutionary movements in cities such as Berlin and Munich. The *Freikorps* also fought the Russian Red Army in the Baltic region, as well as Polish communists and nationalists, and terrorised left-wing activists (such as Rosa Luxemburg and Karl Lieb-knecht, whom they murdered). Theweleit analyses the psychic constitution of these *Freikorps* writers and the cultural frame that had formed them – the socio-historic context that also produced Nazism. Theweleit links these proto-fascist men's fear and oppression of the feminine to the relationship between the sexes in patriarchal society as a whole. In spite of the explicit critique of Freud in *Männerfantasien*, Theweleit's technique of analysis closely parallels Freud's method of uncovering what was hidden behind 'normalcy' by examining those pathological moments in which what was otherwise concealed became visible. For Theweleit, German fascism is one such pathological moment – an extreme manifestation of what was latently there all along. (Replacing Theweleit's psychoanalytical framework with a more Deleuzian language, one could also speak of an actualisation of a virtual potentiality through contingent encounters.) By defining fascism as an extreme form of the patriarchy's phobic relationship to alterity, Theweleit's argument counters the *Sonderweg* view of National Socialism as an aberration of German history, and of German history only.[10]

Theweleit's investigation shares certain traits with the Italian philosopher Roberto Esposito's more recent conceptualisation of totalitarianism as the paroxysm of modern immunitarian thinking. Both writers view fascism as the attempt to establish rigid boundaries designed to defend the self against threatening others. And both writers take account of the modern crisis of male symbolic, i.e. paternalistic (divine, royal, paternal), authority as a central factor contributing to modernity's problematic relationship with the other – Theweleit because he continues the Freudo-Marxist analysis of the 'fatherless society' and Esposito because he views the immunitarian logic of modernity as the result of a post-metaphysical society that does not believe in an afterlife anymore, thus perceives itself at risk and consequently makes biological survival its highest good. In both writers' analysis, fascism is the extreme fear of difference.

The immunitarian threat is a perceived threat to the individual's psychic and bodily autonomy and integrity. As we have seen, in Strindberg's *Creditors* (as in many of his naturalist dramas), the female protagonist constitutes a biological threat to the physical survival of the male protagonist. As an erotic woman, she embodies the border-crossing threat posed by libidinal drives in a modern society marked by abstraction. While the title character causes his victims' death, Brecht's *Baal*, on the other hand, does not enact a biological threat to society's immunity couched in the material problematic of health and pathology. It is this lack of an immunitarian logic that already distinguishes the play from the rhetoric of Nazism.

At the same time, however, border invasion is indeed a central problematic in *Baal*. As Fuegi argues correctly, Brecht does use the same imagery as the proto-fascist texts examined in *Männerfantasien*, which give expression to an extreme fear of feminised libidinal drives and the invasion of the self by the (m)other. What distinguishes Baal from fascist texts, however, is most importantly the value assigned to this feminised threat of invasion. Whereas fascist thinking is based on rigid binaries that aim to fend off one side of the opposition, Brecht's anti-hero celebrates abjection – the transgression of social, psychic and ultimately ontological boundaries. Brecht's play is both a satire of the bourgeois moral code and a parody of the dramatic tradition, a parody that (I argue) ultimately already announces the theatre of the absurd that was to come decades later.

Border Violations

Even beyond the simple fact of the close historical proximity of Brecht's early plays and the proto-fascist texts studied by Theweleit, Brecht's enactment of the feminine as threatening at first seems to establish a parallel between *Baal* and the texts written by the *Freikorps* men – although not in the reductive biographical way suggested by Fuegi. My own reading looks beyond the many well-known investigations of women figures in Brecht's plays by not restricting the conceptualisation of the feminine to women characters alone, but by examining the feminisation of libidinal drives or the more-than human, material energy (what Spinoza would have called *conatus*) in *Baal*. In contrast to many other plays of the patriarchal tradition (including Strindberg's and Sartre's), in Brecht's play it is not women who pose a deadly threat to the male protagonist, but the male protagonist himself whose libidinal energy – or, depending on one's philosophical paradigm, the life force with which he engages – constitutes a lethal threat, the threat of border-crossing abjection or the flesh.

The play starts, however, with almost conventional images of threatening female sexuality. Brecht's colour tropes are again reminiscent of the *Freikorps* men's dichotomy between 'white' (idealised and sexually pure, devitalised) mother and sister figures on the one hand and the 'red' (eroticised communist) women who fought against the right-wing *Freikorps*. The poem that has preceded Brecht's play since 1919, 'Der Choral vom großen Baal' ('Hymn of Baal the Great'), posits the maternal womb as a 'white' space. It similarly refers to sexually pure women as (white) swans ('Schwäne'), to the point where 'white' becomes a leitmotif emblematising originary innocence. While in their autobiographical writings Theweleit's proto-fascist men try to conceal the erotic attraction they feel for their sisters through the very rigidity of the opposition established, Brecht, however, at the very opening of *Baal*, collapses the Madonna–whore dichotomy that pervades the history of the patriarchal tradition by openly eroticising the maternal womb: 'das große Weib Welt, das sich lachend gibt / Dem, der sich zermalmen läßt von ihren Knien / Gab ihm einige Ekstase, die er liebt' (Brecht 1967: I, 3). ('The large big woman World, who gives herself with a laugh / to the one who lets himself be crushed by her knees / gave him some ecstasy that he loves'). Brecht thus uses the title 'Choral' with its semantic link to the Christian mass and Christian ethics ironically. The play itself also collapses the dichotomy between sexually pure 'white' women and sexual drives. The virgins that Baal seduces are more than willing to be victimised by him. And ultimately the play associates both the colours black (visualising abjection) and white (visualising sexual purity) with death and decay, for instance in the *Fronleichnam* (Corpus Christi Day) scene (Brecht 1967: I, 27) or the leitmotif of the white Johanna rotting in the dark river. Lynda Hart observes that 'to violate borders is to *reveal how a system is constructed*' (1994: 98, emphasis in original). Brecht's play enacts the violation of the basic categories of bourgeois society and collapses its dichotomies.

Similar to Theweleit, Kristeva's *Powers of Horror* (1982), another controversial but nevertheless classic and important analysis of fascism,[11] describes the phobic patriarchal subject as marked by the uncertainty of his borders, by a frail 'identity' continuously threatened with disintegration.[12] Kristeva posits that abjection occurs when the rules of classification peculiar to a given symbolic system – when the binary hierarchical separations constitutive of masculine society – cannot be maintained, i.e. when 'leakage' occurs. She writes: 'It is thus not lack of cleanliness or health that causes abjection but what disturbs identity, system, order. What does not respect borders, positions, rules. The in-between, the ambiguous, the composite' (Kristeva 1982: 4). The transgression of established separations, the impossibility of keeping these strict separations intact, in other words, produces what Kristeva calls the 'abject'. The abject is both the zone where contamination occurs and the contaminating matter itself. The reaction to the abject is ambiguous, comprising fear, disgust, repulsion, as well as attraction and fascination. Abjection, in short, is the mechanism by means of which patriarchal society, in the interest of establishing a clear inside/outside division, constructs the 'feminine' as its other – as everything that threatens this distinction. My own debt to Kristeva's work includes not only the concept of abjection, but also this use of the term 'feminine' – a concept conceived large enough to include varying forms

of difference not necessarily based on a binary distinction of anatomi-
cal attributes. (*Powers of Horror* is in fact a study of male authors read
as exponents of 'feminine' writing.) This distinction between biological
women and the feminine, and ultimately the annihilation of fixed genders (that is pre-given qualities), is also central to my understanding of
Brecht's early dramatic work.[13]

The problematisation of feminised difference and tropes of fluidity
in particular is a trait that links Strindberg's *Creditors* and Brecht's
early plays, including *Baal*, to the work of both Kristeva and Theweleit.
All four of these writers are interested in the role played by fluids –
mud, swamp, slime, excrement, pulp, menstrual blood – and examine
floods and fluids as border transgressions. Floods and fluids transgress
the limits of masculine consciousness and its rigid hierarchical classifications. It is in the context of Theweleit's and Kristeva's discussion of
fluidity that one also starts to understand the Nazis' horror of *Rassen-
vermischung*, of the mixing of different races, as part of a more general
resistance to the transgression of static identity classifications. Similarly,
Hitler's later obsession with Marxism (which he saw as a Jewish conspiracy) makes more 'sense' (if such a term can be applied in the context
of homicidal madness) when one recognises communism as a programmatic violation of both national and class boundaries. The Nazis saw
the perceived enemies of the regime – Jews, communists, capitalists,
trade unions, Sinti and Roma – as cosmopolitans with no respect for
national borders, just as they perceived homosexuals as transgressing
the boundary between the sexes. To counter the threat posed by the
other – a threat that links the dramas included in this study – fascist
ideology established a biopolitical binary caesura between different
population groups, a dividing line that could only be transgressed at
the expense of encountering creaturely life or abject flesh. Although, as
we have seen, Brecht wrote *Baal* before adopting Marxism as his political and aesthetic programme and the play therefore does not address a
political problematic, it does enact a transgressive homosexuality and
a questioning of the status of the human. Lacassagne's 1886 entry on
'Péderastie' (that is homosexuality) in the *Dictionnaire encyclopédique
des sciences médicales* calls the ancient cult of Baal nothing but 'une
prostitution masculine' (1886: 241).

Animals, Plants and Water

Brecht's play enacts feminised (though not necessarily female) sexuality on the other hand – the excessive processual energy associated
with nonhuman materiality – as posing a lethal threat ('zermalmen':

'crush' or 'pulverise'). The opening, 'Der Choral vom großen Baal', already links sexual ecstasy ('Wollust') to corpses ('Leichen'). Baal's friend Johannes chimes in with the title character's song about love, associating sexuality with the vagina dentata: 'Ihre Zähne sind wie die eines Tieres: graugelb, massiv, unheimlich' (Brecht 1967: I, 12). ('Love's teeth / your teeth resemble those of an animal: greyish-yellow, massive, uncanny'). Throughout the play, Brecht associates teeth with strength.[14] His title character's description of love teems with ambiguous tropes of animals, plants, fluids and wind invading the body and its boundaries – materialities that enact both the more-than-human world and the human/nonhuman borderline itself. The abject thus described provides both pleasure and pain:

> Und die Liebe ist, wie wenn man seinen nackten Arm in Teichwasser schwimmen läßt, mit Tang zwischen den Fingern; wie die Qual, vor der der trunkene Baum knarzend zu singen anhebt, auf dem der wilde Wind reitet; wie ein schlürfendes Ersaufen in Wein an einem heißen Tag, und ihr Leib dringt einem wie sehr kühler Wein in alle Hautfalten, sanft wie Pflanzen im Wind sind die Gelenke, und die Wucht des Anpralls, der nachgeben wird, ist wie Fliegen gegen Sturm, und ihr Leib wälzt sich wie kühler Kies über dich. (Brecht 1967: I, 12)[15]

> (And love is like letting one's naked arm drift in the pond water, with seaweed between one's fingers; like the pain that makes the drunken tree on which the wild wind is riding start to sing, creaking; like a slurping drowning in wine on a hot day, and her body driving like a very cool wine into all of one's skin folds, soft like plants in the wind are the joints, and the impact of the collision that will give is like flies against the storm, and her body rolls over you like cool pebbles.)

In another, similar passage Baal associates feminised sexuality and motherhood with images of animals and water threatening invasion, disintegration and death:

> Wenn der bleiche milde Sommer fortschwimmt und sie sind vollgesogen wie Schwämme mit Liebe, *dann werden sie wieder Tiere*, bös und kindisch, unförmig mit dicken Bäuchen und fließenden Brüsten und mit feuchtklammernden Armen wie schleimige Polypen, und ihre Leiber zerfallen und werden matt auf den Tod. (Brecht 1967: I, 11; see also 12, 16, my emphasis)

> (When the pale mild summer swims away and they are full like sponges with love, then *they become animals again*, evil and childish, bloated with thick bellies and flowing breasts and with wet and clinging arms like slimy polyps, and their bodies fall apart and become feeble to death. my emphasis)

In contrast to bourgeois theatre, what Brecht's title character fears most in love is not male rivals[16] but a becoming-animal that is somehow linked to motherhood/pregnancy and children, constituting a threat to his personal autonomy as a human (Brecht 1967: I, 4, 12). Kristeva points out that abjection is linked to the archaic mother, that the mother is 'the first pre-object (abject) of need' (1982: 118). Brecht's play also links abjection to the maternal: 'unförmig mit dicken Bäuchen und fließenden Brüsten' ('bloated with thick bellies and flowing breasts' – see above). This enactment of the threat of ego invasion by the maternal does at first glance again resemble Strindberg.

In spite of Fuegi's account of Brecht's fear of Marie Aman's devouring sexuality (Fuegi 1994: 37) and Arnold Heidsieck's discussion of the distrust of the mother's power of seduction in Brecht's early poetry and the original 1918 version of *Baal* (Heidsieck 1975), we will see upon closer inspection, however, that Brecht's play enacts the maternal abject in ways that differ significantly from its portrayal in Theweleit's texts[17] or, for that matter, from the bourgeois immunitarianism in Strindberg. While texts of the patriarchal tradition typically feminise the feared abject, Brecht associates not only motherhood and female sexuality with water, death and creaturely life,[18] but also his male protagonist, Baal: 'Zu zweit dem in seinem Teich liegen?' (Brecht 1967: I, 22) ('The two of us lying in his pond?') The basic gender dichotomy of patriarchal society collapses.

On the one hand Brecht's use of water imagery is thus reminiscent of Kristeva's and Theweleit's discussions of fluids and floods as displacements of the flows of desire and the threat of border transgression. Brecht uses the colours black or purple and the trope of darkness (in contrast to whiteness, blue sky and light) to describe creaturely life outside human society – a literal sphere embodied by trees/plants/the forest, animals, rivers, rain and sky – and ultimately to connote death. It is, however, Baal himself who poses the most lethal threat to the figurative white 'swans' whom he systematically rids of their virginity (Brecht 1967: I, 23) and who end up drowning themselves (Brecht 1967: I, 21–2), again reinforcing the threat posed by water:

> EKART Geh mit mir, Bruder! Zu den Straßen mit hartem Staub: abends wird die Luft violett. Zu den Schnapsschenken voll von Besoffenen: in die schwarzen Flüße fallen Weiber, die du gefüllt hast . . . Zu den Kuhställen, wo man zwischen Tieren schläft: sie sind finster und voll vom Gemuhe der Kühe. Und zu den Wäldern, wo . . . man das Licht des Himmels vergißt: Gott hat einen vergessen. (Brecht 1967: I, 16)

> (EKART: Go with me, Brother. To the streets with hard dust: in the evening the air becomes purple. To the schnaps bars full of drunkards: women that you

have filled fall into the black rivers . . . To the cattle barns, where one sleeps amongst animals: they are dark and full of the moo-ing of the cows. And to the forests, where . . . one forgets the light of the sky: God has forgotten us.)

While Theweleit's proto-fascist men suffer from an extreme phobia of maternal engulfment and while *Männerfantasien* posits this fear as part of not only the fascist psychological constitution, but also of the constitution of the male patriarchal subject, Brecht enacts the transgression of boundaries as positive. Theweleit himself acknowledges that Brecht seems to be an exception:

> Not so Brecht. During his refugee years, he talked of government as the regulation of flowing. He saw good government, however, not as dambuilding (or even making cuts for dams), but as the leveling of obstacles that block the flow of streams. (Theweleit 1987: 385)

Brecht allows the rivers, the unconscious drives, to flow. In a letter dated 28 April 1919, Brecht wrote:

> die Liebe muß alle Schranken durchreißen und auf sich tragen. Wie der Strom das Wehr durchdonnert, sprengt, und auf massigen Schultern mit sich trägt. Sieh, ihr junger schmaler Leib windet sich einmal in Schmerz und die köstlichen Hüften zucken von Wehen. (Brecht 1988: XXVIII, 28, quoted by Jordheim 1999: 104)

> (Love must tear through and carry all barriers. Like the stream thundering through the dam, exploding it, and carrying it onwards on its massive shoulders. Look, her [love's] young narrow body is twisting once in pain and the delicious hips are twitching in labor.)

In opposition to fascism's rigid biopolitical defensiveness, Brecht here extols fleshy abjection, deploying a language of fluidity, border transgression/explosion and childbirth (the maternal), and mixing images of pleasure and pain. Fuegi's assertion that 'German scholar Klaus Theweleit sees Brecht's fantasies reflected in a generation of German men who were almost ubiquitously protofascist and misogynist' (Fuegi 1994: 72) consequently seems inaccurate.

Against Naturalism and Expressionism

In *Baal* as well, Brecht conceived his title character after the French poets François Villon and Paul Verlaine as a vagabond, a liminal figure living outside the conventions of bourgeois society and law, embodying evil (Brecht 1967: I, 43). As a writer, Brecht saw his own models in Villon, the *poète maudit* Arthur Rimbaud and his lover Verlaine – all social outsiders.[19] The motif of drowned women featured in *Baal* – the Ophelia motif in other words – can also be found in Rimbaud's 'Ophélie' (Rimbaud 1963: 51–2). Brecht, moreover, cites Rimbaud in his play *Im Dickicht der Städte* (*Jungle of Cities*). In *Baal*, Brecht develops the protagonist's chosen marginalisation: 'Mörder. Zuvor Variétéschauspieler und Dichter. Dann Karusselbesitzer, Holzfäller, Liebhaber einer Millionärin, Zuchthäusler und Zutreiber' (Brecht 1967: I, 63) ('Murderer. Before music hall actor and poet. Then merry-go-round owner. Lumber jack, lover of a millionaire, convict, and pimp.')

Agamben writes that both the *homo sacer* and the bandit live at the threshold of indistinction between animals and human law, dwelling 'paradoxically within both while belonging to neither' (1995: 105). This space between beast and man – between natural life (*zōē*) and the political-discursive realm (*bíos*), or between the king's mortal body and his sublime body – only becomes problematic in modernity. In modern democratic society, sublime sovereignty 'declines', that is it transforms from the embodied authority of the king to the abstract sovereignty of the body politic/the people. Accordingly, Baal's strength in Brecht's modern play is more of a parody (of the heroes of contemporary Expressionist dramas) than an enactment of sublime, transcendent male authority.

Baal is, apparently by design, a repulsive anti-hero with whom it is difficult to identify. During the time he first wrote *Baal*, Brecht was already working on a conception of theatre that goes beyond the identificatory drama of both Naturalism and Expressionism and would lead to his anti-Aristotelian *Verfremdungseffekt* (estrangement effect) only a few years later. In a note from early 1922, Brecht discusses his two recent plays and his efforts to create the distantiation that would later make his theory of theatre famous:

> Einen großen Fehler sonstiger Kunst hoffe ich im *Baal* und *Dickicht* vermieden zu haben: ihre Bemühung mitzureißen. Instinktiv lass ich hier Abstände . . . Die 'splendid isolation' des Zuschauers wird nicht angetastet. (*Tagebuch*, 10 February 1922 Brecht 1988: XXVI, 271)

> (In *Baal* and *Jungle of Cities* I hope to have avoided a grave mistake common in other art: its effort to carry away. Here I instinctively leave distance: . . . The 'splendid isolation' of the spectator remains intact.)

Gudrun Tabbert-Jones has written on the distantiating effect of the *Lieder* (songs) in *Baal* (Tabbert 1984: 54). Rather than identification, one of the play's (and its protagonist's) primary goals seems to be to shock the bourgeois audience – 'épater le bourgeois', as Gustave Flaubert had called it. The *Fuhrleute* (drivers) in the play, however, whom Johannes idealises as 'das einfache Volk' (the simple people), celebrate and share Baal's crudeness (Brecht 1967: I, 13–16). Unlike the Expressionist heroes of Georg Kaiser, Ernst Toller, Walter Hasenclever and others, who renewed the Romantics' ideal of the artist as visionary and saviour, Brecht's title character nevertheless does not lead humanity (or the working class) to a new reality. In contrast to Expressionist plays, *Baal* does not provide us with a viable alternative to the social status quo. Instead, Brecht's play parodies the Expressionist sense of mission (Sokol 1963: xxiii, xxiv).

Brecht initially wrote his drama as a reaction to the minor Expressionist playwright Hanns Johst's *Der Einsame: Ein Menschenuntergang* (1917) (*The Loner*), which enacts the life of the German playwright Christian Dietrich Grabbe and received a very favourable reception in Nationalist circles when first published and performed. Johst himself would later become one of the best-known Nazi writers as well as president of the *Reichsschrifttumskammer* (Reich Chamber of Written Works), one of the seven divisions of the *Reichskulturkammer* (Reich Chamber of Culture), the instrument for Nazi cultural politics founded by Joseph Goebbels in 1933. In *Der Einsame*, Johst idealises the writer into a fragile and handsome revolutionary melancholic representing the loneliness of the 'higher' individual. While *Baal* and Expressionism share a focus on the intensity of a Dionysian life, Brecht's play and its repulsively ugly protagonist who is keen on egotistically satisfying his physical needs clearly differ from the ecstatic and melodramatic pathos of *Der Einsame* and the theme of love and brotherhood of Expressionism. Taking the tools of distortion and caricature characteristic of the best works of Expressionism, Brecht exaggerates the outsider status of the dissolute poet to such an extreme that his play becomes a cynical, sardonic parody consistent with Brecht's later expectation of the spectator's critical distance to the characters and the plot.

In spite of Brecht's rejection of Expressionist idealisation and pathos in *Baal* as well as his second full-length play, *Trommeln in der Nacht* (*Drums in the Night*) (written in 1918–19 and first performed in 1922), *Baal* resembles many Expressionist plays of the day in its episodic and theme- rather than conflict-centred structure. Following the model of the Christian passion play, this structure connects a series of life stations. The archetype of this structure in Expressionist drama is Strindberg's late trilogy *To Damascus*. In *Baal*, this structure goes against the inevitability of fate and the necessity of dramatic structure inherent in Aristotelian drama, again prefiguring Brecht's Epic Theatre with its lack of action-driven suspense. In *Baal*, each scene stands more or less on its own without any clear references to what goes before or after, and only following a general direction – symbolised by the four seasons – through Baal's life towards his death. Like many Expressionist dramas, finally, Brecht's play favours an anti-naturalistic acting style and features tragicomic elements. In contrast to the dramatic tradition, it abandons psychology in the portrayal of characters and dramatises – both in terms of dramatic action and aesthetics/theatrical vision – the struggle against bourgeois values and institutions, established authority and convention in life and in art, such as the standards of verisimilitude and *bienséance* or good taste.

Society without Parents

While Expressionist dramas often enact this struggle against authority as a conflict with a father figure, however, the society enacted in *Baal* is already what the first generation of the Frankfurt School would call a fatherless society. In ancient Middle Eastern mythology, the Baal figure vanquishes and castrates the previous ruler, the father of gods and humans.[21] In Brecht's play, when the young Johannes, who loves the sexually innocent Johanna, states that the law and parents punish extra-marital sex, Baal responds: 'Deine Eltern . . . das sind verflossene Menschen' (Brecht 1967: I, 11) ('Your parents . . . those are bygone people'). Similar to Johanna, the women whom Baal exploits sexually are originally white sister figures in Theweleit's sense. In a society without parents, Brecht's Housewife character (Baal's landlady) refers to these young women as 'orphans', threatens them with vicarious parental punishment and sends them home to their mothers:

> Und die jungen Dinger! Ihr seid wohl arme Waisen, wie, weil ihr gleich Wasser heulen wollt. Ich prigle [sic] euch wohl? Eure weißen Leiber? . . . Jetzt aber Beine gekriegt ihr und heim zu Muttern, ich gehe gleich mit! (Brecht 1967: I, 23)

> (And the young things! You must be poor orphans, the way you want to cry water right away. Should I spank you? Your white bodies? . . . But hurry up now and go home to your mothers, I'll go right along with you.)

Similarly, when Sophie, one of Baal's victims (and later his wife), tries to fend off his advances by stating that she has to go home to her mother, Baal responds that since Sophie's mother is seventy years old, she is used to evil (Brecht 1967: I, 27). The reference to her mother, in other words, does not protect Sophie from Baal. Sophie later thinks of her mother as mourning her assumed death (Brecht 1967: I, 29) and Baal (unsuccessfully) tries to send the pregnant Sophie home to her mother (Brecht 1967: I, 44–5).

The absence of parental authority in Brecht's play enacts the social and material changes in Germany at the beginning of the twentieth century. The country's defeat in the First World War had profoundly damaged the authority of the fathers' generation. Rather than a society based on paternal authority, Germany would become a society of brothers, a patriarchal society no longer controlled by a mythical father and his secular representatives. While the mothers' position is weak in *Baal*, Brecht's characters never even mention fathers, and the internalisation of moral commands that the Freudian tradition associates with the father's influence – guilt in other words – hardly registers in Baal's mind. At the same time, Brecht does not supplant parental authority with any other institutions of human sociality – whether it be heterosexual love, marriage or a new family. He replaces the idealising veneration of parents in the bourgeois sentimental family with images of the abject, such as the transgression of the boundary between the corporeal inside and outside by excrement:

> Orge sagte mir: Der liebste Ort, den er auf Erden hab/Sei nicht die Rasenbank am Elterngrab. / . . . Orge sagte mir: der liebste Ort / Auf Erden war ihm immer der Abort . . . Ein Ort sei einfach wundervoll, wo man / Selbst in der Hochzeitsnacht allein sein kann. (Brecht 1967: I, 15)

> (Orge told me: The dearest place that he has on earth / Is not the lawn bench at his parents' grave / . . . Orge told me: the place dearest to him / On earth has always been the loo . . . He said a place is simply wonderful where one / can be alone even during one's wedding night.)

The stylistic juxtaposition of often vulgar everyday speech ('der Abort': the loo) with references to objects of Christian or bourgeois veneration (the parents' grave, the wedding night, i.e. marriage) is itself abject in Brecht's play and crosses the boundaries of bourgeois sensibility.

There is a brief moment of hope in 'Mainacht unter Bäumen' ('May Night Under Trees') when Baal expresses his love for his wife, Sophie, and she says: 'Es ist gut, so zu liegen wie eine Beute, und der Himmel ist über einem, und man ist nie mehr allein' ('It is good to lie here like prey, and the sky/heaven is above and one will never be alone again'). But the word 'Beute' (prey) already disturbs this idyll, and the scene has more to do with the fact that Sophie and Baal make love in the roots of a tree – symbolising the return to natural life that Baal longs for – than with successful object relations between husband and wife in the human realm. Later Baal says to his male lover, Ekart, about his wife, whom he (Baal) has chased off in the pouring rain: 'Sie läuft uns nach wie verzweifelt und hängt sich an meinen Hals' (Brecht 1967: I, 42) ('She runs after us in despair and weighs me down'). Baal even compares Sophie, his wife who is pregnant with his child, to a 'Mühlstein' (millstone), again invoking the threat of drowning, and then calls her the most pejorative of names, 'Kanaille' (scum) (Brecht 1967: I, 44).

Zōē, or beyond the Symbolic

While there is no mention of a father figure anywhere in Brecht's play, the references to the maternal that start and end the play suggest, however, that in this modern fatherless society, mothers have not completely lost their power. In the 1919 and 1920 versions of *Baal*, the mother's judgement still pervades the text. Baal, otherwise beyond the boundaries of the bourgeois moral code, cries for his mother's forgiveness and receives it in a tearful maternal embrace. Yet, in a letter from 1920, Brecht remarks that he has taken out all scenes with the mother.[22] The mother as a character in the play or as a female super-ego thus disappears after 1920.

What remains even in the later versions of Brecht's play are references to the pre-symbolic mother. In contrast to Theweleit's proto-fascists and Strindberg's male characters, who share a fear of maternal engulfment and ego invasion, Baal longs for a return to the symbiosis with the mother. He sings: 'O ihr, die ihr aus Himmel und Hölle vertrieben . . . / Warum seid ihr nicht im Schoß eurer Mütter geblieben? / Wo es still war und man schlief und war da' (Brecht 1967: I, 60) ('Oh you who have been chased from heaven and hell . . . / Why did you not stay in your mothers' wombs? / Where it was still and one slept and was there). Baal and Johannes search for an oceanic, pre-symbolic self in yet another fluid: alcohol. Baal sings: 'Er aber sucht noch in absynthenen Meeren / Wenn ihn schon seine Mutter vergißt' (Brecht 1967: I, 61) ('But he is still searching in oceans of absinth / When even his mother is already forgetting him'). Baal's death finally constitutes such a return to the maternal. 'Der Choral vom großen Baal' at the beginning of the play already describes death as a welcome 'dark womb' ('der dunkle Schoß': Brecht 1967: I, 4) and the dying Baal at the end of the play then calls for his mother like a small child: 'Mama!' (Brecht 1967: I, 66). Reinforcing the central role of water imagery and its link to the loss of self, Baal's last word is 'rain': 'ich horche noch auf den

Regen' (Brecht 1967: I, 67) ('I am still listening to the rain'). Rain water is the border-crossing fluid that facilitates Baal's crossing of the threshold from life to death, a death resonant with a Spinozist/Deleuzian/new materialist view of death as ontological transition rather than as anthropocentric finitude.

Brecht's title character, Baal, is thus an antisocial and ultimately ontological outsider who has chosen his exclusion from the human social-political sphere or *bíos*, instead living Rimbaud's *dérèglement de tous les sens* ('the derangement of all senses'). The play enacts libidinal or energetic/ontological excess: the excess of the drives beyond what Brecht identified as the repressive confines of bourgeois society, and the excess of the more-than-human beyond the limits of human finitude. Similar to Kragler, the central character in *Trommeln in der Nacht*, Brecht's Baal speaks a poetic, musical and visual (colour-filled) language of the body – 'Tanz und Musik und Trinken! Regen bis auf die Haut!' (Brecht 1967: I, 16) ('Dance and music and drinking! Drenching rain! [literally 'to the skin]') – a language that expresses the intensity of sensuous, physical-material experience. Images of light and darkness pervade the play, progressing from the light of birth and spring season to the darkness of death and winter, and any theatrical production worth its name would have to pick up on the materiality of these images. Charles Lyons has also spoken of the 'rhythmic structuring of the play in the pattern of appetite, consumption, satisfaction' (Lyons 1968: 8). Baal is associated with childhood, with not having fully entered human sociality, the discursive sphere of logos: 'Dabei ist er ganz kindisch' (Brecht 1967: I, 63) ('At the same time he is quite childish'). According to Sue-Ellen Case, Brecht's early plays enact the alternative (poetic) discourse of desire and corporeality called for by theorists such as Hélène Cixous, Luce Irigaray and Kristeva (Case 1983). Baal's enactment of abjection positions him in close proximity to the primary abject or 'other' – the mother. His death is a return to the maternal and to natural-material life.

Towards Non-Anthropocentric Theatre

Structurally as well, Brecht's *Baal* goes beyond a human discursive semioticity. Although Hans-Thies Lehmann counts Brecht as part of the 'dramatic', realist-humanist theatrical tradition, the associative structure of Brecht's *Baal* moves away from a mimetic plot driven by the linear logic of cause and effect and the imitation of external facts. In spite of Brecht's parodic stance towards Expressionism, *Baal* shares with Expressionist drama the dramatisation of fantasy and daydream inspired by Freud and by Strindberg's post-naturalist 'dream plays'. The fact that Brecht reworked this play repeatedly throughout his entire life suggests that the play's structure is only seemingly random. The later versions in particular eliminate scenes that might provide a sense of continuity (such as the prison scene, after Baal fails to honour his contract). Breaking with Aristotle's unity of place, each scene is set in a different locale. Continuity is mainly provided by recurring motifs and tropes. Structurally, Brecht's first full-length play is thus – in contrast to his later, more didactically oriented work – a non-linear intra-active, productive assemblage rather than a receptacle of 'content'. While Baal still centrally features a human character and is thus not an example of Una Chaudhuri's 'Theater of Species' (Chaudhuri 2017a: e.g. 182 ff.), the dynamic structure of the play intra-relates with the play's thematic enactment of the world as a live natural-biological system or relational ecology from which the title character comes and to which he returns.

Even in a play that still precedes Brecht's theory and practice of epic theatre, the spectators' attitudes or experiences – their inability to identify with the play's central character – are a central part of Brecht's theatrical ecology, though in a way quite different from the immersive experience of Artaud's audience explored later in this project. As a parody of Johst's idealisation of his protagonist in *Der Einsame*, Brecht's *Baal* instead creates a proto-epic distance between his protagonist and the play's audience.[23] The play's discontinuous structure also contributes to this distantiation heightening the spectators' critical awareness. According to Brecht's theory of acting, the distance between actor and role should also be heightened by the distance between spectator and actor:

> Nicht nahekommen sollten sich Zuschauer und Schauspieler, sondern entfernen sollten sie sich voneinander. Jeder sollte sich von sich selbst entfernen. Sonst fällt der Schrecken weg, der zum Erkennen wichtig ist. (Brecht 1963: 212)

> (Spectator and actor are not to approach one another but to move apart. Each ought to move away from himself. Otherwise the element of terror necessary to all recognition is lacking.) (Brecht 1964: 26)

Brecht here posits not only a distance between actor and spectator, but also a split within each person. The gap at the centre of this split causes terror, he says, the terror of recognition – a key component of Aristotelian theatre, the theatre that Brecht otherwise seeks to replace. While

Brecht's theatre is, in contrast to Artaud's work discussed later, usually seen as primarily cognitive, what links both playwrights, surprisingly, is the goal of the spectator's anxiety. This turn towards the spectator constitutes a paradigmatic shift in terms of theatrical vision beyond the mere enactment of the characters' anxiety in Strindberg, although this latter anxiety is also the expression of the contemporary public's ontological anxiety.

The distance most readily associated with Brecht's theory of acting is of course the distance between actor and character or role, between what Erika Fischer-Lichte calls the actor's 'phenomenal body' and her abstract 'semiotic body' (2014: 26). I argue that this distance is ultimately the same as the gap between the king's two bodies – between the king's physical body and his sublime body – a gap that is not perceived as such in premodern Europe, but only opens up in modernity, with the loss of embodiment in democratic modernity's transition to the people's abstract body. With his theory of the *V-Effekt* (estrangement effect), Brecht gives material expression to the gap between physical embodiment and abstraction on the modern stage.

Even though Brecht thus differentiates between the phenomenal body and the semiotic body – incarnated minds and abstract meaning – both are nevertheless linked, not only in more traditional, Aristotelian theatre, but even in Brecht. As Fischer-Lichte points out, actors' bodies and their meanings are in a constant state of becoming or a continual process of transformation (2014: 25) as part of a relational and dynamic network. The *gestus* so central to Brecht's theory of acting – codified gestures marking recurrence and difference – enact this dynamic system, a system that constitutes a bodily negotiation of meaning. In *The Politics of Affect*, Brian Massumi conceptualises the gesture as more than secondary or supportive. It is a call to affective attunement and an aesthetic act of political resistance:

> The only power it has is exemplary. It cannot impose itself. It can only catch on . . . Its power is of contagion. The gesture of resistance is a micro-gesture of offered contagion . . . there is an aesthetic dimension – of allure, of style, of gesture – that is not an added dimension but is absolutely integral to the very operation of resistance, one with its politicality. (Massumi 2015b: 105–6)

Although *Baal* precedes Brecht's development of his theory of the *gestus*, Brecht's gestic theories of the differentiated relationships between actor and role, actors and audience, and actors and stage can also be put in conversation with the different (natural and, in his later work, socio-political) ecologies created in the play. In *Baal*, theatrical and natural-material ecology meet. Commenting on Brecht's theory of the *gestus*, Devin Fore writes:

> The social relations depicted do not 'belong' to any single character, but are instead rendered through the features of the surrounding space ... Brecht wrote an entire series of studies exploring how to translate the principles of *gestic* dramaturgy into the architecture and contents of the stage. The system required above all overcoming the boundary that separated the actor from the objects and space around her, as he declared in a 1937 essay on stage design. (Fore 2015: 174)

In *Baal*, this relationship (1) between actor and theatrical space and (2) the title character's relationship to natural-material life form a mesh. Brecht conceives his protagonist less as a heroic human individual in the Expressionist tradition than as part of a natural ecology. In his later, Marxist plays as well, Brecht is less interested in individual characters than in the transindividual conditions of capitalism. While the naturalist tradition exemplified here by Strindberg and Sartre problematise the threatened boundary between humans and nonhuman matter, Brecht observed that 'our representations of the human environment are formed by a knowledge of the "metabolism between nature and man" as a social process that is historically variable' (Brecht 1988: XXII, 227, trans. in Fore 2015: 174). Ontology and socio-politics meet in Brecht's theatrical vision.

Fore follows Brecht's argumentation that '[d]epicting this open metabolism required a stage design that viewed space not as an indifferent container for dramatic action, but as a dynamic system that responds in dialogue with its human contents' (Fore 2015: 174). Lehmann points out that the term 'dramatic theatre' that he himself uses (in opposition to his term 'post-dramatic theatre') was first coined by Brecht. It was a tradition that Brecht aimed to replace with his epic 'theatre of the scientific age' (Lehmann 1999: 20). In Brecht, the setting goes beyond its function as decor and illustration of an anthropocentric thematic familiar from realist-humanist drama. Instead, as Brecht puts it, the 'environment acquires the quality of a process' (Brecht 1988: XXII, 238), an integrated, constantly changing mesh of agentive organic and inorganic bodies (Brecht 1988: XXII, 229). Like the *gestus* of the actor's speech, '*gestic* dramaturgy frees the events depicted on stage from attribution to any particular individual, replacing the ontology of character' (Fore 2015: 174). While the actor was for Brecht still 'the most important of all the pieces of scenery' (Brecht 1988: XXII, 229), Brecht 'destabilized a realist mode of figuration that required on principle the integrity and autonomy of the human body' (Fore 2015:

175), instead making the actor a co-constitutive element of the materiality of the stage. Fore writes:

> If, as the Prague School structuralist Jiří Veltruský observed in an important essay from 1940, 'Man and Object in the Theatre', traditional realist drama arrests all 'fluctuation between man and object' that could potentially impugn the ideology of heroic humanism', Brecht's *gestic* stage, by contrast, liquefies these terms, restoring the dynamic metabolism between the individual and his environment. (Fore 2015: 175)

Brecht himself notes that 'humans have ceased to exist as autonomous beings who have things at their disposal; in particular the human as *such*, as a finished concept, has ceased to exist' (Brecht 1988: XXI, 320–2; quoted and trans. Fore 2015: 175). In this context, Fore (2015: 176) speaks of the 'psychic dedifferentiation' in Brecht's work, the erosion of the boundary between ego and other.[24] It is this erosion of the boundary between ego and other that is at stake in all of the plays examined in this study.

Because of the apparent randomness of the play's formal structure as well, we can argue that Brecht's *Baal* appears already kindred in spirit not only to his later epic theatre, but also to the eco-drama of our own age, to the new theatrical genre that Chaudhuri calls the 'Theater of Species', which aspires to unsettle the assumptions of the long theatrical or aesthetic tradition based on anthropocentrism and biopolitics. Like recent eco-drama, Brecht tries to increase the critical awareness of the audience, putting in question the ontological status of the human.

Within the theatrical tradition, the status of the human in the universe is of course also already at stake in absurd theatre. We can therefore also argue that Brecht's *Baal* already anticipates absurd theatre with its enactment of the loss of transcendental, anthropocentric meaning. Indeed, Brecht's play already eschews meaning-making as the play's primary purpose at a time – the end of the First World War – when traditional symbolic authorities have lost credibility, both in the metaphysical/theological/ontological and socio-political realms. The closest Brecht's play comes to meaning – in terms of the play's meaning as well as the meaning of life – is the following passage about bodily sensation, the animalistic struggle for survival and the relative insignificance of humans in the universe, their position as part of a more-than-human materiality:

> Wenn man nachts im Gras liegt, ausgebreitet, merkt man in den Knochen, daß die Erde eine Kugel ist und daß wir fliegen und daß es auf dem Stern Tiere gibt, die seine Pflanzen auffressen. Es ist einer von den kleineren Sternen. (Brecht 1967: I, 10)

(Lying in the grass at night, spread out, one feels in one's bones that the earth is a ball and that we are flying and that there are animals on this star that eat its plants. It is one of the smaller stars.)

In *Baal*, as in absurd drama (or as in Lehmann's 'post-dramatic theatre'), dialogue or language in general does not serve as a means of communication to resolve the dramatic conflict, drive the plot forward or bridge the characters' existential isolation.[25] Instead, in the section 'Hölzerne braune Diele', the Beggar says 'Nichts versteht man. Aber manches fühlt man. Geschichten, die man versteht, sind nur schlecht erzählt' (Brecht 1967: I, 48) ('We understand nothing. But some things we feel: stories that one understands are only badly told'). Brecht gives feeling primacy over logic and understanding, at a time in which human reason and the positivism of the nineteenth century had just led western societies into the abyss of the First World War.

The absence of all metaphysical, anthropocentric justifications for living thus distinguishes Brecht's play from Expressionist plays and announces existentialist and ultimately absurd theatre. While 'Himmel' (interpretable as either 'sky' or 'heaven') is a central image in *Baal*, humans are without a metaphysical home, 'aus Himmel und Hölle vertrieben' (Brecht 1967: I, 60) ('chased from heaven and hell').[26] Since Baal does not believe in God, 'Himmel' as 'sky' – and 'sky' only – is, together with trees, the only constant in Baal's life,[27] even paralleling Baal's moods in a spoof on Romantic imagery:

Nachts er violett und trunken Baal
Baal früh fromm, er aprikosenfahl [sic]
    (Brecht 1967: I, 3)

(At night he violet and drunk Baal
Baal early pious, he apricot-pale [*sic*])

Following in the steps of Friedrich Nietzsche's *Zur Genealogie der Moral* (1887) (*On the Genealogy of Morality*), Brecht's *Baal* subverts any idealist value system and does not anthropomorphise images of nature and the maternal. In 'Hölzerne braune Diele', the Beggar tells the story of a man who addressed a tree, contrasting his own description of the tree as a physical entity with Goethe's classic idealist poem *Wanderers Nachtlied* (*Wanderer's Night Song*), known for its beginning 'Über allen Gipfeln ist Ruh' ('Over all the hills / Peace comes anew').

Er lehnte sich an ihn, ganz nah, *fühlte das Leben in ihm*, oder meinte es und sagte: Du bist höher als ich und stehst fest und *du kennst die Erde bis tief hinunter* und sie hält dich. Ich kann laufen und mich besser bewegen, aber ich

stehe nicht fest und kann nicht in die Tiefe und nichts hält mich. Auch ist mir
die große Ruhe über den stillen Wipfeln im unendlichen Himmel unbekannt.
(Brecht 1967: I, 48, my emphases)

(He leaned against it, closely, *felt the life in it*, or thought so, and said: You are
taller than me and stand firm and *you know the earth down deep* and it holds
you. I can run and move better, but I do not stand firm and cannot go down
deep and nothing holds me. Also, the great calm above the still tree tops in the
unending sky is unknown to me' (my emphases).

In *Baal*, the tree, a live body, possesses a knowledge and a grounded-
ness that are not available to humans. In contrast to Strindberg's or (as
we will see) Sartre's enactment of the threat of ego dissolution, Brecht's
main character is intimate with plants on a corporeal level without
perceiving this proximity as a threat to his own human identity or difference.[28]

Given the absence of divine transcendence, the references to the
devil and God in earlier versions of Brecht's play[29] thus become a
curse and a self-invocation in the last version: 'Verflucht! Lieber Baal!'
(Brecht 1967: I, 66) (Cursed! Dear Baal!). The only meaning of life
is the corporeal enjoyment that biological life brings. Brecht replaces
the emphasis on suffering in the Christian faith with Baal's espousal
of hedonism.

> Unter düstern Sternen in dem Jammertal
> Grast Baal weite Felder schmatzend ab
> Sind sie leer, dann trottet singend Baal
> In den ewigen Wald zum Schlaf hinab.
> (Brecht 1967: I, 4)

> (Under dark stars in the Vale of Tears
> Baal is grazing wide fields with smacking lips
> When they are empty, Baal trots down to the eternal forest to sleep.)

It was Nietzsche who characterised the superman who replaces the
faith in God as 'Bestie' (beast) (Nietzsche 1980: 2, 64) and it is in this
sense as well – in the sense of the flesh, of creaturely excess after the loss
of sublime authority – that one needs to understand the host of animal
tropes that Brecht uses for his protagonist. What is interesting here, and
again kindred in spirit to the Theater of Species, is that these images
are, in my view, more than metaphors. In Brecht's play, Baal is indeed
an animal, a human animal. His position on the margins of human
society enacts the ontological position of humans in a modern godless
universe, their position as flesh or creaturely excess.

In this natural universe, therefore, even though the protagonist is a murderer, there is no place for tragic guilt or punishment. In the first version of the play, Baal expresses remorse, but these passages are cut from the second version already. Instead, there is a nostalgic yearning[30] for a return to natural life, for a small meadow '[m]it blauem Himmel drüber und sonst nichts' (Brecht 1967: I, 61) ('with blue sky above and nothing else') or the permanence of a tree. Biological life – sexuality, animals and trees – replaces traditional divinity[31] and, with it, human exceptionalism. The world, in Baal's words, is 'das Exkrement des lieben Gottes' (Brecht 1967: I, 53) ('God's excrement'), a world filled with creaturely abjection.

The God of Excess

The mythological Baal is a figure of abjection that precedes and traverses the binary thinking of Judaism and Christianity. In the Old Testament, Baal – literally 'Master' or 'Owner' in Semitic – is the god of the Phoenicians and Canaanites, the pre-Israelite population of Palestine.[32] The ancient cult of Baal had traits of orgiastic ecstasy and lends Brecht's drama similar overtones. Baal is a god of the storm, rain, sky, sun and fertility in a religion that also venerated trees, stones and (water) sources. Trees are a central live presence in Brecht's *Baal* – a play that, I argue, is a deviation from what Chaudhuri calls 'the claustrophobic, anthropocentric socio-psychologism that has made theater the least environmentally aware, most eco-alienated, and nature-aversive of all the arts of the Western World' (Chaudhuri 2017a: 102).

Brecht's protagonist associates trees with ontological permanence and sees the forest as a place of refuge from society. He considers the felling of trees for the Catholic *Fronleichnam* (Corpus Christi Day; literally 'worship of the corpse') procession as evil, an evil tantamount to the murder of humans ('Baumleichen' [tree corpses], 'Baumkadaver' [tree cadavers], 'Jesus liebt das Böse' [Jesus loves evil]) (Brecht 1967: I, 27–8). As Ronald Speir points out, the conflict between Baal and the merchant Mech at the beginning of the play is ultimately a clash between life and death (Speir 1989: 22). Mech has become rich in the timber business, by cutting down trees, the embodiment of life or permanence: 'Ich kaufe Zimthölzer. Ganze Wälder Zimthölzer schwimmen für mich brasilianische Flüsse abwärts' (Brecht 1967: I, 5) ('I buy cinnamon woods. Whole forests of cinnamon woods swim down Brazilian rivers for me'). Similarly, Baal's own death as part of the natural realm takes place in a hut used by lumberjacks, the ultimate purveyors of death.[33]

In the ancient world from circa 1200 BCE, Baal was in competition with Jahweh, who opposed polytheistic vice and excess with Jewish monotheism, which ultimately gained cultural dominance in the seventh century BCE. It was at this point that the upper and the lower world, life and death, were separated, that the dualism of good and evil and linear temporal thinking (the hope of the arrival of the Messiah) were implemented. This shift signified a devaluation of the nature gods and a transvaluation of nature, including human nature. The nature gods were banned to the underworld, to the realm of devilish evil. As the story of Adam and Eve's eviction from Paradise exemplifies, in the Christian conception the realm of evil is feminised and sexualised – or, to put it the other way around, sexuality and the feminine are demonised. The pre-Christian unity of nature is destroyed. Jahweh is a patriarchal God, a God of the Fathers. In Exod. 3: 6, he reveals himself to Moses as 'the God of thy father, the God of Abraham, the God of Isaac, and the God of Jacob' (King James Bible).

In contrast to the linear thinking of Christianity, Brecht's play follows the natural cycle of birth and death: 'der Wind geht weiter, alles geht weiter' (Brecht 1967: I, 40) ('The wind goes on, everything goes on'). The 'Choral' at the beginning of the play already emphasises the cyclical structure of Baal's life, with its almost identical first and last stanzas about Baal's birth and death, respectively.

> Als im weißen Mutterschoße aufwuchs Baal
> War der Himmel schon so groß und still und fahl
> Jung und nackt und ungeheuer wundersam
> Wie ihn Baal dann liebte, als Baal kam . . .
> Als im dunklen Erdenschoße faulte Baal
> War der Himmel noch so groß und still und fahl
> Jung und nackt und ungeheuer wunderbar
> Wie ihn Baal einst liebte, als Baal war.
> (Brecht 1967: I, 3–4)

> (When Baal grew up in his mother's white womb
> the sky was already so big and still and pale
> Young and naked and immensely wonderful
> Like Baal would love it when Baal came . . .
> When Baal rotted in the dark womb of the earth
> The sky was still so big and still and pale
> Young and naked and immensely wonderful
> Like Baal used to love it when Baal was.)

Similarly the description of Baal's death at the end of the play is full of birth imagery:

> Mama! ... der Himmel ist auch so verflucht nah da, zum Greifen, es ist wieder alles tropfnaß. Schlafen. Eins. Zwei. Drei. Vier. Man erstickt hier ja. Draußen muß es hell sein. Ich will hinaus. *Hebt sich.* Ich werde hinausgehen. Ich werde hinausgehen ... Es muß draußen hell sein ... Zur Tür kommt man noch. Knie hat man noch, in der Tür ist es besser ... *Er kriecht auf allen vieren zur Schwelle.* Sterne ... hm. *Er kriecht hinaus.*' (Brecht 1967: I, 66)

> (Mom! ... the sky is also so damn close, close enough to touch, everything is dripping wet again. Sleeping. One. Two. Three. Four. It is suffocating in here. It must be light outside. I want to go outside. *He gets up.* I will go outside. I will go outside ... It must be light outside ... One can still make it to the door. One still has knees, in the door it is better ... *He crawls on all fours to the threshold.* Stars ... hm. *He crawls outside.*)

Brecht's Baal is an Anti-Christ figure whose status as part of natural-biological life stands in stark contrast to the Christian injunction to have dominion over the earth (Gen. 1: 28).

Baal's character thus enacts Nietzsche's conception at the end of the nineteenth century of the Dionysian in *Ecce homo* (Nietzsche 1980: 6.1, 369–72). In the Nietzschean juxtaposition of Apollo and Dionysus, Apollo embodies the principle of individuation (Nietzsche 1980: 3.1, 28). Dionysus stands not only for the reunion of humans themselves, but also for the reunion of humans with a previously alienated, hostile or oppressed nature: 'auch die entfremdete, feindliche oder unterjochte Natur feiert wieder ihr Versöhnungsfest mit ihrem verlorenen Sohne, dem Menschen' (Nietzsche 1980: 3.1, 29) ('alienated, hostile or subjugated nature as well again celebrates its reconciliation with its prodigal son, the human', my trans.). In this context, there is a link between Nietzsche's dichotomy between Apollo (as the principle of individuation) and Dionysus (as offering reconciliation and community) and the tension between *immunitas*/individualisation and *communitas* as described by Esposito. Whereas the immunitarian inside/outside logic of modernity – and its extreme, fascism – tries to fend off threats to autonomy inherent in community, Brecht's Baal celebrates the transgression of binary frameworks and in particular the dualism between nonhuman nature and the human.

Dionysus is the god of ecstasy and orgiastic cult, and the symbol of life and eternal return. The mythological figures Baal, Dionysus, Persephone and Osiris all descend to the underworld and return to life, symbolising the annual cycle of death/winter and resurrection/

spring. Also in Brecht's play, time is cyclical. Replacing the Christian dichotomy of good and evil, Brecht's play willfully breaches binary oppositions and the play's godless universe is filled with images of abject border transgression (wind/storm, corpse, cloud), with a natural materiality whose role in the play goes beyond the purely metaphorical and assumes a live presence not in opposition to but continuous with the human:

> Tanz mit dem Wind, armer Leichnam, schlaf mit der Wolke, verkommener Gott!' (Brecht 1967: I, 51)
>
> (Dance with the wind, poor corpse, sleep with the cloud, rotten God!)

Homoeroticism

While Brecht's *Baal* is thus not primarily focused on a dramatic inter-personal conflict inspired by a central moral dilemma and instead enacts the contrast between an eco-cidal society and a protagonist close to (and part of) the natural word, the most important interpersonal dynamic in Brecht's play is – more explicitly than in Strindberg's work discussed earlier – the homosexual relationship between two men of similar age,[34] a relationship that Brecht modelled on the love affair between Rimbaud and Verlaine.[35] Baal and Ekart's roving life outside society mimics Rimbaud and Verlaine's late nineteenth-century vaga-bondage through Belgium and England and another one of Brecht's models', Villon's, life as a fifteenth-century Breton highwayman. In typical patriarchal fashion, Baal and Ekart (like Shlink and Garga in Brecht's *Im Dickicht der Städte*) use and exchange women to seal their homoerotic bond. Reinforcing the brother imagery, Ekart repeatedly calls Baal Brother.[36] Freud as well notes the homoerotic nature of the brother clan in modern society.[37]

Thematically, the tension between two men links Brecht's *Baal* to his *Trommeln in der Nacht* and especially *Im Dickicht der Städte*, as well as to the tradition of the bourgeois drama (including Strindberg's work).[38] Similar to Shlink in *Im Dickicht der Städte*, Baal sleeps with women who have ties to the man he desires. Baal's real object of desire is another man, and his only non-instrumentalised object relation is this love for Ekart. Out of jealousy, Baal rapes a young woman that Ekart sleeps with (Brecht 1967: I, 54–5). And it is also in a fit of jealousy of women that Baal kills Ekart, a murder that leads to Baal's flight from society and ultimately to his death (Brecht 1967: I, 62). Reminiscent of the homoerotic undertones in Strindberg and in Brecht's own *Im*

Dickicht der Städte, Baal instrumentalises women in his pursuit of Ekart as the true object of his desire. The women in the play are masochistic, self-destructive[39] and humiliated sex objects. For Baal, women are faceless, that is lacking individual human identity, after the sexual act: 'ein Haufen Fleisch, der kein Gesicht mehr hat' (Brecht 1967: I, 11) ('A heap of flesh that does not have a face anymore').[40] Baal compares sleeping with women to necrophilia, *Leichenschändung*. After he has slept with them, women lose their identity and interest to him and literally become corpses.

> *Ekart*: Dich ließen meine Geliebten kalt, du fischtest sie mir weg, obgleich ich sie liebte.
> *Baal*: Weil du sie liebtest. Ich habe zweimal Leichen geschändet, weil du rein bleiben solltest.
>
> (Brecht 1967: I, 44)

> (*Ekart*: My lovers left you cold, you snatched [literally, fished] them away from me, although I loved them.
> *Baal*: Because you loved them. I have violated corpses twice, because you were meant to remain pure.)

It is tempting to read Baal's phallic narcissism as an act of male self-affirmation, which only lasts when he endlessly repeats the act of seduction, from woman to woman. Both Freud and Lacan view this dynamic as the basis of patriarchal gender relations, and as far as the treatment of women is concerned, Brecht's *Baal* is certainly a profoundly patriarchal play. In this phallic theatre (arguably also exemplified by Strindberg), men use women to attempt to heal their damaged male identity, their castration (Böhme 2012: 380–1). As I have argued, however, this 'social', anthropocentric problematic is ultimately not the primary or exclusive focus of Brecht's play. Instead, this social problematic intra-acts with Brecht's problematisation of the ontological status of the human. Both realms are intimately linked.

Instrumentalisation

On the socio-political level, as we have seen, the sense of 'damaged' male identity intensifies in modernity. The use/abuse of women that is enacted in *Baal* is exacerbated by a modern rationality that becomes increasingly instrumental. Brecht, in other words, depicts women as victims of an instrumental rationality that – according to his fellow Marxists Max Horkheimer and Theodor Adorno's analysis in *Dia-*

lectic of Enlightenment – is the result of the transition in democratic modernity from a paternalistic society to a fatherless society of brothers (whose motto is *liberté, égalité, fraternité*). Horkheimer has shown that the form of domination characteristic of the modern era manifests no longer directly as a binary authority structure – as in premodern times between subject and ruler, or between the father and the other family members – but indirectly as the transformation of all relationships and activities into instrumental, depersonalised forms. Substantive reason, a rationality that judges moral values and goals, is superseded (although not completely replaced[41]) by the principle of instrumental reason, by a rationality of efficiency, calculation of self-interest and acceptance of necessity (Horkheimer 1987). Given the changes in authority structures in modern society, we can find this rationality enacted in many of the plays presented in this study. As in Strindberg, the question is again whether Brecht is critical of this instrumentalisation.

Brecht's play enacts both the instrumentalisation of women by his protagonist and bourgeois society's – more explicitly criticised – instrumentalisation of its material environment. Although the first two versions of *Baal* were written before Brecht's discovery of Marxism as his political mantra in 1926 (when Brecht first read Marx's *Das Kapital*), the play contains the beginnings of a critique of capitalism and of the *Vermarktung*, the instrumentalisation of art. At the beginning of the play, Baal gets himself thrown out of the house of the merchant and publisher Mech, since he is uncooperative in Mech's endeavour to honour him in the exalted bourgeois language of honour and genius (5)[42] and market his poetry. At this early, pre-Marxist point in Brecht's career, his protagonist Baal is equally opposed to any politicisation of his poetry. In contrast to the utopia typically propounded by Expressionist theatre or poetry (see the poems 'Vorbereitung' by Johannes R. Becher and 'Der Baum' by Georg Heym recited, if not named, in the section of *Baal* entitled 'Speisezimmer'), Baal criticises the use of poetry in the interest of a political utopia or revolution (Brecht 1967: I, 6–7). At the end of *Trommeln in der Nacht* as well, first performed in 1922, the protagonist Kragler does not participate in the armed Spartakus uprising that took place in Berlin in 1919 and forms the background of the play. Instead Kragler goes home at the end. The focus of Brecht's *Baal* is the enactment of a libidinally or conatus-driven life from birth to death in the cycle of nature, a life outside bourgeois society. Brecht's protagonist opposes both his own instrumentalisation as an artist and the instrumentalisation of the natural environment through Mech's lumber business, for instance.

Although *Baal* does not lend itself to the critique of capitalism typical of Brecht's later plays, the problematisation of the instrumentalisation of women and nature places the play firmly and paradoxically (given the protagonist's goal of stepping outside the human social sphere) within the history of capitalism. As Jessica Benjamin, following Horkheimer and Adorno, has demonstrated, 'the transformation of all relationships and activity into . . . instrumental, depersonalised forms' has become the dominant rationality under bourgeois capitalism (Benjamin 1978: 35), a rationality that renders human beings incapable of establishing any 'real', that is non-instrumentalised, contact with the other. In a capitalist society dominated by abstraction, in other words, any expression of libidinal desire is regarded as a threat, unless directed at and transformed into commodities. Feminised alterity and the alterity of animals, the structural others of a patriarchal and anthropocentric society, become encoded as the libidinal drives. Brecht's male protagonist enacts a libidinal or energetic alterity that crosses the threshold to the nonhuman.

In *Männerfantasien*, Theweleit argues that the simultaneous repression and controlled incitement of feared libidinal drives is a key trait that bourgeois patriarchal society has in common with its extreme manifestation, fascism. In *Anti-Oedipe*, Gilles Deleuze and Félix Guattari conceptualise fascism mainly as a deformation in desire and a psychological condition produced under capitalism. By enacting libidinal drives and alterity in a way that discourages identification, Brecht's 'pre-Marxist' play *Baal* puts the psychological structures of capitalist modernity up for critical discussion. It becomes clear that this psychological critique and a move away from anthropocentrism are not mutually exclusive but that they productively intra-act.

Nature AND History

Brecht's Baal, a protagonist with whom it is difficult to identify and to whom nothing is sacred[43] has replaced the Judeo-Christian God with social Darwinism. He says: 'ich mag die Pfäfferei nicht. Es muß immer Klügere geben und Schwächere im Gehirn. Das sind dafür die besseren Arbeiter' (Brecht 1967: I, 41) ('I do not like the holier-than-thou attitude. There always have to be smarter ones and weaker-minded ones. Those will in turn be the better workers'). In the Darwinian world of Brecht's play, the borderline between humans and animals has become porous. At the beginning of the play, Mech calls Baal an animal with whom one cannot negotiate (Brecht 1967: I, 9). As we have seen, Baal's liminality is that of the werewolf, an animalistic libidinality on the out-skirts of human society, capitalist instrumentalisation and law. In spite of his aversion to psychological readings of his own work, Brecht's enactment of his protagonist's life is thus congruent with Freud's inter-pretation of animals as the dream manifestation of unconscious libidi-nal drives (Freud 1960: 337).

There are several things that intrigue me here. Apparently, moder-nity perceives libidinal drives as so threatening because they are what is excluded from/by modern abstraction. According to the Frankfurt School, the perception of non-commodified libido as threat is – like instrumental rationality itself – a thoroughly modern, historically pro-duced socio-political problematic. At the same time, however, this libidinality is also the excessive drive energy ontologically inherent in materiality, a materiality that stands in stark contrast to modernity's increasing abstraction. Materiality's dynamic, live energy and the threat of the libidinal in a modernity increasingly marked by abstraction – itself the result of socio-historical developments – intra-act. With the enactment of animality, Brecht's *Baal* is thus the point where the socio-historical problematic of modern abstraction (and the exclusion of libid-inal drives) meets the biological problematic of the interaction of species and the ontological problematic of a live more-than-human materiality.

As in Brecht's *Im Dickicht der Städte*, in *Baal* homosexuality becomes the only site of libidinal relations uncorrupted by instrumentality – but, as Ekart's murder by Baal shows, not a site excluded from the violence inherent in the natural world. The connection between this murder and the natural world becomes clear when Baal has to leave the realm of the law, human society, because of this murder. Interestingly, Brecht's enactment of homosexuality as the site of libidinal object relations contradicts Freud's interpretation of homosexuality as narcissism,[44] as the overall failure to cathect, and also questions Adorno's later confla-tion of homosexuality and fascism (theorised as group narcissism).[45] Homosexuality was of course long excluded from the conventions and social institutions of the human social sphere, including the bourgeois family. Whereas the 'domestic' drama of the nineteenth century (such as Strindberg's naturalist work) dramatises the crisis of the bourgeois family, *Baal* – situated at a historically already more removed point – enacts a social structure where the family has increasingly lost social and moral relevance. Although, as Brecht's drama shows, post-pater-nalistic society has increasingly overcome oedipal authority structures, it is, however, still a form of patriarchy and still shares with the latter the exploitation of women.[46]

Brecht's Baal is thus an ambivalent figure in a variety of ways. He places himself outside the moral codes of the bourgeoisie and bourgeois family structures, instead coming from and cyclically re-entering the natural world. But while embodying a threatening liminal identity on the border to the outside coded (by human society) as abject or evil, he repeats – in his treatment of women – the instrumentalisation that more than anything marks modern, i.e. bourgeois, capitalist society. Similarly, his characterisation of women as 'faceless' after they have given up their virginity runs the risk of reaffirming bourgeois standards of feminine virtue (as problematised for instance in the bourgeois drama of the eighteenth century).[47] This representation of women in Brecht's play as lacking identity recalls Strindberg's problematisation of this issue and the patriarchal tradition as a whole. Reminiscent of the patriarchal tradition in yet another way, not only the abject male protagonist but also the object of Brecht's criticism – bourgeois society – is feminised.[48] The 'white', virginal women that Baal corrupts in the play are all members of the bourgeois society that Brecht and his title character target.

The Fascist Brecht?

Does the controversial representation of women in many of his plays, including *Baal*, then make Brecht a fascist, in congruence with the long-standing discussion of Brecht's imputed quasi-fascist and misogynist tendencies rehearsed above? I argue, first, that the way that Brecht's protagonist in *Baal* uses and abuses women's bodies can be linked to the thematic of sacrifice already discussed in relation to Strindberg's work. In crises of symbolic investiture – such as the crisis of paternalistic society in Germany at the beginning of the twentieth century – human bodies serve as 'backing' to re-establish credibility. In *The Body in Pain*, Elaine Scarry writes:

> At particular moments when there is within society a crisis of belief – that is, when some central idea or ideology or cultural construct has ceased to elicit a population's belief either because it is manifestly fictitious or it has for some reason been divested of ordinary forms of substantiation – the sheer material factualness of the human body will be borrowed to lend that cultural construct the aura of 'realness' and 'certainty'. (Scarry 1985: 14)

Santner reads the First World War and its 'mania for the ultimate sacrifice' as the product of modern Europe's loss of firm foundations, as the attempt to re-establish lost credibility through such 'contact with the real' (Santner 2011: 172).

The First World War itself further destroyed the social fabric of pre-1914 Germany and led to a loss of psychological, economic and national security and identity. The search for credibility, for certainty and for a foundation of knowledge, can provide fertile ground for authoritarian regimes. During the Weimar Republic (1918–33), Germany's first democracy, part of the German population felt disconcerted by the new political freedoms and reassured by the law-and-order platform of the National Socialist Party. The inflation of the early years of the Weimar Republic caused the middle class and rural farmers to lose their savings, further adding to their social and economic dislocation. Six years later, the Great Depression then hit Germany hard. With the advent of the Third Reich finally, the admired *Führer* and the community of the *Volk* again provided 'totality', i.e. identification and identity. While Nietzsche had diagnosed and announced the death of God, the fascist state took the place of God, as Ernst Cassirer already observed in *The Myth of the State* (1946). The NS regime relieved the loss of a spiritual sense of belonging and the modern loss of community by creating a homogenous, idealised national community linked to a mythical Germanic past and common racial heritage, and a charismatic leader who provoked a quasi-religious adulation in his followers. While Christianity finds its grounding in the sacrifice of Christ's body, the persecution of certain marginalised groups under National Socialism gave the new religion of the NS state and its leadership the 'backing' provided by the sacrifice of 'real' bodies.

Can we then also read Brecht's enactment of corporeality in *Baal* in the same vein? I believe that we can answer this question in the negative. While Brecht's play enacts the loss of parental authority and conventional bourgeois values, it does not attempt to re-establish the authority lost. Rather than backing up social credibility through real bodies, Baal rejects the human sphere and occupies the liminal zone close to animality, namely bare life. It is true that Baal sacrifices women's bodies. But there is simply too much critical distance between Brecht's spectators and his protagonist for a reading of the sacrifice of women's bodies as a redemptive strategy. What distinguishes Brecht from fascist rhetoric, in other words, is that he does not try to redress the modern lack of orientation with a semantics of sacrifice.

In addition to Adorno's and Fuegi's accusations already discussed, in his article 'Brecht and Postmodernism' (1999: 51) Rainer Friedrich furthermore accuses the early Brecht of an alleged proximity to 'the death cult and kitsch of fascism'. He associates Brecht's Baal character with the 'Nietzschean vitalism' adopted by fascist movements and Baal's ego dissolution in death with the 'notorious "vive [*sic*] la muerte!" with which the fascist general Millan Astray used to conclude his addresses to his troops during the Spanish Civil War'. Friedrich accuses Brecht's work as a whole of a 'totalitarian logic' and the author himself of succumbing to 'the totalitarian temptation'. In addition to simplistically conflating Nietzsche's philosophy with fascism, Friedrich in one fell swoop finds both Brecht and postmodernism guilty of totalitarianism due to – Friedrich argues – their common erasure of the subject.[49]

As I have demonstrated, both Brecht's play and the proto-fascist texts analysed by Theweleit thematise the transgression of established (psychic and social) boundaries and materially present this abjection in tropes of fluidity, excrement, putrefaction, sexuality and death. But whereas fascist subjects perceive difference as an extreme threat to their own self and psychic survival and attempt to fend off this difference through rigid binarisms, Brecht's play creates an atmosphere of ironic fascination with its protagonist's animalistic strength and stature as an outsider who transgresses the boundaries of bourgeois society. In spite of shared images of abjection, in other words, Brecht's enactment of anti-bourgeois alterity in *Baal* differs from the phobic fear of the other in fascism by not offering an immunitarian logic as a defence. Given the play's 'proto-epic' distantiation or estrangement, we can argue that Brecht does not appeal to the spectator to share the male protagonist's misogyny.

In addition, the enactment of Baal's death, with Baal crawling back into nature like a rat, has nothing in common with the fascist idealisation of death, Expressionist apotheosis or the beautiful deaths of Romantic literature. While, especially in the fascist context, such idealisations of death are often linked to the cult or celebration of masculinity, one of the lumbermen present in the hut where Baal is close to death characterises the weakened Baal as a 'Kapaun' ('capon') (Brecht 1967: I, 66). While Baal once embodied unchecked libidinal energy, he is now a castrated rooster whose death is far from celebration of any kind. In contrast to Johst's *Der Einsame*, the play Brecht intended to parody, the protagonist's death (or any other death) in *Baal* lacks transcendence. In the section 'Ahorn im Wind' ('Maple in the Wind'), Baal sings his *Lied* entitled 'Der Tod im Wald' ('Death in the Forest'). It tells the story of a dying man, who is addressed as a lethal threat and an animal:

> Unnütz bist du, räudig, toll, du Tier!
> Eiter bist du, Dreck, du Lumpenhaufen!
> Luft schnappst du uns weg mit deiner Gier
> Sagten sie. Und er, er, das Geschwür:

. . .
Das war etwas, was kein Freund verstand
Daß sie zitternd vor dem Ekel schwiegen.
                    (Brecht 1967: I, 56)

(You are useless, mangy, rabid, you animal!
You are pus, dirt, you heap of rags!
You snatch away the air from us with your greed
They said. And he, he, the ulcer
. . .
That was something that no friend understood.
That they remained silent in the face of disgust.)

The dying man is described in tropes of abjection – storm, wind, contagion, pus, dirt, repulsion – that transgress the boundaries of human
propriety and comprehension. *Viva la muerte*? I think not. While the
Expressionist heroes can depend on their work to provide them immor-
tality, the central problematic in *Baal* is exactly the issue of death in a
secular, radically immanent, ultimately posthuman universe.[50]

In spite of such passages describing humans' ontological vulnerability,[51] the play's distantiation from its protagonist – even before the formal development of Brecht's theory of the estrangement effect – differs
substantially from the cathartic identification typically encouraged in
the bourgeois dramatic tradition (and in the Aristotelian tradition in
general) and by fascist mass events. As Theweleit has demonstrated,
NS mass rallies were supposed to shore up the fascists' ego armor and
protect their participants from the invasion of their ego by the feminised Other. If this immersion in the feminised mass was a return to the
maternal womb, it was a very staged, controlled return. Baal's return to
the feminine semiotic, however, is anarchic and deadly.

Almost diametrically opposed to Friedrich's interpretation, finally,
another – less reductive – way to link Brecht and fascism is to give
the sphere of the more-than-human enacted in *Baal* another look.
Totalitarianism as a thanato-political regime reduces the life of certain
members of the population to bare or creaturely life. These humans
are excluded from the space of representation and the rights that are
granted to members of the qualified, political in-group. What Baal is
reduced to at the end of the play is indeed the vulnerability, bareness,
and nakedness of our mortal lives. What speaks against the political
reading of Baal as embodying bare life under totalitarianism, however,
is that he is not a victim of biopolitical oppression.

At the same time, although Brecht's play is not based on an immunitarian logic, its male title character's association with the feminine

abject, which transgresses the divisions of bourgeois ideology, fits Michael Hardt and Antonio Negri's description of what constitutes a biopolitical event: 'The biopolitical event, in fact, is always a queer event, a subversive process of subjectivisation that, shattering ruling identities and norms, reveals the link between power and freedom, and thereby inaugurates an alternative production of subjectivity. The biopolitical event thus breaks with all forms of metaphysical substantialism or conceptualism' (Hardt and Negri 2013: 242–3). It is in this sense that Brecht's *Baal* is not only subversive, but queer, again establishing a proximity to recent discussions of queer eco-drama. Brecht's title character lives and participates in an intra-active ecology whose co-constituted relations are not fixed but fluid.

As we have seen, in spite of Baal's role as an outsider at the juncture of nature and the law, Brecht's play itself is in dialogue with the socio-historical and material developments that characterise post-eighteenth-century European modernity. At the same time, the anarchy Brecht establishes in the play is not the political anarchy of a state of exception. With his concept of creaturely life, Santner also speaks less of a political than an *ontological* vulnerability (Santner 2011: 216), a vulnerability that becomes more acute under the conditions of modernity. Linking creaturely or bare life as both a political and ontological condition, however, Santner does draw a parallel between the stateless *homine sacri* of twentieth-century Europe and the characters of absurd theatre: 'Recalling Hannah Arendt's account of the stateless, one could say that Beckett's characters acquire their particular strangeness by being rendered *merely human*. One could further say that Beckett has gone the greatest distance among modern artists in the process of *figuring out abstraction*' (Santner 2011: 251, emphasis in original). Absurd theatre thus enacts both the growing abstraction of modern society and what seems like its opposite – a corporeality that links human and nonhuman animals. Santner writes: 'In Beckett's theatre, the time of creaturely life invades the space of the play' (2011: 251). I argue that Brecht's *Baal* already prefigures this development.

Notes

1. My reading is mainly based on the last version, prepared in 1953 and published in 1955, at the end of Brecht's life. This is also the version the Suhrkamp Verlag chose for its 1967 *werkausgabe* edition of Brecht's *Gesammelte Werke*.
2. See, for instance, Simmel (1918: 107).

3. Like the writer who inspired Brecht, namely the French poet Arthur Rimbaud (see below). Cf., for example, the 'Mauvais sang' section of Rimbaud's *Une Saison en enfer*.

4. 'Ja, werden denn Sie von dem Fleisch nie satt?' (Brecht 1967: I, 22) ('Well, is the flesh/meat never going to fill you up?'). See also Brecht (1967: I, 37).

5. Translations of Brecht in this chapter are mine.

6. Baal is repeatedly called strong (like an elephant: Brecht 1967: I, 37, 63) and the women he seduces are weak (see, for instance, Brecht (1967: I, 26).

7. See also Fraunhofer (1997 and 2000). The title character of *Baal* also shares traits with many later Brechtian characters.

8. Cf. Santner (2006).

9. See Wright (1989: 84–5) for a refutation of Adorno's argument.

10. The most famous expression of the *Sonderweg* view, of a view that posits a specifically *German* cultural connection to the Holocaust, are Thomas Mann's post-war essays and novels.

11. In *Powers of Horror* (1982), Kristeva reads texts by male writers – among them the French fascist writer Louis-Ferdinand Céline – as examples of 'feminine' or abject writing. Kristeva has, among other things, been criticised for her reading of Céline as an exponent of poetic language, which is a positive concept in her work. Nevertheless, a facile reading of *Powers of Horror* as an advocacy or apology of fascism, by simplistically conflating aesthetics and politics, in my view misses the mark.

12. Cf. Kristeva (1982: 67) and the section on Céline (133–210).

13. Theweleit's analysis of the fear of the feminine as well is not limited to the fear of biological women and includes the fear of feminised libidinal drives. Nevertheless, Theweleit's exclusive focus is the psychic constitution of the male subject. In contrast to Kristeva, the essentialism of Theweleit's approach limits his investigation to a critique of patriarchal – and, by extension, fascist – society exclusively as the society of men. Put differently, Theweleit's work would clearly profit from a more qualified and fluid understanding of sexual difference.

14. When Baal is approaching his death, a man tells him 'Du hast keine Zähne mehr' (Brecht 1967: I, 64) ('You have no teeth left').

15. See also 'Mainacht unter Bäumen' (Brecht 1967: I, 29).

16. 'Fürchtet Männer nicht beim Weib, die sind egal' ('Do not fear men when going to women; those do not matter').

17. My reading of *Baal* does not claim general validity for Brecht's work as a whole. Unlike Fuegi or Theweleit, I am, in other words, not positing a stable authorial subject. For instance, Brecht's *Im Dickicht der Städte* (written shortly after *Baal* and *Trommeln in der Nacht*, from 1921 to 1924) enacts the threat posed by the feminine as the *negativised* effects of capitalism and thus differs from the earlier plays.

18. 'O Johanna, eine Nacht mehr in deinem Aquarium und ich wäre verfault zwischen den Fischen!' (Brecht 1967: I, 24) ('Oh Johanna, one more night in your fish tank and I would have rotted to death amongst the fish!')

19. Verlaine is mentioned in the section 'Speisezimmer' ('Dining Room') of Brecht's play in a comparison of Baal's and Verlaine's similar physiognomies (Brecht 1967: I, 6). Following the nineteenth -century criminologist Cesare Lombroso, who is also mentioned in the play, these physiognomies are read as indications of these characters' personalities (and their common criminal nature). Lombroso's 1864 book, *Genio e follia* (*Genius and Madness*), which linked genius to insanity, was widely read and discussed after the end of the First World War.

20. As developed in the poem 'Vom ertrunkenen Mädchen' ('Ballad of the Drowned Girl') (1919/20).

21. In the mythological texts of the twelfth to the fourteenth centuries BCE, Baal attacks El, the previous ruler and father of gods and humans, and castrates him, a mutilation that subsequently excludes El from ruling. Instead of killing his opponents, the mythological Baal incorporates and co-opts them (Clos 1999: 113). In Brecht's play, the protagonist is portrayed as an ogre figure who instrumentalises others.

22. Brief 81, Mitte Januar 1920 (Brecht 1988: XXVIII, 81; quoted by Jordheim 1999: 103).

23. The production of *Baal* that premiered at the Deutsches Theater in Berlin on 28 November 2014 emphasised this proto-epic estrangement inherent in the text through the use of white face paint and Harlequin costumes. See <https://www.youtube.com/watch?v=nrZWImuXyV8> (last accessed 26 July 2017).

24. According to Fore (2015: 176), this psychic dedifferentiation can be simultaneously found in Brecht's work not only in the non-anthropocentric understanding of theatrical spatiality and materiality, but also on the metatextual and linguistic registers (i.e. in Brecht's use of quotation and grammatical shifters).

25. My reading of Brecht's *Baal* as not belonging to the text- and dialogue-based 'dramatic' tradition differs from Lehmann's assessment of Brecht (Lehmann 1999: 87–8).

26. Cf. also 'Denn er hatte weder Heim noch Erde' (Brecht 1967: I, 56) ('Because he had neither home nor earth'), forgotten by God: 'Gott hat einen vergessen' (Brecht 1967: I, 16) ('God has forgotten us').

27. 'Und der Himmel blieb in Lust und Kummer da' (Brecht 1967: I, 3) ('And the sky remained there in pleasure and sorrow'). Cf. also Brecht (1967: I, 10: 'Schwimmst du hinunter mit Ratten im Haar: / Der Himmel drüber bleibt wunderbar' ('If you swim down with rats in your hair: / The sky above remains fair').

28. See also Baal on p. 29 (Brecht 1967: 1): 'Warum kann man nicht mit den Pflanzen schlafen?' ('Why can one not sleep with plants?').

29. 'Teufel! Lieber Gott!' (Brecht 1988: I, 82) ('Hell! Dear God!').

30. 'Heimweh ohne Erinnerung' (Brecht 1967: I, 61) ('home sickness without memory').

31. 'Wenn du die jungfräulichen Hüften umschlingst, wirst du in der Angst und Seligkeit der Kreatur zum Gott. Wie der Machandelbaum viele Wurzeln hat, verschlungene, so habt ihr viele Glieder in einem Bett, und darinnen schlagen Herzen und Blut fließt durch' (Brecht 1967: I, 11) ('When you encircle the virginal hips, you become God in the creature's fear and bliss. Just as the juniper tree has many roots, intertwined, you have many limbs in one bed, and in it hearts beat and blood flows). See also the beginning of 'Mainacht unter Bäumen' (Brecht 1967: I, 29) ('May Night Under Trees').

32. As Jan Knopf and others have pointed out, there were also other, more local models for Brecht's protagonist. See, for instance, Knopf: 'Inzwischen ist aber nachgewiesen, dass Brechts Vorbild ein heruntergekommener Augsburger Dichter mit Namen Johann Baal war, der als verkrachtes Genie durch die Augsburger Kneipen zog' (Knopf 2006: 77) ('In the meantime it has been shown that Brecht's model was an Augsburg poet down on his luck by the name of Johann Baal who made his rounds through the pubs in Augsburg': my trans.).

33. 'Es steht noch ein ganzer Haufen Stämme, die abends liegen müssen' (Brecht 1967: I, 67) ('There are still a whole bunch of stems standing that will have to lie in the evening').

34. Baal also appears as a figure in several literary works of the nineteenth century and Expressionism: Christian Friedrich Hebbel's drama *Judith* (1841), Georg Heym's poem 'Der Gott der Stadt' (1911), Paul Zech's narrative *Das Baalsopfer* (1917), his collection of novellas, *Der schwarze Baal* and Andreas Thom's novella *Baals Anfang* (published in 1920). Together with other details taken from Zech's novella, Baal's homosexuality and his rape of a minor are elements in both Thom's and Brecht's works.

35. 'Du weißt doch, daß ich dich liebe' (Brecht 1967: I, 35) ('But you know that I love you').

36. 'Bruder' (Brecht 1967: I, 16, 17, 33, 35).

37. Cf. Freud (1965: 72): 'It may also be assumed that the sons, when they were driven out and separated from their father, advanced from identification with one another to homosexual object-love and in this way won freedom to kill their father.'

38. In spite of the importance of the homoerotic desire between the two male protagonists, however, *Baal* is no longer centrally focused on a conflict between two antagonists. As in Expressionist plays (see Sokol 1963: xxi), the play's central focus is the protagonist, and the other characters more or less function only as foils.

39. See, for instance, Brecht (1967: I, 43).

40. This motif of facelessness also shows up in *Im Dickicht der Städte*. Cf. again Fraunhofer (2000).

41. Instrumental rationality does not replace earlier forms of traditional authority or patriarchal morality. It is, rather, an extension or generalisation of

tendencies within them; an instrumental orientation always existed alongside the idealised imagery of western patriarchy. However, according to Horkheimer, capitalist society has dispensed even with the appearance of substantive rationality and is openly, cynically instrumental.

42. See in contrast Baal's statement: 'Ich habe Lieder auf dem Papier. Aber jetzt werden sie auf dem Abort aufgehängt' (Brecht 1967: I, 28) ('I have songs on paper. But now they are being hung in the bathroom'). We can read Johannes's statement that he has been more creative since becoming a drunk as ironic: 'früher hatte ich nie solche Einfälle, so schnurrige, als es mir gut ging in den bürgerlichen Verhältnissen. Erst jetzt habe ich Einfälle, wo ich Genie geworden bin' (Brecht 1967: I, 59) ('I used to never have such ideas, such good ones, when I was living comfortably in bourgeois circumstances. Only now do I have ideas in which I have become a genius').

43. Brecht (1967: I, 41).

44. Freud (1975b). On the link between homosexuality and narcissism established by Freud and other early psychoanalysts see also Rupprecht (2006: 10).

45. See Adorno et al. (1950) and Adorno (1974). See also Hewitt's chapter on 'The Frankfurt School and the Political Pathology of Homosexuality' (in Hewitt 1996) and Halle (1995: 300), which points to the link established by Fromm between authoritarian submissiveness and homosexuality.

46. The term 'post-patriarchal' used by both Adorno and MacCannell is thus misleading.

47. Whereas the bourgeois code of feminine virtue was supposed to guarantee the legality of the heirs as the husband's own children, Baal's repudiation of women after the sexual act, however, has no concern for heirs. In fact, he is afraid of children (Brecht 1967: I, 4).

48. Here one can see a link between *Baal* and the feminisation of capitalism in *Im Dickicht der Städte*.

49. See also Friedrich (1990). Interestingly Colebrook also establishes a connection between totalitarianism and postmodernism, both of which she reads as examples of 'equivocity' (2014: 214).

50. Gougou, nicknamed 'der Madensack' (literally 'sack of maggots', with 'Maden' ('maggots'), suggesting death), sings: 'Es ist wie zitternde Luft an Sommerabenden, Sonne. Aber es zittert nicht. Nichts. Gar nichts. Man hört einfach auf. Wind geht, man friert nimmer. Regen geht, man wird nimmer naß. Witze passieren, man lacht nicht mehr. Man verfault, man braucht nicht zu warten. Generalstreik.' ('It is like air trembling on summer nights. Sun. But it does not tremble. Nothing. Nothing at all. One simply stops. There is wind, one is no longer cold. There is rain, one does no longer get wet. Jokes happen, one does no longer laugh. One rots, one does not have to wait. General strike.') When Maja asks: 'Und was kommt am Schluß?' ('And what comes at the end?'), Gougou

grins: 'Nichts. Gar nichts. Es kommt kein Schluß. Nichts dauert ewig' (Brecht 1967: I, 49) ('Nothing. Nothing at all. There is no ending. Nothing lasts forever'). See also Brecht 1967: I, 38, where Baal says about the dead lumberjack, Teddy, contrasting him with the lazy Baal: 'Teddy hingegen war fleißig. Teddy war freigebig. Teddy war verträglich. Davon blieb eines: Teddy war.' ('Teddy on the other hand worked hard. Teddy was generous. Teddy was easy to get along with. Of these one remained: Teddy was.') In other words, having lived a morally good life makes no difference after death. When a second lumberjack asks 'Wo er jetzt wohl ist?' ('I wonder where he is now?'), Baal responds by pointing to the dead man, 'Da ist er.' ('There he is.') There is no transcendence. The dying man described in Baal's song 'Der Tod im Wald' ('Death in the Forest') who is buried by people 'voll von Ekel' ('full of disgust') and 'kalt von Haß' ('cold with hatred') is the only figure whose death has some transcendence, expressing Baal's hope for some light after death: 'Wenn ich nachts nicht schlafen kann, schaue ich die Sterne an' ('When I cannot sleep at night, I look at the stars'). When the dead man's survivors ride away in silence and look back at the tree under which they buried the man, the top of the tree is filled with light (Brecht 1967: I, 57).

51. 'Ihr Mörder, denen viel Leides geschah!' (Brecht 1967: I, 60) ('You murderers who have suffered much!')

CHAPTER 4

Flies vs. the Fetishisation of Consciousness

Reality is composed not of things-in-themselves or things-behind-phenomena but of things-in phenomena. The world is a dynamic process of intra-activity and materialization in the enactment of determinate causal structures with determinate boundaries, properties, meanings and patterns of marks on bodies ... It is through specific agential intra-actions that a differential sense of being is enacted in the ongoing ebb and flow of agency. (Barad 2007: 140)

In Jean-Paul Sartre's play, *Les Mouches* (*The Flies*), the city of Argos is infested with flies. As Jupiter points out, the 'mouches à viande' (flesh flies) are attracted by flesh/meat and were drawn to the city of Argos by a strong smell of putrefaction after Agamemnon's return to Argos and his murder by his wife, Clytemnestra, mother to Orestes and Electra. The eyes of the Idiot at the beginning of the play – a figure at the margins of the diegetic world opening on the stage – are covered with flies. His eyes secrete a white liquid resembling sour milk (Sartre 1947: 107), enacting the theme of the mother as primary abject. The Tutor (Pédagogue) who travels with the protagonist, Orestes, calls the old women of Argos '[v]ieilles carnes' (Sartre 1947: 104), literally 'pieces of old, spoiled meat', establishing a link between the flies, putrefaction, mothers and feminised flesh). When Orestes is bothered by the flies, the Tutor chases them, saying: 'Allons, paix! paix! pas d'effusions!' (Sartre 1947: 107) ('Hey, peace! Peace! No outpourings!').[1] Like fluids (effusions) that transgress boundaries and contaminate the binary categories of the symbolic system causing pollution, the flies in Argos do not fit conventional categories: They are bigger than ordinary flies and more invasive. The Tutor says: 'Elles font plus de bruit que des crécelles et sont plus grosses que des libellules' (Sartre 1947: 107) ('They make more noise than rattles and are fatter than dragonflies'). The city is beset by abjection. Not only is it filled with flies, rats and lepra (Sartre 1947: 244), but the towns around it view the repentance of the inhabitants of Argos as a plague and are afraid of being infected by it.

In the context of her discussion of Eugène Ionesco's *The Rhinoceros* in *The Stage Lives of Animals*, theatre scholar Una Chaudhuri remarks

that '[t]he fact that an animal can *fail* to register in the critical reception and scholarly discussion even of a play named for an animal is in
itself an interesting phenomenon' (Chaudhuri 2017a: 114, emphasis
in original). According to Chaudhuri, this critical omission has to do
with the western theatre's traditional emphasis on human characters
and drama as verbal text. Even when animals feature in this tradition,
they do so as symbols or metaphors for a human problematic. In contrast to this verbal and metaphorical emphasis in the critical reception
of plays, Chaudhuri proposes focusing on 'the rich materiality that is
the hallmark of theater: its seductive traffic in bodies, objects, spaces,
and sounds' (Chaudhuri 2017a: 114). As my own reading will show,
both aspects – language and physical materiality – are in fact deeply
enmeshed in Sartre's play.

First performed in Paris in 1943 under German occupation and one
of Sartre's best-known works, *The Flies* is generally considered 'a work
of political protest' (Pucciani 1985: 159).[2] Sartre himself repeatedly
emphasised the antifascist intentions of this modern Oresteia adaptation and David Carroll, in his excellent study *French Literary Fascism*,
counts Sartre, together with Adorno, as an important antifascist theorist
(Carroll 1995: 12). While the validation of *Les Mouches* as an antifascist and antipaternalistic text has largely remained unquestioned in
Sartre scholarship,[3] I argue that a reading of the 'excess' of Sartre's play,
however, reveals a language that is not only profoundly patriarchal, but
whose immunitarian, defensive dualistic logic is reminiscent of the rhetoric of fascist texts. As we will see, the role played by the nonhuman title
characters of Sartre's play – the flies – is central to this reading.

Not only German writers like Bertolt Brecht, but European writers of the twentieth century have often had to explain or justify their
relationship to the fascist ideologies of their time. The same also holds
true for nation states. In the French context, it has often been argued
that Sartre embodies the twentieth century better than anyone. The
prominent French philosopher Bernard-Henri Lévy's book published
in the year 2000, for instance, is entitled *Le siècle de Sartre*. While
Germany's role in National Socialism and the Shoah is undeniable, this
chapter explores France's relationship to fascism through a reading of
the work of Sartre as one of France's leading intellectuals of the twentieth century. Notwithstanding Sartre's role in the intellectual Résistance
and his reputation as a celebrated antifascist writer and activist, I want
to explore the relationship of Sartre's work to the biopolitical, dualistic
thinking of the early twentieth century. It was Theodor Adorno who,
in his *Negative Dialektik*, insisted on the inescapability of dialectical

contradiction, on the 'remainder' inevitably excluded in all conceptual identity. Adorno was interested in the part of the object that is not included in the identifiable thought; he was interested in the specific, concrete and individual – if you want 'material' – particularity that is covered up by generalising concepts. Conceptual thinking, in other words, does not readily acknowledge the intra-active multi-valence of experience. I argue that this insight also applies to the concepts 'fascism' and 'antifascism'.

In their anthology of theoretical readings of the Shoah, Neil Levi and Michael Rothberg cite Adorno's equally famous – and often misunderstood – statement that 'to write poetry after Auschwitz is barbaric'. They correctly explain that '[w]hat initially concerned Adorno . . . was less the impropriety of any artistic response to the Holocaust than how culture in general and poetry in particular failed to recognize their own implication in the "sinister" forces of total social integration that made the barbarism of Auschwitz possible in the first place' (Levi and Rothberg 2003: 12). I suggest that Sartre's work as well, while claiming fascism as its absolute other, is also implicated in its structures.

To begin with, I argue that Sartre's early work demonstrates a problematic co-extensiveness with the modern western, Cartesian tradition, that Sartre's notion of human consciousness enacts the anthropocentric subjectivism of this rationalist philosophical tradition. While for Descartes, the human cogito controls nonhuman matter, in Sartre existence or matter precedes human consciousness. In order to become truly human, in other words, the human must break from and leave behind his origin in nature. Sartre's work presented here enacts the threat of a materiality that comes alive, that does not retain the passivity assigned to it by this rigid but illusory Cartesian duality of mind and matter. As I will show, the sense of threat, of the danger posed by the contingent internal productivity of natural life – a threat incarnated by the flies – is a trait that Sartre ultimately shares with fascism. Sartre's dualistic worldview blocks the impersonal energy that traverses the human self, and it is this phobic blockage – together with a restrictive, biopolitical definition or internal caesura of what or who qualifies as truly human – that is reminiscent of fascism.

As in the rest of this book, my argument here points to the transnational intra-activity between western modernity and the catastrophe that was early twentieth-century totalitarianism. As I will demonstrate, Sartre's early work establishes a defensive, immunitarian logic based on gender and nation as quasi-biological criteria. I argue that this immunitarian thinking produces a problematic relationality between Sartre's work and – in its extreme – the thanato-politics of fascist thought. I would like to emphasise clearly, however, that I am not suggesting that any of the writers included in this study were fascists. Instead, I aim to point to the problematic nature of an 'othering' of fascism. Such an 'othering' of fascism has marked both Sartre's early work and – until rather recently – France's official stance towards its role in the Second World War.

For the discussion of fascism, it is important not to completely conflate fascism, patriarchal modernity and othering, however. As Michel Serres points out, 'our collective is the expulsion of the stranger, of the enemy, of the parasite' (2007: 56). As Lynda Hart observes, the formation of subjectivity – the formation of *any* subjectivity – is based on the process of othering, on the establishment not only of an ego position different from the (m)other, but also on the differentiation from the 'alien' within (Hart 1994: 98). Jane Bennett thinks of this alien within human subjectivity in terms of a 'vital materiality' akin to the nonhuman:

> Vital materiality better captures an 'alien' quality of our own flesh, and in so doing reminds humans of the very *radical* character of the (fractious) kinship between the human and the nonhuman. My 'own' body is material, and yet this vital materiality is not fully or exclusively human . . . In a world of vibrant matter, it is not enough to say that we are 'embodied.' We are, rather, an array of bodies, many different kinds of them in a nested set of microbiomes. (Bennett 2010a: 112–13)

It is this materiality that is at stake in Sartre.

In the terms of Niklas Luhmann's system theory, in which

> the environment of any system is always already of overwhelmingly greater complexity than the system itself . . . [t]he system's inferiority in complexity must be counterbalanced by strategies of selection . . . Under pressure to adapt to a complex and changing environment, systems increase their selectivity . . . by means of self-referential closure and the reentry of the system/environment distinction within the system itself in a process of internal differentiation. (Wolfe 2010: 14–15, paraphrasing Luhmann)

The more complex the environment, the greater a system's selectivity and self-referential closure have to be, leading even to differentiation within the system itself. As Esposito notes, without immunitarian protection, 'individual and common life would die away' (Campbell xxvii). Agamben defines the fundamental alterity within us as an animality that is 'the ur-form of any state of exception' (Agamben 2004: 37). In an argument for the posthuman, Claire Colebrook posits that there is no (human) subjectivity without normativity: 'Without some minimal ongoing normativity "I" would have no being . . . the stabilization of the self through a repeatable norm . . . sacrifices or mourns that which is occluded or not taken up as worthy of recognition' (Colebrook 2014: 40). Given the constitutive dependence of human subjectivity on the exclusion of difference, Rosi Braidotti similarly deplores 'an alterity which has to be included as necessarily excluded in order to sustain the framing of the subject in the first place.' Braidotti (2010: 211) consequently advocates moving beyond the critical focus on human subjectivity and identity.

While differentiation, self-referential closure or 'othering' are thus fundamental to human – and possibly even any system's – thinking, in systems theory this self-referential closure at the same time does not preclude the system's openness vis-à-vis the environment (Wolfe 2010: 14–15). Fascism's immunitarianism, however, is an attempt to completely close the connection to the environment. Whether or not we can move beyond our anthropocentrism, what distinguishes totalitarianism from more 'benign' othering is thus the former's totality – the absolute character of its immunitarian system. Totalitarian thanato-politics takes the defensive logic of immunitarian protection to its extreme.

Although it is equally important not to conflate the ambiguities of antifascist texts with fascism itself, Sartre's gendered treatment of alterity does fit the description Carroll gives of the gender ideology and the literary fascism of a Drieu la Rochelle:

> Such an ideology is constituted by the project to establish both genders as distinct and totalizable identities, to make man as such or woman as such either an ideal type or the representative of absolute negativity, of a pathological deviation from and threat to the norm or ideal represented by the other. If this is so, no approach that accepts such distinctions and the hierarchies they impose, no matter which term is privileged or how vigorously the masculinist ideology of fascism is opposed, can effectively undermine the ultimate gender ideal of literary fascism: to be 'total'. (Carroll 1995: 169–70)

Similar to Strindberg, Sartre establishes an immunitarian logic based on a strict gender dichotomy and posits both female and male identity as (ideally) biological and stable. At the same time, however, woman is enacted as a negativised threat to the norm represented by man and to male consciousness. It is the totality, the absoluteness, of the representation of gender in Sartre that is reminiscent of totalitarianism.

Given this link between fascism and gender, my examination of the rhetoric of alterity in Sartre's early work is also in dialogue with and extends the long-standing critical debate concerning Sartre's 'sexism'. Hazel Barnes (1990) and Bonnie Burstow (1992) discussed allegations of Sartre's 'sexism' and both concluded that these allegations are untenable – an assertion that my reading will refute. I argue instead that the devaluation of difference is systemic in Sartre. While many critics have done important work documenting the sexism in Sartre's *oeuvre*, I want to additionally explore the link between Sartre's treatment of difference on the one hand and fascism on the other. I am interested, in other words, in the limits of antifascism.

Contagion

As Julia Kristeva has pointed out in *Pouvoirs de l'horreur* (*Powers of Horror*), the continually endangered boundary between the inside and the (ultimately illusory) outside of a given symbolic system (such as the nation) can, like human subjectivity, only be maintained through a process of othering. Kristeva has theorised 'abjection' as a contamination of boundaries, of the 'proper' centre by the outside. In comparison, Esposito reads Nazism as the paroxysm of the logic of modernity, which is based on the protection of the population from a perceived biological threat to its immunity – the threat of contamination or contagion. The rhetoric of the pollution of traditional European values and purity by immigrant outsiders that has constituted one of the central themes of the European far right (as well as the US debate about immigration) or the earlier National Socialist rhetoric of the threat of contamination (of the Aryan race by the Other) illustrate this mechanism of abjection. Anxieties about the loss of national or racial identity – for instance in today's context of globalisation and European integration – are expressions of the fear of ego disintegration brought on by invasive difference. In his 1945 article, 'Qu'est-ce qu'un collaborateur', Sartre discusses collaboration with the Nazi occupiers as an *illness* ('une maladie'), psychic disintegration ('un fait de désintégration') (Sartre 1949a: 46), i.e. an extreme danger exerted by the foreign Other and its collaborators resulting from the disintegration of the French nation. In Sartre's essay, collaborators are described as threatening the purity – the clean and proper nature of the symbolic inside – with contamination, excess and waste ('déchet') (Sartre 1949a: 48, 49). According to Sartre, they therefore have to be ab-jected. As we will see, in Sartre, the immunitarian line of defence is based not only on the concept of nation, but also gender.

As I have demonstrated elsewhere,[4] the extreme fear of contamination of the *Volkskörper* (the body politic of the people) is characteristic of dramatic and other texts from the era of National Socialism. Although Sartre *critiques* exactly this fear of contamination (by the Jewish body) in *Réflexions sur la question juive (Anti-Semite and Jew)*,[5] the same fear is central to an understanding of his contemporaneous 'Qu'est-ce qu'un collaborateur?' written the same year. As we will see in the brief discussion of Sartre's homophobia that follows and my longer exploration of the gender ideology in Sartre's work, the national body politic itself is clearly gendered (as well as racialised, although race is not the primary focus of this chapter).

What is most threatening, of course (as we have established above), is that – as is the case in autoimmune diseases – the other is really first and foremost inside – inside the community and inside the body or the ego – and this threatening inside can only be 'projected' outside. Sartre as well establishes a link between collaboration and the collaborator's 'inner nature', which is latent but manifests itself under certain circumstances (Sartre 1949a: 43). Sartre's collaborators, in other words, were already subject to the disintegration of the self before they succumbed to the integrative forces offered them by the National Socialist community (which provided them with what Klaus Theweleit calls an 'ego armour'). Sartre describes this inner nature as inherently traitorous.

The repression that Sartre consequently advocates is clearly part of the deformation in desire that Deleuze and Guattari's *Anti-Oedipe* identifies with fascism, and part of the simultaneous repression and controlled incitement of libidinal drives in modern society. As Theweleit has demonstrated, fascist thinking takes the fear of the (feminised) inner drives and the ensuing repression and controlled incitement to an extreme level. Whereas Sartre argues that the collaborator tries to 'kill off the human in himself and others' ('anéantir l'humain en lui et chez les autres') (Sartre 1949a: 60), he (Sartre) does not seem to be aware that his own essay, submitting to fascism's rigidity and restrictiveness, targets inner human nature and its disintegrative pull as the very source of the described problem (collaboration). Without elaborating further, Sartre advocates repressive laws that would keep what he describes as the femininised drives of democracy – 'un ennemi que les sociétés démocratiques portent . . . en leur sein' (Sartre 1949a: 60) ('an enemy that democratic societies carry in their bosoms') – under control: 'il convient qu'on fasse enfin des lois restrictives: il ne doit pas avoir de liberté contre la liberté' (Sartre 1949a: 60) ('it is fitting that we finally make restrictive laws: there must be no liberty against liberty'). On the intra-psychic level, the mechanism – the defence against difference – is the same for both the collaborator as described by Sartre and for Sartre himself. This mechanism also finds expression in Sartre's dualistic and hegemonic language, when he consistently refers to the collaborator as an essentialist 'il' (he) who is then continuously – but ultimately in vain – opposed to the 'nous' (we) of the article.

Enacting patriarchal societies' feminisation of difference and reminiscent of the problematic discussed in Strindberg's work, the Sartre of 'Qu'est-ce qu'un collaborateur? – in clearly misogynist and homophobic fashion – moreover discusses collaborators with the German occupation force as weak, effeminate men, as women and/or as homosexuals[6] and as social misfits ('les éléments marginaux') (Sartre 1949a: 46; 'les ratés', 47). The collaborator, according to Sartre, uses 'the weapons of the weak, of woman' ('les armes du faible, de la femme'), that is 'cunning, shrewdness . . . charm and seductiveness' ('la ruse, l'astuce . . . le charme et la seduction') (Sartre 1949a: 58). As we can see from the syntactic juxtaposition of 'femininité' ('femininity') and 'haine de l'homme' ('the hatred of man/mankind') in the essay (Sartre 1949a: 60), the target of the perceived threat posed by the feminine is man.

En-soi and pour-soi, or zōē and bíos

The defensive stance against feminised difference that characterises Sartre's essay 'Qu'est-ce qu'un collaborateur' is also a trait of his play *Les Mouches* (*The Flies*), first performed two years earlier (in 1943). In addition, *Les Mouches* clearly complements Sartre's first major philosophical treatise, *L'Etre et le néant* (*Being and Nothingness*), published the same year. In this treatise, Sartre develops his famous distinction between *être-en-soi* (being-in-itself) – which is based on Kant's 'Ding an sich' and stands for matter, that is inanimate, nonhuman objects or pregiven 'nature' – and *être-pour-soi* (being-for-itself), human consciousness. My investigation of *Les Mouches* focuses on the representation of the female protagonist, Electra, but in contrast to earlier, at times essentialist studies of Sartre's 'sexism', I again also want to look beyond female characters.

As I will show, existence, 'nature', the fluvial facticity of the *en-soi*, sexuality, maternal engulfment, and feminised border transgression are what Sartre's characters fear, what causes their nausea and what – like Kristeva's abject or the 'flesh' of the phenomenological tradition – fascinates them at the same time. Sartre's work establishes a rigid, binary philosophical system to fend off the perceived threat posed by material difference, by a materiality that does not remain passive 'matter'. Instead of thinking life as unity across all its forms or manifestations,

Sartre's philosophy is based on the separation of *en-soi* and *pour-soi* – or, in Aristotle's terms, the separation of *zōē* (natural, biological life) and *bíos* (qualified life). It is a biopolitical, immunitarian distribution that in its extreme led to the Nazi thanato-normative project.

The Nazi euthanasia programme was called *Dasein ohne Leben* (Existence without Life) – a phrase oddly reminiscent of Sartre's terminology. According to Sartre, existence (natural-zoological life established through birth) comes before essence (the qualified human life established through a conscious choice or action). Nazism was a biopolitical system that excluded some lives from the community – thus reducing them to bare life and dealing them death – in order to protect from contagion the immunity of those enjoying qualified life. In Sartre's *Les Mouches*, Electra is expelled from the city and is thus reduced to bare life. By the end of the play, the threatening femininised material force embodied by Electra has been contained, appropriated and absorbed by the male hero, Orestes.

In opposition to a negative biopolitics or thanato-politics that uses exclusion or death to protect or immunise life, Esposito proposes an affirmative biopolitics that abolishes the distinction between *zōē* and *bíos*. Esposito argues that all life is formed life (*bíos*) from the beginning, that there is no such thing as a simple, bare life. Instead, every life is pushed by something beyond itself, following its own possibilities of development. Such an affirmative biopolitics is not possible in Sartre's universe, given the strict separation between *en-soi* and *pour-soi*, existence and essence, matter and mind.

Gender Binarism

As in Strindberg, the dualistic role distribution between Electra and Orestes in *Les Mouches* enacts the binary structure of patriarchal thought, where the devalued side of oppositions such as weakness/strength, nature/culture, and matter/mind are associated with the feminine. In Sartre's play, women are assigned the role of inefficiency and impotence. In contrast to the title character of Jean Giraudoux' Oresteia adaptation, *Electre* (written six years earlier), Sartre's Electra is depicted as clearly weaker than her brother Orestes. At the beginning of the play, she declares herself too weak to deal with Jupiter, the representative of paternalism, on her own. She waits for Orestes, the male phallic hero ('avec sa grande épée') (Sartre 1947: 125) ('with his big sword'), to reveal the hollowness of divine authority and to kill her hated mother and stepfather. After Orestes has arrived and declared his determination to kill his mother and Aegisthus,

Electra accepts Orestes as her brother and she accepts his male authority: 'Oreste, tu es mon frère aîné et le chef de notre famille, prends-moi dans tes bras, protège-moi, car nous allons au-devant de très grandes souffrances' (Sartre 1947: 182) ('Orestes, you are my older brother and the head of our family, take me in your arms, protect me, since great suffering is ahead of us'). Electra sketches the picture of a patriarchal family in which authority is based on gender and age and entails the protection of the 'weaker sex'.

The same gendered duality also structures the rest of the play. In contrast to Orestes, who represents metaphysical freedom and authenticity, Electra is shown as ultimately still embroiled in negativised paternalistic authority structures. In spite of her initially very vocal and determined opposition to Jupiter, her latent entanglement in paternalistic conventions becomes manifest when, ravaged by remorse after the murder of her mother and stepfather, she accepts Jupiter's interpretation of her act as that of a child who does not bear responsibility. By accepting this interpretation, Electra falls back into paternalistic – i.e. divine, royal and paternal – authority structures, the master–slave dichotomy, and the state of an object – in Sartre's terminology, the state of *en-soi*:

> Au secours! Jupiter, *roi* des *Dieux* et des hommes, mon roi, prends-moi dans tes bras, emporte-moi, protège-moi. Je suivrai ta loi, je serai *ton esclave* et *ta chose*, j'embrasserai tes pieds et tes genoux. (Sartre 1947: 239, emphases added)

> (Help! Jupiter, *king of Gods and men*, my king. Take me in your arms, take me away, protect me. I will follow your law, I will be *your slave and your thing*, I will embrace your feet and your knees. (emphases added)

As Ninette Bailey (1977) and Stuart Zane Charmé (1991) have demonstrated, this binary distribution or split between privileged virility and deprivileged/negativised femininity is representative of Sartre's work as a whole.

Although existentialist philosophy is based on the assumption of radical metaphysical immanence, Sartre's distinction between feminised *en-soi* (bio-zoological life) and masculinised *pour-soi* (human consciousness) still very much enacts the distinction between bio-zoological life and anthropo-transcendental life that is fundamental to religious belief systems (Campbell 2008: xv). This distinction is part of an immunitarian logic that calls forth bodily *sacrifices* in order to maintain the difference between the two categories and fend off the threat of contagion. As in Strindberg, the threat posed and the sacrifices that it demands are both feminised in Sartre's work.

Rotting Flesh

In the passage from pre-given existence to essence – from *en-soi* to *pour-soi*, from natural to symbolic surroundings, in this passage constitutive of the human subject in the anthropocentric narrative – there is a gap that can only be overcome through the violence of a decision: the violence of an existentialist act such as Orestes' murder of his mother. The gap opening up in modernity concerns the privilege of the human condition. Eric Santner suggests in *The Royal Remains* that the gap between immanent embodiment or materiality on the one hand and symbolic identity on the other hand informs modern lives in general. Modern humans who do not believe in an embodied sublime or transcendental authority any more – humans who face the existential meaninglessness of life – all of a sudden face the question of their own ontological status, of their own position in the natural world. To preserve human exceptionalism even after the loss of divine transcendence, they attempt to ontologically and psychologically distance themselves from zōē. In modernity, as Santner puts it, 'our finite life as embodied subjects in a material world . . . is fundamentally and internally out-of-joint' (2011: 207). This modern disjuncture, this sense of unease, is ultimately what Sartre's fellow existentialist, Albert Camus, in *Le Mythe de Sisyphe* (*The Myth of Sisyphus*), called 'the absurd'. While the existentialists defined this modern disjointedness as transcendental homelessness (Orestes, in *Les Mouches*, is searching for his home), Santner similarly speaks of an ontological vulnerability. This ontological vulnerability 'takes on a particular acuteness under conditions of modernity' (Santner 2011: 216) and expresses itself in the soma, in psycho-somatic symptoms that are enacted on the modern stage. In Sartre, the excess of an immanent and live materiality in an absurd universe threatens to engulf masculinised human consciousness, bringing with it connotations of rotting, abject flesh: the flesh that attracts the flies in *Les Mouches*.

What separates and distances Orestes from (devalued, feminised) natural-biological life or pure existence in Sartre is his consciousness, the result of his modern alienation from and dismissal of divine authority. Orestes draws a line between humankind and the rest of nature: 'Tu es le roi des Dieux, Jupiter, le roi des pierres et des étoiles, le roi des vagues de la mer. Mais tu n'es pas le roi des hommes' (Sartre 1947: 232) ('You are the king of the Gods, Jupiter, the king of stones and stars, the king of the ocean waves. But you are not mankind's king'). The difference between natural life and Orestes is that he is free and knows it. Orestes's murder of his mother – a crime against nature – further reinforces his alienation from natural life: 'Etranger à moi-même, je sais. Hors nature, contre nature, sans excuse, sans autre recours qu'en moi' (Sartre 1947: 235) ('A stranger to myself, I know. Outside nature, against nature, without excuse, without any other recourse than myself'). Jupiter, on the other hand, offers Sartre's protagonist a return to the *en-soi* of unconscious natural life, to *zōē*. He tries to persuade Orestes to leave Argos by illuminating a stone (Sartre 1947: 177). Sartre's stone imagery, which can also be found in some of his other works[7] and which is used here as a trope for the *en-soi*, establishes an intertextual link to Martin Heidegger, who famously argued as part of his 1929–30 lecture course, *Die Grundbegriffe der Metaphysik: Welt – Endlichkeit – Einsamkeit* (*The Fundamental Concepts of Metaphysics: World, Finitude, Solitude*) that the stone is worldless (*weltlos*), the animal is 'poor in world' (*weltarm*) and humans are world-forming (*weltbildend*) (Heidegger 2004: 290–3). Leaving Argos would deter Orestes from finding his human essence or identity and lead him back to mere existence, to the assumed lifelessness of a stone, which does not have access to what Heidegger calls 'world' (that is, future possibilities).

Contrary to Orestes, Electra, at the end of the play, chooses to return to the unreflective state of *en-soi*, the state in which the feminised inhabitants (women) of Argos find themselves throughout the play. The female protagonist – like many of the women characters in Sartre's dramas[8] – comes to embody what Sartre in *L'Etre et le néant* criticises as bad faith (*mauvaise foi*), dishonesty, self-deception. In *Being and Nothingness*, Sartre associates both women and homosexuals ('a *paederast*') (Sartre 1992: 107, emphasis in original) with bad faith.[9] Sartre's homophobia becomes obvious in passages such as the following: 'The homosexual recognises *his faults* [my emphasis], but he struggles with all his strength against the crushing view that *his mistakes* [my emphasis] constitute for him a *destiny*.' With regard to 'the homosexual', Sartre's appeal for openness is couched in the following terms: 'A *sin* [my emphasis] confessed is half pardoned.' And he refers to the homosexual as 'the guilty one' (Sartre 1992: 108). At the end of *Les Mouches*, Electra falls prey to bad faith. Like Daniel in Sartre's 1945 novel *Le Sursis* (*The Reprieve*) or the Autodidact and the bourgeois in his most famous novel *La Nausée* (1938), Electra accepts the calm and permanence of an object, delivered of freedom, responsibility and existential anxiety. She uses her submission to God (Jupiter) as an escape from the modern human condition, from facing the ontological problem of the relationship between nature and human culture, the gap between embodied and abstract authority that opens in modernity. As an object, Sartre's Electra is consequently associated with the threat posed by nonhuman difference. She embodies the threat of the disintegration of the human self.

While existentialist philosophy is based on the notion that there is no escape from a meaningless universe, Sartre's fetishisation of consciousness in the binary opposition between *pour-soi* and *en-soi* at the same time contradicts this basic assumption of complete immanence. In the terminology developed by Camus (again in *Le Mythe de Sisyphe*), Sartre's call for an action that defines the modern (male) individual's 'heroic' identity (essence) is ultimately a leap (*un saut*), an escape from the absurd condition. As we have seen, Santner suggests that the fetishised 'flesh' that was once housed in the King's sublime body emerges in modernity as surplus or excess. Going beyond the pure animality of the soma, this flesh thus 'actually challenges the entire ideology of disenchantment and secularization' (Santner 2011: 98). Sartre's *pour-soi* is a case in point.

The fetishisation of consciousness as the highest human quality is a trait that Sartre shares with the western Cartesian tradition, and with the work of the Viennese writer Otto Weininger, discussed earlier. Sartre's enactment of consciousness as essentially male and lacking in women mirrors Weininger's ideas. The view of woman as *tabula rasa* that we encountered in Strindberg is a result of this alleged lack of consciousness.

Libidinal Drives

Like the western rationalist tradition and (as Theweleit has shown) like fascism, Sartre's *Les Mouches* devalues not only women but also feminised inner and outer nature (that is libidinal drives as well as the natural environment). Since the drives, which inhabit the 'fleshy' threshold between nature and culture, pose the lethal threat of feminised invasion, Sartre's play advocates an ideology of emotional restraint. Orestes, the male hero, thinks rationally and therefore does not come to repent what he has done. Electra, however, is consumed by feelings of guilt, because her participation in the murder was – like her mother's murder of Agamemnon – an act of passion, of hatred. In *L'Existentialisme est un humanisme* (*Existentialism Is a Humanism*), Sartre denigrates passion, giving expression to the patriarchal and specifically bourgeois distrust of libidinal drives:

> L'existentialiste ne croit pas à la puissance de la passion. Il ne pensera jamais qu'une belle passion est un torrent dévastateur qui conduit fatalement l'homme à certains actes, et qui, par conséquent, est une excuse. Il pense que l'homme est responsable de sa passion. (Sartre 1970: 37–8)

(The Existentialist does not believe in the power of passion. He will never think that a beautiful passion is a devastating torrent that fatally leads man to certain acts and that consequently is an excuse. He thinks that man is responsible for his passion.)

'Passion', according to Sartre, is an escape, an excuse. Electra consequently cannot escape the plague of the city of Argos, namely the flies, which, attracted by rotting flesh, arrived at the same point in time as the city's guilt and repentance. Orestes, on the other hand, does not feel bothered by the flies, nor by guilt and repentance (Sartre 1947: 209). In contrast to Electra's miserable fate at the end of the play, the last sentence of Act II has Orestes say: 'Demain je parlerai à mon peuple' (Sartre 1947: 210) ('Tomorrow I will speak to my people'). Orestes is the new king of Argos, the new – male – authority.

Establishing a link between animals, feminised sexuality and violence, Sartre enacts the threat of border transgression posed by feminised libidinal drives, by the creaturely excess ('inner nature') threatening to invade human consciousness, the 'new sublime'. In *Powers of Horror*, Kristeva links animals to the abject: 'The abject confronts us, on the one hand, with those fragile states where man strays on the territories of *animal*. Thus, by way of abjection, primitive societies have marked out a precise area of their culture in order to remove it from the threatening world of animals or animalism, which were representative of sex and murder' (Kristeva 1982: 12–13). It is above all women who are associated with unreflective nature and nonhuman animals in *Les Mouches*. Whereas Orestes senses his alienation from natural life, Electra is still part of zoological life. She says to Orestes, for instance:

Tu étais mon frère, le chef de notre famille, tu devais me protéger; mais tu m'as plongée dans le sang, je suis rouge comme un boeuf écorché; toutes les mouches sont après moi, les voraces, et mon coeur est une ruche horrible. (Sartre 1947: 280)

(You were my brother, the head of our family, you were supposed to protect me: but you have plunged me in blood, I am red like a skinned cow, all the flies are after me, the voracious flies, and my heart is a horrible beehive.)

What is again interesting here is that Electra does not compare herself to animals. Instead, her centre *is* a multitude of animals. (Her heart is a beehive.) She is followed closely by the flies. She is the flesh that attracts the flies, a materiality that tries to claim her. On the one hand, Strindberg, Brecht, and Sartre have long been considered part of the anthropocentric theatrical tradition, and the fetishisation of consciousness in Sartre confirms this assessment. On the other hand, however, the fact that the animal images in these writers' work go beyond the use of mere metaphors has clear implications, I argue, not only for the reading of the dramatic texts provided here, but also for the performance of these plays.

In addition to Electra's closeness to the natural-zoological world, the women of Argos in their black mourning attire resemble the flies of the play's title. The association between animals and feminised lack of consciousness also becomes clear when Aegisthus calls his subjects (the women of Argos), whom he keeps in a state of fear and does not want to know that they are free, 'chiens' (Sartre 1947: 165) ('dogs'). In addition, the apathy of the people of Argos, who fail to warn the returning Agamemnon of the impending violence and danger to his life, is linked to 'volupté' (voluptuousness) and 'une femme en rut' (a woman in heat). In the same passage, Jupiter then refers to an old woman – again *literally*, not just metaphorically – as an insect and a fish, as

> cette vieille cloporte, là-bas, qui trottine de ses petites pattes noires, en rasant les murs; c'est un beau spécimen de cette faune noire et plate qui grouille dans les lézardes. Je bondis sur l'insecte, je le saisis et je vous le ramène . . . Voilà ma pêche . . . Voyez ces soubresauts de poisson au bout d'une ligne. (Sartre 1947: 111)

> (this old wouldlouse (also: caretaker/concierge) that trots with its little paws closely along the walls, that's a beautiful specimen of this black and flat fauna that crawls in the cracks. I jump on the insect, I seize it, and I bring it back to you . . . That is my sin . . . Look how fish jump at the end of the line.)

The woman's 'voluptuousness' and silence are held responsible for Agamemnon's death and thus ultimately for bringing the flies to Argos. Referring to the murder of Agamemnon, Jupiter says to the old woman: 'Tu as rudement bien dû faire l'amour cette nuit-là' (Sartre 1947: 112) ('You must have made great love that night'). Uncontrolled, unmastered, abject sexuality and nonhuman nature are what Sartre's characters fear – a fear expressed in physiological nausea – and what at the same time exerts a deadly fascination on them.

Nausea, Mothers and Flies

The flies in Sartre's play are of course not the first insects we encounter in this study. You will recall that Strindberg's female protagonist in *Creditors* already appeared on stage as a thinly disguised predatory insect. Braidotti points to the qualities that make insects paradigmatic and that are, for our purposes, shared by Strindberg's Tekla: 'the fast rate of metamorphosis, the talents for parasitism, the power of mimetism or blending with their territory and environment . . . [t]heir hyperactive sexuality' (Braidotti 2011: 103–4). In her essay 'Bug Bytes: Insects, Information, and Interspecies Theatricality', Chaudhuri also asks about what accounts for not only playwrights' but our general human obsession with insects. Chaudhuri argues that this obsession has to do with insects' small size and their vast numbers – both traits that make insects mobile, hard to see, hard to control and thus threatening. Due to our sensory limitations, Braidotti argues, '[t]hey are a radical form of otherness' – an alien life form we can neither perceive, nor assimilate or expel. Having lived on earth for 300 million years, insects have an impressive pedigree in literature, philosophy and culture, from the Bible to their contemporary role as phobic objects in science fiction narratives and film, where they transgress the ontological boundaries between biology and technology, human and machine. Braidotti also refers to 'the insectoid and arachnoid terminology so often used to describe advanced technologies', including the World Wide Web and the role of insects (especially the fruit fly) in molecular research. Braidotti, in sum, sees insects as 'powerful indicators of the decentring of anthropocentrism (Braidotti 2011: 103–5). We will remember that this was the threat already enacted in Strindberg.

Insects are boundary crossers par excellence. They pollinate other species (plants). They invade other organisms' body boundaries or skins with poison, bites and stings, sometimes carrying deadly illnesses such as malaria (Braidotti 2011: 111). They easily transcend the most emotionally fraught boundaries – ontological as well as, given their size and mobility, spatial. Chaudhuri writes: 'Insects flout the boundaries we guard most obsessively: the walls of our homes – *home* is, of course, the most emotionally turbulent of geopathological sites – and the skin that encases our bodies.' As boundary invaders, insects are also agents of contamination or disease (Chaudhuri 2017a: 136). While Strindberg's women characters have invaded the home – the site central to bourgeois ideology and bourgeois domestic drama, the thematic of home is also central to the myth of an exile, Orestes, returning to the city of his birth in Sartre's play. Sartre's flies incarnate creaturely excess, the ontological fear of invasion by what is only projected outward – teeming animality – in *Les Mouches* as well as in other texts such as *La Nausée*. In *La Nausée*, cities – the phobically clean/sanitised and 'safe' space established exclusively by and for humans – figure as protection from an unruly and live 'wild nature', whose most threatening components are Vegetation (with a capital V) and animals:

> J'ai peur des villes. Mais il ne faut pas en sortir. Si on s'aventure trop loin, on rencontre le cercle de la Végétation. La Végétation a rampé pendant des kilomètres vers les villes. Elle attend. Quand la ville sera morte, la Végétation l'envahira, elle grimpera sur les pierres, elle les enserrera, les fouillera, les fera éclater de ses longues pinces noires; elle aveuglera les trous et laissera pendre partout des pattes vertes. Il faut rester dans les villes, tant qu'elles sont vivantes, il ne faut pas pénétrer [!] seul sous cette grande chevelure qui est à leurs portes: il faut la laisser onduler et craquer sans témoins. Dans les villes, si l'on sait s'arranger, choisir les heures où les bêtes digèrent ou dorment, dans leurs trous, derrière des amoncellements de détritus organiques, on ne rencontre guère que des minéraux, les moins effrayants des existants. (Sartre 1938: 217–18)

> (I am afraid of cities. But one must not leave them. If one ventures out too far, one encounters the circle of Vegetation. Vegetation has crawled for kilometers towards the cities. She waits. When the city is dead, Vegetation will invade it, she will climb on stones, she will encircle them, search them, she will make them burst with her long black pincers; she will block the holes and will let her green paws dangle everywhere. One has to stay in cities as long as they are alive, one must not penetrate [!] by oneself under this great mane that is at our doorstep; one must let her undulate and split things open without witnesses. In cities, if one knows how to manage and choose the hours when the animals digest or sleep in their holes, behind the heaps of organic garbage, one encounters hardly anything but minerals, the least scary of things alive.)

Sartre also addresses the unpredictabilty of what escapes the laws of the city – the threat of *live*, femininised nonhuman nature – in the following passage:

> Cependant, la grande nature vague s'est glissée dans leur ville, elle s'est infiltrée, partout, dans leurs maisons, dans leurs bureaux, en eux-mêmes. Elle ne bouge pas, elle se tient tranquille et eux, ils sont en plein dedans, ils la respirent et ils ne la voient pas, ils s'imaginent qu'elle est dehors, à vingt lieues de la ville. Je la *vois*, moi, cette nature, je la *vois* . . . Je sais que sa soumission est paresse, je sais qu'elle n'a pas de lois: ce qu'ils prennent pour sa constance . . . Elle n'a que des habitudes et elle peut en changer demain. (Sartre 1938: 221, emphasis in original)

> (Nevertheless big vague nature slid into their city, she seeped in, everywhere, into their houses, their offices, into their bodies. She does not move, she keeps quiet and they . . . they are fully inside, they breathe her and they do not *see* her, they imagine that she is outside, twenty leagues from the city. I do *see* her, this

nature, I *see* her . . . I know that her submission is laziness, I know that she does not have any laws: They take that for her dependability. She only has habits and she can change them tomorrow.)

Sartre's worldview is based on and depends on the material and ontological isolation of the human from the rampant physicality of the natural world. While Strindberg enacts the perceived threat posed by the disappearing dividing line between animality and humanity at the end of the nineteenth century, Sartre problematises the threat to human identity posed by the excluded other of modern discourses, namely vegetal life. As Nealon points out, for Hegel '[a]nimal desire is 'superior' . . . because that desire can be repressed, sublated, trained.' The Nazis would later speak of *Züchtung* (breeding). On the other hand, '[p]lant desire merely grows without telos, without a proper end', i.e. uncontrollably (Nealon 2016: 68). Pointing out the distinctions between 'wild' and domesticated plants, Nealon notes: 'It is this "wild" essence of *uncontrolled growth* [my emphasis] that earns plants their position as the "lowest" or most basic form of life (precisely insofar as growth and the ability to reproduce and die are the rudimentary markers for life in Western thinking' (2016: 31). The uncontrolled growth of plants, the unpredictability of a live materiality, threatens humans' exclusive claim to agency and their perceived autonomy.[10] When Nealon explains that 'on land the vegetable kingdom makes up 99 percent of the total biomass, and the ocean floor is home to ten million trillion microbes for every human on the planet' (Nealon 2016: 109), we realise that the threat to human dominance is real, so to speak. Not only that, but Sartre's description gives plants animal traits and movement (crawl, paws, mane, slid), establishing a continuity or coalition between plants and the animal kingdom. For Hegel, 'the plant must be "animalized" in the same way that the woman must be manned, the family must be nationed, and mere matter must be lifted up by spirit: without that sublating moment there is nothing but cancerous "natural" growth, without regard to betterment or higher ends: nutritive life without "world"' (Nealon 2016: 68–9). As Nealon writes and as we have seen in Strindberg, 'animals are figured as other not because of their absolute distance from modern definitions of 'man' but precisely because of their intimate, hidden subtending proximity' (Nealon 2016: 33). Sartre's protagonist ultimately only considers minerals as sufficiently removed from the human realm not to pose any lethal harm. Only minerals are 'the least scary of things alive' in the passage cited.

Nutritive life without a Heideggerian 'world', the *en-soi*, is the main threat in Sartre's early work, a threat that, as in Hegel, must be sublated or absorbed by the *pour-soi*, matter by spirit. In his summary of Derrida's *Glas*, Nealon encapsulates perfectly the threat enacted in Sartre's early work as well:

> Are humans ever lifted to the level of being 'for themselves [*pour-soi*],' giving themselves their own place? Or are humans somehow akin to plants – at the end of the day subject wholly to their environments, living, growing without entelechy, and dying indifferently: responding as they can to the events that happen around them, events or emergences within a physical world largely indifferent to any particular life-form 'as such' [*en-soi*]? (2016: 71)

What is at stake is human agency and human exceptionalism. Sartre shares Hegel's dream for philosophy and for the human in general: 'an originary force that in fact constitutes and lords over everything, all the rest' (Nealon 2016: 74). This dream is still possible in Sartre's early work, such as *Les Mouches*. His later work, such as his play *Les Séquestrés d'Altona* (*The Condemned of Altona*), for instance, shows us, however, that we are all *en-soi*. There, the protagonist, Frantz, will argue in his final words that any distinction between (violent, evil) animality and humanity is illusory, 'a misunderstanding'.[11]

Sartre's early work resembles Strindberg's plays in that the ontological threat of overproximity and indifferentiation posed to the (male) human is not only enacted or represented as an animal or plant threat, but is also feminised. The *patronne* (inn owner) of *La Nausée*, not only because of her skin colour, but also due to her maternal traits a 'white woman' in Theweleit's sense, conjures up the fear of the devouring mother. Her scent, the scent of 'a newborn child', links her to maternity. Whereas this mother figure smothers the narrator, pressing him against her maternal breast, he rescues himself psychologically by 'distractedly' evoking the image of another male figure and 'intellectual' pursuits. The narrator's reaction to feminised sexuality – again expressed in tropes of lower flora and fauna – is a feeling of disgust and physiological sickness. The verb 'vomir' not only evokes physiological disgust, vomiting also marks a border transgression, the transgression of the bodily boundary between inside and outside and, thus, abjection.

> J'ai dîné au *Rendezvous des Cheminots*. La patronne étant là, j'ai dû la baiser, mais c'était bien par politesse. Elle me dégoûte un peu, elle est trop blanche et puis elle sent le nouveau-né. Elle me serrait la tête contre sa poitrine dans un débordement de passion: elle croit bien faire. Pour moi, je grapillais distraitement son sexe sous les couvertures; puis mon bras s'est engourdi. Je pensais a

M. de Rollebon: après tout, qu'est-ce qui m'empêche d'écrire un roman sur sa vie? J'ai laissé aller mon bras le long du flanc de la patronne et j'ai vu soudain un petit jardin avec des arbres bas et larges d'où pendaient d'immenses feuilles couvertes de poils. Des fourmis couraient partout, des mille-pattes et des teignes. Il y avait des bêtes encore plus horribles: leurs corps était fait d'une tranche de pain grillé comme on en met en canapé sous les pigeons; elles marchaient de côté avec des pattes de crabe. Les larges feuilles étaient toutes noires de bêtes. Derrière des cactus et des figuiers de Barbarie, la Velléda du Jardin public désignait son sexe du doigt. 'Ce jardin sent le vomi', criai-je. (Sartre 1938: 88–9)

(I had dinner at the *Railway Workers' Meeting Place*. The manager was there, I had to sleep with her, but it was only out of politeness. She disgusts me a bit, she is too white and she also smells like a newborn baby. She pulled my head against her chest in an excess of passion: she thought she was doing the right thing. As for me, I distractedly picked her genitals under the covers, then my arm fell asleep. I thought of Monsieur Rollebon: After all, why should I not write a novel about his life? I let my arm slide down the manager's side and I suddenly saw a little garden with small and tall trees from which enormous leaves were hanging, covered with hair. Ants were running everywhere, millipedes and ringworms. There were animals that were still more horrible: their bodies were made of grilled bread slices like those we put under roasted pigeons; they walked to the side with crab legs. The large leaves were all black with animals. Behind the cacti and fig trees of the Maghreb, the Velleda moth of the City Garden was pointing to its genitals. 'This park smells like vomit,' I cried.)

As Kristeva explains, citing similar passages, the expulsion of what is inside – nausea/vomiting – is a protective mechanism necessary to the subject's ego formation.[12] In the passage quoted, vomiting is a protective mechanism that abjects the threatening inner drives and protects the ego from dissolution, from being engulfed by the devouring mother, re-establishing a 'safe distance'. The link that Sartre establishes between abjection and plants, animals and women to a certain extent puts in question Nealon's argument of the categorically different treatment of animals and plants in modern philosophy.[13] As we have seen, Brecht's *Baal* also establishes the ontological continuity between animals and plants (and natural forces such as the wind). My argument concerning Strindberg resonates with Nealon's diagnosis of the animal's overproximity in modernity. In Sartre's early texts (countering Nealon's argument), this overproximity does also apply to plants (and, as in Strindberg, to women). In contrast to Strindberg and Sartre, as I have shown, Brecht on the other hand establishes an *affirmative* intimacy with the natural world (and the maternal as part of this natural-biological world).

In contrast to Brecht but again similar to Strindberg, matrophobia, the fear of the archaic mother as primary abject, finds its expression in

Les Mouches, where the feminised Erinyes constitute a perversion of maternal love and are linked to animals, fluids, floods and inundation. At the beginning of the first scene of Act III, the Erinyes sleep standing up 'comme des échassiers', like waders, a kind of bird. The First Erinye speaks of the 'délices de se sentir griffes et mâchoires' (Sartre 1947: 214) ('the delight of feeling one's claws and jaws'). The Erinyes also describe themselves as dogs ('molosse'), insects ('bourdonnement', the humming of flies, bees), forest animals and they state that they will only give up their place to the worms in the grave. When Electra wakes up, Orestes says: 'Tu étais si belle, hier. On dirait qu'une bête t'a ravagé la face avec ses griffes' (Sartre 1947: 218) ('You were so beautiful yesterday. You look like some wild animal has *ravaged* [my emphasis] your face with its claws'). The wild animals in question are the Furies. Orestes calls them 'chiennes' (female dogs) and orders them to go to their 'niche', their kennel (Sartre 1947: 218). In Aeschylus' version of the Oresteia, the Erinyes incarnate spirit. In Sartre's adaption, the First Erinye, conjuring up images of the engulfing and suffocating mother, declares that she will roll on Orestes' and Electra's stomachs and chests 'comme *un torrent* sur des cailloux' (Sartre 1947: 213) ('like a *torrent* under pebbles', emphasis added) and further states: 'La haine *m'inonde et me suffoque*, elle monte dans mes seins *comme du lait*' (Sartre 1947: 214, emphasis added) ('Hatred *inundates* and *suffocates* me. It [literally 'she'] climbs up into my breasts *like milk*', emphasis added). The Erinye then further predicts her penetration of Electra's body: 'J'entrerai en toi comme le mâle en la femelle, car tu es mon épouse, et tu sentiras le poids de mon amour' (Sartre 1947: 214) ('I will enter you like the male the female, because you are my wife, and you will feel the weight of my love'). Similar to fluids, the Erinyes, who are (traditionally and also in Sartre) depicted as women, overstep and blur boundaries – including bodily boundaries and the boundaries between male and female sexuality. Moreover, as in Aeschylus, the Erinyes are associated with putrefaction and pus (Sartre 1947: 216), a contamination of clean, proper matter with improper matter.

In *Les Mouches*, the threat posed by abjection is embodied not only by the Erinyes, but also by the flies that give the play its name. The link between Electra, animals and feminised abjection becomes even clearer when Aegisthus orders Electra to leave town. He declares that if she is still inside the city walls – i.e. the masculinised inside or centre – the next day at dawn, she will be slaughtered like a mangy sheep (Sartre 1947: 166). Electra, who, like a mangy sheep, is threatening contamination, needs to be expelled from the centre, ab-jected. After this abjection, she is – like Agamben's *homo sacer* – outside human law. When Electra's dance is interrupted by Jupiter, the people call Electra a seductress and a witch: 'Nous n'avons rien fait, ça n'est pas notre faute, elle est venue, elle nous a séduits par ses paroles empoisonnées! A la rivière, la sorcière, à la rivière! Au bûcher!' (Sartre 1947: 164–5) ('We have done nothing wrong, it is not our fault, she came, she seduced us with her poisonous words! To the river, witch, to the river! To the stake!'). Hans Peter Duerr (1985) analyses the witch as a woman who continually crosses the boundary between inside and outside, culture and nature, civilisation and wilderness,[14] the human and the nonhuman realms.

Because she is still representing Agamemnon's masculine claim until Orestes comes to replace her in that role, the Electra of the beginning of *Les Mouches* and finally Orestes, the male hero who has recognised his existential freedom, are the only two instances in the play where abjection seems to be presented as a positive force. As the discussion of the viscous and of sexual desire in *L'Etre et le néant* will show as well, Sartre's work gives expression to the extreme fear of feminised abjection and nonhuman materiality that marks the anthropocentric patriarchal western philosophical tradition. While Sartre's atheist existentialist work opposes the idea of divine transcendence, it posits a transcendence of immanence based on human consciousness. In Sartre, this humanist transcendence is threatened, however, by what Vicky Kirby calls, in *Telling Flesh*, 'the primeval ooze of nature's sticky immanence', an immanence associated, in the Cartesian patriarchal tradition, with women's bodies (Kirby 1997: 59). As an attempt to fend off this threat, Sartre's work is an example of the modern and ultimately fascist immunitarian logic discussed by Esposito – a paradigm that defends against the perceived threat of contagion.

Slime

Given recent discoveries in the sciences of our own time, it is highly ironic that Sartre chooses slime as the substance that threatens to blur the boundaries of his rigid anthropocentric philosophical system, the boundaries between feminised dead matter and human masculinised consciousness or cognition. As Jacqueline Dalziell explains in her brilliant contribution, 'Microbiology as Sociology: The Strange Sociality of Slime' (2017), *Physarum polycephalum*, an acellular slime mould, has in recent years been the object of much scientific study, 'due in part to its unexpected level of cognitive literacy', including '[i]ts ability to consistently calculate and take the shortest path to any destination . . . a surprising level of sophistication for a brain-less organism without a nervous system'. In experiments that, for the most part, test forms of intelligence

> [r]esearch has discovered that slime moulds 'learn', 'memorise' events and routes, 'make decisions', 'form preferences', selectively forage for food, and solve with unexpected accuracy a range of complex challenges that scientists have set them. So far *Physarum* has accurately anticipated the itinerary of the Silk Road, outwitted human engineers in transport network organization, solved puzzles which supercomputers cannot, replaced machines to control microchips, and driven robots. (Dalziell 2017: 154–5)

As it turns out, in terms of 'what is classically thought of as intelligence (memory, rationality, forethought)', *Physarum* 'measure[s] up rather well' (Dalziell 2017: 155). In fact, this brainless slime's body is 'directly cognizant'; 'its intelligence is immediately corporeal' (Dalziell 2017: 170). It is thus an organism that, in all of its stages, completely blurs the distinction between body and consciousness. As Dalziell puts it: 'matter is the capacity to think, to cognize. Put differently, cognizing is a material imperative. If matter is always already thoughtful, and biology intellectually animated from its genesis, then mindfulness must appear through, and as, embodiment' (Dalziell 2017: 170–1). Mind and biological body are one.

In this context, Sartre's aversion to slime specifically, his view of border-crossing slime as the ultimate threat to human exceptionalism, then seems almost visionary. More than Sartre could fully realise at his time, slime as a nonhuman substance appears indeed to be in a prime position to put in question humanity's claim to uniqueness and the fundamental binary categories on which Sartre's philosophical system is based. Consciousness is not the result of a human choice or quality that separates humans from mere matter, as claimed by Sartre or the Cartesian tradition as a whole. Consciousness *is* the body. The implications of Dalziell's investigation do not stop with slime or even with living, biological organisms: 'If slime can cognize, can a drop of oil? Can a particle of light?' (Dalziell 2017: 171). Dalziell ends her argument by asking: 'what *if* Nature thinks?' (Dalziell 2017: 173). And what if, as Astrida Neimanis (following Kirby's work) puts it, '*everything is representation*' (Neimanis 2017: 183, emphasis in original)? What if everything is meaning, or meanings? What if the cosmos or Being is nature self-representing itself in its modes of becoming?

Sartre himself sees the opposition between the human or consciousness and materiality or nature as deeply threatened. When it comes to the thematisation of slimy viscosity, Sartre's *Les Mouches* again clearly complements *L'Etre et le néant*. In the subchapter 'La Psychanalyse existentielle' ('Existential Psychoanalysis') of the latter, Sartre describes the threat posed to the *pour-soi* (for-itself) by the viscous, a clearly negativised, 'hostile' and 'horrible' state. The slimy, despite its repulsive character, exerts a deadly, trap-like fascination, posing the threat of fusion, degradation, ego-dissolution,[15] and again engulfment by the (m)other. Sartre conjures up the threat of the sugary death of the for-itself, which is compared to a wasp drowning in jam. The physiological reaction to the viscous is 'a sweetish sort of disgust' (Manser 1962: 12), nausea.[16] Like the abject or the flesh, what Santner calls 'this gelatinous stuff' (Santner 2016: 134), the slimy, is essentially ambiguous, a 'substance between two states' (Sartre 1992: 607), in this case between solid and liquid matter.

Again, the science of the twenty-first century confirms the taxonomic confusion posed by slime, by *Physarum*:

> *Physarum* was initially thought to be a kind of fungus, but it was later discovered to be a protist. According to biologist Chris Reid of The Social Insects Laboratory, this taxonomic group embraces 'everything we don't really understand' . . . In terms of both taxonomisation and species being it is, for scientists, unsettlingly indeterminate. (Dalziell 2017: 155)

'[S]patially plural, yet ontologically singular', *Physarum*, the 'many headed slime', poses a problematic of identity and individual or collective agency, negating any notion of 'either a strict social determinism, or free will' (Dalziell 2017: 155, 156, 159). It problematises, in other words, the very concepts that are central to Sartre's work, challenging his phobic separation of androcentric and anthropocentric individual identity from the feminised or nonhuman collective. For Sartre, the encounter of for-itself and in-itself is an encounter between masculinised mind (solid) and feminised and sexualised[17] matter (liquid). The ensuing matter, the viscous or slimy, as well is feminised: 'It is a soft, yielding action, a moist and feminine sucking.'[18]

Whereas the masculinised *pour-soi* attempts to absorb and possess the feminised *en-soi* (in-itself), the slimy resists this project of assimilation and turns the tables on the for-itself, in turn appropriating it. The clear distinction between the in-itself and the for-itself, the clear delineation of classificatory boundaries, is thus impossible to maintain. Abjection sets in. In this context, it is interesting to compare the reaction to the viscous – which is ultimately the reaction to abjection and the threat of maternal engulfment and sexuality – to Sartre's description (also in *L'Etre et le néant*) of sexual desire, which is associated with fear, the fear of the erasure of the rational, conscious ego and 'une douceur lourde et pâteuse' (a heavy and thick sweetness). Sexual desire, due to the threat it poses to consciousness of being invaded, *submerged* by the fluvial facticity of the *en-soi*[19] – as opposed to the 'dry' characteristics of hunger – has to be subdued, repressed.

By the end of *Les Mouches*, the threatening force embodied by Electra has been contained and transferred to – not to say absorbed by – the male hero. Nature, the *en-soi*, has been raised and transformed in the Hegelian dialectic and has become culture.[20] *Masculinised* violence and sexuality, however, are depicted as positive. In the following passage Orestes addresses his sister, who here is identified with the feminised city. For Sartre any encounter with the feminised other is a project of forceful appropriation, not to say rape.

> Viens Electre, regarde notre ville. Elle est là, *rouge sous le soleil, bourdonnante d'hommes et de mouches*, dans l'engourdissement têtu d'un après-midi d'été; *elle me repousse* de tous ses murs, de tous ses toits, de toutes ses portes closes. *Et pourtant elle est à prendre*, je le sens depuis ce matin. *Et toi aussi, Electre, tu es à prendre. Je vous prendrai. Je deviendrai hache et je fendrai en deux ces murailles obstinées, j'ouvrirai le ventre de ces maisons bigotes*, elles exhaleront par leurs plaies béantes une odeur de mangeaille et d'encens; *je deviendrai cognée et je m'enfoncerai dans le coeur de cette ville comme la cognée dans le coeur d'un chêne.* (Sartre 1947: 179, my emphasis)

> (Come, Electra, look at our city. It/She is there, *red* under the sun, *humming with men and flies*, in the stubborn numbness of a summer afternoon; *she repels me* with all her walls, with all her roofs, with all her closed doors. And *still, she must be taken*, I have sensed it since the morning. *And you as well, Electra, you must be taken. I will take you both. I will become the ax and I will split these obstinate walls in two, I will open the belly of these sanctimonious houses*, they will exhale an odor of grub and incense through their gaping wounds; *I will become the hatchet and will thrust myself in the heart of this city like the hatchet in the heart of an oak tree.*) (My emphasis)

Reinforcing again the philosophical proximity of *Les Mouches* and *L'Etre et le néant*, the theme of appropriation also gains particular insistence in Part Four of the latter.

Sartre in the end critiques neither the *pour-soi*'s attempt to establish mastery nor the basic binary and oppositional structure of patriarchal immunitarian thinking. Instead, his work is itself a product of the logic of mastery and domination: the power struggle between the for-itself and the in-itself in Sartre's philosophy and theatrical *oeuvre* is a variation of the struggle for domination and immunity protection against contagion that characterises both modern thought and practice and its extreme expression, totalitarian thanato-politics. This struggle negates playful ambivalence, abjects it and affirms dualistic structures.

Antithetical Rigidity

The fundamental concepts of Sartre's philosophy in *L'Etre et le néant*, namely *pour-soi*, *en-soi*, *pour-autrui* and *en-soi-pour-soi* are based on Hegel (*Fürsich, Ansich, Für-Andere, An und für sich*).[21] It was Hegel who in *Phänomenologie des Geistes* theorised the master–slave dialectic, the dichotomy between 'Herr' (master) and 'Knecht' (slave, servant). He distinguishes between two forms of consciousness ('zwey entgegengesetzte Gestalten des Bewußtseyns'): 'die eine das selbständige, welchem das Fürsichseyn, die andere das unselbständige, dem das Leben oder das Seyn für ein anderes, das Wesen ist; jenes ist der Herr, diß der Knecht' (Hegel 1980: 112) ('the one/first is the independent one, to which the being-for-itself is the essence, the other is the dependent one, to which the life or the being-for-others is the essence: the former is the master, the latter the slave'). Contrary to Hegel, however, Sartre denies the possibility of a synthesis or mediation between the subject (*pour-soi*) and the object (*en-soi*).

Although the goal of the for-itself's totalising appropriation is the establishment of the in-itself-for-itself, although, according to Sartre, man's desire is to be simultaneously *en-soi* and *pour-soi* – self-sufficient like a thing, but endowed with the freedom human consciousness provides – the totality of *en-soi-pour-soi*[22] is ultimately illusory. In Sartre's philosophy, the higher dialectical synthesis which Christianity identifies with God[23] and Hegel with Absolute Knowledge remains an unachievable ideal. As Sartre's drama *Huis clos* (*No Exit*) – the offspring of Strindberg's *Creditors* and *The Dance of Death* – with its famous proclamation 'L'enfer c'est les autres' ('hell is other people') demonstrates, for Sartre, the basic relationship with others or the Other/alterity consists of irreconcilable conflict:

> Pendant que je tente de me libérer de l'emprise d'autrui, autrui tente de se libérer de la mienne; pendant que je cherche à asservir autrui, autrui cherche à m'asservir. Il ne s'agit nullement ici de relations unilatérales avec un objet-en-soi, mais de rapports réciproques et mouvants . . . Le conflit est le sens originel de l'être-pour-autrui. (Sartre 1943: 431)

> (While I try to free myself from the control of the other, the other tries to free himself from mine: while I seek to enslave the other, the other seeks to enslave

me. There is no question whatsoever here of unilateral relations with an object-in-itself, but of reciprocal and moving relations ... Conflict is the original meaning of the being-for-the-other.)

In contrast to a Hegelian recognition of the self in the other and an ensuing reconciliation, in Sartre, Dominick LaCapra correctly notes, 'the dialectic of self and "other" remains open at the price of total war' (LaCapra 1978: 135). In Sartre's dualistic ontology, mutual influence or exchange – intersubjectivity in Jessica Benjamin's sense or Karen Barad's intra-activity – does not take place: 'Les subjectivités demeurent hors d'atteinte et radicalement séparés' (Sartre 1943: 498) ('Subjectivities remain out of reach and radically separate'). In *No Exit*, Anthony Manser observes, 'all three characters are in hell precisely because they are prevented by their own choices from establishing any proper relations with those around them' (Manser 1962: 98). The inability to form object relations is also one of the dominant features of the fascist psychological constitution as analysed by Theweleit. Esposito discusses the threat community poses to individual autonomy as central to the modern biopolitical immunitarian paradigm that ultimately led to the thanato-politics of totalitarianism. As he puts it, 'relation carries mortal danger' (Esposito 2010: 29).

The fetishisation of consciousness in Sartre is an attempt at redemption, an attempt in other words to imagine the human body as the master of its metaphysical destiny and of the material, more-than-human conditions and agents that surround, drive and form it.[24] The result of Sartre's fear of difference and of the antithetical rigidity that ensues from it, the result of the fight for the subject position at the expense of the other's reduction to bare life, however, is isolation. The pattern of domination prevalent in patriarchal society 'leaves the self encapsulated in a closed system' (Benjamin 1988: 67). As Esposito points out, the loss of community is the price to be paid for immunity. Although existential freedom is a key term in his work, for Sartre the problem does not consist in realising human freedom in the world, but in defending it from the world. He writes in *La Nausée*, for example:

Le voilà encore qui me regarde. Cette fois il va me parler, je me sens tout raide. Ce n'est pas de la sympathie qu'il y a entre nous: nous sommes pareils, voilà. Il est seul comme moi, mais plus enfoncé que moi dans la solitude. Il doit attendre sa Nausée ou quelque chose de ce genre. Il y a donc à présent des gens qui me *reconnaissent*, qui pensent, après m'avoir dévisagé: 'Celui-là est des nôtres.' Eh bien? Que veut-il? Il doit bien savoir que nous ne pouvons rien l'un pour l'autre. Les familles sont dans leurs maisons, au milieu de leurs souvenirs. Et nous voici, deux épaves sans mémoire. S'il se levait tout d'un coup, s'il m'adressait la parole, je sauterais en l'air. (Sartre 1938: 97, emphasis in original)

(There he is looking at me. This time he is going to speak to me, I feel all stiff. What there is between us has nothing to do with liking each other: we are similar, that's all. He is alone like me, but sunk deeper into loneliness than me. He must be waiting for his Nausea or something of that sort. So there are right now people who *recognise* me, who think, after having stared at me: 'That one is one of us.' And so? What does he want? He must well know that we cannot do anything for each other. The families are in their houses, in the middle of their memories. And we are here, two shipwrecks without memory. If he got up all of a sudden, if he started to speak to me, I would jump.)

Tied as it is to the control or threat exerted by the other, Sartre's concept of freedom is thus reactive and secondary. As such it precludes true autonomy.[25] As an existentialist, Sartre belongs to what Elizabeth Grosz describes as 'those philosophical traditions in which the questions of freedom and autonomy are irremediably tied to the functioning and deprivatory power of the (oppressive or dominant) other – that is, the tradition of dialectical phenomenology that dates from Hegel, through Marxism, and influences and inflects existentialism, structuralism and poststructuralism' (Grosz 2010: 140). As I have argued above in the context of Hegel, however, these traditions also emphasise an *Aufhebung* or synthesis (or in the case of poststructuralism a deconstruction) of binary or dialectical relationships. Even the cultural universalism of structuralism had its impetus, in the work of its maybe most famous proponent, the anthropologist Claude Lévi-Strauss, for instance, in the attempt to overcome the binarism between 'high' and 'primitive' cultures. As my comparative references to Camus also show, moreover, all existentialisms are not the same. Sartre's early work, however, clearly fits Grosz's description.

Because of his ontological, inherent dependence on the ability to defend against an unmasterable, threatening other, true autonomy or agency in other words eludes Sartre's subject: 'Autrui est par principe l'insaisissable: il me fuit quand je le cherche et me possède quand je le fuis' (Sartre 1943: 479) ('The other is by definition elusive: he escapes me when I look for him and possesses me when I flee from him'). Human solidarity and identification with the other in Camus's sense cannot be realised in Sartre's system of thought.[26] Here it becomes clear that the universal responsibility that Sartre advocates, the Kantian 'universality of man',[27] in fact only consists of a fending off of the others' threat to one's own subjectivity, an absorption instead of others' subject positions, and an imposition of one's own choice on them: 'Tout ce qui vaut pour moi vaut pour autrui' (Sartre 1943: 431) ('Anything that is true for me is true for him').[28] In *Les Mouches*, Orestes appropriates Electra's freedom. His project, the existentialist project of recovering himself, is ultimately a project of absorbing the other, an absorption of the negative that is paradigmatic of the Hegelian dialectic and required to give consciousness greater strength.[29] Since human empathy is unachievable, however, Orestes remains free, but alone. At the end of the play, he again leaves Argos. His hero's displacement and homelessness in an absurd, radically immanent universe is Sartre's modern enactment of tragedy. The community that is (arguably) restored at the end of Attic tragedy, however, has been lost in Sartre.

Contrary to Sartre's claim to an unequivocally antifascist ideological stance, his early work[30] thus shows traits that are reminiscent of the characteristics of fascist texts. Sartre establishes a dualistic, immunitarian philosophical system as a protective armour against the perceived threat that feminised border-crossing abjection and nonhuman materiality pose to hegemonic human/male consciousness. If, as Esposito has argued, totalitarian thanato-politics constitutes the paroxysm of the immunitarian structures of European modernity, modern France also bears the roots of fascism within it. The exploration of the work of one of France's most influential writers and leading intellectuals of the twentieth century confirms this assessment.

Notes

1. Since I am interested in literal (rather than metaphorical) readings, I am choosing to provide my own translations of Sartre's texts in an attempt to stay as close to the original as possible. I will, however, additionally be using Hazel Barnes's translation of *L'Etre et le néant* (*Being and Nothingness*) (and will indicate when I do so). Barnes's translation is generally considered the gold standard.

2. Following Sartre's essay 'Paris sous l'Occupation' ('Paris Under Occupation') (1949b), which describes the Vichy regime's cult of remorse and national defeat, the attitude (in Sartre's play) of the people of Argos, who live in fear and remorse, can indeed be read as a critique of the attitude of the French people during the Nazi occupation. Moreover, it is possible to interpret the character of Jupiter as Hitler and Aegisthus as the Vichy government or Pétain. In his Sartre biography, Ronald Hayman furthermore argues that Clytemnestra represents a collaborator: 'The queen represents the docile conformism of occupied France: "For fifteen years we have kept silent, and only our eyes betray us"' (Hayman 1987: 187). Hayman's reading makes Orestes and Electra into something like Resistance fighters.

Like Orestes' liberation of Argos, the *Résistance* was 'a movement not of revolution but of revolt. It had no intention of taking power after the war; its single goal was to liberate France from the occupying Nazi forces' (McCall 1967: 23). Finally, we can also read the critique of paternalistic authority structures in Sartre's play as a critique of Pétain's speeches proclaiming the renewal of France along the lines of a clerical and restorative paternalism (Kohut 1971: 158).

3. One notable exception is Joseph (1991).
4. See Fraunhofer (1997).
5. Cf. Sartre (1976a: 34): 'The first thing the Germans did was to forbid Jews access to swimming pools; it seemed to them that if the body of an Israelite were to plunge into that confined body of water, the water would be completely befouled. Strictly speaking, the Jew contaminates even the air he breathes.'
6. As Carroll points out, 'Sartre was certainly not alone among political theorists of the left in characterizing the fascist as a "failed male" or homosexual. Theodor Adorno, in a section of *Minima Moralia* . . . [w]ritten in 1944 and entitled "Tough Baby," made the sweeping claim that "totalitarianism and homosexuality belong together"' (Carroll 1995: 152). See also Hewitt (1996). Theweleit takes up – and for a long and disturbing time goes along with – the conflation of homosexuality and fascism in order eventually to prove it wrong.
7. The stone imagery is also used in Sartre's *Le Sursis* (*The Reprieve*). Cf. Sartre (1945: 285 and 1976a: 18–19).
8. Cf. Léni in *Les Séquestrés d'Altona*, Estelle or Inès in *Huis clos* (*No Exit*), Jessica in *Les Mains sales* (*Dirty Hands*), Lizzie in *La Putain respectueuse* (*The Respectful Prostitute*) and Catherine in *Le Diable et le bon dieu* (*The Devil and the Good Lord*).
9. In the section 'Patterns of Bad Faith' of *Being and Nothingness*, Sartre poses the question: 'What must be the being of man if he is to be capable of bad faith?' When he starts to answer this question in the next paragraph, his first sentence starts: 'Take the example of a woman' (Sartre 1992: 96). On the following page, Sartre predictably concludes: 'We shall say that this woman is in bad faith' (1992: 97). 'Man' on the other hand is associated with candour, sincerity, with the opposite of bad faith: 'If man is what he is, bad faith is forever impossible and candor ceases to be his ideal and becomes instead his being' (Sartre 1992: 101).
10. Elaine Miller writes: 'The plant is radically opposed to the figure of the organism as autonomous and oppositional' (Miller 2004: 116).
11. Cf. Sartre (1960a: 222 and 1960b: 374–5).
12. Cf. Kristeva (1982: 2–3):

> Loathing an item of food, a piece of filth, waste, or dung. The spasms and vomiting that protect me. The repugance, the retching that thrusts me to the side and turns me away from defilement, sewage, and muck

> . . . Food loathing is perhaps the most elementary and most archaic form of abjection . . . I experience a gagging sensation and, still farther down, spasms in the stomach, the belly . . . *nausea* makes me balk at that milk cream, separates me from the mother and father who proffer it. 'I' want none of that element, sign of their desire; 'I' do not want to listen, 'I' do not assimilate it, 'I' expel it. But since the food is not an 'other' for 'me,' who am only in their desire, I expel *myself* out, I abject *myself* within the same motion through which 'I' claim to establish myself . . . that trifle turns me inside out, guts sprawling; it is thus that *they* see that 'I' am in the process of becoming an other at the expense of my own death. During that course in which 'I' become, I give birth to myself amid the violence of sobs, of vomit. (Emphases in original)

13. Cf., for example, Nealon (2016: 33–4).
14. Duerr (1985: 46):

> As late as the Middle Ages, the witch was still the *hagazussa*, a being that sat on the *Hag*, the fence, which passed behind the gardens and separated the village from the wilderness. She was a being who participated in both worlds. As we might say today, she was semi-demonic. In time, however, she lost her double features and evolved more and more into a representation of what was being expelled from culture, only to return, distorted, in the night.

15. Cf., for example, Sartre (1943: 701:

> Si j'enfonce dans l'eau, si j'y plonge, si je m'y laisse couler, je ne ressens aucune gêne car je n'ai, à aucun degré, la crainte de m'y diluer: je demeure un solide dans sa fluidité. Si j'enfonce dans le visqueux, je sens que je vais m'y perdre, c'est-à-dire me diluer au visqueux, précisément parce que le visqueux est en instance de solidification.

> (If I submerge myself in water, if I dive into it, if I let myself flow there, I feel no discomfort since I have no fear whatsoever of becoming diluted there; I remain a solid mass in its fluidity. If I submerge myself into the viscous, I feel that I will lose myself there, that is become diluted in the viscous, precisely because the viscous is undergoing solidication.)

16. Cf. Sartre (1943: 404):

> Cette saisie perpétuelle par mon pour-soi d'un goût *fade* et sans distance qui m'accompagne jusque dans mes efforts pour m'en délivrer et qui est *mon* goût, c'est ce que nous avons décrit ailleurs sous le nom de *Nausée*. Une nausée discrète et insurmontable révèle perpétuellement mon corps à ma conscience: il peut arriver que nous recherchions l'agréable ou la douleur physique pour nous en délivrer, mais dès que la douleur ou l'agréable sont existés [*sic*] par la conscience, ils manifestent à leur tour sa facticité et sa contingence et c'est sur fond de nausée qu'ils se dévoilent. Loin que nous devions comprendre ce terme de *nausée* comme une métaphore tirée de nos écoeurements physiologiques, c'est, au contraire, sur son fondement que se produisent toutes les nausées concrètes et

empiriques (nausées devant la viande pourrie, le sang frais, les excréments, etc.) qui nous conduisent au vomissement.

This perpetual apprehension on the part of my for-itself of an insipid taste which I cannot place, which accompanies me even in my efforts to get away from it, and which is my taste-this is what we have described elsewhere under the name of Nausea. A dull and inescapable nausea perpetually reveals my body to my consciousness. Sometimes we look for the pleasant or for physical pain to free ourselves from this nausea; but as soon as the pain and the pleasure are existed [*sic*] by consciousness, they in turn manifest its facticity and its contingency; and it is on the ground of this nausea that they are revealed. We must not take the term nausea as a metaphor derived from our physiological disgust. On the contrary, we must realize that it is on the foundation of this nausea that all concrete and empirical nauseas (nausea caused by spoiled meat, fresh blood, excrement, etc.) are produced and make us vomit. (Sartre 1992: 338–9)

17. Cf. again the animal imagery ('leech-like', 'suction cups' (Sartre 1992: 608).

18. Cf. also Sartre (1943: 699: 'comme l'étalement, le raplatissement des seins un peu mûrs d'une femme qui s'étend sur le dos' ('like the spreading, the flattening of the somewhat ripe breasts of a woman who lies down on her back').

19. Cf. Sartre 1943, p. 457:

> [o]n sait que dans le désir sexuel la conscience est comme empâtée, il semble qu'on se laisse envahir par la facticité . . . on dit (. . .) qu'il *vous submerge* . . . le plus faible désir est déjà submergeant . . . La conscience alourdie et pâmée glisse vers un alanguissement comparable au sommeil.

> (One knows that in sexual desire . . . consciousness is as if thickened, it seems that one lets oneself be invaded by facticity . . . one says . . . that it *submerges you* . . . the weakest desire is already submerging . . . Weighted down and lost consciousness slides towards a languid state comparable to sleep.)

20. Cf. Nealon (2016: 67).

21. Aronson also points out that '*L'Etre et le Néant* bears the traces of [Heidegger's] *Being and Time* on virtually every page . . . Heidegger's *Dasein* becomes Sartre's *pour-soi*, inauthenticity becomes bad faith, facticity and thrownness (*Geworfenheit*) become contingency. Sartre also takes over Heidegger's distinction between fear and anguish and his notion of *Dasein* existing in terms of its possibilities' (Aronson 1980: 94). Cf. also Aronson (1980: 95): 'Taking the term being-in-itself (*être-en-soi, an-sich-sein*) directly from Heidegger, he reverses its meaning.' Contrary to Heidegger, Sartre stresses the primacy of the thing; the in-itself is prior to consciousness.

22. Sartre's term is obviously a translation of Hegel's *an-und-für-sich*.

23. Cf. Sartre (1943: 653):

> La valeur fondamentale qui préside à ce projet est justement l'en-soi-pour-soi, c'est-à-dire l'idéal d'une conscience qui serait fondement de son propre être-en-soi par la pure conscience qu'elle prendrait d'elle-même. C'est cet idéal qu'on peut nommer Dieu. Ainsi peut-on dire que ce qui rend le mieux concevable le projet fondamental de la réalité humaine, c'est que l'homme est l'être qui projette d'être Dieu.

> (The fundamental value presiding over this project is exactly the in-itself-for-itself, in other words the ideal of a consciousness that would be the foundation of its own being-in-itself through the pure consciousness that it would have of itself. It is this ideal that can be called God. Thus we can say that what makes the fundamental project of human reality best conceivable is that man is the being that contemplates being God.)

24. Cf. Orlie (2010): 'The "mind" is the means by which the body imagines itself as master of the conditions of its experience' (123).
25. Cf. Grosz (2010): 'If we rely on a concept of freedom that is linked to the controlling power of the other . . . we abandon in advance the concept of autonomy . . . Such an understanding of freedom . . . is reactive, secondary, peripheral' (153).
26. Cf. Sartre (1943: 501–2):

> Vainement souhaiterait-on un nous humain dans lequel la totalité intersubjective prendrait conscience d'elle-même comme subjectivité unifiée, un semblable idéal ne saurait être qu'une rêverie . . . L'essence des rapports entre consciences n'est pas le Mitsein, c'est le conflit.

> (In vain would one wish for a human us in which intersubjective totality would become conscious of itself as a unified subjectivity; such an ideal would only be a dream . . . The essence of relations between different consciousnesses is not the being-together, it is conflict.)

27. Cf., for example, Sartre (1970: 70): 'En ce sens nous pouvons dire qu'il y a une universalité de l'homme; mais elle n'est pas donnée, elle est perpétuellement construite. Je construis l'universel en me choisissant' ('In this sense we can say that there is a universality of man, but it is not given, it is forever being constructed. I construct the universal by choosing me') and Sartre (1970: 74): 'il engage par son choix l'humanité entière, et il ne peut pas éviter de choisir' ('he engages all of mankind through his choice, and he cannot avoid choosing').
28. Cf. also, for example, Sartre (1970: 26):

> Si l'existence, d'autre part, précède l'essence et que nous voulions exister en même temps que nous façonnons notre image, cette image est valable pour tous et pour notre époque tout entière. Ainsi, notre responsabilité est beaucoup plus grande que nous pourrions le supposer, car elle engage l'humanité entière.

> If existence, on the other hand, precedes essence and if we want to exist
> at the same time that we are fashioning our image, this image is valid for
> all and for our entire age. Thus our responsibility is much bigger than we
> could think, since it engages all of humanity.

29. Cf. Nealon (2016: 63), discussing Derrida's *Glas*: '. . . Hegel is a thinker
of animal desire as the engine of knowledge and progress, but this animal
desire must be negated and raised – made culturally respectable by spirit.'

30. My reading does not automatically claim validity for Sartre's later work,
such as *Critique de la raison dialectique* and *L'Idiot de la famille*. Brosman argues that in his later work, Sartre does indeed perceive the possibility of genuine reciprocity: 'In *L'Idiot de la famille*, he goes so far as
to say that reciprocity, even if hidden and alienated, is the fundamental
relationship among men' (Brosman 1987: 68; see also 69). Cf., however,
Bailey (1977) and Charmé (1991).

CHAPTER 5

Artaud and the Plague: A Posthumanist Theatre?

> Representationalism and Newtonian physics have roots in the seventeenth century. The assumption that language is a transparent medium that transmits a homologous picture of reality to the knowing mind finds its parallel in a scientific theory that takes observation to be the benign facilitator of discovery, a transparent lens passively gazing at the world . . . In the twentieth century, both the representational or mimetic status of language and the inconsequentiality of the observational process have been called into question. (Barad 2007: 97)

> Representationalism, metaphysical individualism, and humanism work hand in hand. (Barad 2007: 134)

The remaining part of my project is dedicated to the theatrical work of the French writer Antonin Artaud (1896–1948), an *oeuvre* that differs markedly from the representationalist theatre explored so far, from what theatre scholar Hans-Thies Lehmann, in his well-known book on *Postdramatic Theatre*, calls the 'anthropocentric', 'dramatic' tradition.[1] It is a theatre that poses a radical challenge to Cartesian epistemology and to what Barad calls 'its representationalist triadic structure of words, knowers, and things' (Barad 2007: 97).

Artaud's key theoretical writings on the 'theatre of cruelty', written between 1931 and 1937 and first published together in 1938[2] in *Le Théâtre et son double* (*The Theatre and Its Double*), are typically considered the 'bible of modern theatre' (Scheer 2004: 5). Here Artaud argues that in contrast to Asian theatre, the western dramatic tradition leaves in the background everything not expressed by 'la parole', by words, anything that is not contained in the dialogue. As a member of what Lehmann calls the 'historical avant-garde' of the early twentieth century, Artaud announces and pre-figures a deep caesura or radical transformation of scenic practice in the western theatrical tradition. This caesura is the shift from the focus on the text, mimetic action or plot and the representation of human conflicts in the 'dramatic' tradition since the Renaissance on the one side to, on the other side, the heterogeneity of theatrical performance in the 'post-dramatic' theatre after the 1960s.[3]

While the primarily verbal theatre of the 'dramatic' western tradition leaves behind even the *sound* of the dialogue itself, Artaud posits that the dialogue belongs to the book and is not specifically theatrical (Artaud 1976: IV, 45). In Artaud's work sound and the space of the performance become actors themselves. The *spatiality*, *corporeality* and *tonality* of the play speak a concrete and physical, specifically *theatrical* language that addresses the senses. These are the elements of Artaud's language: music, dance, rhythms, the musical *tempo* of passions, vibrations, physical bodies ('plastique'), bodily attitudes or postures, pantomime, facial expressions, masks, gestures, laughter, screams, the voice and its modulations, intonations, the particular pronunciation of words, repetitions, onomatopoeia, mispronunciations or Freudian slips ('les dérisoires lapsus de la langue') (Artaud 1976: IV, 86), all kinds of sounds amplified by loudspeakers across the entire theatrical space and surrounding the audience (Artaud 1976: II, 148–9), dissonances, truncated or garbled ('tronquées') melodies, silences, volumes, architecture, costumes, colours, lighting and decor (Artaud 1976: IV, 45, 47, 48, 49, 61, 67, 68, 82, 107, 108, 111, 145, 149, 150, 153, 157, 163).

Moving beyond the European realist dramatic tradition focused on verbalised psychological conflicts, beyond a theatre that (as we have seen) starts to address ontological questions concerning the status of the human, but is at least formally often still humanist, Artaud's work takes the materiality of theatre to a different level. In opposition to a dramatic tradition focused on discursivity, Artaud argues that drama cannot be separated from performance (Artaud 1976: IV, 82). The materiality of Artaud's stage is more than the simple reflection of the text and takes on an agency of its own. As we have seen in Strindberg and Sartre, the 'dramatic' theatrical tradition had used the consistent recourse to logos and mimesis to defend against the threat of the corporeal – a corporeality that had to be sublimated and subordinated to the word. Strindberg had seen his role as playwright as that of a hypnotist controlling the spectator's mind and body. While also playing on the audience's nervous systems, Artaud's work nevertheless marks a rupture: the eruption of aesthetic sensory perception, of heterogeneous experiential contingency. In Artaud's *oeuvre*, the mastery of/by humans, the reassurance provided by understanding/representation/logos is no longer only in crisis, as it is in Strindberg or Sartre. Instead, in Artaud's theatre of cruelty, this reassurance is gone. Artaud's work resonates with new materialism in that, as Florence Chiew argues, 'perception is not the primordial substrate of cognition but a site where the eye/I (the Subject) is constantly renegotiated through, and as, diffracted sensory modalities' (Kirby summarising Chiew's argument in *What If Culture Was Nature All Along?* (xi)). What is at stake in both new material-ism and Artaud is the renegotiation of the traditionally ocular-centric, human subject through heterogeneous sensory modalities. Anna Gibbs points to the important role affect plays in this renegotiation, stating that 'affect seems to act as a switchboard through which all sensory signals are passed' (Gibbs 2010: 192). Daniel Stern similarly calls affect 'the 'supramodal currency' in which experience in any sensory modality may be translated' (53). Heterogeneous sensory perception and affect are also central to Artaud's theatre of cruelty.

The Theatre and Culture

In 'On Not Becoming Man: The Materialist Politics of Unactualized Potential', Claire Colebrook (2008) discusses two different ways of approaching literary (or here, scenic) materiality. She notes: 'The first is to see the text as a signifier, as the mark or trace through which communicative and lived relations are organized; the aim of reading is actualization – to take the matter of the text and unfold it in all its potentialities' (Colebrook 2008: 76). This is how scholars have typi-cally read the dramas of the 'psychological' western tradition described so far. In this study, we have re-lived and re-transcribed these realist dra-mas as co-constitutive parts of socio-material relations that include the scientific, economic, socio-historical and psychoanalytical discourses and material practices of the late nineteenth and early twentieth centu-ries – discourses and practices that reverberate in the practices and dis-courses of our present moment (and vice versa). Here my methodology has been inspired by Gilles Deleuze and Félix Guattari's understanding of assemblage[4] (itself informed by Artaud's work) and Karen Barad's related work on intra-active relationality. I argue that this methodol-ogy can be applied even if the texts of the realist-humanist tradition themselves seek to erect biopolitical walls and a linear plot against such simultaneous flowing.

As a second alternative, Colebrook proposes reading a text as 'a frag-ment of "time in its pure state"; rather than extending itself through time, the text is intensive.' In this context, Colebrook understands the text as 'a style or noise that organizes bodies', refuting 'the idea of lan-guage as the expression *of* life' (emphasis in original). Such an approach 'tear[s] the matter of language from its relations'. Isolating language from reference, 'we are given the expression of matter itself' (Colebrook 2008: 76). While tearing language from the web of relations seems problematic and exclusionary to me (given the central argument of my project concerning the intra-activity of materiality and representation), and while Colebrook has an avowed preference for the second type of reading (the expression of matter), I argue – with this book – that the two approaches described can lend themselves to different kinds of plays, acting styles and productions. Erika Fischer-Lichte agrees: 'We can assume that theatre performances that involve a realistic-psychological style of acting invite the spectators to privilege the perceptual order of representation, while experimental theatre and performance art draw the spectator toward the perceptual order of presence' (Fischer-Lichte 2014: 40). As I will show, Artaud's work resonates especially well with the second kind of approach: a reading of his performative work as the expression of presence, materiality and intensities themselves, as pure affect.[5]

Fischer-Lichte is of course correct in adding that '[n]evertheless it is almost impossible to imagine a performance that an audience would perceive exclusively through one of these orders . . . in every performance the perception of each spectator oscillates between different modes of perception' (Fischer-Lichte 2014: 40–1). Maaike Bleeker (2008: 21) and Liesbeth Groot Nibbelink (2019: 50) have also argued that it is impossible for theatre to completely do without representation. As Groot Nibbelink puts it: 'I do not think that an emphasis on process, experimentation, or continuous differentiation leads us beyond representation' (Groot Nibbelink 2019: 51). Colebrook on the other hand stipulates that reading in the second way 'isolates style from reference – the world from which it emerged – and intuits its sense' (Colebrook 2008: 77). Colebrook's approach in other words establishes a split between affect and world. Artaud's theoretical statements, by contrast, oppose any kind of isolation or separation and advocate an overcoming of the binary opposition between materiality and mind or meaning. If, as Colebrook writes, '[t]o be human is to be burdened with giving oneself a world, with framing oneself and deciding on one's own being' (Colebrook 2008: 79) – if in other words the human and his/her world are co-extensive, the question concerning the role of mimetic reference becomes the question of exploring to which extent Artaud's work is posthumanist (in this sense). Posthumanist and post-dramatic (non-mimetic) then become synonymous, as Lehmann also argues. At the same time, however, in contrast to Martin Heidegger's work for instance, posthumanism is founded on the assumption that the world is/worlds are not necessarily and always human, but rather more-than-human. Colebrook's understanding of 'world' is in fact reminiscent of what Artaud calls 'culture', a realm that both Artaud and Colebrook distrust.

As Susan Sontag remarks, 'Artaud imagines the theatre as the place where the body would be reborn in thought and thought would be reborn in the body' (1999: 89). Given the close relationality between materiality and ideas in Artaud's work, any reading of Artaud's *oeuvre* needs to be put in conversation with his groundbreaking theoretical statements. Artaud's Preface to *Le Théâtre et son double* starts with the author's expression of his distrust of culture or civilisation, a culture that, he says, has never coincided with life ('la vie'), but instead is designed to rule or govern ('régenter') life. Put differently, he bemoans the split between culture or thought systems and a materially understood 'life'. Artaud remarks that culture has never saved anybody from material concerns such as hunger. Instead of the creation of a cultural project per se, his own goal is instead to extract the live energy ('la force vivante') of ideas from what we call culture (Artaud 1976: IV, 11). (Somehow contradictorily, this statement suggests that there must be some life in culture after all.) Can we then read this goal of extracting live energy from culture as the objective of collapsing the dichotomy between materiality and culture that has long marked western thinking and theatre? Artaud's statement that he sees an undesirable rupture between things on the one side and words/ideas/representations on the other as the source of the 'contemporary confusion' does indeed suggest so. Artaud's view of life seems to resonate with a Deleuzian framework (and Deleuze himself was of course influenced by Artaud.). Rosi Braidotti, herself a student of Deleuze's at the Sorbonne, also sees controlling reason as impeding the sensorial perception or life: 'In those moments of floating awareness, when rational control releases its hold, "Life" rushes on toward the sensorial/receptive apparatus with exceptional vigor and higher degrees of definition.' What follows the vigorous onslaught of life is then what Deleuze describes as 'the folding in and out of perception', a 'holding' of affectivity that 'does not occur on the paranoid or rapacious model of a dominant, dialectically driven consciousness' (Braidotti 2011: 152) – the model followed, for instance, by Sartre.

Uniting culture and materiality, Artaud proposes as a solution a 'culture in action' that becomes in us 'like a new organ', a kind of second breath. Artaud's objective is the presence of the mind ('l'esprit') in things (Artaud 1976: IV, 12), a presence that again transverses/cuts

through the dichotomy between matter and mind: 'One does not separate the body from the mind, nor the senses from the intellect' ('On ne
sépare pas le corps de l'esprit, ni les sens de l'intelligence'). Artaud's
theatre instead addresses the entire organism (Artaud 1976: IV, 104).
In lieu of the dichotomies that have marked western thinking, Artaud
proposes *an equation*: 'a kind of enthralling equation between Man,
Society, Nature, and Things' ('une sorte d'équation passionnante entre
l'Homme, la Société, la Nature et les Objects') (Artaud 1976: IV, 107).
This infusion of materiality into culture, or (vice versa) of the mind
into materiality, constitutes a 'constant magic', an animated witchcraft:
'cette sorcellerie objective et animée' (Artaud 1976: IV, 88).

In the essay 'L'Athlétisme affectif' ('An Affective Athleticism'), written
in 1935, Artaud argues that the knowledge that *passions are matter*
gives us (humans) a control that 'extends our sovereignty' (Artaud
1976: IV, 157). At first, this passage seems to reassert ('extend') the
idea of human control over materiality and realms previously excluded
(magic, witchcraft) instead of bridging the dichotomies of western
philosophy and theatre. But then Artaud adds: '*rejoining* the passions
through their *forces* instead of considering them as pure abstractions
gives the actor the mastery of *a true healer*' ('*Rejoindre* les passions par
leurs *forces*, au lieu de les considérer comme des abstractions pures,
confère à l'acteur une maîtrise qui l'égale à *un vrai guérisseur*') (Artaud
1976: IV, 157, my emphases). Artaud retains the notion of human (the
actor's) 'mastery', while at the same time emphasising 'rejoining' and
'healing' in his approach to affect ('passions'). He understands affect
as a material (human or more-than-human) force, as 'the capacity to
affect and be affected before and below consciousness' (Pitts-Taylor
2016: 6). But Artaud also does not exclude the mind. Artaud's theatre
is a therapeutic theatre that aims to close the gap between abstraction
and material forces. His emphasis on healing and compassion can be
put in productive conversation with the more recent emphasis in new
materialist philosophies such as Braidotti's on an affirmative politics
and critical practice.[6]

When in the same essay, on the other hand, Artaud speaks of emotion ('sentiment') and materiality – which are positive terms in Artaud's
work – as feminine (Artaud 1976: IV, 161), he again follows the gendered distribution of western philosophy (which feminises both matter
and emotion). But he is also reclaiming/giving priority to the threat
that the patriarchal tradition has attempted to avert and exclude:
'I want to try my hands on a terrible femininity. The scream of the slow,
shuffling revolt, of the armed anxiety of war, and of the demand' ('Je

veux essayer un féminin terrible. Le cri de la révolte qu'on piétine, de l'angoisse armée en guerre, et de la revendication') (Artaud 1976: IV, 175). Similar to Brecht's early work, but in clear contrast to Strindberg and Sartre, who also see the feminine as terrible but negativise anxiety, the feminine is here seen as positive, exceeding the constraints of western patriarchal structures and the western dramatic tradition.

In the Preface to *Le Théâtre et son double*, however, Artaud posits that it is this very 'infection' of the human that 'ruins' for us ideas that 'should have remained divine' (Artaud 1976: IV, 13). What are we to make of this biological-immunological choice of words (infection) and the mention of the divine, a divinity that for Artaud is a human invention? Why is Artaud, as we have seen, speaking of (human) sovereignty? In the Preface, he again mentions a split or separation ('scission') from life as the root of what he sees as the contemporary problem, as the reason why things are 'taking revenge' and why, he says, we can no longer find poetry in ourselves nor in things. The gratuitously bizarre crimes that Artaud says we are witnessing today – enacted on the stage, for instance as Count Cenci's criminal, incestuous desire for his daughter in Artaud's most famous play, *Les Cenci* (*The Cenci*) – these contemporary bizarre crimes are, according to Artaud, a result of our human powerlessness to possess life. Is this another stab at human sovereignty and another reiteration of the threat of materiality after all (things taking revenge)? For Artaud, the task of the theatre, however, is not the mastery of/by human consciousness that we have witnessed in Sartre. The task of theatre is instead to allow our repressions to come alive in a kind of 'atrocious poetry' enacting the intensity of life (Artaud 1976: IV, 13). Whereas the western biopolitical tradition attempts to defend against the threat of contamination or infection arising from the material 'outside' of human culture by erecting walls, Artaud sees the split between a live, agential materiality and human culture as leading to the familiar threat of things 'taking revenge' and wants to overcome this split in his work.

The host of immunological images in Artaud's theoretical writings, in other words, suggest that he does take note of some sort of threat. But what is threatened is not human eurocentric male privilege. While Artaud laments our 'deep-rooted absence of culture' ('notre absence enracinée de culture') (Artaud 1976: IV, 13), he then signals a threat that does not menace this culture, however, but instead endangers the natural world. For instance, Artaud imagines an island without any contact with contemporary civilisation, an island that is infected with illnesses previously unknown to the native population through the simple passing-by of a ship carrying only healthy people. He lists these infectious illnesses: shingles, influenza, rheumatism, sinus infection, polyneuritis – an inflammation of nerves that can be caused by Vitamin B deficiency, by a toxic substance or (most relevant in Artaud's context) by an infectious disease. While western colonial discourses perceive non-European populations as the threat to the white norm and white hegemony, Artaud here reverses the racially charged dichotomy, positing anything that is white as the excess that threatens 'extreme decomposition': 'tout ce qui est excessif est blanc; et pour un Asiatique la couleur blanche est devenue l'insigne de la plus extreme decomposition' (Artaud 1976: IV, 14). ('All that is excessive is white; and for an Asian the color white has become the emblem of the most extreme decomposition.')

Continuing to grapple with an understanding and valuation of 'culture' that does not just perpetuate the humanist eurocentric Cartesian tradition, Artaud criticises culture's 'insane shrinkage' ('rétrécissement insensé') and its separation from life, 'comme s'il y avait la culture d'un côté et la vie de l'autre' (Artaud 1976: IV, 14) ('as if there were culture on one side and life on the other'). What interests Artaud are the 'forces' and energies that he sees underlying cultural artifacts such as the library of Alexandria and its papyrus rolls (Artaud 1976: IV, 14–15). This concept of culture needs neither a specific space nor time and instead contains our 'nervous capacity', an anxiety that reappears with increased energy. For Artaud and his theatre of cruelty, this anxiety is not a negative thing but an expression of life energy, and culture is not necessarily subject to human space or time scales. Artaud associates life with the natural world. He laments what the separation or scission he has just discussed has turned into dead things ('une chose morte'): the old totemism of animals, stones, objects charged with lightning, 'bestially impregnated costumes' ('des costumes bestialement imprégnés') (Artaud 1976: IV, 15). In contrast to the Cartesian tradition, which sees matter as dead and in Artaud's view has also damaged or 'shrunk' culture, he instead envisions a live materiality.

Giving Artaud's collected theoretical work its title, *Le Théâtre et son double*, these 'bestially impregnated' costumes give actors a 'double body, double members' ('un double corps, de doubles membres') (Artaud 1976: IV, 70). In general, the live materiality that Artaud envisions and that expresses itself in Artaud's theatre acts as the Double of the human, 'like a perpetual specter where the forces of affectivity manifest' ('glow/shine', 'rayonnent'). It is of course interesting that Artaud speaks of the affectivity of live materiality as a *spectre*, a term with a long philosophical heritage from Marx to Derrida. The actor imitates this material 'world of affect' through his/her own senses (Artaud 1976: IV, 156). The senses in other words provide the liminal meeting point of the human and its material and affective double. Mimesis now includes the imitation of a sensory affectivity.

Artaud, for whom true culture acts through its exaltation and its force, argues that the European ideal of art (which in his usage includes theatre) has aimed to separate mind ('l'esprit') and force, only exalting the mind. Before long, in his view, this separation leads to death – to Cartesian 'dead' matter, but also to the impairment of culture. In this study, we have already mapped (as enacted in modernist drama) the relationality between the biopolitical view of matter in the rationalist philosophical tradition and the politics of death of twentieth-century totalitarianism. Artaud argues that his own understanding of culture on the one side and (this kind of) traditional art cannot go together (Artaud 1976: IV, 15). Instead of the 'old totemism', Artaud advocates a totemism – a barbarism or primitivism marked by spontaneity and 'savage life' ('la vie sauvage') – that actively moves and thus lends itself to theatre. He writes: 'it moves, and it is made for actors' ('il bouge, et il est fait pour des acteurs'). To replace the 'inert and disinterested' western conception of art, Artaud proposes an authentic culture exemplified by Mexico and inspired by magic and engaged interest, a culture where elemental forces and forms inhabit a 'magical identification' and communication (Artaud 1976: IV, 16). While Brecht wrote a play about Baal, the border-crossing Middle Eastern nature god, Artaud uses a mythical animal as an example of this suggested 'primitivism': the feathered, dragon-like snake Quetzalcoatl that in Aztec mythology marked and crossed the boundary between sky and earth, its boundary transgression leading to the creation of humankind (Artaud 1976: IV, 15). Reminiscent of Brecht, Artaud then goes on to list the nature gods of ancient mythologies (Artaud 1976: IV, 16). He describes these gods of the natural world in terms of visuality (colours, 'jade verte'), auditory sense experience ('sonne'), smell ('aromes') and a materiality of objects that come alive due to the positive influence of humans ('a world where the stone becomes animated because it has been properly hit') ('un monde où la pierre s'anime parce qu'elle a été frappée comme il faut'), resulting in a world of 'perpetual exaltation'. In Artaud's worldview, the intensity of forms only exists to capture the force of life. This force evokes 'un déchirant clavier' (a harrowing keyboard), i.e. disharmonious music or sound (Artaud 1976: IV, 15).

Together with his focus on magic, Artaud also goes beyond the rationalist tradition by establishing a contrast between a positive valuation of dreams (eyes turned towards the inside) as a truly awake state ('éveiller') on the one hand against, on the other hand/negatively, sleeping in full consciousness with eyes open ('dormir, en regardant avec des yeux atttachés et conscients') (Artaud 1976: IV, 16). This Freudian and post-Surrealist emphasis on the unconscious, on the release from the dominance of the censorship of the conscious mind, clearly establishes a difference from Brecht's work. At the same time, however, Artaud also opposes 'this empiricism of images that the unconscious brings forth randomly' ('cet empirisme des images que l'inconscient apporte au hazard') (Artaud 1976: IV, 96), in other words surrrealist automatic writing.[7] He instead aims for a more rigorous total art (or post-Wagnerian *Gesamtkunstwerk*) in which emotions are grounded in the physical organism (Artaud 1976: IV, 163), an art that overcomes modernity's growing abstraction.

Linking affect and *physis*, Artaud speaks of the 'affective muscle structure' of the actor, who is 'an athlete of the heart' (Artaud 1976: IV, 154). As Matteo Colombi and Massimo Fussilo write, in Artaud's theatre 'trained actors are indispensable in freeing the disruptive and chaotic forces of the unconscious in conjuring and transmitting energy flows which might traverse human dreams, nightmares, instincts, and hopes – the actor's task requiring a corporal discipline akin to that of an elite sportsman or [sports]woman' (Colombi and Fussilo 2013: 4). But it is the spectator who is ultimately central to Artaud's theatre (Artaud 1976: IV, 98) and who goes from the relatively passive position of onlooker or viewer (in the western theatrical tradition) to being exposed as an active participant in Artaud. While theatre typically gathers bodies in a communal space, Artaud asserts that community in a new way. In a time that he perceives as deeply neurotic, Artaud views the theatre (as we have seen) in therapeutic and sacred terms as the only place or means left that allows us to directly access communal organisms (Artaud 1976: IV, 97, 102, 163).[8] Julia Kristeva also speaks of the sublimation of abjection that marks Artaud's work as 'a substitute for the role formerly played by the sacred' (1982: 26). Like Chinese acupuncture, the theatre must touch myriad points of the body in order to put the audience in a magical trance affecting the whole nervous system (Artaud 1976: IV, 162–3).

It is in this context of dreams and 'the unleashed unconscious' ('L'inconscient déchaîné') (Artaud 1976: IV, 66) that Artaud uses the term 'shadow' and again the notion of 'doubling' ('Toute vraie effigie a son ombre qui le double') (Artaud 1976: IV, 17) ('Every true effigy has a shadow that doubles it'). The theatre returns to us in a physical manner some of the most secret (and therefore unconscious) perceptions of the mind (Artaud 1976: IV, 73–4). Artaud describes the theatre as the only language and as the only art that still has shadows that break limitations, as the only language and art that from the start has not tolerated limitations. Artaud's theatre, in other words, is excess.

In short, Artaud opposes what he calls the 'empty' tradition of the rationalist philosophical tradition and the western theatrical tradition, a theatre of the past addressed to a cultural elite and incomprehensible to the people today ('la foule') (Artaud 1976: IV, 88). While Sophocles' *Oedipus Rex*, for instance, enacts an incest and a plague epidemic (two themes that interest Artaud as well), Artaud finds that its language has lost touch with the 'epileptic' rhythm of contemporary times (Artaud 1976: IV, 17). As we have seen, Strindberg also enacts modern times as epileptic. Artaud himself produced and directed works by Paul Claudel and Strindberg (*A Dream Play*, *Ghost Sonata*) when he founded and led the critically acclaimed and influential Théâtre Alfred Jarry in Paris during its brief history from 1926 to 1928. The theatrical tools used by Artaud in his own work and by Strindberg (even the post-Inferno, i.e. post-naturalist, Strindberg) differ greatly, however. Artaud's theatre makes the heterogeneous elements of the performance themselves come alive and act. In Artaud's theatre, the mind uses all languages – gestures, sounds, words, fire, cries – to manifest itself. When the theatre fixates on one language, however, whether it be written language, music, lights or noise, this dried out or limited language, according to Artaud, indicates the theatre's imminent doom (Artaud 1976: IV, 17). Artaud thus advocates a theatre and an understanding of culture that do not formally stagnate in verbal language, but lead the way to a true performance of life: 'To break language to touch life is to make or remake the theatre' ('Briser le langage pour toucher la vie, c'est faire ou refaire le théâtre') (Artaud 1976: IV, 18).

In spite of his opposition to what Lehmann considers the 'humanist' or anthropocentric 'dramatic' theatrical tradition, Artaud's materialism, his rejection of the restriction to one type of language and form, is not completely anti- or posthumanist. Like surrealism, Artaud understands his theatre as a rejection of the usual limitations of mankind and its powers, as an infinite expansion of the borders of reality. Contrary to his existentialist contemporaries, who thematise the absurdity of life, Artaud advocates a theatre that renews the meaning of life. As he puts it, he 're-installs mankind as the master of things that are to come because of him' (Artaud 1976: IV, 18). Here Artaud thus continues to claim human agency and sovereignty. His material theatre and the exalted role of the human do not seem to exclude each other. Nevertheless, Artaud ends his Preface by underlining his understanding of 'life' ('la vie'), not as the life of external facts (i.e. realism or mimesis), but as a kind of fragile and shifting home or hearth ('foyer') that 'forms' alone cannot touch. In a famous passage, Artaud links his theatre to a crisis, to pain and urgency, to the urgency of human torture victims who are burning and signalling from the stakes (Artaud 1976: IV, 18), unsuccessfully attempting to establish meaning or communication. As we will see, Artaud's play *The Cenci* enacts such mental and physical torture and also extends this tonality to the spectators.

The Theatre and the Plague

At the beginning of the twentieth century, when the deadly influenza pandemics at the end of the First World War had claimed as many as one hundred million lives worldwide and close to a quarter of a million people succumbed to the disease in France alone (Stanton 1992: 8), contagion continued to be a central threat to public health. In the first essay of *Le Théâtre et son double*, 'Le Théâtre et la peste' ('The Theatre and the Plague'), Artaud returns to the imagery of the immune system already evoked in the Preface. He tells the story of a vice-king whose people are threatened by a particularly pernicious virus coming from the East, an epidemic, and by the vertiginous loss of matter: the plague, 'le virus d'origine' (Artaud 1976: IV, 19–21), the 'original virus', the 'pathogen *par excellence*' (Podd 2018). The Vice-King, who has been exposed to the virus in a dream, without any physical contact, autocratically and at the same time 'miraculously enlightened', does not allow the ship carrying the virus to approach his kingdom (Artaud 1976: IV, 21–2). Artaud discusses the epidemic as 'the direct instrument or the materialisation of an intelligent force in close contact with what we call fate' ('l'instrument direct ou la matérialisation d'une force intelligente en étroit rapport avec ce que nous appelons la fatalité') (Artaud 1976: IV, 22). He links 'intelligence', i.e. some sort of cognition, and its materialisation in the biological-natural phenomenon of the plague. For Artaud, contagion, already an element of the semioticity of Sophocles' *Oedipus Rex*, is the modern trope of fate. Like Sophocles' play, Artaud's *Les Cenci* is a five-act tragedy. Artaud's emphasis on fate resonates with new materialist conceptualisations of what Braidotti calls *amor fati*, of 'catch[ing] the wave of life's intensities and rid[ing] it out, exposing the boundaries or limits as we transgress them' (Braidotti 2011: 361). Indeed, Lehmann (2013), in his book on tragedy, speaks of tragic theatre as having qualities that can be grasped better with the help of Deleuze than with classic drama theory. Lehmann sees theatre as the enmeshment of heterogeneous elements: gestures, bodies, looks and words, language, ideas.

Reminiscent of the Vice-King, whose contact with the virus is not a bodily contact, Artaud proceeds to discuss the plague as an illness of a psychic nature not caused by a virus or actual contact and whose symptoms manifest before any physiological or psychological sense of not being well (Artaud 1976: IV, 24). The most severe case of plague, according to Artaud, is the one that does not show any symptoms (Artaud 1976: IV, 25). The organs that are affected the worst are the brain and the lungs (i.e. thinking and breathing), which, he says, both directly depend on consciousness and will (Artaud 1976: IV, 26). From the bio-material symptomology, Artaud (joining materiality and the human realm) then moves on to the history of the virus's discovery in 1880 by a French doctor named Yersin on the bodies of Indo-Chinese victims. Artaud nevertheless sees the plague as an illness whose scientific mechanisms ('lois', 'laws') remain vague and whose geographic origin, due to its great variety, remains unknown (Artaud 1976: IV, 27). He instead focuses on the 'spiritual or intellectual physiognomy' ('la physionomie spirituelle', itself a boundary-crossing term) of this illness as a pain that grows in intensity as it multiplies in areas affected.

Slowly returning to the discussion of the theatre, Artaud sees this illness as a 'spectacle' (Artaud 1976: IV, 28). The plague destroys human institutions, the institutions of the sphere of culture: 'Once the plague is established in a city, the regular institutions collapse, there are no longer a highways department, an army, a police, a municipality' ('La peste établie dans une cite, les cadres réguliers s'effondrent, il n'y a plus de voirie, d'armée, de police, de municipalité') (Artaud 1976: IV, 28). The corpses it produces form a double assemblage ('agencement', the term later used by Deleuze) of wooden slabs (Artaud 1976: IV, 29), like a stage. This is the point in time when the theatre establishes itself: the theatre as a gratuitous, frenetic immediacy, as absurd, useless actions or crimes (Artaud 1976: IV, 98) without any current benefit or meaning, similar to the reviled erotic fever that those cured of the plague seek to satisfy with the dying or the dead (Artaud 1976: IV, 30). Again, the theatre is excess or surplus.

The state of the plague victim who dies without material, bodily destruction, 'with, within himself, all the stigmata of an absolute and almost abstract evil, is identical to the state of the actor' ('avec en lui tous les stigmates d'un mal absolu et presque abstrait, est identique à l'état de l'acteur'), an actor completely overcome by his gratuitous emotions. Like a plague victim chasing his hallucinations, the poet (i.e. playwright) invents and delivers his characters to spectators who are themselves both inert and hallucinatory. Like a plague victim, Artaud writes, the actor similarly 'chases his sensitivity' in the middle of an audience constituted by corpses and delirious madmen (Artaud 1976: IV, 30–1). For Artaud, the theatre and the plague both amount to a true epidemic. In Artaud's theatre, this epidemic affects the playwright, the actors and the spectators.

While Artaud describes the plague as a powerful state of physical disorganisation as well as the last eruptions of an intellectual force ('force spirituelle') that is exhausting itself, in theatre poetry is an intellectual force that also starts its trajectory in the sensory realm but leaves mimetic reality behind. Both the plague ('fuseés', 'rockets') and the theatre ('fureur', 'furor') are marked by an intense violence, a violence that, according to Artaud, takes the actor to a level where he needs more virtue in order not to commit a crime than the criminal needs courage to commit his. Here, Artaud says (somewhat channelling Aristotle's argument of the greater truth of tragedy over history), in its gratuitousness (the lack of value or profit), the action of an affect on the theatre appears as infinitely more valuable than an affect that becomes reality (Artaud 1976: IV, 31). In contrast to the furor of the assassin, which exhausts itself, the furor of the tragic actor remains in a 'pure and closed circle'. Unlike the action of the criminal, a force that has discharged and thus is lost, the affect on stage takes on a form, the form of the actor, who denies herself the more this form is released and becomes universality. We are here approaching a depersonalising affect that goes beyond the human.

Confusingly, since my argument is that Artaud represents a more 'material', increasingly post-anthropocentric theatre, Artaud ultimately sees the plague (and with it the theatre) as 'spirituelle' (spiritual/intellectual), in spite of, he says, the solidified and material face of a disorder that on another level corresponds to the conflicts caused by events. Interestingly, Artaud claims this 'spirituality' for a nonhuman entity (the plague). Rather than focusing on biomedical material causes, he even conjectures that affects ('le désespoir inutilis[é] et les cris d'un aliéné') ('unused despair and the cries of a madman') can cause the plague. At the same time, however, he does not exclude external events. The affect he describes is a sensory (i.e. material in that sense) affect:

Artaud argues that external events – political events as well as natural disasters, that is a linked materialsemiotic – can pass the plague on to the theatre 'with the force of an epidemic', through a sensory discharge in the spectators who watch these events. Artaud thus follows the analogy that Saint Augustin establishes between the plague, which kills without destroying any organs, and the theatre, which – while not lethal – provokes highly mysterious changes in the mind (Artaud 1976: IV, 31–2).

Linked to our focus on anxiety in the modern theatre and theorising the contagiousness of affects, Artaud conceives of his theatre as a 'contagious delirium' ('délire communicatif') of the nervous system ('l'organisme nerveux') (Artaud 1976: IV, 33), as an exploration of our 'nervous sensitivity' (Artaud 1976: IV, 104). Artaud is less interested in what causes this delirium than in the fact, as he keeps repeating, that *the theatre is a delirium* and that *it is contagious*. He adds that there is something victorious and something vengeful in both the theatre and the plague. (Earlier, you will remember, he was talking of 'things taking revenge'.) Collapsing the distinction between materiality and the social, Artaud describes the plague as a spontaneous fire, an immense liquidation, a complete social disaster. It is an organic disorder, an overflow of vices, a total exorcism that pushes the soul to the end, an extreme force in which the powers of nature meet, raw, at the point in time where nature will accomplish something essential (Artaud 1976: IV, 33). Even in plays outside the 'dramatic' tradition not typically based on human psychological conflicts, theatre is the genre where (human or nonhuman) conflicts or antagonisms meet at their point of rupture, at or close to an affective climax point. The heightened affect explored in my project is the extreme anxiety affecting (and co-constituting) modern bodies. In Artaud's theatre this affect reaches the intensity of an epidemic. Instead of trying to fend off this modern anxiety with dramatic representations, Artaud prefers instead, as Herbert Blau puts it, to stare this anxiety down (Blau 2004: 77).

While postmodernism or the linguistic turn associates representation with the symbolic sphere of human sociality, Artaud differentiates between symbols and the social. He describes his theatre as a theatre of intensely felt symbols, of symbols that give expression to actions that are by nature hostile to social life (Artaud 1976: IV, 34). Artaud's symbols, in other words, are not primarily products of the symbolic sphere, but oppose the symbolic. Reflecting his surrealist beginnings and his positive assessment of primitivism, Artaud's theatre wakens the senses, frees the unconscious, pushes to a sort of virtual revolt, imposing on society in the form of spectators ('les collectivités rassemblées') a heroic and difficult attitude. In this context, Artaud also speaks of the 'disrespectful demand of incest' ('une revendication insolente d'inceste') (Artaud 1976: IV, 34), a foundational social taboo centrally enacted in *The Cenci*. The absoluteness of this revolt, of this 'exemplary love without respite', makes the spectators anxiously hyperventilate ('haleter d'angoisse') at the idea that this 'absolute liberty' and danger are forever unstoppable (Artaud 1976: IV, 35). This anxiety is also expressed by Cenci's daughter, Béatrice, at the end of the play. According to Artaud, when we have arrived at the paroxysm of horror and blood, of fundamental social laws that have been trampled (through patricide, filicide and incest in *The Cenci*), at the paroxysm of the poetry that crowns/rages (the double meaning of 'sacrer'), we are obliged to go even further in a vertigo that nothing can stop (Artaud 1976: IV, 36). In Artaud, the inevitability of tragedy no longer finds closure. The therapeutic effect that Artaud envisions for his theatre (a goal, *catharsis*, again shared with ancient tragedy) is achieved exactly through this lack of closure.

If the 'essential theatre' is like the plague, Artaud says, it is not because it is contagious (Artaud here contradicts himself), but because it is, like the plague, a revelation of, an emphasis on, a latent fundamental cruelty that pushes towards the exterior. In this cruelty, all the perverse possibilities of the mind manifest themselves. Like the plague, the theatre is for Artaud the triumph of evil, of black forces fed by an even deeper force to extinction. Here the abnormal – the difficult and the impossible – becomes the norm (Artaud 1976: IV, 37). But this cruelty does not necessarily have much to do with sadism or with blood (Artaud 1976: IV, 120–1). Artaud's concept of cruelty is linked to consciousness, to the awareness that living is cruel because life always comes at the cost of somebody else's death (Artaud 1976: IV, 121) – an insight that resonates in contemporary times as we humans try to rethink our relationship to the more-than-human world. With Artaud's notion of theatre as plague, the theatre as a performance of the spectators' bourgeois politeness comes to an end and the border between the more-than-human stage and the spectators, the immunitarian border shielding the spectators from contagion and violence or cruelty, collapses.

Posthumanist Tragedy

In spite of the role of gratuitousness in Artaud's work, the role of cruelty in his magical, ritualistic theatre and his concept of cruelty as inevitable cosmic necessity ('rigueur cosmique', 'nécessité implacable') (Artaud

1976: IV, 122) are reminiscent of the role of fate in Greek tragedy. In Artaud's theatre as well humans meet their fate. Lehmann refutes the well-known German theatre scholar Peter Szondi's argument (1965) concerning the 'historical impossibility' of tragedy in modernity, granting, however, that tragedy only lends itself 'with effort' to dramatic forms of theatre (Lehmann 2013: 28). Instead, tragedy has an affinity to Artaud's project of overcoming the 'dramatic' theatrical tradition. Lehmann associates the tragic with the experience of excess: 'the tragic as manifesting the energy of transgression, rupture, overstepping, immoderation and excess, insofar as it involves self-endangerment or actual annihilation'. This is also Artaud's project, as Lehmann agrees as well. In Lehmann's words, Artaud 'views the "transgression" of nervous and mental constitution designated by the word "cruelty" as "inexorable necessity" and, in so doing, accepts the danger that such efforts at liberation mean risking self-destruction. Here, mental excess does not shake the foundation of inherited theatre alone, but also the whole of standing culture' (Lehmann 2016: 390–1). Artaud's theatre is a revolt not only against the dramatic tradition, but against the entire traditional western understanding of culture.

If both ancient tragedy (as 'pre-dramatic' theatre) and Artaud's work differ from the anthropocentric tradition of the modern 'dramatic' theatre, as Lehmann argues, what exactly is the role of humans in these two alternative theatrical visions? In contrast to Attic tragedy, in Artaud's work humans meet their fate 'not to suffer if, but to measure up to it' (Artaud 1976: IV, 130). (This is what Blau called 'staring it down'.) Whereas the hero's death in Greek tragedy arguably restores divine laws (as Hegel argued in his theory of tragedy), for Artaud 'evil is permanent law' ('le mal est la loi permanente') (Artaud 1976: IV, 124). Artaud, moreover, is not only inspired by Greek tragedy but also by Plato. While Artaud criticises the Freudian concept of *libido* as everything that is dirty and abject in living (in a way reminiscent of the plays discussed so far), he contrasts it with the Platonic concept of *eros*, the 'reproductive sense', the freedom of life, a natural and – perplexingly also impure – vigour and constantly renewed life force covered up by libido (Artaud 1976: IV, 37–8). Artaud, in other words, sets up an opposition between two kinds of 'impurities' – one that he opposes (human libido) and one that he endorses (an impersonal *eros*). While both ancient tragedy and Artaud's theatre centrally require human bodies, Artaud does not understand life ('la vie') as individual life or individual dramatic characters, but as a pre-personal or impersonal force.

In ancient Greece, as enacted in Attic tragedy, humans were part of a communal existence and a collective destiny, a society based on profound interdependence, as well as on an interconnected metaphysical universe. As Lehmann points out, early ritual forms of theatre united dance, music and role play with the help of masks, costumes and props, enacting affectively charged processes like the hunt or fertility. In Baroque theatre (circa 1575–1725), texts were still linked to musical language, dance gesture and the splendour of optical and architectonic decoration. In bourgeois 'literary' theatre, i.e. since at least Lessing, however, any theatrical tools had to serve and were controlled by the text as rational, anthropocentric meaning (Lehmann 1999: 74). 'Dramatic' theatre was marked by the abstraction that increasingly defines capitalist modernity. By contrast, like the ancient Greeks, Artaud is instead interested in a mythical theatre where life is 'translated' materially in its universal sense (Artaud 1976: IV, 139).[9] In spite of passages speaking of human mastery and the positive influence of humans, and in spite of the central role of human spectators in Artaud's theatre, it is here, in his view of life as a universal force and in the use of heterogeneous theatrical tools, that Artaud becomes posthumanist.

Ironically, given Artaud's opposition to the realist or naturalist dramatic tradition focused on human conflicts and motivations, the justification he gives for the 'blackness' of his theatre resembles the French novelist Stendhal's famous defence of the nineteenth-century realist novel as a mirror that only reflects the existing dirt of the road (i.e. the negative sides of contemporary society). Artaud writes: 'The theatre, like the plague, unleashes forces, it opens possibilities, and if these possibilities and forces are black, it is not the fault of the plague or of the theatre, but of life' ('Le théâtre, comme la peste . . . dégage des forces, il déclenche des possibilités, et si ces possibilités et ces forces sont noires, c'est la faute non pas de la peste ou du théâtre, mais de la vie') (Artaud 1976: IV, 38).[10] The theatre, like the plague, only enacts the blackness of the forces that constitute life.

Continuing the analogy between the theatre and the plague, Artaud describes the therapeutic function of the theatre as the collective emptying of abscesses. Speaking again in terms of immunity or contagion, he refers to the theatre as a poison 'thrown into the social body' that might disintegrate or break apart that social body. The theatre does so like the plague, a 'vindictive' and at the same time a 'life-saving' scourge that, according to Artaud, is the application of the natural law that every gesture is compensated by another gesture and every action by its reaction. Like the plague, Artaud's theatre is a crisis that is only resolved by death or by the restoration of health (Artaud 1976: IV, 38). Artaud sees both the plague and the theatre as a 'superior evil' because it only leaves behind either death or an extreme purification or supreme balance (here again reverberating with Greek tragedy). Unlike 'biopolitical' plays, in other words, Artaud does not attempt to defend against this evil. For Artaud, the theatre, like the plague, ultimately has a positive influence, inviting the mind to a delirium that exalts its energies (Artaud 1976: IV, 39). Like both ancient Greek theatre (based on identification) and Strindberg, but in clear contrast to Brecht's epic, cognitive theatre, Artaud sees the effect of the theatre in terms of the audience's hypnosis, where the spectator's mind is affected by 'a direct pressure on the senses' (Artaud 1976: IV, 150). In her analysis of Artaud, Kristeva speaks of 'an asymbolic pulsation whose tremors are recorded on the body' (Kristeva 2004: 120) – both the actors' and the spectators' bodies. Artaud describes this intended effect on the audience as immediate and violent and opposes it to the 'inefficient numbness' caused by cinema (Artaud 1976: IV, 101).

Any theatre addressed to a human audience, even the theatre as envisioned by Artaud, is of course arguably still a humanist theatre. Revealing their hidden force, Artaud encourages human communities to face destiny with a heroic attitude. Artaud ends his essay on the plague by asking whether in this world that is 'committing suicide without knowing it', there will be humans who are capable of imposing this superior notion of the theatre. This theatre, he argues, will return to us the natural and magical equivalent of dogmas in which we no longer believe (Artaud 1976: IV, 39). In modernity, where male symbolic authority – from divine authority to the authority of the king or the father in the family – is one of the dogmas in which we no longer believe, Artaud proposes a theatre that replaces this symbolic authority – 'the abominable institutions that enclose us' ('Lettre à André Breton', quoted by Kristeva 2004: 124) – with a magical equivalent, that is with the magic of dreams (Artaud 1976: IV, 103). In this magic of dreams, mankind finally does lose its central role: 'humankind can only resume its place between the dream and events' ('il ne reste plus à l'homme que de réprendre sa place entre le rêve et les événements') (Artaud 1976: IV, 111). Whereas the early Artaud of the 1930s was most likely not thinking in terms of climate crisis but rather in terms of the destruction caused by war and totalitarian regimes when he was speaking of a world that is committing suicide without realising what it is doing, the relevance of his assessment for our contemporary times is clear.

The *Mise-en-Scène*

Artaud is often inspired by paintings.[11] In his essay 'Metaphysics and the *Mise en Scène*', he discusses Renaissance Dutch painter Lucas van den Leyden's work *Lot and His Daughters*, again expressing his own interest in the incest thematic. According to Artaud, this supremely material and anarchic painting that shows us the uselessness of words ('la Parole') is what the theatre should be 'if it spoke the appropriate language' ('s'il parlait le langage qui lui appartient'). In opposition to 'la Parole' ('Language') with a big P, that is the logocentrism of human, verbal language, Artaud proposes a different, material and anarchic language. He wants to re-establish the link between words and physical movements and make the logical and discursive side of language disappear under its physical and affective side. Put differently, Artaud wants words to be understood less in terms of their meaning than in terms of their physicality, as movements (Artaud 1976: IV, 143–4).

In this context, the question of breath in particular seems to be central to Artaud's theatre. For every movement of the mind and for every leap of affect there is, according to Artaud, a corresponding breath (Artaud 1976: IV, 155). Breath gives life (Artaud 1976: IV, 159). This corporeal-material language, these signs instead of words (Artaud IV: 65), is based on the actual performance: on the actions and movements not only of human bodies, but also of plants, body parts and the 'cries', 'sighs' or 'breaths' of instruments (Artaud 1976: IV, 67). This language is based on moments and movement in time and on an active use of space that leaves no portion of the stage unused (Artaud 1976: IV, 55, 56, 65). This language, Artaud states, is only truly theatrical to the degree that the thoughts that it expresses escape articulated language (Artaud 1976: IV, 45). At the same time, however, and most importantly for us, this focus on the senses does not preclude this language from subsequently developing its intellectual consequences and meaning ('sens précis') (Artaud 1976: IV, 65), on all levels and in all directions (Artaud 1976: IV, 46). It does not preclude this language from elucidating a state or an intellectual problem (Artaud 1976: IV, 74), as my reading of *The Cenci* will show in the next chapter. The language Artaud advocates does not exclude meaning or knowledge. While losing its decorative function, it is 'directly communicative' (Artaud 1976:

IV, 128). Again, materiality and consciousness ('esprit'/'mind/intellect') are not mutually exclusive.[12]

What is reversed in Artaud is the primacy of mind or verbal language over matter that marks the western philosophical tradition and western theatre. Artaud writes:

> In the realm of the affective imponderable, the image provided by my nerves takes the form of the highest intellectuality, which I refuse to strip of its quality of intellectuality. And so it is that I watch the formation of a concept which carries within it the actual fulguration of things, a concept which arrives upon me with the sound of creation. No image satisfies me unless it is at the same time Knowledge, unless it carries with it its substance as well as its lucidity. My mind, exhausted by discursive reason, wants to be caught up in the wheels of a new, an absolute gravitation. For me it is like a supreme reorganization in which only the laws of illogic participate, and in which there triumphs the discovery of a new Meaning . . . But it does not accept this chaos as such, it interprets it, and because it interprets it, it loses it. It is the logic of Illogic. And this is all one can say. My lucid unreason is not afraid of Chaos. (Artaud 1999: 108, quoted by Kristeva 2004: 120)

Artaud's understanding of the concept and the image breaks down the dichotomy between nerve sensation, sound and things/substance on the one hand and intellect/mind/knowledge/lucidity on the other. Interestingly, Artaud makes a distinction between discursive reason and (his) mind. Artaud's 'objective and concrete' language breaks with the hegemony of discursive reason or conceptual language ('l'asujetissement intellectuel au langage') (Artaud 1976: IV, 108) ('the intellectual subjection to language').[13] He aims for a language that leads not to anti-intellectualism, but instead gives voice to a new and deeper intellectuality not averse to the lack of logical coherence,[14] to affect, materiality ('things', 'substance'), and to more acute perception (Artaud 1976: IV, 108). In the passage quoted, the terms used ('the laws/logic of illogic' or 'lucid unreason') figure as transversals since usually, laws and illogic are considered opposites. In Artaud, meaning and chaos become one.

Artaud and Brecht

While Artaud's and Brecht's projects are in many ways diametrically opposed and Brecht targets the spectators' minds instead of their senses and affects, both writers are inspired by Asian, and in particular Balinese, theatre and dance. Artaud saw the latter performed at the Paris Colonial Exposition in 1931 (Artaud 1976: IV, 47, 53, 57; see also 'Sur le théâtre balinais').[15] Brecht also uses corporeal and material techniques (gestures, physical attitudes, disharmonious songs and stage decor) for his project of estrangement, of breaking the spectator's illusion. While Artaud approvingly mentions the French playwright Alfred Jarry (Artaud 1976: IV, 68), whose work is considered a forerunner of Dadaism, surrealism and absurd theatre, my chapter on Brecht's *Baal* has argued that the (in Kristeva's sense) poetic, semiotic or extra-symbolic language of Brecht's early work already foreshadows the theatre of the absurd. As we will see, we can also find such poetic language in Artaud. When Artaud speaks of actors as 'these mechanized beings to whom neither their joys nor their pain seem to belong' (Artaud 1976: IV, 70), these mechanised actors are also reminiscent of the Brechtian *gestus*. Whereas Brecht, however, wants to achieve the audience's critical distance, Artaud wants to cause terror (Artaud 1976: IV, 70).

Artaud's theatre of cruelty is a theatre where objects exercise cruelty and a certain eroticism on human spectators (Artaud 1976: IV, 95, 102, 119). While Artaud speaks of the objects exercising agency over human spectators, the spectators themselves are also part of this open, moving system, themselves in turn affecting the tonality of the performance and the agential spatiality around them. In her discussion of Artaud's work, Kristeva speaks of the eroticism of this dynamic performativity in terms of an excessive (excessive because extra-symbolic) *jouissance* (Kristeva 2004: 123).[16]

Both Brecht and Artaud see the common people rather than the bourgeoisie as their intended audience. Targeting the people's (and spectators') senses instead of their understanding (as Brecht does, although Artaud's understanding of the psychological, 'realist' tradition as based on understanding seems a bit questionable, given for instance Strindberg's view of the playwright as hypnotist), Artaud's goal is the 'convulsion' of agitated masses:

> Pénétré de cette idée que la foule pense d'abord avec ses sens, et qu'il est absurde comme dans le théâtre psychologique ordinaire de s'adresser d'abord à leur entendement, le Théâtre de la Cruauté se propose de recourir au spectacle de masses; de rechercher dans l'agitation de masses importantes, mais jetées l'une contre l'autre et convulsées, un peu de cette poésie qui est dans les fêtes et dans les foules, les jours, aujourd'hui trop rares, où le people descend dans la rue. (Artaud 1976: IV, 102)

> (Filled with this idea that the masses think first of all with their senses, and that it is absurd to address above all their understanding as does the psychological theatre, the theatre of cruelty proposes to return to the mass spectacle, to search in the agitation of substantial masses, thrown against each other and convulsive, for a bit of this poetry that one finds in festivals and in crowds on those days, too rare today, when the people go out into the streets.)

In 1933, the year of publication of this section of *Le Théâtre et son double* ('Le Théâtre et la cruauté') ('Theatre and Cruelty'), this kind of language could of course remind one of the fascist rhetoric concerning masses, and (again reminiscent of Brecht's reception) certain critics have indeed accused Artaud of totalitarianism (for instance Jannarone 2010: 118 and Vork 2013: 310).

But in contrast to Brecht – whose theatre is also, as I have argued, *not* totalitarian – Artaud's theatre is not a political theatre.[17] Like Brecht's early work, Artaud's theatre is anarchic in a social sense; Artaud writes 'that the current state of society is unjust and should be destroyed ('l'état social actuel est inique et bon à détruire') (Artaud 1976: IV, 50). But Artaud first and foremost sees his theatre as a mystical, hallucinatory, magical and 'cosmic' theatre focused on the universal themes of love, crime, war and madness (Artaud 1976: IV, 90, 102, 104, 105).[18] In contrast, Brecht's theatrical vision eschews any mysticism. While Brecht, moreover, wants to create a distance between the stage and the audience, Artaud aims to physically and affectively immerse his audience in the sensory materiality and perpetual movement of the performance (Artaud 1976: IV, 103, 150), doing away – historically at the same time as the quantum revolution proposes to do so in physics – with 'the classical ontological condition of exteriority between observer and observed' (Barad 2007: 140). Artaud produces spectators that experience themselves as physically and ontologically vulnerable in their relationality to performative heterogeneity.

In spite of their differences, Artaud and Brecht are, as Sontag writes, the only writers whose work on theatre 'had an impact so profound that the course of all recent serious theatre in Western Europe and the Americas can be said to divide into two periods': before Artaud/Brecht and after Artaud/Brecht. In other words, according to Sontag, 'Brecht is the century's only other writer on the theatre whose importance and profundity conceivably rival Artaud's.' Nevertheless, in contrast to Brecht's later work, Artaud's practical work as a theatre director in the years between 1926 and 1935 was marked by commercial failure and public rejection. As Sontag reminds us, 'Artaud's most ambitious, fully articulated production of the Theatre of Cruelty, his own *The Cenci*, lasted for seventeen days in the spring of 1935' (Sontag 1999: 94), and he subsequently abandoned the theatre and the idea of an ideal art form. Artaud's project of overcoming the separation of art and life, however, persisted throughout his life (Sontag 1999: 95), and his influence on the theory and practice of performance that succeeded him has indeed been extraordinary. Leo Bersani writes: 'Perhaps the most fundamental aspect of theatrical reform in the twentieth century has been the devaluation of the written theatrical text. And of course the figure most intimately connected with this project is Antonin Artaud' (Bersani 2004: 97).

Artaud, Posthumanist?

Artaud compares the signs used in his theatre to hieroglyphs, 'where humans, to the extent that they help form them, are only one form among others' ('où l'homme, dans la mesure où il contribute à les former, n'est qu'une forme comme une autre') (Artaud 1976: IV, 48). I have argued above that Artaud's work as described in 'The Theatre and the Plague' (a talk given at the Sorbonne on 6 April 1933) (Artaud 1976: IV, 344) is not yet fully posthumanist. At the same time, however, his essay 'Metaphysics and the *Mise en Scène*' – a talk originally given at the Sorbonne on 10 December 1931 (Artaud 1976: IV, 345), i.e. a year and a half *earlier* – does propose a theatre where material objects become the primary actors and are not reduced to human purposes (Artaud 1976: IV, 117). This theatre abolishes the primacy of the human over non-human matter, doing away with human exceptionalism and notions of human freedom or control (Artaud 1976: IV, 95). As we have seen, Artaud elsewhere writes of humans' beneficial influence (and sees epidemics as therapeutic). Here, however, we read: 'we have only left . . . to recognize that we are no longer good for anything except disorder, famine, blood, war and epidemics' ('nous n'avons plus . . . qu'à reconnaître que nous ne sommes plus bons que pour le désordre, la famine, le sang, la guerre et les epidemies') (Artaud 1976: IV, 96). According to Artaud, it would be futile to erect immunitarian borders or walls. We have seen the enemy, and it is us.

At the same time, Artaud does not give up completely on humans. He speaks of humans' 'nature double' (Artaud 1976: IV, 49, 75), a 'double nature' that provides the basis of his theatrical vision and gives his collected theoretical writings their title. This double nature includes both the symbolism of natural-material, more-than-human life on the one side and – on the other side – human 'esprit'/mind/intellectual and verbal language ('la Parole'). The signs used on the stage are hieroglyphs, because for Artaud clarity equals death and limitation: 'Because for me, clear ideas are dead and finished ideas, in the theatre as well as elsewhere' ('Car pour moi les idées claires sont, au théâtre comme partout ailleurs, des idées mortes et terminées'). Artaud's hieroglyphic language is a language of excess, exceeding not just articulated human language but also the limits imposed on human emotions: 'an active language, active and anarchic, where the usual limits of emotions and words are abandoned' ('un language actif, actif et anarchique, où les délimitations habituelles des sentiments et des mots soient abandonnées') (Artaud 1976: IV, 49).

According to Artaud, this excess or anarchy is at the base of any true poetry (Artaud 1976: IV, 51). Following a passage on the arbitrariness of form worthy of the linguistic theories of Ferdinand de Saussure,[19] Artaud's explains that the anarchy he advocates is a linguistic anarchy. He describes this anarchy as follows: 'poetry is anarchic insofar as it questions all the relations of object to object and of forms to their meanings' ('la poésie est anarchique dans la mesure où elle remet en cause toutes les relations d'objet à objet et des formes avec leurs significations') (Artaud 1976: IV, 52). Again, this linguistic anarchy is ultimately also a questioning of the relation of human-as-object to other objects. This anarchy, 'these displacements of meanings' ('ces déplacements de significations'), is the modern questioning of the reliability of representation, of any stable or closed sign system. It is a questioning of what Max Horkheimer and Theodor Adorno, in their *Dialectic of Enlightenment* (*Dialektik der Aufklärung*) called 'spezifische Vertretbarkeit' ('specific representability'). Here, in 'Metaphysics and the *Mise en Scène*', Artaud's theatre is indeed evolving into a posthumanist theatre. As Artaud himself says, 'Everything in this poetic and active manner of contemplating expression on the stage leads us to turn away from the human, current and psychological meaning of the theatre in order to rediscover the religious and mystical meaning with which our theatre has completely lost touch' ('Tout dans cette façon poétique et active d'envisager l'expression sur la scéne nous conduit à nous détourner de l'acception humaine, actuelle et psychologique du théâtre, pour en retrouver l'acception religieuse et mystique dont notre théâtre a complètement perdu le sens') (Artaud 1976: IV, 56).[20] Rather than on dichotomies, Artaud's border-crossing theatre is based on 'synthesis and analogy' (Artaud 1976: IV, 57) and goes beyond the human.

Opposing the Cartesian hegemony of consciousness, Artaud urges that the theatre address the spectator's unconscious and not limit itself to the conscious realm (Artaud 1976: IV, 57), the realm negatively described as 'our logical and abusive intellectualism' ('notre intellectualisme logique et abusif'), an intellectualism also associated with the naturalist-mimetic dramatic tradition that Artaud seeks to overcome. Instead, Artaud's theatre enacts an intensity, a violence (Artaud 1976: IV, 65) that makes the actors and the audience sense ('sentir') 'the subterranean threats of a chaos that is as decisive as it is dangerous'. Explaining the title of his theoretical work based on the notion of 'the double', Artaud speaks of 'the essential drama', the drama of matter and the 'thickening' (materialisation) of the idea (Artaud 1976: IV, 61). What is at stake is ultimately more than the human; it is the cosmos ('la formidable tempête cosmique') (Artaud 1976: IV, 81). Artaud's 'essential drama' is, finally, an 'essentialist' drama, a drama whose materiality is not situated. Put differently, the materiality in Artaud's work is a materiality across timescales or space; Artaud is exclusively interested in the cosmic, universal scale. At the same time, his theatre is indeed focused on process, on the iterative performative making and remaking of matter and affect.

In his discussion of Balinese theatre in 'Metaphysics and the *Mise en Scène*', Artaud also addresses in further depth the question of affect in his theatre. He speaks of a 'mysterious fear' ('cette peur mystérieuse'), a corporeal fear to be unleashed, as one of the most effective and essential elements of theatre (Artaud 1976: IV, 53, 68). Greek tragedy was of course already based on fear or *phobos*. While the ancient Greeks saw tragedy as a cleansing (*catharsis*) from negative emotions, Artaud speaks of exorcism – a Christian term (Artaud 1976: IV, 73). As we have seen, the European psychological dramatic tradition so despised by Artaud also enacts the anxiety that pervades modern Europe, although with different tools.

But is the fear or 'angoisse ineffable' ('inexpressible anxiety') that Artaud speaks of (for instance Artaud 1976: IV, 76, 101) itself different from enactments of anxiety discussed so far or is it simply expressed differently in his theatre? While key exponents of the European realist dramatic tradition from Strindberg to Sartre enact immunitarian systems to fend off perceived psychic and material threats in the hope of diminishing any related anxieties, Artaud's border-crossing theatre is based on 'synthesis and analogy' (Artaud 1976: IV, 57) rather than dichotomies and goes beyond the human. Artaud also speaks of anxiety – agitation and worry ('inquiétude') – as characteristic of contemporary times. But in contrast to the writers explored so far, he is not interested in enacting economic, utilitarian or technical issues (Artaud 1976: IV, 147). Instead of a theatre that voyeuristically displays modern anxieties (Artaud 1976: IV, 93) and attempts to defend against these anxieties, Artaud sees these anxieties as related to ecstasy ('l'extase'),[21] an affect that links humans ('l'homme total' instead of 'l'homme social') to plants and animals on a universal, cosmic, ontological and mythical level (Artaud 1976: IV, 79, 147).

Artaud's theatre thus aims to overcome the separation of art and life. He refers to this separation as a 'castration' and instead sees his own theatre as an expression of 'vital force' ('la force vitale') (Artaud 1976: IV, 93–4) or a 'blind appetite for life' ('appétit de vie aveugle') (Artaud 1976: IV, 122). Artaud sees 'gestures' in painting or theatre and 'gestures' in natural-material life ('un geste fait par la lave dans le désastre d'un volcan') (Artaud 1976: IV, 96) ('a gesture made by lava in the disaster of a volcano') in terms of analogy. In both cases, *objects act*. In spite of the emphasis on the mythical in Artaud's work, his understanding of objects or materiality also includes material manifestations that have become available due to recent advances in science ('[les] manifestations matérielles obtenues par des moyens scientifiques nouveaux') (Artaud 1976: IV, 147). Like Brecht, who wanted to create a 'theatre for the scientific age', Artaud says that in theatre, poetry and science must henceforth be the same (Artaud 1976: IV, 163).

Fusions

Artaud's theatre is in many ways a theatre of analogies, the threshold ('lieu de passage') where divergent realms meet (Artaud 1976: IV, 130). In his essay 'Le Théâtre alchimique' ('Theatre as Alchemy'), Artaud again establishes such an analogy: this time the analogy is not between theatre and the plague, but between the theatre and alchemy – the physical transformation of ordinary metals into gold – and Artaud points out that many books about alchemy express their affection for theatre (Artaud 1976: IV, 59). Like the theatre, alchemy, this physical transformation, is also based on symbols and is thus again double in Artaud's sense. Alchemy leads us to 'a different typical and dangerous reality' ('une autre réalité dangereuse et typique') (Artaud 1976: IV, 58), a reality that exceeds the realm of human culture. Artaud describes this ultimately posthuman reality in the following terms: 'this reality is not human but inhuman and man with his customs or his character, one must admit, counts for little there' ('cette réalité n'est pas humaine mais inhumaine, et l'homme avec ses mœurs ou avec son caractère y compte, il faut le dire, pour fort peu'). Restricting the theatre to purely human means, Artaud says, will lead it to miss out on aberrations, fantasies, illusions and hallucinations, and thus on true theatre: 'the alchemical symbol is a mirage, as the theatre is a mirage' ('le symbole alchimique est un mirage comme le théâtre est un mirage' (Artaud 1976: IV, 59). In spite of his opposition to the rationalist tradition, Artaud here follows this tradition by associating the human exclusively with consciousness.

In contrast to the Cartesian tradition, however, the symbolism that Artaud advocates is a material symbolism, '[un] symbolisme materiel' (Artaud 1976: IV, 60). Artaud's theatre is a theatre that creates gold (Artaud 1976: IV, 62), a materiality that nevertheless draws its value from the human sphere. According to Artaud, just as the symbols of alchemy settle and transfuse matter, the mind/spirit ('l'esprit') also transfuses matter (Artaud 1976: IV, 63). Artaud's theatre is a materialsymbolic theatre that inextricably fuses the abstract and the concrete (Artaud 1976: IV, 63, 72, 77), the mental and the physical realms (Artaud 1976: IV, 72,110). In this way, Artaud's theatre stands in opposition to the plays presented so far (Strindberg, Sartre) in which fusion is problematised as a biopolitical threat. Moreover, Artaud's 'essential' or 'pure', universalist theatre confronting 'the absolute' ('l'absolu') (Artaud 1976: IV, 84) diverges from the western 'dramatic' tradition in that the latter is based on contemporary social thematics ('cette sorte de théâtre social ou d'actualité') (Artaud 1976: IV, 60, 93). The goal of Artaud's theatre is not to resolve human social or psychological conflicts or to serve as the battleground for anthropocentric 'moral passions', but to objectively express secret truths, 'reconcil[ing] [theatre] with the universe' (Artaud 1958: 70).

Coining yet another term that would become central to Deleuze's philosophy, 'le Devenir' ('becoming'), Artaud speaks of the secret universal truths that he aims to express as hidden under forms in their encounter with becoming (Artaud 1976: IV, 84). Artaud defines 'le Devenir' as the passage or transmutation of ideas into things ('la transmutation des idées dans les choses') (Artaud 1976: IV, 130). As we have seen, the mainstream European dramatic tradition had indeed enacted what Artaud calls 'the conflicts produced by the antagonism between matter and mind'. As the close reading of Artaud's best-known play, *The Cenci*, will show in the next chapter, Artaud instead proposed melting these disparate components – matter and mind – into one expression (gold), an expression resembling a materiality that has been distilled ('spiritualisé' – i.e. intellectualised as well as spritualised) (Artaud 1976: IV, 63).

For Artaud, abstraction is thus ultimately not the crisis of representation gone wild – symbolic authority's increasing loss of embodiment in modernity as discussed in previous plays from the European 'dramatic' tradition. In Artaud, abstraction instead starts out from a state of mind and, by a 'mental alchemy', is turned into the materiality of the stage, in order to finally return to thought (Artaud 1976: IV, 77, 80). Rather than a defensive movement away from materiality followed,

paradoxically, by the attempt to again ground abstraction in materiality, this movement is instead – as *The Cenci* will show – circular and
recurring in Artaud.

Whereas the dramas described so far, and in particular Strindberg
and Sartre's work, problematise the *threat* posed by abstraction, by
the gap that opens up in modernity between an increasingly disembodied sublime political authority and natural-material life, Artaud
embraces the void ('le vide') that for him characterises both material nature ('[le]vide réel de la nature') and thought,[22] explaining that
'a sunset is beautiful because of everything it makes us lose' ('un
soleil couchant est beau à cause de tout ce qu'il nous fait perdre')
(Artaud 1976: IV, 86). What Artaud's work and the other modern
plays studied so far nevertheless have in common is a sense of loss,
a sense of lack shared with the epistemological/psychoanalytic tradition. Artaud's work, however, gives expression to this modern sense
of loss and anguish in a performative vision that clearly differs from
the plays discussed so far.

Notes

1. Even though my discussion has tried to qualify Lehmann's assessment of
   anthropocentrism for Brecht in particular.
2. All translations of Artaud are my own, unless otherwise noted.
3. Cf. Lehmann (1999).
4. 'An assemblage, in its multiplicity necessarily acts on semiotic flows,
   material flows, and social flows simultaneously' (Deleuze and Guattari
   1987: 71).
5. For Brian Massumi, 'affect is precisely a matter of how intensities come
   together, move each other, and transform and translate under or beyond
   meaning, semantics, fixed systems, cognitions' (Bertelson and Murphy
   2010: 147).
6. Cf., for instance, Braidotti (2013: 215).
7. As Sontag (1999: 90) points out, even before his 1926 rupture with the
   surrealist movement, Artaud did not engage in automatic writing. For
   more on differences between surrealism and Artaud see also Sontag
   (1999: 90).
8. Cf. Erin Manning referencing Guattari's sense of the 'therapeutic' in Massumi (2015b: 166).
9. Cf. Sontag (1999: 91): 'Artaud's argument in *Le théâtre et son double*
   is closely related to that of the Nietzsche who in *The Birth of Tragedy*
   lamented the shriveling of the full-blooded archaic theatre of Athens by
   Socratic philosophy – by the introduction of characters who reason.'

For other affinities between Artaud and Nietzsche see also Sontag (1999: 91).

10. In his novel *Le rouge et le noir*, Stendhal famously writes: 'Ah, Sir, a novel is a mirror carried along a high road. At one moment it reflects to your vision the azure skies, at another the mire of the puddles at your feet. And the man who carries this mirror in his pack will be accused by you of being immoral! His mirror shows the mire, and you blame the mirror! Rather blame that high road upon which the puddle lies, still more the inspector of roads who allows the water to gather and the puddle to form' (Stendhal 1926: 166–7).

11. Cf., for example, Artaud (1976: IV, 144).

12. See also Artaud (1976: IV, 54, 76).

13. Cf. Artaud (1999: 109): 'The truth of life lies in the impulsiveness of matter. The mind of man has been poisoned by concepts.'

14. Cf. Artaud (1976: IV, 39: 'Because for me clear ideas, in the theatre as in everything else, are ideas that are dead and finished' (quoted by/trans. in Derrida 2004a: 130).

15. As Garner points out, '[t]he Dutch East Indian Pavilion, where Artaud saw the Balinese dancers perform at the 1931 Colonial Exposition, included a display on the fight against plague and other diseases' (Garner 2006: 8).

16. In contrast to Kristeva, Artioli (2004: 144) argues that 'there is never jouissance' in Artaud. Cf. on the other hand Vanoye's discussion of the *jouissance* in Artaud (based on Roland Barthes's understanding of the term) (Vanoye 2004: 181).

17. Cf. Sontag (1999: 92): 'Dismayed when Breton attempted to link the surrealist programme with Marxism, Artaud broke with the surrealists for what he considered to be their betrayal into the hands of politics of an essentially "spiritual" revolution.'

18. In Artaud's 1925 play *Jet de sang* (*Jet of Blood*), for instance, the characters do not have individual names, but are 'The Young Man', 'The Young Woman' and so forth. One of the characters, finally, is a disembodied 'A Thunderous Voice'.

19. 'La nature quand elle a donné à un arbre la forme d'un arbre aurait tout aussi bien pu lui donner la forme d'un animal ou d'une colline, nous aurions pensé *arbre* devant l'animal ou la colline, et le tour aurait été joué' (Artaud 1976: IV, 51) ('When it gave a tree the form of a tree, nature could have just as well given it the form of an animal or a hill, and we would have thought 'tree' in front of an animal or a hill, and that would have been that.')

20. This and the following chapter are primarily concerned with the 'early' Artaud, that is with Artaud's theoretical writings and theatrical work of the 1930s. Concerning the late or 'final' Artaud, whose opposition to representation grew ever stronger in the 1940s during and after his

stay at the psychiatric hospital at Rodez from 1943 to 1964 and before his death in 1948, Murphy states: 'His ferocious disintegration of the hieroglyph and representation goes hand-in-hand with his shredding of any mystical or religious belief' (Murphy 2015: 16). Cf. also Murphy (2015: 17): 'With the late Artaud categories of sacred/profane are of little utility. With his visit to the Tarahumara Indians in September 1936, Artaud became inducted into a universe of sorcery and counter-sorcery he never left.'

21. In relation to Artaud, Kristeva spoke of 'jouissance'.

22. See Blanchot's analysis of Artaud's letters on the erosion of thought experienced by Artaud (Blanchot 2004).

CHAPTER 6

Where Does the Body End? Artaud's Materialsymbolic Theatre

Grace passes in the fuzzy area between words and things, between the canals where substantial foods and sonorous voices flow, between the exchanges of energy and information, an intermediate space, a space of equivalence where language is born, where fire is born, where it makes the things of which its speaks appear, an unstable distance of ecstasy and existence, of incarnation and ascension, of breads and birds . . . I hear the invitation to live together in the space in which the material and the logical are exchanged. The third appears; the third is included. Maybe he is each and every one of us. (Serres 2007: 47)

When things like that happen, it deserves to be called an event. Events are always transindividual, bringing out potentials that could never have been arrived at individually . . . what will transpire has not been predetermined, but has to eventuate, and how it eventuates is up for relational grabs, and will only be clear as the event unfolds. (Massumi 2015b: 172)

An adaptation of Percy Bysshe Shelley's 1819 verse drama first performed in 1922 and of Stendhal's 1837 novella of the same name, Artaud's most famous play, *Les Cenci: Tragédie en quatre actes et dix tableaux d'après Shelley et Stendhal*, is considered 'the most complete, concrete example ever produced of his theatrical vision' (Vork 2013: 308). The only play in Artaud's career over which he had exclusive artistic control (if such a thing exists), it was first performed, with the author himself as Count Cenci, in 1935 – thirteen years after the premiere of Shelley's play, and seven years after Artaud's infamous and short-lived production of Strindberg's post-naturalist *Dream Play* at the Théâtre Jarry. Although Artaud considered the production of his play a success, it was a commercial failure and had to close after only seventeen performances. Considered 'a precipitating event in the collapse of Artaud's mental health' (Curtin 2010: 250), it ultimately proved to be Artaud's last theatrical production. In the intervening years since then, Artaud's *Les Cenci* has had a reputation as a theatrical failure and has only rarely been staged. The reception in English-speaking countries in particular was also long hampered by what many considered a less than exciting translation of the play into English. In 2008, however, John Jahnke, the artistic director of the acclaimed Hotel Savant theatre company, staged *Les Cenci* based on a new translation by the scholar Richard Sieburth (the first American to translate the play), the play's first major New York production in more than thirty years (Artaud 2008). Positing that the play's reputation as a theatrical flop was unfair ('I don't believe in judging something by the standards of its day'), Jahnke is quoted as saying: 'Is it a difficult piece? Yes. Is it a flawed piece? Absolutely. But does that detract from the fact that it's exciting onstage? No, not at all. It's worth a second look' (Blankenship 2008). With this chapter, I join Sieburth and Jahnke in encouraging cultural theorists and theatre practitioners to take a second look.

As even just production clips (for instance by Theatre Artaud/Berlin 1986–91) show, Artaud's *Les Cenci* is certainly not an easy play to watch – or listen to. Like Shelley's Romantic verse tragedy, Artaud's play integrates 'the monstrous, the uncanny into modern aesthetics, admitting all that is shocking and painful to common perception' (Roussetzki 2000: 2). At the same time Artaud's tools in what he calls his 'theatre of cruelty' differ greatly from Shelley's. To achieve the shock and pain central to his theatre, Artaud created in *Les Cenci* an innovative design that foregrounded sound and included the first stage use of the *Ondes Martenot* (an electronic instrument).[1] Artaud thus displaced the primacy of visuality or scopic exclusivity typical of traditional western theatre, the imperative of the human eye that has marked the humanist tradition since Plato.[2] As Timothy Morton puts it, Plato sought 'to separate the language of seeing, of insight into truth, of clarity, from the haptic confusion of the cave's interior' (Morton 2016: 71). Vision has been central to the western concept of the subject. With his displacement of the centrality of vision, by enmeshing vision with the intensity of sound, Artaud therefore ultimately also displaces western anthropocentric subjectivity.

The goal of Artaud's theatre is in fact the confusion not only of vision, but of all senses. As Anna Gibbs remarks, while 'sight is in fact neurologically dominant in the so-called higher primates [including the human], it rarely operates in isolation from the other senses' (Gibbs 2010: 202). Intensifying the actors' and spectators' confusion, the production by the Hotel Savant included a set designed by Peter Ksander that featured a maze that ran through the entire theatre, abandoning the traditional proscenium (Hetrick 2008). Artaud himself had called for abandoning theatres for more quotidian structures such as hangars, barns or factories and for putting the audience in the middle (as the playwright Robert Wilson would do in the 1970s). For their production, the Hotel Savant company used the Ohio Theater, one of the last warehouse-style theatres in Manhattan (Lockwood 2008), where the maze of the set design consisted of twisting paths bounded by low walls that the actors had to navigate in every scene. Breaking down the separation between actors and audience and the illusion of realist-mimetic theatre, the cast members dove under the spectators for many of their exits and spoke some of their lines at a 'rapid, unnatural pace'. The production was also 'peppered with blasts of recorded sound and live onstage music, and there [were] plenty of pauses for dance breaks, simulated orgies and comedic entrances from the stage manager.' The purpose of the Hotel Savant's production was the creation of a physical language that expressed the mania of Artaud's theatrical vision (Blankenship 2008).

The space created in Artaud's avant-garde theatre already fits the description Liesbeth Groot Nibbelink gives of another, contemporary/twenty-first-century performance that she analyses in her book *Nomadic Theatre*, namely the Flemish company Ontoerend Goed's *The Smile Off Your Face*: 'it deterritorializes the theatre as a *theatron* – a place for looking and watching – and instead reterritorialises the theatre as a *sensorium*, as the theatre space becomes an environment in which all of the senses are addressed simultaneously' (2019: 115). In *Les Cenci*, Artaud creates an all-encompassing energetic exchange between space, sounds, rhythms, things, tonality, visual perceptions, actors and spectators. Artaud's redistributed stage is what Deleuze and Guattari would later call a 'smooth space': 'Smooth space is filled by events . . . far more than by formed and perceived things. It is a space of affects, more than one of properties. It is . . . occupied by intensities, wind and noise, and sonorous and tactile qualities' (Deleuze and Guattari, quoted by Groot Nibbelink 2019: 102; cf. also Groot Nibbelink 2019: 185 n. 4). The fact that the spectator as 'embodied mind' (Fischer-Lichte 2014: 34) is literally surrounded by the material intensities of the performance, becoming part of this multisensory world, contributes to the atmosphere of terror, the physiological affective impact, of Artaud's work. As Brian Massumi writes, 'affect is synesthetic, implying a participation of the senses in each other' (Massumi 2002: 35). Artaud's goal is sensory cross-modalisation, 'perception as an aggregate of different sensory modalities' (Chiew 2017: 48).[3] In *The Parasite*, Michel Serres writes about the harrowing effect of disharmonious sound in particular: 'We are surrounded by noise . . . It is our apperception of chaos, our apprehension of disorder, our only link to the scattered distribution of things. Hearing is our heroic opening to trouble and diffusion' (Serres 2007: 126). Artaud's work thus reconfigures the spectator's relationship to her sensory environment in a not primarily representational, non-hegemonic/non-anthropocentric mode. As Serres puts it, 'our chance is on the crest'; while '[n]oise destroys or terrifies' and 'order and flat repetition are in the vicinity of death' (a view shared by Artaud), '[o]rganization, life and intelligent thought live between order and noise, between disorder and perfect harmony' (Serres 2007: 127). The fact that Artaud's work pushes us off the crest, making us (the audience) lose our human sense of control, is the interest – and the threat – of Artaud's immersive theatre of affect.

In his *Ethics* (Part III Definition 3), the seventeenth-century Dutch philosopher Baruch Spinoza defines 'affects' as (a) the variations produced in bodies through their interactions with other bodies, and (b) the ideas of these variations. Spinoza writes: 'By affect I understand affections of the body by which the body's power of acting is increased or diminished, aided or restrained, and at the same time, the ideas of these affections' (Spinoza 1994: 154).[4] An affect is a vital force that increases or diminishes the body's power to act. In Artaud's *Les Cenci*, Count Cenci describes himself as such a vital force. The main force resonating with and responding to the Count, his main antagonist, is his daughter Béatrice. But the forces or bodies that act on each other in Artaud are not limited to humans. The many heterogeneous, human and nonhuman elements that compose the performance intra-act with each other, co-creating the affective intensities of this encounter. In Artaud's ecology of terror, in a circularity that replaces the conventional frontality of theatre, escape – the affective refrain that pervades and structures *Les Cenci* – becomes impossible for both the characters and the spectators. While Artaud's theatre of cruelty targets his (human) spectators, affect in Spinoza's sense is ultimately impersonal and goes beyond human consciousness; the live forces or bodies that act on each other instead co-constitute the cosmos.

Les Cenci, an Event

Artaud's contemporary, the surrealist painter and sculptor Marcel Duchamp, characterised art as 'a road which leads towards regions that are no longer governed by time and space' (quoted by Murphy 2015: 4). Guattari would later define an 'event' as 'a rupture with the coordinates of time and space'. Mixing past, present and future, an event is 'outside time', it 'crosses time' and it is 'transversal to all the measures of time' (Guattari, *Chaosmosis*, quoted by Murphy 2015: 4). Aiming for a universalist, ontological theatre, Artaud's *Les Cenci* creates a chronologically and geographically non-descript setting. In contrast to Shelley's play, which was itself inspired by the real-life story of a Renaissance family by the name of Cenci, Artaud's adaptation gives us few if any clues as to the time or place of the action. The stage directions at the beginning of the first act specify 'Une galerie en profondeur et en spirale.' What exactly is 'une galerie'? The meanings of this word range from an underground tunnel, a mining drift, an art gallery, a covered passage, to an upper balcony at the theatre or a shopping mall. Whatever it is, this 'galerie' is described as deep and as a spiral, specifications that do not add much further clarification or precision. Artaud's *Les Cenci* is thus an event in Guattari's sense. Given the importance of the spectators in Artaud, *Les Cenci* can incidentally also be considered an event in theatre scholar Erika Fischer-Lichte's sense: 'A performance can be seen as an event rather than an artwork because it is created through the interaction of actors and spectators (i.e. an autopoetic feedback loop). The autopoetic process is the process of the performance' (Fischer-Lichte 2014: 41).[5] In Artaud, the theatrical performance is a self-producing and self-sustaining process, an impersonal autopoetic feedback loop that goes beyond human time and space.

Let us then give this performance a closer look in a postcritical/descriptive intimate reading that, instead of imposing hegemonic mental concepts, respects the materiality and temporal axis of the text itself. While the verbal dialogue of Artaud's play sets in first at the beginning of the play, it problematises right from the start the dichotomy of the soul or mind and the body that has marked western philosophy and art, juxtaposing 'the life of souls' ('la vie des âmes') and 'a body'. Human dialogue is of course the primary theatrical tool used in the anthropocentric dramatic tradition that preceded Artaud, serving as an apparatus of a Cartesian worldview. In *Les Cenci*, Artaud puts this theatre in question by first mimicking its techniques. Camillo, a member of the papal conclave and thus a representative of traditional religion (Catholicism), argues that the soul is more valuable than the body (and that therefore a murder is nothing). He proposes an economic deal between Count Cenci and the Pope that would give Cenci absolution in exchange for a third of his possessions. Not only does the beginning of the play thus immediately problematise western binary thinking (the dichotomy of body and soul), but it also brings two male figures representing patriarchal authority and their economic interests into play: the head of the Catholic Church and Count Cenci, the head of the noble family that gives the play its title. Artaud presents the conflict between the two men as long-standing. Depreciating and objectifying again the value of human life as Camillo had done before him, Cenci argues that the life of a man is not worth such a great amount of land with vineyards, and he expresses his wish to declare war against the Pope (Artaud 1976: IV, 187–8). The very first scene of Artaud's play thus puts in play already the value of human life (in an almost Marxian take), patriarchal institutions and the binary division of body and soul – that is, socio-economic and political as well as ontological questions.

Enacting Artaud's theory of theatre as the expression of inevitable natural forces, Cenci then declares himself as more than a man, as a force of nature or destiny – as we have seen both crucial concepts in Artaud's understanding of theatre. Vork writes: 'The raw physical power of kinetic motion is here invoked – unstoppable, radically impersonal . . . This radical conception of action is incompatible with action viewed as the practical expression of subjective agency or will' (Vork 2013: 314). Announcing and at the same time annulling the key themes of the play, Cenci declares that for him – as for a force of nature – (human) life, death, god, incest, repentance or crime do not exist. While Camillo conveys the Pope's offer of a truce, stating that 'the world is weak: it wants peace' (Artaud 1976: IV, 189),[6] Cenci prefers war and vice. He is a force not only of nature, but of evil: 'I am a true monster . . . I do evil' ('je suis un vrai monstre . . . je fais le mal') (Artaud 1976: IV, 190–1). As we have seen, Artaud sees (ontological) evil as permanent or inevitable and praises its purifying effect on the audience.

In a self-reflective meta-discourse that is frequently a trait of the historical theatrical avant-garde of the early 1900s, Cenci's monologue (after Camillo has left the stage in Scene I) comments on the difference between theatre and life: In life, one acts more and speaks less; in theatre, one talks much and does little. In accordance with Artaud's opposition to the realist 'dramatic' theatrical tradition based on dialogue and with Artaud's own theatrical vision, Cenci declares his intention to re-establish the balance, promising more action (instead of words) on the stage. While Artaud wants more 'life' ('la vie') in theatre, Cenci here declares that his re-establishment of balance will come at the cost of human life. As we have seen, Artaud does not understand 'la vie' as individual life or individual dramatic characters, but as an impersonal life force. In Artaud's play, this life force comes at the cost of individual human lives.

Using a horticultural image that sees human life as part of the more-than-human world (here: plant life) and thus ultimately breaking down the distinction between human and nonhuman life, Cenci declares that he will 'prune' his abundant family (Artaud 1976: IV, 192). Collapsing the opposition between soul and body without conflating the two, Cenci says that he will torture the soul of his daughter through her body. As for Guattari (his later work influenced by Artaud), in Artaud the soul is 'not an immaterial soul in opposition to or in contradiction with matter. On the contrary, it is *matter itself that is infused with soul*' (Eduardo Viveiros de Castro on Guattari, quoted by Murphy 2015: 19, my emphasis). Count Cenci then again self-reflexively breaks the dramatic illusion by speaking of his 'taste for theatre', thereby conflating not only body and soul but also theatre and life.

Underlining the primacy of physical gestures in Artaud's work, Cenci makes a hand gesture (showing his dangling little finger) to underline his only subsequently verbally stated intention to spare his young son, Bernardo – not out of mercy, but so Bernardo can cry for his lost family members, in other words in order to cause his young son psychic suffering. Enacting the importance of breath in Artaud's theatre, Cenci then breathes into the air, addressing matter (air) as a quasi-human, personal entity and underlining his own intimacy with matter: 'Air, I am confiding my thoughts to you.' He subsequently also anthropomorphises and addresses the echo of his steps and the walls (Artaud 1976: IV, 193). The ending of this monologue is punctuated by another physical gesture followed by verbal instructions: Cenci strikes a gong with his sword, the latter a symbol of his (male) authority, creating a sound that makes a character in a subservient position (the servant Andrea) appear on stage. Enacting the primacy of corporeality or gestural language in Artaud's theatre, in the Hotel Savant's production the actors were instructed to rehearse their 'blocking' (or movements) before working on their (verbal) lines. 'Most of the time telling the story through movement is secondary to telling it through words, but with this we're forced to work in reverse', Anna Fitzwater, who played Count Cenci's wife, said: 'I'm surprised how much I'm able to tell with just a gesture or a head turn, and that starts making me think, "Why do we neglect that so often?"' (Blankenship 2008). Why, in other words, has the humanist theatrical tradition so often neglected the physical aspects of theatre?

In Artaud, however, one does not have to choose between the social and the physical. Artaud merges them both. Since Cenci has just given his servant peremptory orders to tell his daughter to come see him alone at midnight, at the end of Scene I the stage is set for incest. The French structuralist anthropologist Claude Lévi-Strauss considered the violation of this taboo the most important social rule and the foundation of any human society. Count Cenci, a pre-personal vital force, however, does not concern himself with the rules governing human society. In his dialogue with Béatrice, her would-be lover Orsino also speaks of his love for her, a love he claims to be stronger than his adherence, as a priest, to the Church. Social structures, in other words, are weak when compared to the forces of nature (Artaud 1976: IV, 195). In a similar vein, Béatrice tells Orsino that what separates them is neither the Church nor his heart, but – as in Greek tragedy – destiny, a force stronger than mere social obstacles. In *Les Cenci*, this destiny is Béatrice's father ('Mon père'). At the same time, however, Béatrice states that what is forcing her to stay in 'these walls of misery' is 'more than a man' ('plus qu'un homme'). The problematic of the play transcends the personal or human scale (Artaud 1976: IV, 196).

In spite of the primacy of physicality in Artaud's play, verbal language still has an important role to play in *Les Cenci*. The linguistic styles or registers used in the dialogue between Cenci and his daughter enact the difference between elemental nature (Cenci) and Béatrice as a member of human society. Béatrice speaks a refined language that includes a very elegant and rare past subjunctive ('eûmes'), also underlining the fact that the Cenci belong to the Roman upper nobility and that the action is set in the more formal past – although, as we have seen, Artaud never gives his play any social or historic specificity. At this early point in Artaud's play, Béatrice herself still sees the dramatic conflict as the internal conflict between love and duty familiar, for instance, from the neoclassical, seventeenth-century tragedies of Corneille or Racine. Béatrice is staying because of her little brother and her stepmother, who she says are suffering. It is here, however, that Béatrice also raises the stakes of the play by uttering the word that has made Artaud's theatre famous: cruelty ('la cruauté qui m'oppresse') ('the cruelty that oppresses me'). She adds, again channelling Artaud's theory of theatre: 'We have to act.' ('Il faut agir.') When Béatrice describes the upcoming supper with her extended family, the spectators come away from the end of Scene II with a sense of urgency, an urgency to act rather than just talk (Artaud 1976: IV, 195–8). The example of this exchange shows again that in contrast to the primarily verbal theatre of the realist-representationalist tradition, Artaud's theatre is a theatre based on physical action AND dialogue.

In a move away from human characters, Scene III of the first act starts with a staging of the banquet that includes a large number of *mannequins* – puppets as stand-ins for the human guests. The stage directions compare the scene to the biblical Wedding at Cana, 'but more barbaric'. The stage instructions speak of purple curtains that fly in the wind and fall back, in heavy folds, onto the walls. In another self-reference, under one of the lifted curtains – the displaced curtain of Artaud's theatre – a furious orgy scene bursts forth, painted 'comme en trompe-l'oeil'. Is the scene under the curtain painted in the technique of *trompe-l'oeil* or does the 'real' orgy resemble a *trompe-l'oeil* painting? Here Artaud self-referentially enacts the question of representation or reality. The reliable reality on which the naturalist dramatic tradition had been based is no longer available in Artaud.

The bells of Rome then ring at full volume ('à toute volée'), but are somehow muted ('mais en sourdine'), in accordance with the turbulent rhythm of the feast. How does 'muted' match a turbulent rhythm? How can bells ring at full volume in a muted way? According to Artaud's stage directions, the human voices become louder, assuming the 'grave or shrill' tonality of the bells. Human sounds and the sounds of non-organic objects (the bells) merge. But how is this sound? Is it 'grave' or 'shrill' ('suraigu')? From time to time, iteratively, a voluminous sound then spreads and fuses, 'as if [comme] stopped by an obstacle that makes it spill over in sharpened ridges'. Does the sound spread or is it stopped? The repeated use of 'comme' ('as if', 'like') certainly does not help advance any sense of logical clarity in these stage instructions. As we have seen, Artaud does not aspire to clarity, but instead wants what he calls 'hieroglyphs' on the stage. There is no sense of human control of the surrounding sound at the beginning of Scene III, nor any obvious human control of 'meaning', neither on the side of the actors, nor on the side of the audience (Artaud 1976: IV, 199).

Artaud is instead interested in a mythical theatre, a theatre enacting universal, cosmic themes not limited to the individual characters' psychology or contemporary social or political concerns. In *Les Cenci*, Jane Goodall says, 'it is Cenci's role as the father-destroyer which links his story with the 'Great Myths' (Goodall 2004: 72), the mythical fathers of Greek mythology. Reminiscent of these mythical fathers, who aim 'to reverse the process of creation towards a new Chaos' (Goodall 2004: 73), Cenci gets up to deliver a speech, calling himself 'the Myth Cenci' (Artaud 1976: IV, 199). Artaud's Count Cenci is a force of nonhuman, impersonal Chaos. The father gods of Greek mythology – Uranus, Chronos, Thyestes – also include Tantalus, who 'killed his son Pelops and served his body as food at a banquet of the gods' (Goodall 2004: 72). Artaud writes: 'Tantalus is mankind and every man alive is a menagerie of vampires' (Artaud 1976: IV, 60). While 'immunitarian' writers such as Strindberg enact vampire figures as a threat to be defended against, Artaud takes the vampirism of humankind – an ontological evil that transcends the evil threat posed by any single character – as an inevitable fact of nature. In reaction to Cenci's speech, Camillo says that he feels a cold wind – a force of nature – creeping up his back. Indeed, as another guest at the banquet points out, Cenci's introductory remarks presage nothing good. While Count Cenci does not serve his sons' bodies at the banquet as did Tantalus, he instead offers the guests the news of his sons' deaths, which he himself ordered. When Cenci announces his gratification at his sons' deaths, the guests express their disbelief at the nightmarish scene: 'I dream that I have understood well' ('je rêve que j'ai bien entendu') (Artaud 1976: IV, 205). Providing a model for the audience's reaction, the guests' reactions enact the affective impact of a nightmare. As we have seen in his theoretical writings, Artaud wants his theatre to access what the rationalist western philosophical and theatrical tradition had repressed but what is often expressed in myths, namely dreams and the unconscious.

The primary mythical father and linguistic signifier giving meaning to human life, on the other hand, namely God, has been emptied out for Cenci and has become a tool for Cenci's own cynicism. At the beginning of the play, Béatrice still declares her belief in divine justice (Artaud 1976: IV, 203) and the word 'God' ('Dieu') is used in repeated expressive exclamations (Artaud 1976: IV, 201–5). In Scene III, at the banquet, moreover, Cenci re-enacts the transsubstantiation of wine into blood, a process of re-signification. He pretends to drink the blood of his sons (Artaud 1976: IV, 204), whom he had murdered – in a complete mockery of paternal love and the Christian God's sacrifice of his own son – and he now asks the servant to pass the chalice (Artaud 1976: IV, 205). When the guests become frightened and start leaving, Béatrice stands in their way, appealing to their own roles as fathers: 'You are fathers. Do not leave us with this wild animal, or I will never again be able to see a white-haired head without feeling the desire to curse fatherhood' (Artaud 1976: IV, 206). Béatrice warns Cenci, threatening him that God might give the sons the arms to act against bad fathers. As if having received a big punch of the fist in the stomach, the crowd breathes and then exhales a loud scream and quickly and chaotically starts to leave in the direction of all exits (Artaud 1976: IV, 207) – a response more powerful than any verbal exchange. The old men, fathers themselves, in other words choose to protect their own authority over defending Béatrice and her family against a monstrous father. Goodall brilliantly points out that the feast thus does not act 'as a ceremonial reinforcement of communal solidarity, of the strength, security, and benevolence of the social order and its leaders'. Instead, 'the semiotics of the ritual are hijacked and instantaneously converted to their opposite by the revelation of violence' (Goodall 2004: 74). The fathers present at the banquet are indeed only the puppets (manne-quins) – figuratively and literally – that the stage instructions call for. They choose to protect absolutist authority – a premodern authority that cannot be questioned – while Béatrice, Cenci's daughter, is left as the one remaining character to question this authority. In spite of the fact that the father figures are literally only puppets, the scream they emit impresses itself physically onto the spectators. The power struggle enacted in this scene finds its gestural expression when Béatrice and her father face each other and for a long time size each other up with their eyes. As we have seen, in his theoretical writings, Artaud speaks about humans 'measuring up' to their fate (Artaud 1976: IV, 130). He empties out symbolic authority and replaces it with a raw physicality associated with the tragic notion of fate.

In *Tragödie und dramatisches Theater*, Hans-Thies Lehmann describes the shift from post-Renaissance 'dramatic' theatre to the historical avant-gardes of the early twentieth century (with Artaud as one of the major exponents of this latter tradition) as a shift from the primarily verbal conception of theatre based on human dialogue to the equality of space, light, sounds and timescale (Lehmann 2013: 29). The third scene of Act I can be seen as an example of what Lehmann calls 'Sinn- und Klangräume', spaces of meaning and sound that can no longer be attributed to an individual source. When in this scene (I, iii), Cenci finally goes to the table and pours himself another glass of wine, several torches suddenly go out and we hear the 'cavernous voice' of the bells. An unprecedented calm descends on the stage and a sound 'like a violin sound' vibrates very lightly and on a high pitch. The loss of light and the ominous or unidentified sounds announce an acute change in atmosphere/tonality and enact the sense of an imminent threat. Lehmann argues that while in traditional, bourgeois theatre (as exemplified in this project by Strindberg and Sartre), the actor was an agent of the director – who 'repeated' the author's word, which itself was a representation of the outside world – Artaud's stage and the stage of what Lehmann calls 'post-dramatic' theatre are a beginning instead of the location of a copy (Lehmann 1999: 46). Instead of replacing a chain of privileged signifiers (director, author, outside reality) with another privileged signifier ('beginning', that is 'origin', a signifier suggesting a linear timeline), maybe a better way of framing this comparison between bourgeois drama and Artaud would be to say that Artaud enacts a process co-constituted by multiple heterogeneous elements.

While the realist-humanist dramatic tradition was/is based on a teleology of (human) time and narrative, atmosphere or tonality becomes dominant in Artaud. In spite of this theatrical vision, however, *Les Cenci* also still contains plenty of suspense, which is a teleological or linear element. Consistent with the atmosphere of expectation in this scene (I, iii) – one of the play's central scenes, the scene of incest – Béatrice sits down and waits. Her father slowly starts to walk towards her (Artaud 1976: IV, 208). His attitude has completely changed; concordant with the importance Artaud assigns to breath, it now 'breathes' (the French stage instructions say 'respire') a heightened feeling of serenity and a definite change in tonality. Béatrice's distrust as well seems to have suddenly evaporated. Both antagonists' tone now bespeaks great emotion ('un ton ému'). Béatrice addresses Cenci as 'Mon père' ('My Father'). In a sexual image, she then tells him to 'withdraw' from her ('retire-toi de moi') and calls him 'ungodly man' ('homme impie'). Stating that she will never forget that he 'was' her father, she tells him to go away. That way, she says, she might be able to forgive him. Béatrice here voices the reality of what has so far only been hinted at in the play, namely Cenci's incestuous desire for his daughter (Artaud 1976: IV, 209). The female protagonist's shock and terror is the tonality that also affects the spectator in Artaud's play.

At the same time, Cenci's magic spell – in his theoretical writings Artaud speaks of 'witchcraft' – has started to work and Béatrice is already sensing her own loss of (human) control against the elemental force that is her father. Giving gestural expression to this desire, Cenci wipes his hand over his forehead, telling Béatrice that her father is thirsty. Will she not quench her father's thirst? Béatrice chooses to interpret this question literally and gives him an enormous glass of wine. Cenci takes the glass and makes a gesture of touching Béatrice's hair. Indicating that she feels this gesture to be sexual rather than paternal, Béatrice's reaction is physical, instantaneous and determined: She 'violently' moves back ('retire') her head. The word 'retire' (withdraw) of course again has sexual connotations. Cenci now speaks in a low voice and with clenched teeth, physically expressing the violence of this exchange. He calls Béatrice a 'viper' and tells her that he knows a charm (both in the sense of spell and seductiveness) that will tame her. At this point Béatrice is taken by an immense 'panic'. The French word 'affolement' includes the root word 'folie' ('insanity'). She leaves the room: 'elle bondit dehors' – literally, she leaps outside, like an animal (Artaud 1976: IV, 210). Invaded by Cenci's elemental energy, she is forced to abruptly leave the realm of the human. 'Cela me fait bondir' ('this is making me leap') is a French idiomatic expression roughly equivalent to 'That makes me hopping mad.' Madness, insanity is certainly part of Béatrice's reaction here, her reaction to the ambivalence of her abject relationship with her father – a relationship based on both attraction and repulsion. Julia Kristeva describes abjection as follows: 'Apprehensive, desire turns aside; sickened, it rejects . . . But simultaneously, just the same, that impetus, that spasm, that *leap* is drawn toward an elsewhere as tempting as it is condemned . . . Unflaggingly, like an inescapable boomerang, a vortex of summons and repulsion places the one haunted by it *literally beside himself*' (Kristeva 1982: 1, my emphases). In Artaud's play as well, Béatrice 'leaps outside as if she had suddenly understood' (Artaud 1976: IV, 210). The main character's and the spectators' intellectual comprehension is reached through the corporeality of the scene.

As Goodall points out, any 'attempts to withstand the engulfing morass of abjection have no place . . . in the theatre of cruelty' (Goodall 2004: 68). When the servant makes a gesture of stopping Béatrice, Cenci tells him to let her go. After a silence that only gives what follows a greater effect, Cenci says: 'Let her be. The charm is already working. From now on she will not be able to escape me' (Artaud 1976: IV, 210). The effectiveness of this scene, as of Artaud's theatre as a whole, is based on the interplay between materiality and corporeality – sounds, bodily movements, gestures – and the text.

The Loss of Cognitive Control

'In performance', Fischer-Lichte writes, 'participants experience themselves as subjects who partially control, and are partially controlled by, the conditions – neither fully autonomous, nor fully determined' (Fischer-Lichte 2014: 42). At the beginning of the second Act of *Les Cenci*, human logical control has increasingly been lost, both for the characters and the spectators of Artaud's play. Béatrice's 'affolement' at the end of Act I continues when she again enters the stage 'affolée', trying to ascertain her father's whereabouts and thus to avert the threat posed by him (Artaud 1976: IV, 213). Béatrice says that since the previous day (that is since what happened in Act I), she feels him everywhere. She is exhausted and tired of fighting. In a motherly gesture that establishes a contrast to the biological father that Béatrice has to fear, Lucrétia, the stepmother of Cenci's children, takes Béatrice's head between her hands. We hear the birds – the natural realm linked to Cenci – screech ('crier') outside, and we simultaneously hear something like (again, 'comme') the noise of a step coming from above. The 'comme' in this sentence, the uncertainty about what the characters and audience are hearing, only adds to the continued sense of unease of this scene. Béatrice does recognise this step 'that fills the walls' as her father's. She says that she should hate him and that she can't. Instead, she has internalised his criminality as her own guilt: 'His living image is in me as if I were carrying a crime' (Artaud 1976: IV, 214). While Artaud understands his own work as in opposition to the realist-naturalist dramatic tradition's psychologism, there is a remnant of human psychological motivation in Beatrice's internal conflict. Nevertheless, this human psychological conflict and the spectators' identification with this conflict are enmeshed with the play's gestural and sound language, which transcends the human individual.

Artaud's theatre thus troubles the opposition between human mind/representation and more-than-human materiality. Fischer-Lichte describes how the participants, whether spectators or actors, in theatre

> experience performance as an aesthetic and a social . . . process in which relationships are negotiated . . . and communities emerge and vanish. Concepts and ideas that we traditionally see as dichotomous pairs in our culture – such as autonomy and determinism, aesthetics and politics, and presence and representation – are experienced not in the form of *either/or* but as not *only/but also*. Oppositions collapse. (2014: 42)

Fischer-Lichte sees this liminality of performance as tied to the history of theatre as ritual and enactment of 'threshold experiences and rites of passage'. Fischer-Lichte makes this argument for theatre in general, for a theatre that would then by generic definition be anti-dualistic. She is correct in stating that 'different or opposing frames collide in performances'. Spectators enter this liminal situation whenever they attend a theatrical performance, a fact that, according to Fischer-Lichte (2014: 42), then also explains why theatre often enacts taboo violations – as does, of course, Artaud's *Les Cenci*.

I would argue, however, that how (and whether or not) this liminality is resolved differs from theatrical tradition to theatrical tradition. The dramas that are part of the realist-mimetic tradition of 'dramatic theatre' privilege the human (an assessment shared by Lehmann, given his charge of the anthropocentrism of this tradition) and thus, as we have seen, do perpetuate the dichotomy of human/nonhuman. At the same time, however, Strindberg's and Sartre's dramas already problematise this latter dichotomy thematically and the plays of the historical avant-garde of the early twentieth century, including Brecht and Artaud, start to bridge it further in theatrical form. Brecht and Artaud move towards an encounter of equal though heterogeneous, i.e. human and more-than-human, elements, an encounter that blurs the relation between observing subject and observed object.

The gestural language of Artaud's *Les Cenci* is a language of the body that frequently enacts the loss of human control and in this sense also becomes to a certain extent posthumanist. Sensing Béatrice's feeling of foreboding (II, 1), Lucrétia reassures her, as one would a child: 'Enough, enough, little girl. A crime only exists when it is committed' (Artaud 1976: IV, 214). At this point, however, Béatrice is wringing her hands in despair, and a sob suddenly 'rises from her' and becomes louder and louder. Artaud's stage directions do not describe Béatrice as sobbing, as giving expression to her feelings; instead the sob rises from her body, a corporeal expression not controlled by the human from whom it emerges.[7] Nevertheless trying to reassert some sort of human agency over her fate, Béatrice says that she would rather die than give in (further) to her father's monstrous desires (Artaud 1976: IV, 214). Again, however, she also implicates herself: 'He has nourished me with infected dishes' (Artaud 1976: IV, 215). The word used here for 'infected' is 'empesté', derived from 'la peste' ('the plague'). As we have seen in his theoretical writings, Artaud establishes an analogy between the theatre and the plague. In *Les Cenci*, the Father has infected his daughter. Cenci *is* the plague that Artaud discusses in his theoretical work, the purifying force that he aims for in his theatre.

In response to the threat this force poses to human society, Artaud's adaptation is, like Shelley's *The Cenci*, centred on anxiety, an anxiety that the Swedish philosopher Søren Kierkegaard associates with modernity.[8] The stage instructions specifying the play's corporeal language powerfully mould the play's atmosphere. Again linking psychological turmoil with corporeal expression, Béatrice, accusing herself of not having protested what she calls the slow, daily 'martyrdom' ('[le] lent martyre') of her brothers, wrings her hands and sobs even more violently. The heightened corporeal and affective tension of the scene (II, i) finds its material expression when the door opens. Fearing her father's arrival, Béatrice starts and stands straight. When only the chambermaid appears, Béatrice expresses her relief by sitting back down (Artaud 1976: IV, 215). While Artaud is a modern writer and post-metaphysical modernity produces a heightened sense of ontological vulnerability, the anxiety he enacts ultimately has its origins in the *phobos* of Greek tragedy. Reading tragedy in Deleuzian terms, as the enmeshment of heterogeneous elements and excess, Lehmann (2013: 47–8) argues that tragedy meets Freud's definition of the uncanny.

In contrast to the western 'dramatic' and psychoanalytic traditions, however, Artaud, if we are to believe his theoretical writings, has no primary interest in portraying the characters' psychic interiority or the psychological motivations for their actions; instead, the stage directions help establish a tonality, an atmosphere whose main target are the spectators. In *Les Cenci*, not only the characters, but also the audience are immersed in a heightened affective tension, an overriding sense of threat. In contrast to the theatre spaces of the nineteenth century, where electricity made it for the first time possible (or easier) to separate the light on the stage from the darkened *Zuschauerraum* (the space of the audience), Artaud's theatre pulverises the conventional distinction between stage and auditorium. As part of 'one energetic, orgasmic body' (Groot Nibbelink 2019: 37), the spectators are absorbed (Bleeker's term) into the performance in Artaud's theatre of cruelty, which erases any remnants of mediation (Bleeker 2008: 21). In this respect, Artaud anticipates theatrical experiences of our contemporary times, such as the radical and unsettling work of the Italian experimental theatre company *Socìetas Raffaelo Sanzio*, as described by Romeo Castellucci, one of its founding members:

> I believe that today theatrical experience is founded on the intimate experience of each spectator . . . contemporary theatre has become an experience of sensitive awareness. Awareness in the sense of an opening, awareness of what opens up. (Castellucci et al. 2007: 4)

Castellucci posits the primacy of the spectator's experience for contemporary theatre.

In Artaud's *Les Cenci*, even the verbal language used is often expressive or performative rather than communicative, foreclosing reference and representation. Béatrice, who for a long time continues to preserve her faith in God, for instance, frequently uses 'mon Dieu' as an exclamation or an address ('Merci, mon Dieu, ce n'est pas mon père'). These references to God establish Béatrice's adherence to a traditional, faith-based morality that contrasts with her father's moral monstrosity. But 'mon Dieu' also heightens the spectators' sense that what is happening on stage warrants exclamations of shock and fear. On the one hand, to Béatrice, the Church at first provides a sense of security. When Camillo, the papal envoy, requests to see her 'in safety' ('en toute sécurité'), she responds that she will meet him in the evening at the church. From this appeal to an illusory safety, however, we immediately swing around to an intensification ('avec intensité') of the sound of footsteps and an abrupt change in tonality. This change in tonality is again enacted physically: Béatrice again stands up and Cenci enters (Artaud 1976: IV, 214).

The rhythmic exclamations in Artaud's piece have both an affective and corporeal impact on the spectators and they point to what is going on atmospherically in the play. Fischer-Lichte points to the link between rhythm and corporeality: 'One reason that rhythm is such a powerful organizing principle lies in the fundamental connection to the human body, 'which itself follows its own rhythms'. Fischer-Lichte (2014: 37–8) states:

> Indeed the human body is a rhythmical instrument, particularly suited to perceive and be moved by rhythm. In performance, different 'rhythmic systems' come into contact: the rhythms of production with those of the spectators. . . every spectator follows different rhythmic patterns, both internally and externally . . . Autopoesis emerges out of the interplay of actors and spectators . . . out of their rhythmic attunement to one another . . . it can impact other spectators and give new impulses to the actors . . . performance works to a large extent through rhythmic divergences, changes, and shifts. Performance organizes itself through rhythmic calibration, manifest on a physical level. Its transience is reflected in rhythm's dynamism and propensity to change.

All that Béatrice can say at certain moments of extreme tension and fear is: 'Ah!' Cenci repeats the same exclamation ('Ah'), but as an exclamation of surprise at having discovered Béatrice while he was approaching her little brother, Bernardo. Then Cenci emits a third 'Ah!' 'as if he were getting close to making an important decision' ('comme s'il s'apprêtait à prendre une décision importante') (Artaud 1976: IV, 216).

It is clear that the expressive sign 'Ah!' does not determine its own meaning, but that this meaning depends on the context, tonality and rhythm of the enunciations. In Artaud, semioticity or meaning is thus closely linked to the other intra-active elements of the performance.

Congruent with the play's reliance on a language that is not primarily based on human communicative meaning, Béatrice's ontological vulnerability has reduced her to the level of an animal. Béatrice ('dans un coin', 'in a corner') finds herself cornered physically and figuratively and trembles 'comme une biche' (literally, like a female deer). She makes a gesture of wanting to rush outside, but without being able to come to the decision ('sans s'y résoudre'), a decision based on (human) consciousness or will. This cognitive and physical inability to move and flee from her father sums up and corporeally enacts Béatrice's inability to hate her father and stop his highly inappropriate advances. Cenci then approaches her physically ('s'avançant vers elle') and reminds her that the previous night she had dared look him in the face – human to human, or human to elemental force. By now, however, Béatrice 'trembles more and more [and] begins to slide along the wall', like a reptile. Again, no mere words could more powerfully create such a heightened sense of threat to the female protagonist's status as human in the play (Artaud 1976: IV, 215–16).

For the schizophrenic writer Artaud, as well as for Cenci (as we have seen played by Artaud himself in the first production), there are no clear limits separating inside and outside.[9] When Lucrétia tries to intervene with her husband, Cenci makes her responsible for his own guilty thoughts and intentions: 'You have *penetrated* me too well for me to still be able to feel ashamed for what I think' ('Vous m'avez trop bien *pénétré* pour que je puisse encore avoir honte de ce que je pense') (Artaud 1976: IV, 217, my emphases). This penetration has of course a sexual connotation and is thus linked to the thematic of incest in the play. Artaud's play enacts all kinds of border transgressions, both as the performance of heterogenous elements and thematically, i.e. within the diegetic world.

The (verbal) language of Artaud's play links paranoia, penetration and feminised abjection. Cenci uses the term 'penetrate' to establish himself as the (feminised) victim, here claiming an identity with the (female or feminised) members of his family. He blames his wife for his own lack of conscience, his own shamelessness. Cenci then addresses the small child Bernardo, who has stepped behind Lucrétia, whether to hide from Cenci or to help defend Béatrice. Bernardo is the product of Cenci's affair with another woman. Blaming the child, Cenci tells Bernardo that seeing him reminds him of certain 'sordid love affairs' – his own love affairs – that have spoiled his best years. Cenci then tells all three family members to go away: 'I detest feminised beings' ('Je déteste les êtres féminisés'). Cenci is blurring the borderline between himself and the other characters, the border between inside and outside, good and evil. As a consequence, any logic that allows his family members (i.e. other characters) or the spectators to find order in the world is lost. Madness and border-crossing abjection set in. Terror ensues.

Reminiscent of his contemporary's, Jean-Paul Sartre's, work, Artaud has Cenci send Bernardo away, saying that his milky face makes him nauseous (Artaud 1976: IV, 217).[10] Cenci establishes a link between his loathing of femininity and the feeling of nausea. In *Le Théâtre et son double*, Artaud writes:

> This flux, this nausea, this language, here is where the fire starts. The fire of languages, the fire woven into the twists of language, in the brilliance of the earth which opens like a pregnant belly with entrails of honey and sugar ... I look into my throat for names and the vibrative filament of things. The stench of nothingness, a must of absurdity, the dung of total death. (Artaud 1976: I, 141–4, quoted by Kristeva 2004: 119)

Three years after *Les Cenci* was first staged in Paris, Sartre would publish his most famous novel on the absurdity of human existence, *La Nausée*, with similar images of nausea caused by milky maternal images and the threat of flux and materiality ('things') or animality ('dung'), the transgression of human psychic and ontological boundaries. As my project has demonstrated, in spite of a shared thematic (nausea, abjection, femininity), Sartre's and Artaud's theatrical visions are, however, vastly different.

While Sartre represents materiality as the threat to be defended against, heterogeneous materiality is central to Artaud's theatrical work. Anxiety is not something to be avoided, but is intentionally created in Artaud's work. After Béatrice and Bernardo have exited the stage, Cenci lies down comfortably on the bed, gesturally enacting his own lack of emotional tension or anxiety. Cenci is the character who is responsible for the cruelty of the play, for the spectators' immersion in terror, but at this point he does not seem to suffer from it himself. Surprisingly, however, when Lucrétia asks Cenci if he is suffering, he does answer in the affirmative, saying that he is wounded because of his family. He is now no longer extended on the bed, but is sitting on the edge of the bed: 'The family has defiled everything' ('C'est la famille qui a tout vicié'). Again, Cenci manipulatively blames his own perversion on his family. Lucrétia tells him that the family has enabled him to measure his cruelty, that he would be nothing without the family (Artaud 1976: IV, 218). Somehow, in this dialogue between husband and wife, cruelty has become a point of pride, reprising Cenci's clear pride in his previous crimes in his dialogue with Camillo at the beginning of the play (Artaud 1976: IV, 190). In Artaud's theory of theatre as well, cruelty is a positive element, something to which his theatre aspires.

But let us also remember that Artaud wants his theatre to have a therapeutic effect. Does the cruelty and suffering he creates in *Les Cenci* have an ulterior end or is it completely gratuitous? In a version of Plautus' (and Thomas Hobbes's) negative view of human nature, Cenci states in the dialogue at hand, with his wife, that no human relationships are possible between beings, who are only born to replace each other and who cannot wait to devour each other. As we have seen, in *Le Théâtre et son double* Artaud declares that he is interested in the enactment of evil. In an already familiar response, Lucrétia, on the other hand, exclaims: 'Mon Dieu!' Cenci tells her to send her God to the devil. Lucrétia, who was so compassionate towards her husband before, finally shows that she is no dummy: 'But with such words, there is no society anymore' ('Mais avec de paroles pareilles, il n'y a plus de société'). When Cenci replies that the family that he commands and that he has created is his only society, Lucrétia speaks of tyranny (Artaud 1976: IV, 219). Although Artaud sees his work as ontological and as focused on universal themes, *Les Cenci*, a play first performed in 1935, here (and also in the banquet scene already described) problematises the role of society and enacts a version of totalitarianism.

Is Artaud's *Les Cenci* then a political play? Cenci feels that tyranny is the only weapon against the perceived threat (war) posed by his family. When Cenci says (to Lucrétia) that Béatrice turned the previous night's banquet into a reunion of murderers, it becomes clear that he suffers from paranoia. Cenci says: 'When murder does not suffice you, you use criminal slander. Since my perceptive mind gets in your way, you have tried to have me locked up as crazy' ('Quand le meurtre ne vous suffit pas, vous utilisez la calomnie criminelle. Comme mon esprit trop pénétrant vous gêne, vous avez cherché à me faire enfermer comme fou'). He calls his entire family a 'filthy conspiracy' ('de l'immonde complot') (Artaud 1976: IV, 220). The play channels its author's own battles with mental illness. But as the inmate of several asylums throughout his lifetime, Artaud must have also been keenly aware of questions of authority.

Moving the insanity of Cenci's statement in what is ultimately an apolitical play to a corporeal and ontological-mythical level (the level of life), this scene also demonstrates the importance of breath in Artaud's theatre. Lucrétia says she cannot breathe ('J'étouffe'). She is trembling: 'Permets-moi de chercher un lieu où je puisse trembler en paix' ('Allow me to look for a place where I can tremble in peace') (Artaud 1976:

IV, 220). When Cenci tells her that she and Bernardo will need to pack up, Lucrétia breathes a resigned sigh. Establishing a spatial separation between himself and the family that he perceives as a threat, Cenci will force them to leave for Petrella, an abandoned castle he owns where any secrets can be locked away. In response to hearing this news, Lucrétia asks for an opportunity to regain her breath. Cenci exclaims: 'Breathe in this poisonous atmosphere.' The word used (for poisonous) is again, 'empestée', infected. Lucrétia tells Cenci that his sacrilegious imagination has created the atmosphere that makes him suffer. As before, the analogy is between Cenci and the plague ('la peste'). Mixing the language of contagion with Christological imagery, Cenci says that if he suffers, it is up to himself to 'deliver' himself ('me délivrer') (Artaud 1976: IV, 221). Artaud understands his own theatrical work in terms of myth, and Cenci consequently sees himself in mythic terms, as the Saviour – his own Saviour.

This mythic quality and the scene at hand again remind us that Artaud's twentieth-century adaptation is based on Shelley's Romantic play. For the time being, Cenci will lock away, hide away ('mettre au secret') his family, creating an immunitarian separation between himself and the perceived threat. It is here that Artaud's modern tragedy, like a Romantic play, breaks the unities of time and place. After Cenci has declared this intention, the stage directions call for night to fall, materialising the impending secrecy and isolation (Artaud 1976: IV, 221). For now, however, Lucrétia is still at home and Cenci slowly approaches the section – still lit – where his wife just exited the stage. Reminiscent of the apostrophes of nature in Romantic poetry, Artaud now has Cenci address a natural phenomenon as a person. Striking his upper body, Cenci speaks to the literal and emblematic night ('Et toi, nuit'), asking it to enter his chest with the excessive forms ('formes démesurées') of all the crimes that one can imagine. Returning to his paranoia while also describing himself as a force that transcends nature, he tells the night that it cannot chase him away from himself: 'The deed [but also the theatrical act] that I carry is greater than you' ('L'acte que je porte est plus grand que toi') (Artaud 1976: IV, 222). The enactment of madness that dominates Artaud's play, a condition outside society, is a Romantic theme.

At the end of the first scene in Act II, the dramatic use of light and especially darkness, together with this verbal announcement, has affectively prepared the spectators to expect Cenci to commit a crime. Joseph P. Cermatori remarks on the evocativeness of Miranda Hardy's lighting design in the Hotel Savant's 2008 production of Artaud's play. He describes the design as having created

> hot pools of light amid an otherwise darkened space, illuminating the warm browns of the actors' flesh in dramatic juxtaposition to encroaching shadow and recreating the chiaroscuro effect of Rembrandt and Caravaggio. This tenebrism suggested psychic intensity on the part of the characters and a malevolent inscrutability on the part of the universe – both apposite for Artaud. (Cermatori 2008: 670)

When the curtain falls on this scene marked by intense affect, not only the characters, but also the audience are left in a state of fearful suspense.

As we have seen and as Cermatori reminds us, in *Le Théâtre et son double* Artaud emphasises the universal, cosmic character – rather than the specific socio-historicity – of his theatrical work, and like the beginning of the play, the second scene of Act 2 (Artaud 1976: IV, 223–9) is again set at an 'indeterminate place' ('un endroit indéterminé'). According to the stage directions, the location could again be a heath or moor, a hallway, a staircase, an underground tunnel/theatre balcony/art gallery ('galerie') or 'whatever you want' ('Lande, couloir, escalier, galerie, ou ce qu'on voudra'). An ominous, anxiety-producing darkness ('les ténèbres') is now everywhere, an intensification of the 'night' of the previous scene. Camillo is addressing Giacomo, who is quickly identified as a member of the Cenci family who has been dispossessed by his father. In congruence with the physical darkness of the scene, Camillo is encouraging Giacomo to kill Cenci, bringing up the oedipal theme, another universal myth (Artaud 1976: IV, 223).

Giacomo counter-argues that Camillo is asking him to declare war not against his father, but against authority in general. Astonishingly, Camillo, the papal envoy (!), declares that this idea does not frighten him. He calls Cenci diabolical ('ce diable de Cenci') and says that this is a case where the intolerant, sectarian despotism of fathers drives the sons to rebel. For the moment, however, Giacomo is still resisting Camillo's argumentation, expressing his distrust of anarchy and the questioning of authority. He points out that Camillo's own position and the authority of the pope that he serves are indeed based on this very authority. While Camillo is advocating authority as long as it is not based on tyranny – a modern understanding – Giacomo, voicing a premodern position, seems willing to serve any authority, whether grounded/rational or not (Artaud 1976: IV, 224). Without the indeterminate setting in which this scene is embedded, it would be easy to read this dialogue as a political exchange.

Does the juxtaposition of these two historically divergent concepts of authority – premodern and modern – then introduce a certain historicity into *Les Cenci*? The dialogue is followed by stage directions that corporeally enact the lack of progress that Camillo is making in this verbal argument, his inability to convince Giacomo. The two men's legs are moving as if they were marching, but they are not really advancing. Giacomo calls Camillo a 'vipère', a viper or malicious person. Camillo works for the Pope, who suggested to Cenci to disinherit Giacomo. Camillo points out that the fortune of the old Cenci and all his possessions will have to return to the papacy, over the head of his family. Camillo, in other words, advocates revolting against Cenci, but this revolt will benefit the Pope, whom he (Camillo) himself serves. Giacomo correctly calls Camillo cynical. Camillo counters that Popes are made/elected by the Conclave with cynicism (Artaud 1976: IV, 225). In spite of his criticism of the realist or naturalist theatrical tradition's staging of socio-historical problems, Artaud's thematic here is the validity of paternal(istic) power – a socio-political problematic that typifies modernity, but also the ontological stuff of Greek myth. Camillo cannot reach an agreement with Giacomo and the two men again walk without moving forward. Instead of an opposition between the body and verbal discourse, Artaud enacts the confluence of both types of language. In his 'Letter to André Breton', Artaud comments on the materiality or corporeality of his theatrical language and its revolutionary impact. He writes: 'These are not just words, ideas, or any other kind of phantasmatic bullshit, these truly are real bombs, physical bombs' (Artaud 1996: 33–4).

In this scene (II, ii), the problematic seems to transition from kinship to the jealousy between siblings (the younger generation), peer envy, which is ultimately a thematic characteristic of modern literature and theatre. Seemingly contradicting his stated, 'premodern' deference to *any* established authority and indicating a shift in position, Giacomo speaks of his disgust for a country where the old are the norm ('la règle'). He states that he can no longer count on his family and that his father has tried to win his family's love by taking away what Giacomo had. But when Giacomo says that his wife will not forgive him that, together with himself, their sons have also been disinherited (Artaud 1976: IV, 226), this problematic is also still tied to Giacomo's own authority as paterfamilias and thus the question of paternalistic authority.[11]

Like Count Cenci, who had declared himself to embody destiny at the beginning of the play, Orsino then links the Cenci family to the fatality and family curse of Greek tragedy. He says: 'Je veux donner à *cette race maudite* les moyens de se dévorer' ('I want to give *this accursed race* [my emphases] the means to devour each other') – a surprising statement by the man who has earlier claimed to love Béatrice Cenci. To Giacomo, Orsino says about Cenci: 'Il vient de passer sur toute cette *race* une bizarre *fatalité*. Les fils trépassent, le père s'égare, la fille sombre dans une insupportable mysticité' ('He just cast on this entire family ['*race*'] a bizarre *fatality*') (my emphases). The sons pass away, the father loses his mind, the daughter sinks into an intolerable mysticism') (Artaud 1976: IV, 227). Orsino furthermore tells Giacomo, who has been forbidden to enter the Cenci palace, about the scandal arising from the banquet held there the previous night. Again, Orsino reminds Giacomo 'of which tainted blood [he is] descended' ('de quel sang taré vous sortez') (Artaud 1976: IV, 228). Whatever happens to the Cenci is a result of their tainted blood, the curse cast on their family.

At the same time, however, when Artaud then contrasts the thematic of the family curse inherited from Greek tragedy with the modern ideology of progress and individual autonomy, it becomes clear that this play is not exclusively a Greek universalist-metaphysical tragedy any more after all. When Orsino says that the guests are afraid to speak, Giacomo expresses his incredulity, saying that 'today', in the sixteenth century (i.e. in early modernity) marked by progress, such a silence has become impossible to retain ('De nos jours, un tel silence ne serait plus possible à garder. Nous sommes tout de même au XVIe siècle. Et le monde a fait des progrès'). Consistent with the thematic of peer envy in this scene (told that his sister and stepmother are suffering, all that Giacomo has to say is that he is oppressed as well), Giacomo's argumentation is indeed finally modern, based on the idea of transparency, rationally based authority and notions of progress (Artaud 1976: IV, 228). Orsino, as a Catholic priest, says that he has tried to discuss the suffering of this 'terrorised family' with the Pope, but that 'his Holiness' (not surprisingly) has only laughed in his face. As Orsino relates, like the fathers at the banquet, the Pope, a premodern, paternalistic figure, does not for any reason want to question the 'natural' authority of a father, thereby weakening his own authority. Orsino, like Camillo before him, encourages Giacomo – in an emphasis on the modern concept of individual autonomy – to rely on himself: 'Quand la justive s'en va, il est bon que les opprimés se rassemblent hors de toute légalité' ('When justice vanishes, it is good for the oppressed to unite outside of any legality'). While Giacomo confirms that his exasperation is indeed 'ripe', he still hesitates. Orsino tells Giacomo that the interests of the Cenci family and his own (Orsino's) are henceforth the same. Thanks to Orsino's previous aside, the spectator will interpret this ambivalent statement differently than Giacomo. Orsino has an interest in Giacomo rebelling against his father, but only to serve his (Orsino's) employer's, the Pope's, financial gain. Again, the curtain falls with the audience left in a state of suspense and confusion (Artaud 1976: IV, 229) between different forms of authority (premodern and modern), a confusion that any production inspired by Artaud's vision will seek to increase through corporeality and the non-verbal materiality of the stage.

'We Are the Storm'

As we have just seen, Artaud's play veers back and forth between ontological and socio-political emphases and breaks down the psychological borders between characters, the ontological boundaries between good and evil, and the affective and spatial distinctions between stage, actors and audience. Heterogeneous theatrical elements intra-act and support each other: the gestural language of corporeality, including breath and rhythm, sound, light (or darkness) and also – though no longer primarily – words. By now indicative of the spectator's own resulting sense of internal turmoil, Act III – like Act II before – again starts with Béatrice running onto the stage 'affolée'. She is still trying to defend herself against her father's advances, with one difference, however, as she tells her stepmother: 'le pire est réalisé' ('The worst has happened'). Cenci has befouled, polluted ('pollué') his own daughter. To underline the enormity of this act and its affective impact, Béatrice breaks down sobbing. Lucrétia gives expression to her own agitation over this extreme sinfulness by not being able to stand still, but walking across the stage and crossing her chest four times, exclaiming four times: 'Mon Dieu!' Staying with religious imagery, Béatrice, sobbing, in a reference to Christ's last words on the cross says: 'Tout est atteint' ('It is finished'). Leaving no room for doubt, she repeats: 'Tout' ['All'], adding: 'The body is dirty, but it is the soul that has been besmirched' (again, 'pollué'). Béatrice says that there is no small part in her any more to which she can escape. She has become completely, absolutely vulnerable and exposed, modelling Artaud's intended effect on the spectator (Artaud 1976: IV, 233–4).

With physical posture and words spoken reinforcing each other, Lucrétia on the other hand is retaining her corporeal and psychological composure and strength: 'Lucrétia stands upright next to her' ('Lucrétia se tient debout auprès d'elle'). She asks Béatrice to tell her (and the audience) everything that has happened. Giving expression to the unspeakable, Béatrice first answers Lucrétia's question physically, by sobbing four times (i.e. rhythmically) and sighing. She then says: 'My only crime is to have been born' ('Mon seul crime, c'est d'être née') (Artaud 1976: IV, 234). Her assessment of her own individual innocence and her emphasis on her birth (as a member of an accursed race) reprise Orsino's previous remarks about the Cenci 'race' and, in a play set in the Italian Renaissance, the classical/Greek/tragic concepts of fate and family curse. Béatrice herself discusses the question of human freedom or choice, a choice limited to the choice of her own death: 'If I can choose my death, I have not chosen my birth. That's where fate bursts forth' ('Si je peux choisir ma mort, je n'ai pas choisi ma naissance. C'est là qu'éclate la fatalité') (Artaud 1976: IV, 233–5). We sense and fear the approach of the ending that typifies Greek tragedy.

Here Artaud mixes elements of Greek tragedy and Greek mythology with Christian images surrounding Christ's crucifixion and death. While the rape that Béatrice has suffered at the hands of her father was just a minute before associated with Jesus's death on the cross, Béatrice now embraces her stepmother's legs, as Mary Magdalen did the cross. Like Mary Magdalen, Béatrice is now no longer sexually pure. But both women nevertheless remain positive figures and preserve their faith. Lucrétia also, while aware of what has happened, does not want to question a God who allows such evil deeds to happen: 'Tais-toi, tu me ferais accuser la justice qui permet de pareils forfaits' ('Be quiet, you would make me accuse the justice that allows such deeds'). Instead of the 'affolement' of the previous scenes, the result of her desperate attempt to escape her father, Béatrice has now reached 'la folie' ('madness') itself and compares this state to death: 'La folie, c'est comme la mort.' She states that she is dead, but her soul, which does not want to die, cannot be delivered. Béatrice's suffering stems from the separation of her physical being and her metaphysical state. This split affects her stepmother as well, who implores Béatrice to return to herself, lest Lucrétia also 'lose footing' and believe that they are all 'possessed'. Possessed? By the Devil? Again, Christian imagery mixes with the tragic idea of the family curse (Artaud 1976: IV, 235).

Les Cenci has now reached the affective intensity of a nightmare.[12] Béatrice retells a dream that she used to have every night when she

was small: 'I am naked in a big room and a beast like those that tend
to appear in dreams *breathes and breathes*. I become aware that my
body is shining. I want to flee, but I have to cover up my blinding
nudity . . . I am hungry and thirsty and I suddenly discover that I am
not alone' (Artaud 1976: IV, 236, my emphasis). Together with the
breathing beast, there are also other things breathing in Béatrice's
dream. Soon, a whole 'people' of vile objects is swarming around her
feet. As she is herself, this 'people' is also famished. In her dream,
Béatrice tries to find the light, because she senses that the light will
allow her to satisfy her hunger. Meanwhile, however, the beast clings
to her and pursues her from cave to cave. When Béatrice feels it on top
of her, she realises that it is stubborn, like her hunger. When she feels
that her strength is leaving her, she each time awakens. Today, the
day that her father has violated her, Béatrice tells Lucrétia, her dream
has, strangely, been erased (Artaud 1976: IV, 237). Lucrétia responds
that she did not need this dream in order to realise that one does not
escape one's destiny. The recurring dream easily allows the audience
to interpret the beast as Cenci. Béatrice's hunger for love is matched
by Cenci's stubborn pursuit of his daughter. Whether one interprets
the dream, as the ancient Greeks did, as the gods' announcement of
the heroine's predetermined, inevitable destiny or psychoanalytically
as the individual expression of Béatrice's fate based on her emotional
state, this dream clearly underlines that Béatrice's destiny has just
been fulfilled. As in the long tradition of anthropocentric theatre, literature and art, the threat posed by Béatrice's monstrous father is
expressed in terms of animality.

    But Artaud's play also differs from the anthropocentric tradition.
Béatrice verbally articulates her hope that what she is experiencing is
again only her childhood dream and that there will be a knock on the
door telling her that it is time to wake up (literally, in the French original, the door will tell her). Indeed, there is now a gentle knock on the
door. Claiming agency, the door opens almost immediately and allows
Orsino and Giacomo (who hides behind it) to enter. Will this material
intervention or this physical interruption be able to awaken Béatrice
from her psychic nightmare? Béatrice indeed asks Orsino to counsel
her on how to avoid a repetition of what has happened. Lucrétia also
implores Orsino to act. Orsino, who although a priest is more the representative of social than divine authority in this play, advises Béatrice
to file a legal complaint. But Béatrice herself has already chosen her
own, more metaphysical answer: Judges will not be able to return her
soul to her. She has internalised her father's guilt, blaming her blood

and thus again the family curse. But at the same time she will choose her own justice. Even death (i.e. the murder of her father), however, she says, will not be able to atone for this crime. When Béatrice expresses a sense of urgency, Orsino recommends Cenci's secret assassination and now steps aside to reveal Giacomo's presence. Orsino urges all four family members, including Bernardo, to conspire against a perverted authority ('une autorité dévoyée'), stating that he will furnish two mute assassins (Artaud 1976: IV, 238–40). Given that Orsino is a priest and murder is a capital sin, and given that Orsino (like Camillo) represents the Pope's unquestioned and unquestionable patriarchal authority, the spectator's reaction at this point can only be surprise at this patriarchal authority's moral hypocrisy.

The reaction of Béatrice and Lucrétia is also not verbal, but consists of ten exclamation marks each. In other words, both women are speechless. While silences are part of the non-verbal language that Artaud employs, the use of punctuation is ironic here. After all, Artaud opposes a theatre that privileges the written text. And exclamation marks are of course only visible to a reader (unless externalised in stage design). Orsino shows his aristocratic/autocracy-based-on-class-privilege cards when he says that in today's mob there are many 'idiotic and obstinate scoundrels' like the two assassins he is proposing. Mute, the two assassins chosen offer the advantage of not being able to reveal any secrets. The way Orsino talks about 'the mob' ('l'engeance') already reveals that his siding with Béatrice and Lucrétia's revolt against Cenci's autocratic rule might pose some problems (Artaud 1976: IV, 241). Giacomo's motives are more convincing: 'family, gold, justice' (Artaud 1976: IV, 242). Since Artaud's goal is not primarily character motivation, Giacomo's motivation is announced perfunctorily and we have no further exploration at all of Orsino's duplicity.

Again reminiscent of Romantic imagery, Scene ii of Act III starts with stage directions for a storm – marked by a quick succession of several claps of thunder, i.e. rhythm and sound – that go hand in hand with the dark plans for Cenci's assassination (Artaud 1976: IV, 241). 'The scene picks ups without interruption' ('La scène reprend sans interruption') (Artaud 1976: IV, 243) from the discussion of these plans at the end of the previous scene, and Orsini and the two assassins enter 'immediately', enacting the urgency of the attempted coup. Cenci is planning to lock his family away in the horrible, prison-like Petrella Castle and this last-ditch attempt on his life is intended to occur on the journey to this dungeon (Artaud 1976: IV, 241). Upon entering Act III, Scene ii, Orsino and his two men are fighting against a furious wind, this material difficulty already announcing that their undertaking will not be an easy one. Orsino physically positions the assassins and also gives them verbal instructions. Again underlining the close link between the materiality and physicality of the stage and the (com)plot, Orsino explains that 'we are the storm'. Giacomo is already expressing his doubts that the two men will be able to understand and appropriately complete their assigned task. Without any further delay, however, three claps of thunder announce the arrival of the caravan of travellers. Three men covered in iron arrive and move with excessive slowness, 'like the figurines of the big clock of the Strassburg cathedral'. This slow motion underlines the importance of what is going on and, together with the continued, rhythmic succession of thunder claps, increases the spectators' suspense (Artaud 1976: IV, 243–4).

At the same time, the comparison with the figurines of the famous Strassburg chime – while oddly specific geographically in a play focused on a universalist, mythic ontology – enacts Artaud's vision of 'mechanised' actors 'to whom neither their joys nor their pain appear to belong' mentioned in his theoretical writings (Artaud 1976: IV, 70). Like the mannequins of the banquet scene earlier, the stage director will have to make the characters appear somewhat artificial, a distancing device that breaks the suspense and terror central to Artaud's vision (and that we usually associate more readily with Brecht's *gestus*). When Orsino says that all is well ('Everybody knows the role he has to play', a metadiscursive statement), Giacomo, again expressing his doubts, says: 'I am afraid that they might know too well how to play and no longer how to do something for real' (Artaud 1976: IV, 243–4). In other words, the split between theatrical illusion and reality might get in the way of the correct execution of the plan. The characters in the travelling group move in a 'jerky' mechanised or unnatural way ('saccade'), again breaking the audience's illusion. The tempest, the attack, and the assassins' voices become one, a unity to which Cenci responds (in capital letters): 'AND THEN, WHAT!' ('EH BIEN, QUOI!'). We see the shapes of the assassins, who turn like spinning-tops and merge with the lightning. At the same time, we hear two enormous gunshots. Darkness descends, and the lightning stops. Everything disappears. After this materially enacted paroxysm of confusion, the end of the scene, disappointingly, restores verbal clarity. The assassination attempt on the evil force that is Cenci has 'FAILED!' (Artaud 1976: IV, 245).

'The Sufferings of an Imminent Birth'

While the previous scene (III, ii) used distantiation techniques to materialise the difficulty of the coup on Cenci's life, the transitions between scenes in Artaud's play are smooth, ensuring continuity and thus the spectator's immersion in the performance as an affective experience. Given the failure of the assassination attempt at the end of Act III, the beginning of Act IV shows Cenci's unbroken dominance over his family. He is pushing his wife in front of him and, resuming the hunger and thirst imagery already familiar from what has come before, tells her to go get Béatrice: 'I am hungry for her.' Lucrétia, who spoke so compassionately to her husband earlier, calls for air and a respite: 'I want to live. We are not born to be tortured' (Artaud 1976: IV, 249). The situation clearly has not improved from the previous acts: the threat on the family members' lives continues. Artaud's theatre is a theatre of unmitigated and relentless cruelty.

Bringing up the philosophical question of existential meaning and, again, the tragic concept of fate, Cenci asks his wife if she can tell him why he was born. In a tragedy such as *Les Cenci*, somebody – usually the title character – has to die at the end. The play bears the family name in the plural. Does this mean that all the characters will have to die at the end? Lucrétia confirms that Cenci's deeds certainly make him an exposed target (Artaud 1976: IV, 249). Cenci nevertheless asks Lucrétia to fetch Béatrice. After she has left, Cenci suddenly staggers and wipes his hand across his forehead, as if giving credence to Lucrétia's warning. With a kind of laughter – in other words, undaunted – Cenci nevertheless also verbally expresses his refusal to repent. In his typical vein, he instead blames God for his actions, for having him made the father of a daughter he desires. He then performs a thought process that at first seems like a dialectical three-step, but is ultimately completely circular in terms of logic. (1) He first blames fate and rejects the notion of freedom – and thus individual responsibility and guilt. (2) Then, however, the stage direction says: 'Il s'éloigne.' He steps away, physically, but he also steps away or distances himself from the argument he has just made: 'This is why I open the locks, in order not to be submerged.' If all was up to fate (as he has just stated above – see (1)), an individual act of self-protection (opening the locks) would be futile. (3) Next, Cenci states that there is in him a kind of demon chosen to revenge the crimes of the world. Here we are back to fate. Things have been predetermined, chosen. Rather than as a criminal, Cenci sees himself as the chosen tool of a higher force. (4) Finally, Cenci again states that there is no destiny that could prevent him from executing what he has dreamt. We are back to individual choice and responsibility. In sum, Cenci clearly does not follow a logical line of thought, vacillating between notions of fate and individual action (and between Christian and classical mythology). Greek tragedy as well is a product of the tension between fate/family curse and individual responsibility/punishment for the hero's tragic flaw – hubris (Artaud 1976: IV, 250). But in contrast to a Hegelian logic that overcomes the affective excess of hubris in a dialectical *Aufhebung* (synthesis), the logic propounded by Artaud's Count Cenci is enough to make any spectator feel crazed herself.

Like the demon he just declared himself to be, Cenci does not exit like a normal human character, but 'disappears' (Artaud 1976: IV, 250). Béatrice enters with the assassins. In one of Artaud's meaningful and atmospheric silences, a long time passes. One vaguely hears a step ('On croit entendre . . .'). The spectator is again not sure what is going on here. When Lucrétia enters, Béatrice asks her if she thinks that Cenci is asleep: 'Crois-tu qu'il dorme?' Again, no certainty is available here. Lucrétia has put a sleeping aid in his drink, but she divulges that he was still shouting a minute before. Béatrice nevertheless has the assassins move to the front of the stage. This physical move enacts her instruction to them of another assassination attempt. The two assassins laugh, like the 'idiots' that they are, inspiring little confidence in the audience that the outcome will be better this time. To corporeally and materially demonstrate the mentally unfit state of the two men, Béatrice moves around them, tying them up in their coats as if the coats were straight-jackets, leaving only the fists free (Artaud 1976: IV, 251). She brushes her hand across their faces to make them stop laughing. Lucrétia puts two daggers in the men's hands. Béatrice tells them to go, accompanying them off stage before returning to Lucrétia. The fact that the two assassins show such lack of independence does not bode well. Judging from their physical actions and position next to each other, however, Béatrice and Lucrétia are clearly in this effort together. A 'dead silence' ('un silence de mort') falls over the stage, indicating the moment of Cenci's possible death. Enacting the psychological difficulty of the murder of her father and the courage required of her, Béatrice is close to fainting; Lucrétia supports her both physically and emotionally. Time is again passing slowly, enacting the women's (and spectators') heightened anxiety and tension. Indeed, Béatrice exclaims: 'My God! My God! Quick, I don't know if I will be able to stand it . . .' Congruent with Artaud's goal of creating a dream-like atmosphere in his plays, a sigh is rising independently *as if from a voice* – Cenci's – that speaks in its sleep (Artaud 1976: IV, 252). The two assassins reappear, without having had the courage to accomplish the murder. Since they cannot speak, they convey what has happened through a pantomime. Béatrice physically enacts her agitation by running to the back of the stage and then reappearing in front. Having asked the failed assassins where their weapons are, Béatrice runs off, supposedly to look for them. Again, time passes, heightening the intolerable tension and suspense (Artaud 1976: IV, 253).

When Béatrice finally returns, her words start changing the mood or tonality of the scene. Reporting that there are no more weapons and that the window is wide open, Béatrice scolds the assassins for being afraid of 'an old man who dreams and debates his feelings of remorse'. She tells them to go and 'hollow out his head' or she will kill him with whatever she can find and accuse them of his death. Her description of her father as an old, harmless man and her order to kill him in the graphic terms of 'hollowing out his head' all of a sudden make the spectator cringe and shy away from – instead of identifying with – this murder. The words uttered – including the mention of Cenci's remorse – also give expression to Béatrice's own emerging remorse in the dramatic tradition of other women patricides (such as, for instance, Sartre's Electre, as discussed earlier) (Artaud 1976: IV, 253–4).

Artaud's *Les Cenci* follows Shelley in obeying the neoclassical rules of internal and external *bienséance* or decorum. Murder is shown in a teichoscopy, i.e. indirectly, as in classical theatre. The assassins leave again and we hear a loud scream. They then come back on stage, this time covered in blood. Béatrice rewards them by throwing them a gold-gleaming garment, the kind of garment a Catholic priest wears during Mass. The murder of a paternalistic authority figure (the Father) is rewarded with the discarded, disrespected material symbol of such authority. Cenci appears, swaying, with his fist on his right eye, a gesture reminiscent of King Oedipus, who is blinded at the end of Sophocles' tragedy. The scene ends with 'terrible fanfares' that are getting louder and louder – a celebration, but terrible. The spectator is left in emotional turmoil, feeling relief that Cenci can no longer harm his family, pity for an old man, and trepidation and confusion about whether Cenci will recover, take revenge and wreak further havoc (Artaud 1976: IV, 253–4). Artaud's theatre of cruelty has no need for showing murder and violence on the stage to effect the audience's affective immersion. In this modern tragedy, Artaud enacts intense terror based on the violation of human society's greatest taboos – incest and patricide.

After what eventually turns out to have in fact been Cenci's murder (at the beginning of IV, ii), a cloth showing a white sky falls in front of the stage and is immediately 'attacked by lighting'. In spite of all this light and brightness, the scene directions are thus not creating a reassuring atmosphere. Similarly, the fanfare starts up again, but 'extraordinarily close and threatening'. Béatrice then verbally acknowledges the intense materiality of this threat by plugging her ears and urging, again referring to breath: 'Enough! Enough! I cannot breathe with the noise of this trumpet.' Lucrétia confirms that the instrument sounds like the last trumpet. The atmosphere is apocalyptic. Béatrice is wondering if other people already know about her father's death, in addition to her. While the spectator at this point is still to find out in detail what exactly has transpired in the last scene (IV, i), the threat posed to Béatrice by her father has now become the threat of being punished for his murder. There are soldiers everywhere and Bernardo says that he fears for Béatrice, that she should hide quickly (Artaud 1976: IV, 255). Béatrice says that it is too early to be afraid, but too late to cry over what is done. Again, we sense a degree of mourning for her father in Béatrice. After Béatrice and Bernardo have exited, Lucrétia, who was approaching the fanfare, moves away, backward, frightened by a 'blinding and terrible' light that slowly spreads over the entire set. The cloth rises continuously, enacting the inevitability or ineluctability of what is happening and – like the light – taking over, enacting a terrible materiality exceeding the characters' or spectators' control.

Artaud's word choice and the physicality of his theatre are both clearly symbolic, tied to the semioticity of the play. When Camillo enters followed by guards, we realise that the light comes from 'a forest of torches'. The guards follow Camillo, which means that he now is in charge. Camillo and the guards enter from the side *opposing* Béatrice, Lucrétia and Bernardo ('le côté opposé'), making it clear that this arrival does not bode well for these three characters. When Lucrétia calls out his name, Camillo makes a curt, peremptory, 'cutting' ('trenchant') gesture with his left hand, cutting short any hopes based on their previous familiarity. The left (Latin *sinister*) hand of course has more negative symbolic implications than the right hand. The word 'trenchant' announces a certain level of physical violence. Camillo corrects Lucrétia: 'No, not Camillo, but the Legate of His Holiness' ('Non, pas Camillo, mais le Légat de Sa Sainteté'). Even though Camillo had previously (II, ii) himself encouraged Giacomo to rebel against his father, calling Count Cenci 'diabolical', it is clear that neither Lucrétia nor Béatrice will now be able to count on their previous acquaintance with Camillo to protect them. The verbal clarification is in fact no longer necessary after the gestural physicality of this scene.

While Artaud's physical theatre is also an intensely symbolic one, the following scene, arguably more than any other, proves Artaud's theory concerning the superiority of material, physical theatre over a theatre primarily based on the text, on verbal discourse. As one representative of patriarchal power to another, Camillo, as Papal Legate, is request-ing to speak to Count Cenci (Artaud 1976: IV, 256). There is general, immersive relief – among the actors and the spectators – when Camillo states that Cenci is required to respond, urgently, to charges of the highest importance. Béatrice and Lucrétia, in a double entendre, state that Cenci is asleep and that nobody present will be able to waken him. It is here that the spectator realises that Cenci is in fact dead. Camillo still has not caught up to this information; he states his intention to wake Cenci himself. Bernardo has tiptoed and hidden behind Béatrice, who now asks him to lead the Legate to his father's room. Béatrice does not do so herself, but uses a child, the incarnation of innocence, to put some distance between what the Legate is going to discover and her own guilt. Two guards leave with Camillo and Bernardo while the others form a half-circle around the two women. This half-circle enacts a certain amount of surveillance and threat, but only partially so. It is not a full circle or arrest – yet. Lucrétia steps to the centre of the circle, like a sleepwalker. The action again has the dream-like character that Artaud, in his theoretical writings, posits as the goal of his theatre. Béatrice positions herself next to Lucrétia. Her physical attitude is defi-ant (Artaud 1976: IV, 257). Again exclaiming 'Mon Dieu!', Lucrétia states that only a minute before Cenci was still breathing. She adds: 'If we could only go back in time' ('Si le temps pouvait reculer'). If only Cenci could have been arrested instead of having to be killed. Béatrice says that, independent of what is going to happen, she has nothing to mourn or regret ('Pour moi je n'ai rien à pleurer. J'ai fait ce que je devais faire. Ce qui va suivre m'est étranger'). In contrast to Béatrice's calm, fatalistic attitude, Lucrétia is 'desperately' listening. A 'great tumult' erupts, cries calling for the murderers. Lucrétia gives up, calling all lost. Like Jesus on the cross and recalling Béatrice's earlier recounting of the completion of the incest, Lucrétia states: 'All is finished.' Ancient fate and Christian faith again merge (Artaud 1976: IV, 258).

When, surprisingly, the tumult then suddenly stops and there is only silence, there could not be a more powerful tool creating com-plete surprise, shock and suspense in the audience than the silence of this moment. Lucrétia interprets it for us: 'They' – Camillo and the guards – are guessing: 'They are starting to trace the circle where they are going to imprison us.' And in fact, this figurative circle is also starting to close physically; the half-circle around the women is starting to close as Camillo is returning with the guards (Artaud 1976: IV, 258). He is ordering the entire castle searched, the doors guarded. Everybody is now a prisoner. In spite of her earlier fatalism, Béatrice is keeping her wits around her; she is running up to Camillo, asking what is wrong. Bernardo also plays his role well (or truly had no previous knowledge of the murder), telling his sister that he is afraid, that their father has been assassinated. Cenci has been assassinated with a nail to his head. Béatrice is shaking her head, feigning shock at the news (or truly shocked about the specific details). Lucrétia exclaims, feigning surprise, that only they had had the keys to the room, that nobody else had access. She puts her hand over her mouth, realizing that she has said too much. Camillo picks up on this information and Lucrétia's hand gesture right away (Artaud 1976: IV, 259). He goes to Bernardo, supposedly the weakest link. Bernardo says he does not know anything. When Lucrétia and Béatrice are trying to leave, claiming fatigue, Camillo is now treacherously using his previous relationship with the Cenci family – his knowledge of Béatrice's desperate relationship with her father – against her in his role as papal legate (Artaud 1976: IV, 260). Béatrice, calling him 'Monsieur' and 'Monseigneur', tries to re-establish the distance proper for his official role; he insists on calling her by her first name. She shows him her white hands, a gesture of obvious symbolism stronger than any verbal declaration of innocence.

Joining material with verbal violence, Camillo states that there is a secret that he needs to unravel – 'percer', pierce, a verbal choice indicating more material violence than the 'unravel' of the English translation (Artaud 1969: 54), and reminiscent of the nail that pierced Cenci's head. Joining again semioticity with material gesture, Camillo orders the guards to surround the two women completely. In a powerful gesture of solidarity, dependence and love, Bernardo rushes to the middle of the circle and presses himself against Béatrice. Camillo takes Bernardo by the head, gently pulling him outside. He will not implicate the child in the murder. But the circle closes back up around the women. Extending her arms, Béatrice implores Camillo not to take Bernardo away from her. Bernardo, extremely agitated, resists, both physically and verbally (referencing the Bible, Ruth 1: 16), against being taking away from Béatrice: 'Wherever she goes, I will follow her.' He throws himself frenetically against the soldiers and hits them. Lucrétia exclaims, surprisingly: 'My God! But this is Cenci himself. Be quiet,

Cenci' (Artaud 1976: IV, 261–2). Does the violence of the scene extend to diabolical possession?

In *Le Théâtre et son double*, Artaud speaks of his theatre in terms of exorcism (Artaud 1976: IV, 33, 73). When Bernardo states: 'For God's sake, kill me. But give me back my soul' ('Pour Dieu, tuez-moi. Mais rendrez-moi mon âme'), what had at first been a shocking statement on Lucrétia's part now starts to make sense. Bernardo is momentarily possessed by Cenci. Howling desperately, he exclaims rhythmically, three times: 'My soul has been sacrificed. My soul has been sacrificed. My soul has been sacrificed' ('C'est mon âme qui a été sacrifié'). This ending of Act IV, scene ii again takes Artaud's theatre to the mythical level that he declares, in *Le Théâtre et son double*, to be his goal (Artaud 1976: IV, 262).

The mythical and ritual dimension of Artaud's theatrical vision and his use of space – together with Brecht's epic theatre and the theatre of the absurd – constitute the end of what Elinor Fuchs (2011: 69) calls the 'fourth-wall realism' of bourgeois domestic drama and prefigures the post-dramatic theatre of the 1960s to the 1990s. The latter includes the theatre of Robert Wilson, Richard Foreman and other exponents of American avant-garde theatre, a 'dialogue-less theatre' (Lehmann 1999: 45). As we have seen, in his theoretical writings Artaud talks about using all available theatrical space and not just the stage itself. In the stage directions for Scene IV, iii of *Les Cenci*, a wheel turns on the ceiling of the theatre 'as if' ('comme') on an axle that crosses ('traverserait') the diameter of the wheel. The comparison ('comme') and the *conditionnel* of 'traverserait' (literally 'would cross') create a distance between these stage instructions and the reality of production, that is the question of how this play could be produced without actually harming the actors. Suspended by her hair and pushed by a guard who pulls her arms behind her back, Béatrice is following the axle of the wheel. Grammatically, the passive voice used here for Béatrice and the active voice used for the guard, together with the physical posture of Béatrice's hands tied behind her back, clearly encapsulate and enact Béatrice's situation. Every two or three steps that Béatrice takes, a 'cry' ('un cri') rises: the mechanical noise of the winch, of the wheel that is being turned, or of 'quartered beams' ('poutres écartelés') coming from a different part of the stage. The prison in which we find ourselves makes the sound of a factory in full motion ('une usine en plain movement') (Artaud 1976: IV, 262).

The scene encountered here is a prime example of how in theatre '[s]ound creates spatiality' (Fischer-Lichte 2014: 35). The term 'quartered' and the physical presence of the turning wheel to which Béatrice is tied establish this scene as a scene of torture, an outstanding example of what Artaud means when he discusses the role of torture in *Le Théâtre et son double*. While there is no blood spilled on the stage (as Artaud stipulated in his theory), the impact on the audience is clear. The inevitability that characterises tragedy finds its modern expression in the effect of a factory, a tragic machine that in its materiality seems unstoppable. The dialogue that starts the scene only confirms verbally what the stage directions have already shown us physically. Bernardo says: 'There is no corner of this accursed prison where they stop torturing' ('Pas un coin de cette prison maudite où l'on s'arrête de tourmenter') (Artaud 1976: IV, 263–4). Prefiguring and inspiring Deleuze's view of art, Artaud's theatre brings us to the limits of what our embodied selves can endure and to the limits of representation, opening the horizon of death. In this sense, as the experience of limits, theatre is again boundary work.[13]

For Artaud, life is inevitably torture. Béatrice's response to the torture inflicted upon her equates the prison enacted with life itself. While her torture continues – Béatrice and the wheel continue turning as the prison, a live materiality, cries out – Béatrice addresses Bernardo lovingly as the older sister advising her younger brother. She tells Bernardo that she will be leaving him as her inheritance the words of a *music* that heal the 'mal d'exister'. The 'mal d'exister', the 'pain of existing', is of course a term with obvious Romantic and existentialist overtones. Then 'a very soft and very dangerous music rises' ('Une musique très douce et très dangereuse s'élève') (Artaud 1976: IV, 264). Objects or sound – not only the door that opens or the prison that cries, but also the 'dangerous' music – have agency; they are actors on a par with human actors in Artaud's theatre.

Living is nightmarish dreaming. Béatrice recites the words of the 'dangerous music' that speak of living as dreaming: 'accepter de vivre, c'est renoncer à se réveiller' ('accepting to live is renouncing to wake up'). Life is worse than any darkness ('les ténèbres') or nightmare, worse than death. The song rejects the soul that is stained by life – as Béatrice's soul is stained from the murder of her father – as a fire that ought to cure God from creating any more. Acknowledging the power of the song and modelling the spectator's affective reaction, the soldier has now stopped and weeps. As a material expression of the song's rebellion against 'the god ("dieu" with a small d) who has made me', the stage instructions call for the sound of a commotion ('on entend un remue-ménage') in the cellars of the prison that is life (Artaud 1976: IV, 265).

Now that the final act has thus established that life is worse than death, Bernardo says: 'They are coming' ('Ils viennent'). The vagueness of this announcement (who is 'they'?) further builds suspense and fear. Reprising the fire imagery of the song, Bernardo speaks of 'the fire that destroys everything'. He wants to kiss Béatrice before this fire destroys her and before she becomes 'comme un grand vent' ('like a wind'), a force of nature (Artaud 1976: IV, 265). When Camillo enters with Lucrétia, Giacomo and the guards, he says – in another theatrical self-reference – that it is indeed time that the story end. Camillo, Lucrétia and Giacomo all urge Béatrice to confess and save herself from being further tortured. Wiping his face and giving expression to what Artaud intends the spectator to feel at this point, Camillo says: 'I feel sick with horror' ('je me sens malade d'horreur') (Artaud 1976: IV, 266).

The final scene of the play (IV, iii) is a condemnation of all paternal and paternalistic authority as unfounded and corrupt. When Camillo hands her the papal execution order, Béatrice equates the Pope's cruelty with the old Cenci's. Following up on the song's critique of God the Father, Béatrice now accuses the alliance between other figures of paternalistic authority – the Pope ('the father of Christendom', 'le père de la chrétienté') and Cenci as paterfamilias – saying that 'it is not good that the fathers unite against the families they have created'. The Pope's authority is absolutist and absolute: Béatrice's crime 'has already been judged' ('le crime est déjà jugé . . . vous ne fléchirez pas l'autorité'). The Pope himself will economically benefit from the destruction of the Cenci family, whose possessions/land will return to his coffers. God allowing her execution to proceed also invalidates divine authority for Béatrice: 'But what celestial judge could sign mine without blushing?' ('Mais quel juge du ciel a pu signer la mienne, sans rougir de ce qu'il faisait?') Having signed her own execution order, Béatrice tells Camillo to never again talk to her about God (Artaud 1976: IV, 265–8). Artaud's *Les Cenci* is a universal critique of paternalistic authority.

The procession to the execution starts with Bernardo's metadiscourse, a double entendre reminding the readers (!) that they are witnessing a fictional event: 'Quick, quick, turn the page; so that we can believe that all of this has never existed' ('Vite, vite, tournez la page; qu'on puisse croire que tout cela n'a jamais existé'). While the action is set in Renaissance Rome, the march to the execution is furthermore accompanied by an 'Inca rhythm'[14] that also distances the audience from the impending violence. This distancing effect is again an unusual moment in Artaud's theatre, which as we have seen aims to immerse the spectator in the affect created on the stage and is typically opposed to Brecht's theatre of distantiation (Artaud 1976: IV, 269).

As discussed earlier, in his theoretical writings Artaud speaks of the theatre as a fire, 'un incendie' (a theme also already mentioned in the 'dangerous music' described above). While Bernardo's life is spared at the end of *Les Cenci*, Béatrice reminds us that '[e]verything dies, because the world burns, uncertain between good and evil. Neither God, nor man, nor any of the powers that dominate what we call fate, has chosen between good and evil' ('Tout meurt, parce que le monde brûle, incertain entre le mal et le bien. Ni Dieu, ni l'homme, ni aucun des pouvoirs qui dominent ce qu'on appelle notre destin, n'ont choisi entre le mal et le bien'). After a silence – a moment of reflection giving weight to what is to follow – Béatrice says: 'I am dying and I have not chosen' ('Je meurs et je n'ai pas choisi') (Artaud 1976: IV, 270).

This statement transforms the meaning of Artaud's play. It is now no longer a play about a young woman becoming a martyr for the abolition of an unjust tyranny. Without this telos or *Aufhebung* (sublation) in Hegel's sense, without the preservation of a value (justice) that would give her death meaning in a surviving world, 'the world that escapes me will not survive me' ('Le monde qui m'échappe ne me survivra pas'). Béatrice's voice now not only enacts the despair of the modern human condition, but questions human life – or possibly even just 'life' – in general. The stage instructions call for the music to become louder while 'a kind of desperate human voice' ('[u]ne espèce de voix humaine désespérée') mixes with its obsessive rhythm. On the threshold to death, Béatrice wonders if she will not find her father again in the afterlife – obviously a thought leading to despair (Artaud 1976: IV, 269–70). Rather than an ending, her death enacts what Artaud elsewhere called the 'sufferings of an imminent birth' (Artaud 1976: XIII, 43, quoted by Artioli 2004: 139). In 1933, Jay Murphy notes, Artaud had written

> that it is a mistake to see the body as a fixed and impermeable organism; it is, rather, only 'provisional stratifications of states of life.' Early on, Artaud prefigures the body as an image of the inorganic vitality that traverses it . . . For Artaud, it is ever a matter of evoking the movements of the 'life plane'. (Murphy 2015: 3; Artaud 1976: V, 148 and 212)

Artaud's influence on Deleuze is clear here. But given its mythical dimension, Artaud's work, as Murphy (2015: 3) puts it, 'arguably blasts beyond a Deleuzian philosophy of immanence as well'.

For Deleuze's neo-Spinozist ontology, life and creation are not opposed to death.[15] Deleuze instead theorises a 'plane of immanence' that includes both life and death. On this plane of immanence, there are only dynamic networks of forces, relations, affects and becomings:

> There are only relations of movement and rest, speed and slowness between unformed elements, or at least between elements that are relatively unformed, molecules, and particles of all kinds. There are only haecceities, affects, subject-less individuations that constitute collective assemblages . . . We call this plane, which knows only longitudes and latitudes, speeds and haecceities, the plane of consistency or composition (as opposed to a plan(e) of organization or development). (Deleuze and Guattari 1987: 266)

In Artaud, the body is in an ongoing process of transformation. In reference to Artaud's work, Murphy speaks of 'infinity as constant becoming', of 'a release of the body into infinity composed of multiple planes of time' (2015: 4). It is in his later work, *Pour en finir avec le jugement de dieu* (*To Have Done With the Judgment of God*) (1947), that Artaud developed the corresponding concept of the body-without-organs (*le corps-sans-organes*). This concept of a body that is not an organism would later also influence Deleuze and Guattari.[16] This body breaks free from organised efficiency (Braidotti 2013: 92) and can thus be reassembled in new, alternative ways.

For Deleuze, pure immanence and 'a life' – that is a more-than-personal, indefinite life that inhabits all things – suppose each other:

> We will say of pure immanence that it is A LIFE, and nothing else . . . A life is the immanence of immanence, absolute immanence: it is complete power, complete bliss. (Deleuze 2001: 27)

> A life is everywhere . . . an immanent life carrying with it the events and singularities that are merely actualized in subjects and objects. (Deleuze 2001: 29)

While Count Cenci calls himself a force of evil, Artaud at the same time creates an ethics of immanence by steering clear of transcendent judgements of good and evil, blurring Béatrice's 'purity' at the end of the play.

Whereas Brecht's theatre offers the hope of a political solution on a human timescale, in Artaud there is no awakening possible from

Béatrice's nightmare, no knock on the door, even in death. When Béatrice's last two lines give expression to her fear that she will find out in death that she has ended up resembling her father (Artaud 1976: IV, 271), there are no clear distinctions between good and evil left in Artaud's play. As we have seen, some of the other plays discussed in this project (Strindberg, Sartre) enact immunitarian, binary self-defence strategies that are, however, ultimately fruitless (and in Strindberg shown to be fruitless). Artaud's Béatrice also tries to escape the boundary-crossing threat that is her father. But in contrast to Strindberg and Sartre, Artaud understands this violation of boundaries as a cleansing reminiscent of Greek tragedy. He designs his theatre of cruelty to lift all defensive psychic barriers, immersing the audience in the emotional violence or affective intensity of the play's performance. Artaud writes in December 1946: 'The theatre is a passionate overflowing/a frightful transfer of forces/from body/to body' (quoted by Derrida 2004b: 45).

Burnt Flesh

Artaud lets the theatrical world burn in a purifying fire that extends the borders of reality or the mind in an experience that unites non-cognitive affect and materiality. In a letter addressed to Artaud after the 1935 production of *Les Cenci*, a certain Eugène Gengenbach described the play's effect on the audience: 'You are playing with fire . . . Around me spectators were laughing like lunatics, trembling with hysterical laughter' (quoted by Curtin 2010: 255).

But there are also other references to fire. In the preface to his *Collected Works*, written in 1946, Artaud writes of 'the seething of burnt flesh' (Artaud 1976: I, 11, quoted by Finter 2004: 55). Does this reference to burnt flesh, a reference written after the Shoah, establish a relationship between Artaud's work and totalitarianism? Adrian Curtin, for instance, observes, that

> Artaud's conception of a 'cruel' auditory event – sonic bombardment intended to provoke communal *ekstasis* – is uncomfortably close to the way in which the Nazi Party ultilized music and sound in public spaces in Germany in the early 1930s, particularly in urban street environments. In documenting this phenomenon, Carlyn Birdsall has coined the phrase 'affirmative resonances' to refer to the way in which sensory overstimulation and rituals of sonic dominance worked to delineate patterns of belonging (and exclusion), reinforce group identity and (ultimately) affirm the legitimacy of the Nazi Party. (Curtin 2010: 257)[17]

Curtin (following Constance Spreen[18]), however, also points out that 'critics of Artaud, particularly those associated with the reactionary, nationalist movement L'Action française, distrusted and rejected Artaud's theatre aesthetic because it subverted traditional French aesthetic values' (Curtin 2010: 255). Given totalitarian regimes' prototypical distrust of the aesthetic avant-garde (of what the Nazis called 'decadent' art), it is ironic that for economic reasons the première of *Les Cenci* in 1935 took place at the Folies-Wagram Theatre in Paris, which was located next door to the Solidarité française, a right-wing, nationalist organisation. Thus the artistic sound design of Artaud's production 'was potentially crossed with the political dissension and acoustical violence of right-wing protest groups like the Solidarité française' (Curtin 2010: 256). Rather than a fascist spectacle based on mass hysteria that would link Artaud to totalitarianism, however, Artaud's theatre is, on the contrary, a therapeutic theatre of multi-voiced otherness.[19]

Creating an encounter between human and more-than-human sensory elements or qualities as 'the glue of the universe, as the tingling skin through which entities are able to communicate' (Lunning 2016: 85, following Graham Harman), Artaud's theatre breaks down immunitarian walls. The schizophrenic Artaud for whom everything was physical,[20] who experienced verbal signification as false, and who discovered the rich language of the body through his own suffering (Deleuze 2004: 31, 35), this schizophrenic created a work that attacks what Goodall calls 'the fortress of rational, egocentric consciousness from which he is outcast' (2004: 68). Artaud instead designed a carnal theatre that aims to 'heal the split between language and flesh' (Sontag 1999: 89).[21]

Artaud's work thus prefigures the French philosopher Maurice Merleau-Ponty's phenomenology of perception, and most notably his final, unfinished book, *The Visible and the Invisible* (1968), where Merleau-Ponty (1968: 1377) conceptualises the world as 'universal flesh'. Florence Chiew writes:

> By insisting on the world as a general field of sensibility, and sensation as itself a form of apperception, a cognitive act of self-knowledge and realization, Merleau-Ponty unsettles the routine separation between self and other, the body and the environment . . . He argues that any knowledge we have we can only acquire through living our bodies, for . . . 'the world is at the heart of our flesh'. (Chiew 2017: 58, quoting Merleau-Ponty 1968: 136)

Influenced by Artaud, Deleuze and Guattari would similarly theorise in their *Anti-Oedipe* (1972) (*Anti-Oedipus*) that 'man' and nature co-produce each other. Donna Haraway, in her 2003 *Companion Species Manifesto*, speaks of this co-construction and coextensiveness of psychic and somatic forces in terms of *naturecultures*. Today's exploratory cognitive sciences and the discovery of the brain's great neural plasticity have shown the organic body and the mind to be deeply interconnected (or in Karen Barad's words, intra-connected) and anything but static. It is this 'dynamic' plasticity of the brain and its relations that demonstrates the coextensive entanglement of physiology/the body and the social (Murphy 2015: 12–13). This 'intercorporeity', to use Merleau-Ponty's term (1968: 141), challenges the conventional view of the world as constituted by separate, autonomous bodies. As Chiew (2017: 63) puts it, 'the flesh of the body is . . . the flesh of the world'.

Overcoming the division between the realms of materiality and meaning, which are mutually articulated without being reducible to one another (Barad 2008: 140), the schizophrenic Artaud thus leads the way by wanting to infect us with his contagious delirium. Artaud was a mental patient who spent nine years of his life in insane asylums and who died in a psychiatric clinic, a borderline 'non-subject' who could not separate inside and outside (Kristeva 1982: 25).[22] But it was this madman, Artaud, who created a work that, while not yet unambiguously posthumanist itself, shows us the way out of the madness of a philosophical tradition based on the hegemony and immunitarian isolation of human consciousness.

Notes

1. For a detailed description of the acoustics of the first production see M. W. Smith (2018: 187–9).
2. Cf. Braidotti (2011: 107): 'Think, for instance, of the importance of the gaze for phenomenology and psychoanalysis.' Or of Foucault's analysis of the panopticon.
3. While the orthodox account or classic definition of perception relies on the assumption of 'the object's externality from the perceiving subject or body' (Chiew 2017: 48), Florence Chiew's article 'The Sensory Substitution: The Plasticity of the Eye/I' (2017) is an argument against this assumption. In Artaud's theatre of cruelty, the boundaries between spectator and spectacle break down.
4. The terms 'affect' and 'affection' gained prominence through Deleuze and Guattari's *A Thousand Plateaus* (1987) [1980], the second volume of their *Capitalism and Schizophrenia*.
5. Cf. also Lehmann's discussion of the transition from 'dramatic' work to theatrical event, paralleling for theatre Derrida's theory of the closure of the book and the open processuality of the text (1999: 100–1).

6. English translations of Artaud in this chapter are my own, unless marked otherwise.

7. Yampolsky refers to a '"speech-affect," which originates directly from within the body and attains its fullest realization in the scream, the howl, or the groan' (Yampolsky 2004: 170). Yampolsky (2004: 170) quotes Deleuze (1990: 89), who speaks of *language without articulation* (emphasis in original).

8. Cf. Roussetzki's discussion of Shelley's *The Cenci*: '. . . in Fear and Trembling the philosopher repeats that only the strategies aimed at provoking this anxious feeling could be called specific to the "modern," that is, the Romantic tragedy' (Roussetzki 2000: 1).

9. Cf. Deleuze (2004: 31).

10. A short time later, in his dialogue with his wife, Cenci will call Bernardo 'cet avorton' ('this deformed runt') (Artaud 1976: IV, 220), an image of abjection.

11. Here the scene directions – a corporeal language and the language of sound – and the words uttered again coincide: Camillo responds that he is going to suggest something to Giacomo that will have to remain a secret. Giacomo tells Camillo to speak quickly, and we hear hurried steps. Without finishing the conversation, Camillo exits and Orsino enters. Reinforcing again the importance of breath in Artaud's theatre, we hear only Camillo's voice that 'arrives in a breath/little wind' ('souffle'), creating in the audience suspense for the dialogue between Orsino and Giacomo that is to follow: 'Tiens, voilà quelqu'un qui pourra mieux t'éclairer' ('This one [Orsino] will clarify things for you' – 'you' being Giacomo, but of course also the spectator). Speaking in an aside, Orsino then gives the audience an advantage over what Giacomo knows (Artaud 1976: IV, 226).

12. Giving voice to the intensifying tension of this scene, Béatrice states that she feels under her feet the apocalyptic 'forces of the world, a world that is getting ready to take everything with it'. At this point, Lucrétia – linking physical and verbal expression – buries her head in her hands, stating that she fears that the worst is not yet over. She again reinforces the affective intensity of her statement and the spectators' emotional turmoil with the exclamation 'Mon Dieu!', a testament to her continued religious faith in spite of it all and possibly an appeal for divine help in extreme distress. Béatrice, who continues to sob, confirms that while horrible things have happened in this world, their current thoughts are unprecedented: 'Mais jamais la pensée n'a rêvé . . .' ('nobody would have dreamed . . .', with 'thought' as the grammatical subject) (Artaud 1976: IV, 236). We have seen in Artaud's theoretical writings that he wants to give his theatrical work a dream-like quality.

13. Cf. Braidotti (2013: 107), paraphrasing Deleuze and Guattari's (as well as Blanchot's) view of art.

14. Cf. Curtin (2010: 253): 'The 'Inca seven-part time rhythm' may be a misnomer on Artaud's part; as far as I can tell, no such musical trope exists.'

15. See also Braidotti (2013: 115).
16. Cf., for instance, Deleuze and Guattari (1987: 499).
17. In her *Powers of Horror* (1982: 125), Julia Kristeva also investigates Artaud's work as an example of poetic language, a language that she argues 'borders on psychosis . . . and totalitarianism or fascism'.
18. Cf. Spreen (2003: 84 ff.).
19. Cf. also Finter (2004: 56) and Murphy (2015: 21–2, n. 4): 'One has to ask why if Artaud, who traveled often to Germany in the 1930s for film work (and who claimed to have met Hitler at the Romanisches café in Berlin in May 1932, a meeting that was possible), felt Nazi rallies were a fulfillment of his ideas, he never said so.'
20. Cf. Deleuze (1990: 87).
21. Cf. also Derrida (1978: 179), quoted by Yampolsky (2004: 171): 'The integrity of the flesh torn by all these differences must be restored in the theatre.'
22. Cf. Artaud (1995: 278): 'I'm still not sure of the limits at which the body of the human self can stop' (quoted by Murphy 2015: 18).

Conclusion

The reworking of exclusions entails possibilities for (discontinuous) changes in
the topology of the world's becoming. (Barad 2007: 182)

Inspired by the work of Niels Bohr, the physicist-philosopher Karen
Barad refers to apparatuses as 'device[s] for making and remaking
boundaries' (Barad 2007: 201–2). Apparatuses are 'the specific prac-
tices/intra-actions/performances through which specific exclusionary
boundaries are enacted' and 'dynamic (re)configurings of the world'
(Barad 2008: 134). As this book has demonstrated, theatre as an apparatus is in a prime position for such boundary work. Informed by
Barad's work, my project has rearticulated the materialsemiotic practices and open-ended processes through which the modern stage has co-
configured as well as challenged the immunitarian identity boundaries
of nineteenth- and twentieth-century European society. Although, as
Barad points out (2007: 49, 60), theatrical performances are not necessarily the same as the performative enactments she describes, this book
has established a dialogue between (1) Barad's insights garnered from
quantum physics and (2) theatrical practices as products of material
engagements with the world. My project has charted the (not always
chronological) itinerary of modern drama from the representationalist
realist-naturalist tradition based primarily on verbal dialogue, human
meaning-making and abstraction to a theatrical tradition itself close
to Barad's view of performative enactment, namely the theatre of the
historical avant-garde of the early twentieth century. In Artaud's experimental theatre of cruelty in particular, embodied practice becomes
primary or co-constitutive, offering an alternative to the rationalist
philosophical tradition and its emphasis on consciousness as the exclusive site of knowledge.

Given that Bruno Latour has also advised us to think of objects
not in terms of substances but rather as performances (Harman 2009:
47–51), theatre is in a more than advantageous position to benefit
from the philosophical insights of the material turn – and the material
turn from theatre. What is at stake in all of the plays assembled in this

project, in other words, are object relations: relations between hetero-geneous elements, and specifically relations between the human and the more-than-human worlds. The restless, anxious 'flesh', the loca-tion where bodies on the stage and 'culture' intra-act and collapse in a common drive energy or *conatus*, is the very battleground of mod-ern theatre. From at least Lessing to the nineteenth century, western bourgeois theatre enacted the Cartesian-Kantian philosophical tradi-tion's privileging of the human, both in content and in theatrical form. The realism of this theatrical tradition, whose action-based plot was driven by human characters and verbal dialogue, mimetically repre-sented a domestic or outside reality. It enacted an anthropocentric and representationalist worldview in which human culture tried to exert its dominance over inert, 'dead' nonhuman matter, a worldview in which 'nature' served as a mere metaphor to illustrate human emotions, psy-chological motivations and interpersonal conflicts. As we have seen, however, even the realist-naturalist plays presented in this book also enact the biophysical realm as a dynamic threat that goes beyond the purely metaphorical and beyond the passivity of dead matter. Rather than keeping intact the binary division between nature and culture, this study has explored the performativity of theatre in its double sense – as theatrical production and as the intra-activity or enactment of a live, open and dynamic system of multiple relations between co-consti-tutive entities of human and more-than-human actors/actants, energies and affects.

My project has specifically mapped the ontological relationship between nature and culture (or materiality and meaning) in the shift from bourgeois-naturalist drama (Strindberg and Sartre) to the theatri-cal avant-garde of the early twentieth century (Brecht and Artaud). This is the shift from what the German theatre scholar Hans-Thies Lehmann has called 'dramatic' to ultimately 'post-dramatic' theatre (the theatre of the last third of the twentieth century), from (human) emotion to (impersonal) affect, and from the rationalist, humanist philosophi-cal tradition to new materialism and posthumanism. At an important point in this transition, in the theatre of the 'historical avant-garde' of the early twentieth century, whose most important representatives are Brecht and Artaud, the increasing abstraction of capitalist modernity is counteracted by a materialist theatre that instead enacts the entan-gled presence of heterogeneous, human and more-than-human, organic (organism-based) and inorganic agentive elements. Rather than inde-pendently existing 'out there', waiting to be represented, these elements co-produce intra-active performances.

As I have shown, however, the historical avant-garde is not the only or first theatrical tradition that enters into conversation with the beginnings of what we today call posthumanism. While the bourgeois-realist 'dramatic' tradition of the nineteenth century was centrally based on verbal dialogue and human conflicts and Lehmann consequently calls this tradition 'anthropocentric', this project has demonstrated that what these human characters are already talking about in Strindberg and even in Sartre's humanist work are indeed ontological matters: the relationship between the human and the natural-material world. Instead of Lehmann's binary opposition between 'dramatic' (anthropocentric) and 'post-dramatic' (posthumanist) theatre, therefore, my study has found a *continuum*: an emerging and continuing discussion about the status of the human and more-than-human, with increasingly posthumanist tools. We can already locate this ontological discussion, although not yet the same theatrical tools, in Strindberg.

At the turn from the nineteenth to the twentieth centuries, sexual difference, race and the ontological status of the human intersect. In conversation with the post-Darwinian/scientific and economic discourses of his time, Strindberg's naturalist dramatic work displaces the question of the relationship between the human and the more-than-human onto gender. While Strindberg enacts the flesh as passive matter initially awaiting animation by the male human, this feminised materiality then comes alive, posing a lethal threat. Arguably an example of modern immunitarian thinking, Strindberg's preoccupation with questions of individual autonomy – from the host of monstrous mothers in his plays to an explicit thematisation of debt – anchors his naturalist plays within the tradition of bourgeois drama. But his enactment of autonomy and community also already poses ontological questions about the status of the human.

Jean-Paul Sartre's early work establishes a dualistic, immunitarian philosophical system against the perceived threat that feminised border-crossing abjection and nonhuman materiality pose to hegemonic human/male consciousness. This invasive materiality is incarnated by the flies in Sartre's most famous play, *The Flies*. The fetishisation of consciousness in Sartre is an attempt at redemption, an attempt in other words to (re)imagine the human as the master of his metaphysical destiny and as the master of the material, more-than-human conditions and agents that surround, drive and form him. While this attempt still largely succeeds in Sartre's early work, it comes at a much higher cost in his later work.

Instead of trying to fend off the modern fear of border transgressions with dramatic representations, finally, Artaud's theatre of cruelty enacts a modern 'crisis of representation' of its own. Methodologically as well, Artaud's theatre intra-acts especially well with a descriptive, affective reading not primarily focused on ideology critique. Artaud immerses his audience physically and affectively in the sensory materiality and perpetual movement of the performance. Artaud's plays are encounters that cut through or transverse the binary relation between observing subject and observed object, producing spectators that experience themselves as physically and ontologically vulnerable. With Artaud's concept of theatre as plague, the theatre as a performance of the spectators' bourgeois politeness comes to an end and the immunitarian border shielding the spectators from contagion collapses. The border lines between self and other break down and individual subjectivity is decentred and depersonalised. In the end, Artaud's spectators suffer a total sensorial and perceptive immersion in an affective network of heterogeneous, human and inhuman relations. Whereas 'dramatic', realist theatre enacts the abstraction that increasingly defines capitalist modernity, Artaud is, like the ancient Greeks, interested in a mythical theatre that materially 'translates' life in its universal sense (Artaud 1976: IV, 139). Instead of leading to anti-intellectualism, however, Artaud's theatre gives voice to a new and deeper intellectuality not averse to the lack of logical coherence, to affect, to materiality and to acute perception. I argue that in his view of life as a universal force and in the use of heterogeneous theatrical tools, Artaud already becomes posthumanist.

Creating an encounter between human and more-than-human sensory elements or qualities, Artaud's theatre breaks down the immunitarian walls present in Strindberg's and Sartre's work, as well as the physical distance and cognitive distantiation between spectator and stage (and actor and role) of Brecht's epic theatre. Artaud's theatre brings us to the limits of what our embodied selves can endure and to the limits of representation, opening the horizon of death. Here, as the experience of limits, theatre is again boundary work.

What all of the diverse theatrical works presented in this project ultimately put in question is western rationalist philosophy and modern bourgeois ideology's claims to humans' status as autonomous, sovereign subjects. While we have long considered dualism to be one of the hallmarks of modernity, this study has shown post-Enlightenment modernity to be a time that nevertheless begins to collapse many oppositions. Modernist theatre troubles not only the teleological timeline that would depend on the dichotomy between dramatic and post-dramatic theatre or between humanism and posthumanism. It also transverses other dualisms, breaking through the divides between mind and body, political life (*bíos*) and natural life (*zōē*), public and private, the state and the economy, theology and secularism, norm and state of exception, democracy and tyranny,[1] self-preservation and self-destruction, immunity and community, biopolitics and thanato-politics, life and death, human and nonhuman, same and other. As a counter-reaction to the perceived threat of such border invasions, however, modern society established a defensive system of rigid immunitarian, biopolitical lines – a system that ultimately led to totalitarianism but proved illusory nonetheless. This book has followed the contingent journey of transnational European modernity as a history of socio-political and ontological inclusion and exclusion based on quasi-biological criteria designed to defend the health and life of the population against the threat posed by human and nonhuman others – others that ultimately function as displacements of the perceived threats of modernity. While this phobic defensive logic is based on a threatened gender dimorphism in Strindberg's naturalist dramas and on the fetishisation of heroic, autonomous male human consciousness in Sartre's early work, National Socialism would primarily racialise the perceived threat of difference.

This book itself has chosen to go beyond a one-sided, ultimately still binary methodology, arguing that the creative reworking of modernity requires a historically and socially inflected ontology, that is an intra-active approach that transverses the philosophical divide between new materialist ontology on the one side and the critique of subjectivity and identity categories (including historical materialism) on the other. The (largely, though not always chronological) arc mapped in this study starts with the problematic of difference as pejorative identity category, with *zōē* and libidinal drives as the threat of the feminised nonhuman in the plays belonging to the realist-mimetic tradition (Strindberg and Sartre). But the ecology described ultimately extends to difference, sexuality, desire and *zōē* as impersonal forces of intensity and as dynamic relational processes transversing the bounded categories of self and other in the early Brecht and in Artaud. While Foucault's and Agamben's work on biopolitics and biopower lends itself well to a conversation with the former, a Deleuzian framework deterritorialising identities establishes an especially productive dialogue with the early Brecht and with Artaud. The arc described in this study thus also demonstrates the polyvalence of power – enmeshing both restrictive *potestas* and life-affirming or empowering *potentia*.

Openings, or Where Do We Go from Here?

The plays of the 'anthropocentric' realist tradition enact the material –
physical and mental – suffering of human beings, who in modernity are
thrust into lives that continue to claim a status different from the nonhuman (and nonhuman animality in particular), but that at the same
time cannot claim sublime transcendence any more. This confusion of
modern human identity is what we have referred to as 'the flesh'. In
modernity, symbolic authority detaches from natural-biological life (the
king's physical body) in the move towards the people's abstract body
in democracy. At literally the same time, however, the universal human
rights declarations of the eighteenth-century collapse what the Greeks
called *zōē* (zoological-natural life) and qualified, political life. The flesh
is located at the convergence of these two kinds of life into one flow
of life. The flesh, this liminal entity at the disappearing border to the
nonhuman, is what the characters in Strindberg and Sartre perceive as
the greatest threat: the threat of degeneration, of the dissolution of the
specifically human self. Understood this way, the flesh is ultimately the
modern condition, a product of the ontological gap between the material immanence of the modern universe and the unfulfilled longing for
human transcendence that Sartre's contemporary, the French existentialist writer Albert Camus, in *Le Mythe de Sisyphe*, referred to as 'the
absurd'.

This sense of metaphysical alienation in western modernity is the
result of our human *hubris*, our claim – as humans – to a unique status
on earth or in the universe based on the (biblical) assumption that the
earth and all nonhuman life on it are ours to dominate. In his 2012
book *Third Person*, the Italian philosopher Roberto Esposito challenges this human arrogance by exposing the notion of 'personhood'
as inherently violent. He questions, in other words, our need to distinguish between what Aristotle called *zōē* (natural life) and *bíos politikos* (qualified, human life). In contrast to a long line of philosophers
from Aristotle to Immanuel Kant, Hannah Arendt, Martin Heidegger,
Jacques Lacan, Emmanuel Levinas and Jacques Derrida who reject
'biologistic continuism' (Wolfe 2013: 7, 42), I agree with Esposito that
we need to eliminate the dividing line, as Brecht's *Baal* or Artaud's
work have already done. We need to eliminate the dividing line, both
between the human and the more-than-human and between consciousness and materiality. What matters, in other words, is that we enact
a relation, rather than a separation, in ways that 'take seriously the
status – epistemologically and ethically – of different kinds of minds'

(Wolfe 2010: 44) as part of a material ecology. In his book on *Eco-Translation* (2017: 80), Michael Cronin refers to Déborah Danowski and Eduardo Viveiros de Castro's work, which points out that 'for Amerindian peoples, other animals and entities in the world are "political entities"' (Danowksi and Castro 2014: 279). Once we legally – and, most importantly, materially – acknowledge that humans are part of all life forms, that the cosmos is one intra-connected living body or 'collectively distributed consciousness' (Braidotti 2013: 169), the paradigm of inclusion and exclusion explored in this study falls away. The paradigm of (pre-existing) person/subject- and objecthood, and the violence, narcissism and parasitic-extractivist exploitation that accompany this division, fall away. In my view, such an elimination of the biopolitical dividing line is not what Cary Wolfe describes (negatively) as a 'dedifferentiating discourse of life' (2013: 58). I join Timothy Morton, who notes that 'biology does not recognize firm bright boundaries between inside and outside, male and female, life and nonlife, or between and within species . . . At the DNA level, the biosphere is permeable and boundariless' (Morton 2010: 274–5). Abandoning the binary hierarchies that aim to justify violence, in other words, is not the same as overlooking the diversity of beings and their co-productive relations.

As Rosi Braidotti points out in *The Posthuman*, today's global economy and bio-genetic capitalism are already increasingly diminishing the separations between human and nonhuman species whenever they can financially profit from such a blurring of ontological categories (Braidotti 2013: 63). The control of populations in today's society in other words goes beyond human populations to include nonhuman and inorganic entities. Since, as Braidotti points out, 'advanced capitalism reduces bodies to carriers of vital information, which get invested with financial value and capitalized . . . [t]here is a structural isomorphism between economic and biological growth' (Braidotti 2013: 117). Even these different instances of a blurring of the borderlines between the biological and the inorganic, however, continue to work along hierarchical scales and are designed to economically benefit humans (or a financial elite, to be more specific). In my view, the collapse of ontological categories therefore does not necessarily make this work post-anthropocentric.[2] In order to move towards true post-anthropocentrism, I see, in contrast to Wolfe (2013: 60), a need for philosophical approaches based on an ethics of care, or at least of doing less harm.[3]

While the immunitarian threats enacted by the plays of the 'dramatic' tradition discussed in my study are *perceived* threats to the biological survival of the population, our planetary survival as human-and-non-human ecosystems in what Donna Haraway (2016) calls the chthulucene depends in very real, concrete terms on our ability to change the human immunitarian paradigm that I have mapped. For this reason, but not only for this reason, our goal has to be community rather than immunity, an affirmative community that values ethical encounters between entangled selves and others, humans and more-than-humans, a community built on transversal relationality and intra-connectedness that overcomes binary dichotomies. It is time for an opening of systems, for the kind of opening that, I have argued, is already prefigured in Brecht and Artaud. In Brecht, as he himself put it, the 'environment acquires the quality of a process' (Brecht 1988: XXII, 238), an integrated, constantly changing mesh of agentive organic and inorganic bodies (Brecht 1988: XXII, 229).

I share with Rebekah Sheldon the conviction that 'epistemology is an agent with directly material consequences'. As Sheldon writes, this perspective 'begins from the assumption that ideas and things do not occupy separate ontological orders but instead are co-constituents in the production of the real' (Sheldon 2015: 196). Such a perspective resists the operations of a biopolitics based on dualistic oppositions as reworked in this study. Rejecting such binaries, this book has shown materiality and meaning to be entangled in many complex, co-constitutive ways. It has mapped the contingent and transversal material-historical itineraries that have led human and nonhuman life to, ultimately, the ecological crisis of our contemporary times. In Elizabeth Grosz's words, however, 'given that oppressions, harms, injustice have occurred and cannot be undone, the political task is not simply to mourn or lament them, but to use them, their memory, precisely as a spur to transformation, to difference' (2008: 49, n.14).[4] Let us then hope, in a modest utopian gesture, that the memory of the enfleshed suffering and sacrifice that we have reworked can reach beyond western philosophy's focus on mourning and beyond binary reversals, contributing instead to the open-ended task of everyday qualitative transformations. Heeding Barad's advice that '[i]t matters which [subject/object] cuts are enacted: different cuts enact different materialized becomings' (Barad 2007: 361), let us help reconfigure agentive cuts. Let us coexist as affirmative viral forces that rhizomatically and diffractively sidestep immunitarian walls, becoming part of the sticky meshes of alternative social relations, both human and more-than-human.

Notes

1. In his groundbreaking 2016 book, *Plant Theory*, Jeffrey Nealon posits an opposition between Agamben's work on state-based sovereignty and our contemporary times. Recent political developments, however, have again demonstrated the deep enmeshment of democratic modernity and sovereign structures, an imbrication explored throughout my book.
2. Given capitalism's goal of profit for humans, I here differ from Braidotti, who considers what she calls the 'political economy of bio-genetic capitalism' as 'post-anthropocentric in its very structures' since 'it . . . inflicts a blow to any lingering notion of human nature, *anthropos* and *bios*, as categorically distinct from the life of animals and nonhumans, or *zoe*' (Braidotti 2013: 65).
3. Nussbaum speaks of providing 'positive opportunities to flourish' (2006: 349, 351; quoted in Wolfe 2010: 67). Povinelli discusses 'a maximal saturation of the possibility of the object and its assemblage' (Povinelli 2016: 119).
4. Braidotti also proposes 'an ethics that respects vulnerability while actively constructing social horizons of hope' (Braidotti 2013: 122).

Bibliography

Adorno, Theodor W., Else Frenkel-Brunswik, Daniel J. Levinson and R. Nevitt Sanford (1950) *The Authoritarian Personality*. New York: Harper.

Adorno, Theodor W. (1973) *Negative Dialektik*. Frankfurt am Main: Suhrkamp.

Adorno, Theodor W. (1974) *Minima Moralia: Reflections from Damaged Life*, trans. E. F. N. Jephcott. London: NLB.

Adorno, Theodor W. (1980) 'On Commitment', in P. Anderson et al. (eds), *Aesthetics and Politics*. London: Verso, pp. 177–95.

Aeschylus (1952) *The Eumenides*, in *The Complete Plays of Aeschylus*, trans. G. London. London: Allen, pp. 201–53.

Agamben, Giorgio (1995) *Homo Sacer: Sovereign Power and Bare Life*. Stanford: Stanford University Press.

Agamben, Giorgio (2004) *The Open: Man and Animal*, trans. Kevin Attell. Stanford: Stanford University Press.

Agamben, Giorgio (2005) *State of Exception*, trans. Kevin Attell. Chicago: University of Chicago Press.

Agamben, Giorgio (2009a) *The Signature of All Things: On Method*. New York: Zone.

Agamben, Giorgio (2009b) *What Is an Apparatus? and Other Essays*. Stanford: Stanford University Press.

Agamben, Giorgio (2013a) 'Biopolitics and the Rights of Man', from *Homo Sacer*, in T. Campbell and A. Sitze (eds), *Biopolitics: A Reader*. Durham, NC: Duke University Press, pp. 152–60.

Agamben, Giorgio (2013b) 'The Politicization of Life', from *Homo Sacer*, in T. Campbell and A. Sitze (eds), *Biopolitics: A Reader*. Durham, NC: Duke University Press, pp. 145–60.

Ahmed, Sara (2010) 'Happy Objects', in M. Gregg and G. J. Seigworth (eds), *The Affect Theory Reader*. Durham, NC and London: Duke University Press, pp. 30–51.

Alaimo, Stacy and Susan Hekman (eds) (2008) *Material Feminisms*. Bloomington: Indiana University Press.

Aldrich, Robert and Gary Wotherspoon (eds) (2005) [2001] *Who's Who in Gay and Lesbian History: From Antiquity to World War II*. London and New York: Routledge.

Anderson, Ben (2010) 'Modulating the Excess of Affect: Morale in a State of "Total War"', in M. Gregg and G. J. Seigworth (eds), *The Affect Theory Reader*. Durham, NC: Duke University Press, pp. 161–85.

Arendt, Hannah (2013b) 'The Perplexities of the Rights of Man', from *The Origins of Totalitarianism*, in T. Campbell and A. Sitze (eds), *Biopolitics: A Reader*. Durham, NC: Duke University Press, pp. 82–97.

Arendt, Hannah (2013a) 'Selections from *The Human Condition*', in T. Campbell and A. Sitze (eds), *Biopolitics: A Reader*. Durham, NC: Duke University Press, pp. 98–133.

Aristotle (1961) *Poetics*. New York: Hill.

Arons, Wendy and Theresa J. May (eds) (2012) 'Introduction', *Readings in Performance and Ecology*. New York: Palgrave Macmillan, pp. 1–10.

Aronson, Ronald (1980) *Jean-Paul Sartre – Philosophy in the World*. London: Verso.

Artaud, Antonin (1958) *The Theater and Its Double*, trans. Mary Caroline Richards. New York: Grove Press.

Artaud, Antonin (1969) *The Cenci*, trans. S. Watson-Taylor. London: Calder & Boyars.

Artaud, Antonin (1976) [1964] *Oeuvres Complètes*. Paris: Gallimard.

Artaud, Antonin (1995) *Watchfiends and Rack Screams*, trans. and ed. C. Eshleman with B. Bador. Boston: Exact Change.

Artaud, Antonin (1996) 'Letter to André Breton, 28 February 1947', trans. Yvonne Houlton, *Interstice*, 2, Autumn, pp. 33–4.

Artaud, Antonin, *Selected Writings* (1999) [1976], trans. Helen Weaver, ed. Susan Sontag. Los Angeles: University of California Press, <https://www.worldcat.org/title/antonin-artaud-selected-writings/oclc/18134493/viewport> (last accessed 16 August 2019)

Artaud, Antonin (2008) *The Cenci*, trans. R. Sieburth, adapted and directed by John Jahnke, Hotel Savant, Ohio Theatre New York City, 23 February.

Artaud, Antonin. *Jet de sang* <syncself.50webs.com/diyreader/artaudjetsang.htm> (last accessed 14 August 2017).

Artioli, Umberto (2004) From 'Production of Reality or Hunger for the Impossible?', in E. Scheer (ed.), *Antonin Artaud : A Critical Reader*. London and New York: Routledge, pp. 137–47.

Bailey, Ninette (1977) 'Le Mythe de la fémininité dans le théâtre de Sartre', *French Studies*, 21 (3): 294–307.

Balzac, Honoré de (1968) 'Author's Introduction', *The Human Comedy* (last accessed 14 August 2017).

Banville, John (2012) 'Bizarre & Wonderful Strindberg', review of Sue Prideaux, *Strindberg: A Life*, Yale University Press 2012, in *The New York Review of Books*, 21 June, pp. 48–50 <https://www.nybooks.com/articles/2012/06/21/bizarre-wonderful-strindberg/> (last accessed 12 August 2019).

Barad, Karen (2007) *Meeting the Universe Halfway: Quantum Physics and the Entanglement of Matter and Meaning*. Durham, NC: Duke University Press.

Barad, Karen (2008) 'Posthumanist Performativity: Toward an Understanding of How Matter Comes to Matter', in S. Alaimo and S. Hekman (eds), *Material Feminisms*. Bloomington: Indiana University Press, pp. 120–54.

Barad, Karen (2011) 'Queer Performativity', *Qui Parle*, 19 (2): 121–58 <http://ww.jstor.org/stable/10.5250/quiparle.19.2.0121> (last accessed 15 May 2017).

Barnes, Hazel (1990) 'Sartre and Sexism', *Philosophy and Literature*, 14: 340–7.

Barnwell, Ashley (2017) 'Method Matters: The Ethics of Exclusion', in V. Kirby (ed.), *What If Culture Was Nature All Along?* Edinburgh: Edinburgh University Press, pp. 26–47.

Bartov, Omer (2000) *Mirrors of Destruction: War, Genocide, and Modern Identity*. Oxford: Oxford University Press.

Bataille, Georges (1988) *Oeuvres complètes*, XII. Paris: Gallimard.

BBC News (2012), 'Dolphins Deserve the Same Rights as Humans, Scientists Say', 21 February <https://www.bbc.com/news/world-17116882> (last accessed 17 August 2019).

Beard, George M. (1884) *Sexual Neurasthenia*. New York: Treat.

Bederman, Gail (1995) *Manliness and Civilization: A Cultural History of Gender and Race in the United States, 1880–1917*. Chicago: University of Chicago Press.

Behar, Katherine (2016) 'An Introduction to OOF', in *Object-Oriented Feminism*. Minneapolis: University of Minnesota Press, pp. 1–36.

Benjamin, Jessica (1978) 'Authority and the Family Revisited or, A World Without Fathers?' *New German Critique*, 13, Winter, pp. 35–57.

Benjamin, Jessica (1988) *The Bonds of Love: Psychoanalysis, Feminism, and the Problem of Domination*. New York: Pantheon.

Bennett, Jane (2010a) *Vibrant Matter: A Political Ecology of Things*. Durham, NC: Duke University Press.

Bennett, Jane (2010b) 'A Vitalist Stopover on the Way to a New Materialism', in D. Coole and S. Frost (eds), *New Materialisms: Ontology, Agency, and Politics*, Durham: Duke University Press, pp. 47–69.

Bennett, Jane (2015) 'Systems and Things: On Vital Materialism and Object-Oriented Philosophy', in R. Grusin (ed.), *The Nonhuman Turn*, Minneapolis: University of Minnesota Press, pp. 223–39.

Bennett, Jane (2018) 'Vibrant Matter', in R. Braidotti and M. Hlavajova (eds), *Posthuman Glossary*. London: Bloomsbury Academic, pp. 447–8.

Berman, Russell (1986) 'The Wandering Z: Reflections on Kaplan's Reproductions of Banality', foreword to A. Yaeger, *Reproductions of Banality: Fascism, Literature, and French Intellectual Life*. Minneapolis: University of Minnesota Press, pp. xi–xxiii.

Bernheimer, Charles (2002) *Decadent Subjects: The Idea of Decadence in Art, Literature, Philosophy, and Culture of the Fin de Siècle in Europe*, ed. T. J. Kline and N. Schor. Baltimore: Johns Hopkins University Press.

Bersani, Leo (2004) 'Artaud, Defecation and Birth', in E. Scheer (ed.), *Antonin Artaud: A Critical Reader*. London and New York: Routledge, pp. 96–106.

Bertelsen, Lone and Andrew Murphy (2010) 'An Ethics of Everyday Infinities and Powers: Félix Guattari on Affect and the Refrain', in M. Gregg and G. J. Seigworth (eds), *The Affect Theory Reader*. Durham, NC and London: Duke University Press, pp. 138–57.

Best, Stephen (2017) 'La Foi Postcritique, on Second Thought', *PMLA*, 132 (2): 337–43.

Blanchot, Maurice (2004) 'Artaud', in E. Scheer (ed.), *Antonin Artaud: A Critical Reader*. London and New York: Routledge, pp. 109–15.

Blankenship, Mark (2008) 'It's Not Just Cruel; It's Unusual, Too', *New York Times*, 10 February <https://www.nytimes.com/2008/02/10/theater/10blank.html> (last accessed 10 July 2018).

Blau, Herbert (2004) From 'The Dubious Spectacle of Collective Identity', in E. Scheer (ed.), *Antonin Artaud: A Critical Reader*. London and New York: Routledge, pp. 77–82.

Bleeker, Maaike (2008) *Visuality in the Theatre: The Locus of Looking*. Basingstoke: Palgrave Macmillan.

Bogost, Ian (2015) 'The Aesthetics of Philosophical Carpentry', in R. Grusin (ed.), *The Nonhuman Turn*. Minneapolis: University of Minnesota Press, pp. 81–100.

Böhme, Hartmut (2012) *Fetischismus und Kultur: Eine andere Theorie der Moderne*. Reinbek bei Hamburg: Rowohlt.

Braidotti, Rosi (2000) 'Teratologies', *Deleuze and Feminist Theory*, eds I. Buchanan and C. Colebrook. Edinburgh: Edinburgh University Press, pp. 156–72.

Braidotti, Rosi (2006) 'The Ethics of Becoming-Imperceptible', in C. V. Boundas (ed.), *Deleuze and Philosophy*. Edinburgh: Edinburgh University Press, pp. 133–59.

Braidotti, Rosi (2010) 'The Politics of "Life Itself" and New Ways of Dying', in D. Coole and S. Frost (eds), *New Materialisms: Ontology, Agency, and Politics*. Durham, NC: Duke University Press, pp. 201–18.

Braidotti, Rosi (2011) *Nomadic Theory: The Portable Rosi Braidotti*. New York: Columbia University Press.

Braidotti, Rosi (2012) 'Interview with Rosi Braidotti', in R. Dolphijn and I. van der Tuin (eds), *New Materialism: Interviews and Cartographies*. Ann Arbor: Open Humanities Press, pp. 19–37.

Braidotti, Rosi (2013) *The Posthuman*. Cambridge: Polity.

Brandes, Georg (2017) 'The 1872 Introduction to *Hovedstrømninger I det 19de Aarhundredes Litteratur (Main Currents of Nineteenth-Century Literature)*', intro. and trans. Lynn Wilkinson, *PMLA*, 132 (3): 696–8.

Brecht, Bertolt (1963) 'Dialoge über Schauspielkunst', *Schriften zum Theater I. 1918–1933*. Frankfurt: Suhrkamp.

Brecht, Bertolt (1964) 'A Dialogue about Acting', *Brecht on Theatre: The Development of an Aesthetic*, ed. and trans. John Willett. New York: Hill & Wang.

Brecht, Bertolt (1966) *Jungle of Cities and Other Plays*, trans. N. Goold-Verschoyle. New York: Grove Press.

Brecht, Brecht (1967) *Gesammelte Werke*, 20 vols. Frankfurt am Main: Suhrkamp.

Brecht, Bertolt (1988) *Werke: Große kommentierte Berliner und Frankfurter Ausgabe*, ed. Werner Hecht et al., 30 vols. Frankfurt: Suhrkamp.

Breu, Christopher (2016) 'Why Materialisms Matter', *Symploke*, 24 (1–2): 9–26.

Brosman, Catherine Savage (1987) 'Seeing Through the Other: Modes of Vision in Sartre', *South Central Review*, 4 (4): 61–73.

Bryant, Levi R., Nick Srnicek and Graham Harman (2011) *The Speculative Turn: Continental Materialism and Realism*. Melbourne: re.press.

Bryant, Levi R. (2016) 'Knots: Notes for a Daemonic Naturalism', *Symploke*, 24 (1–2): 27–45.

Burstow, Bonnie (1992) 'How Sexist Is Sartre?', *Philosophy and Literature*, 16: 32–48.

Campbell, Timothy (2008) 'Translator's Introduction', in R. Esposito, *Bíos: Biopolitics and Philosophy*. Minneapolis: University of Minnesota Press, pp. vii–xlii.

Campbell, Timothy and Adam Sitze (eds) (2013) *Biopolitics: A Reader*. Durham, NC: Duke University Press.

Canetti, Elias (1962) *Crowds and Power*, trans. Carol Stewart. New York: Viking.

Canetti, Elias (1980) *Masse und Macht*. Frankfurt am Main: Fischer.

Carroll, David (1995) *French Literary Fascism: Nationalism, Anti-Semitism, and the Ideology of Culture*. Princeton: Princeton University Press.

Case, Sue-Ellen (1983) 'Brecht and Women: Homosexuality and the Mother', *Brecht Yearbook*, 12: 62–74.

Casper, Stephen T. (2016) 'The *Political* Without Guarantees: Contagious Police Shootings, Neuroscientific Cultural Imaginaries, and Neuroscientifc Futures', in K. Nixon and L. Servitje (eds), *Endemic: Essays in Contagion Theory*. London: Palgrave Macmillan, pp. 169–90.

Cassirer, Ernst (1946) *The Myth of the State*. New Haven: Yale University Press.

Castellucci, Claudia, Romeo Castellucci, Chiara Guidi, Joe Kelleher and Nicholas Rideout (2007) *The Theatre of Socìetas Raffaello Sanzio*. London: Routledge.

Cermatori, Joseph P. (2008) Rev. of *The Cenci*, *Theatre Journal*, 60 (4): 668–70.

Le Chagrin et la pitié: Chronique d'une ville française sous l'occupation, film, dir. Marcel Ophuls, prod. A. Harris and Alain de Sedouy. Productions Télévision Rencontre, 1969.

Chaudhuri, Una (1997) *Staging Place: The Geography of Modern Drama*. Ann Arbor: University of Michigan Press.

Chaudhuri, Una (2003), 'Zoo Stories: "Boundary Work" in Theater History', in W. B. Worthen, with Peter Holland (eds), *Theorizing Practice: Redefining Theatre History*. Basingstoke: Palgrave Macmillan, pp. 136–50.

Chaudhuri, Una (2017a) *The Stage Lives of Animals : Zooësis and Performance*. London: Routledge.

Chaudhuri, Una (2017b) 'Bug Bytes: Insects, Information, and Interspecies Theatricality', in U. Chaudhuri, *The Stage Lives of Animals: Zooësis and Performance*. London: Routledge, pp. 133–52.

Charmé, Stuart Zane (1991) *Vulgarity and Authenticity: Dimensions of Otherness in the World of Jean-Paul Sartre*. Amherst: University of Massachusetts Press.

Chiew, Florence (2017) 'Sensory Substitution: The Plasticity of the Eye/I', in V. Kirby (ed.), *What If Culture Was Nature All Along?* Edinburgh: Edinburgh University Press, pp. 48–69.

Clos, Annett (1999) 'Bertolt Brechts *Baal* oder Kann denn Sünde Liebe sein?', in T. Jung (ed.), *Zweifel–Fragen–Vorschläge: Bertolt Brecht anläßlich des Einhundertsten*. Frankfurt am Main: Peter Lang, pp. 111–24.

Colebrook, Claire (2008) 'On Not Becoming Man: The Materialist Politics of Unactualized Potential', in S. Alaimo and S. Hekman (eds), *Material Feminisms*. Bloomington: Indiana University Press, pp. 52–84.

Colebrook, Claire (2014) *Sex after Life: Essays on Extinction, Vol. 2*. Ann Arbor: Open Humanities Press.

Colombi, Matteo and Massimo Fusillo (2013) 'Artaud, Barney, and the Total Work of Art from Avant-Garde to the Posthuman', *CLCWeb: Comparative Literature and Culture*, 15 (7), at <https://docs.lib.purdue.edu/clcweb/vol15/iss7/18/> (last accessed 6 April 2020).

Coole, Diana and Samantha Frost (eds) (2010) *New Materialisms: Ontology, Agency, and Politics*. Durham, NC: Duke University Press.

Coole, Diana (2013) 'Agentic Capacities and Capacious Historical Materialism: Thinking with New Materialisms in the Political Sciences', *Millennium – Journal of International Studies*, 41 (3): 451–69.

Corning, Leonard (1884) *Brain Exhaustion*. New York: D. Appleton.

Cronin, Michael (2017) *Eco-Translation: Translation and Ecology in the Age of the Anthropocene*. London and New York: Routledge.

Curtin, Adrian (2010) 'Cruel Vibrations: Sounding Out Antonin Artaud's Production of *Les Cenci*', *Theatre Research International*, 35 (3): 250–62.

Danowski, Déborah and Eduardo Viveiros de Castro, 'L'Arrêt du monde', in E. Hache (ed.), *De l'univers clos au monde infini*. Bellevaux: Editions Dehors, pp. 221–339 <https://www.academia.edu/7512791/De_lunivers_clos_au_monde_infini_Editions_Dehors_2014> (last accessed 13 September 2019).

Dalziell, Jacqueline (2017) 'Microbiology as Sociology: The Strange Sociality of Slime', in V. Kirby (ed.), *What If Culture Was Nature All Along?* Edinburgh: Edinburgh University Press, pp. 153–78.

Darwin, Charles (1859) *On the Origin of Species: Or the Preservation of Favoured Races in the Struggle for Life*, at <https://www.gutenberg.org/files/1228/1228-h/1228-h.htm> (last accessed 21 March 2020).

Darwin, Charles (1898) [1871] *The Descent of Man, and Selection in Relation to Sex*. New York: Appleton.

Davis, Noela (2017) 'Material Culture: Epigenetics and the Molecularisation of the Social', in V. Kirby (ed.), *What If Culture Was Nature All Along?* Edinburgh: Edinburgh University Press, pp. 111–33.

DeFazio, Kimberly (2014) 'The Spectral Ontology and Miraculous Materialism', *The Red Critique*, at <http://redcritique.org/WinterSpring2014/spectralontologyandmiraculousmaterialism.htm> (last accessed 20 March 2020).

Deleuze, Gilles and Félix Guattari (1983) *Anti-Oedipus: Capitalism and Schizophrenia*, trans. Robert Hurley, Mark Seem and Helen R. Lane. Minneapolis: University of Minnesota Press.

Deleuze, Gilles and Félix Guattari (1987) *A Thousand Plateaus: Capitalism and Schizophrenia*, trans. of *Mille Plateaux* (1980). Minneapolis: University of Minnesota Press/Paris: Les Editions de Minuit.

Deleuze, Gilles (1990) *Pourparlers*. Paris: Les Editions de Minuit.

Deleuze, Gilles (2001) *Pure Immanence: Essays on a Life*, intro. J. Rajchman, trans. A. Boyman. Cambridge, MA: MIT Press.

Deleuze, Gilles (2004) 'Thirteenth series of the schizophrenic and the little girl', in E. Scheer (ed.), *Antonin Artaud: A Critical Reader*. London and New York: Routledge, pp. 27–36.

Derrida, Jacques (1978) 'La Parole soufflée', in J. Derrida, *Writing and Difference*, ed. and trans. A. Bass. London: Routledge.

Derrida, Jacques (1994) *Specters of Marx: The State of the Debt, the Work of Mourning, and the New International*, trans. Peggy Kamuf. New York: Routledge.

Derrida, Jacques (2002) 'The Animal That Therefore I Am (More to Follow)', *Critical Inquiry*, 28 (2): 369–418.

Derrida, Jacques (2004a) From 'To Unsense the Subjectile', in E. Scheer (ed.), *Antonin Artaud: A Critical Reader*. London and New York: Routledge, pp. 125–36.

Derrida, Jacques (2004b) From 'The Theatre of Cruelty and the Closure of Representation', in E. Scheer (ed.), *Antonin Artaud: A Critical Reader*. London and New York: Routledge, pp. 39–46.

Derrida, Jacques (2008) *The Animal That Therefore I Am*, ed. M.-L. Mallet, trans. D. Wills. New York: Fordham University Press.

Dijkstra, Bram (1986) *Idols of Perversity: Fantasies of Feminine Evil in Fin-de-Siècle Culture.* New York: Oxford University Press.

Dijkstra, Bram (1996) *Evil Sisters: The Threat of Female Sexuality in Twentieth-Century Culture*. New York: Holt.

Dolphijn, Rick and Iris van der Tuin (2012) *New Materialism: Interviews and Cartographies*. Ann Arbor: Open Humanities Press.

Donzelot, Jacques (1997) *The Policing of Families*, foreword by G. Deleuze, trans. R. Hurley. Baltimore: Johns Hopkins University Press.

Druon, Maurice (1997) 'Derniers Témoignages des partisans de Maurice Papon', *Le Monde*, 24 October, p. 10.

Duerr, Hans-Peter (1985) *Dreamtime: Concerning the Boundary between Wilderness and Civilization*, trans. F. Goodman. Oxford: Blackwell.

Eder, Franz X. (2002) *Kultur der Begierde: Eine Geschichte der Sexualität*. München: Beck.

Eilemann, Johannes et al. (1940) *Hirts Deutsches Lesebuch*. Breslau: Hirt.

Eloy, Geoff (2010) *Fascism and the Historians: Past, Present, and Future*. Birkbeck Institute for the Humanities – Department of History, Classics and Archaeology and Institute of Historical Research's Rethinking Modern Europe Seminar, Backdoor Broadcasting Co., 24 May 2010 <http://backdoorbroadcasting.net/2010/05/fascism-and-the-historians-past-present-and-future/> (last accessed 1 June 2011; no longer available).

Emden, Christian J. (2017) 'Normative Matters: Philosophical Naturalism and Political Theory', in S. Ellenzweig and J. H. Zammito (eds), *The New Politics of Materialism: History, Philosophy, Science*. London and New York: Routledge, pp. 269–99.

Engels, Friedrich (1972) *The Origin of the Family, Private Property, and the State*, trans. Alec West. New York: International Publishers.

Esposito, Roberto (2008) *Bíos: Biopolitics and Philosophy*. Minneapolis: University of Minnesota Press.

Esposito, Roberto (2010) *Communitas: The Origin and Destiny of Community*, trans. T. Campbell. Stanford: Stanford University Press.

Esposito, Roberto (2012) *Third Person*. Cambridge: Polity.

Esposito, Roberto (2013a) 'Biopolitics', from *Immunitas* (2011), in T. Campbell and A. Sitze (eds), *Biopolitics: A Reader*. Durham, NC: Duke University Press, pp. 317–49.

Esposito, Roberto (2013b) 'The Enigma of Biopolitics', from *Bíos* (2008), in T. Campbell and A. Sitze (eds), *Biopolitics: A Reader*. Durham, NC: Duke University Press, pp. 350–85.

Felski, Rita (2008) *Uses of Literature*. Malden: Blackwell.

Felski, Rita (2015) *The Limits of Critique*. Chicago: University of Chicago Press.

Felski, Rita (2017) 'Response', *PMLA*, 132 (2): 384–91.

Finter, Helga (2004) From 'Antonin Artaud and the Impossible Theatre: The Legacy of the Theatre of Cruelty', in E. Scheer (ed.), *Antonin Artaud: A Critical Reader*. London and New York: Routledge, pp. 47–58.

Fischer-Lichte, Erika (2014) *The Routledge Introduction to Theater and Performance Studies*, eds M. Arjomand and R. Mosse, trans. M. Arjomand. London: Routledge.

Fore, Devin (2015) *Realism after Modernism: The Rehumanization of Art and Literature*. Cambridge, MA: MIT Press.

Foucault, Michel (1977), *Discipline and Punish: The Birth of the Prison*, trans. Alan Sheridan. New York: Vintage Books.

Foucault, Michel (1980a), *The History of Sexuality. Volume I: An Introduction*. New York: Vintage.

Foucault, Michel (1980b) *Power/Knowledge: Selected Interviews and Other Writings 1972–1977*, ed. C. Gordon, trans. C. Gordon et al. New York: Pantheon Books.

Foucault, Michel (2013) '*Society Must be Defended*': Lectures at the Collège de France, 1975–1976, in T. Campbell and A. Sitze (eds), *Biopolitics: A Reader*. Durham, NC: Duke University Press, pp. 61–81.

Fraunhofer, Hedwig (1997) 'The Fascist Brecht? The Rhetoric of Alterity in *Drums in the Night*', *Brecht Yearbook*, 22: 357–73.

Fraunhofer, Hedwig (2000) 'Fear of the Feminine: Sexuality and Economics in Brecht's *Jungle of Cities*', *Women in German Yearbook*, 15: 117–35.

Fraunhofer, Hedwig (2007) 'Gender and the Abject in Sartre', *Gender Forum*, 18 <http://www.genderforum.uni-koeln.de/abject/article_fraunhofer.html> (last accessed 17 September 2011).

Freedman, Barbara (1991) *Staging the Gaze: Postmodernism, Psychoanalysis, and Shakespearean Comedy*. Ithaca: Cornell University Press.

Freud, Sigmund (1905) 'Fragment of an Analysis of a Case of Hysteria', *Complete Works 1890–1936*, at <http://staferla.free.fr/Freud/Freud%20complete%20Works.pdf> (last accessed 21 March 2020).

Freud, Sigmund (1959) 'Medusa's Head', *Collected Papers 5*, ed. J. Strachey. New York: Basic Books, pp. 105–6.

Freud, Sigmund (1960) *Die Traumdeutung*. Frankfurt am Main: S. Fischer.

Freud, Sigmund (1965) *Group Psychology and the Analysis of the Ego*, trans. J. Strachey. New York: Bantam.

Freud, Sigmund (1974) *Moses and Monotheism: Three Essays*, trans. and ed. J. Strachey. London: Hogarth.

Freud, Sigmund (1975a) *Studienausgabe, Vol. 3: Psychologie des Unbewußten*. Frankfurt am Main: S. Fischer.

Freud, Sigmund (1975b) 'Zur Einführung des Narzißmus', in S. Freud, *Studienausgabe, Vol. 3*. Frankfurt am Main: S. Fischer, pp. 37–68.

Friedman, Susan Stanford (2017) 'Both/And: Critique and Discovery in the Humanities', *PMLA*, 132 (2): 344–51.

Friedrich, Rainer (1990) 'The Deconstructed Self in Artaud and Brecht: Negation of Subject and Antitotalitarianism', *Forum for Modern Language Studies*, 26 (3): 282–97.

Friedrich, Rainer (1999) 'Brecht and Postmodernism', *Philosophy and Literature*, 23 (1): 44–64.

Fuchs, Elinor (2011) 'Postdramatic Theatre and the Persistence of the "Fictive Cosmos": A View from America', in I. Medenica (ed.), *Dramatic and Postdramatic Theater Ten Years After: Conference Proceedings*. Belgrade: Institute of Theatre, Film, Radio and Television, Faculty of Dramatic Arts, pp. 63–71.

Fuegi, John (1994) *Brecht and Company: Sex, Politics, and the Making of the Modern Drama*. New York: Grove.

Galster, Ingrid (2001) *Sartre, Vichy et les intellectuels*. Paris: L'Harmattan.

Garner, Stanton B., Jr (2006) 'Artaud, Germ Theory, and the Theatre of Contagion', *Theatre Journal*, 58 (1): 1–14.

Ghosh, Amitav (2016) *The Great Derangement: Climate Change and the Unthinkable*. Chicago and London: University of Chicago Press.

Gibbs, Anna (2001) 'Contagious Feelings: Pauline Hanson and the Epidemiology of Affect', *Australian Humanities Review*, 24 <http://www.australianhumanitiesreview.org/> (last accessed 20 February 2018).

Gibbs, Anna (2010) 'After Affect: Sympathy, Synchrony, and Mimetic Communication', in M. Gregg and G. J. Seigworth (eds), *The Affect Theory Reader*. Durham, NC and London: Duke University Press, pp. 186–205.

Giraudoux, Jean (1942) *Littérature*. Paris: Gasset.

Goldstein, Amanda Jo (2014), 'Old Materialism', Society for the Humanities and College of Arts & Sciences Sesquicentennial Conference at Cornell University, 31 October–1 November, https://vimeo.com/112213361 (last accessed 18 July 2018).

Goodall, Jane (2004) 'The Plague and Its Powers in Artaudian Theatre', in E. Scheer (ed.), *Antonin Artaud: A Critical Reader*. London and New York: Routledge, pp. 64–76.

Goodman, Kevin (2016) 'Introduction', in E. Santner, *The Weight of All Flesh*. New York: Oxford University Press, pp. 1–19.

Graeber, David (2011) *Debt: The First 5,000 Years*. Brooklyn: Melville.

Greenblatt, Stephen (2009) *Cultural Mobility: A Manifesto*. Cambridge: Cambridge University Press.

Gregg, Melissa and Gregory J. Seigworth (eds) (2010) *The Affect Theory Reader*. Durham, NC and London: Duke University Press.

Groot Nibbelink, Liesbeth (2019) *Nomadic Theatre: Mobilizing Theory and Practice on the European Stage*. London: Methuen.

Grossberg, Lawrence (2010) 'Affect's Future: Rediscovering the Actual in the Virtual', in M. Gregg and G. J. Seigworth (eds), *The Affect Theory Reader*. Durham, NC and London: Duke University Press, pp. 309–38.

Grosz, Elizabeth (2008) 'Darwin and Feminism: Preliminary Investigations for a Possible Alliance', in S. Alaimo and S. Hekman (eds), *Material Feminisms*. Bloomington: Indiana University Press, pp. 23–51.

Grosz, Elizabeth (2010) 'Feminism, Materialism, and Freedom', in D. Coole and S. Frost (eds), *New Materialisms: Ontology, Agency, and Politics*. Durham, NC: Duke University Press, pp. 139–57.

Guattari, Félix (1995) *Chaosmosis: An Ethico-Aesthetic Paradigm*, trans. P. Bains and J. Pefanis. Bloomington: Indiana University Press.

Habermas, Jürgen (1987) *Strukturwandel der Öffentlichkeit: Untersuchungen zu einer Kategorie der bürgerlichen Gesellschaft*. Darmstadt: Luchterhand; *The Structural Transformation of the Public Sphere: An Inquiry into a Category of Bourgeois Society*, trans. T. Burger and F. Lawrence, Cambridge, MA: MIT Press.

Halle, Randall (1995) 'Between Marxism and Psychoanalysis: Antifascism and Antihomosexuality in the Frankfurt School', *Journal of Homosexuality*, 29 (4): 295–317.

Haraway, Donna (2003) *Companion Species Manifesto: Dogs, People, and Significant Otherness*, Chicago: Prickly Paradigm Press.

Haraway, Donna (2013) 'The Biopolitics of Postmodern Bodies: Constitutions of Self in Immune System Discourse', in T. Campbell and A. Sitze (eds), *Biopolitics: A Reader*. Durham, NC: Duke University Press, pp. 274–309.

Haraway, Donna (2016) *Staying with the Trouble: Making Kin in the Chthulucene*. Durham, NC: Duke University Press.

Hardt, Michael and Antonio Negri (2013) 'Biopolitics as Event', from *Commonwealth*, in T. Campbell and A. Sitze (eds), *Biopolitics: A Reader*. Durham, NC: Duke University Press, pp. 237–44.

Harman, Graham (2009) *Prince of Networks: Bruno Latour and Metaphysics*. Melbourne: re.press.

Harman, Graham (2011) 'On the Undermining of Objects: Grant, Bruno, and Radical Philosophy', in L. R. Bryant, N. Srnicek and G. Harman, *The Speculative Turn: Continental Materialism and Realism*. Melbourne: re.press, pp. 21–40.

Harris, Gardiner (2011) 'Head of Surgeons Group Resigns Over Article Viewed as Offensive to Women', *New York Times*, 18 April, p. A16.

Hart, Lynda (1994) *Fatal Women: Lesbian Sexuality and the Mark of Aggression*. Princeton: Princeton University Press.

Hayman, Ronald (1987) *Sartre: A Life*. New York: Simon & Schuster.

Hegel, Georg Wilhelm Friedrich (1980) *Phänomenologie des Geistes*, eds Wolfgang Bonsiepen and Reinhard Heede, Vol. 9 of *Gesammelte Werke*. Hamburg: Meiner.

Heidegger, Martin (2004) *Die Grundbegriffe der Metaphysik: Welt – Endlichkeit – Einsamkeit. Gesamtausgabe 29/30*. Frankfurt am Main: V. Klostermann.

Heidsieck, Arnold (1975) 'Psychologische Strukturen im Werk Bertolt Brechts bis 1932', in *Ideologiekritische Studien zur Literatur: Essays II*. Bern: Lang.

Hetrick, Adam (2008) 'Artaud's *The Cenci* Gets New Adaptation from Hotel Savant Feb. 5', *Playbill*, 16 January <http://www.playbill.com/article/artauds-the-cenci-gets-new-adaptation-from-hotel-savant-feb-5-com-146888> (last accessed 7 July 2018).

Hewitt, Andrew (1996) *Political Inversions: Homosexuality, Fascism, and the Modernist Imaginary*. Stanford: Stanford University Press.

Highmore, Ben (2010) 'Bitter after Taste: Affect, Food, and Social Aesthetics', in M. Gregg and G. J. Seigworth (eds), *The Affect Theory Reader*. Durham, NC and London: Duke University Press, pp. 118–37.

Hollande, François (2012) 'The 'Crime Committed in France, by France', *New York Review*, 17 September, pp. 40–1.

Hooker, Claire, Chris Degeling and Paul Mason (2016) 'Dying a Natural Death: Ethics and Political Activism for Endemic Infectious Disease', in K. Nixon and L. Servitje (eds), *Endemic: Essays in Contagion Theory*. London: Palgrave Macmillan, pp. 265–90.

Horkheimer, Max (1974) *Eclipse of Reason*. New York: Seabury Press.

Horkheimer, Max (1987) 'Autorität und Familie in der Gegenwart', in M. Horkheimer und T. Adorno, *Dialektik der Aufklärung und Schriften 194–1959*, Vol. 5 of *Gesammelte Schriften*, ed. G. Schmid Noerr. Frankfurt am Main: Fischer, pp. 47–128.

Irigaray, Luce (1985) *Speculum of the Other Woman*, trans. Gillian C. Gill. Ithaca: Cornell University Press.

Jacobson, Louis (n.d.) 'Yes, U.S. suicides have risen by 30% in past decade and a half', at https://www.politifact.com/truth-o-meter/statements/2019/may/20/amy-klobuchar/yes-us-suicides-have-risen-30-past-decade-and-half/> (last accessed 23 August 2019).

Jacoby, Russell (2015) 'The Object as Subject', *Chronicle Review*, 24 April <https://www.chronicle.com/article/The-Object-as-Subject/229587> (last accessed 12 August 2018).

Jagoda, Patrick (2017) 'Critique and Critical Making', *PMLA*, 132 (2): 356–63.

Jameson, Frederic (1982) *The Political Unconscious: Narrative as a Socially Symbolic Act*. Ithaca: Cornell University Press.

Jannarone, Kimberly (2010) *Artaud and His Doubles*. Ann Arbor: University of Michigan Press.

Johst, Hanns (1917) *Der Einsame: Ein Menschenuntergang*. Münche: A. Langen.

Jordheim, Helge (1999) 'Gefährlicher Nihilismus: Eine Analyse der Mutterfigur in Brechts *Baal*', in T. Jung (ed.), *Zweifel–Fragen–Vorschläge: Bertolt Brecht anläßlich des Einhundertsten*. Frankfurt am Main: Peter Lang, pp. 99–110.

Joseph, Gilbert (1991) *Une si douce occupation: Simone de Beauvoir, Jean-Paul Sartre, 1940–1944*. Paris: Albin Michel.

Jung, Thomas (ed.) (1999) *Zweifel–Fragen–Vorschläge: Bertolt Brecht anläßlich des Einhundertsten*. Frankfurt am Main: Peter Lang.

King James Bible <https://www.kingjamesbibleonline.org/> (last accessed 23 April 2019).

Kinetz, Erika (2006) 'Is Hysteria Real? Brain Images Say Yes', *New York Times*, 26 September 2006 <https://www.bbc.com/news/world-17116882> (last accessed 31 August 2018).

Kirby, Vicky (1997) *Telling Flesh: The Substance of the Corporeal*. London and New York: Routledge.

Kirby, Vicky (2011) *Quantum Anthropologies: Life at Large*. Durham, NC: Duke University Press.

Kirby, Vicky (2017) 'Matter out of Place: "New Materialism" in Review', in V. Kirby (ed.), *What If Culture Was Nature All Along?* Edinburgh: Edinburgh University Press, pp. 1–25.

Kissler, Alexander (2016) 'Ein Held für jede Gegenwart', Interview with Horst Bredekamp, Constanze Pers and Eberhard Knobloch, *Cicero*, 8, August, pp. 18–30.

Knopf, Jan (2006) *Bertolt Brecht*. Frankfurt am Main: Suhrkamp.

Kohut, Karl (1971) 'Jean-Paul Sartre: *Les Mouches*', in W. Pabst (ed.), *Das Moderne Französische Drama: Interpretationen*. Berlin: Schmidt, pp. 154–73.

Krafft-Ebing, Richard von (1993) *Psychopathia Sexualis. Mit besonderer Berücksichtigung der konträren Sexualempfindung. Eine klinisch-forensische Studie*. München: Matthes & Seitz.

Kristeva, Julia (1980) *Desire in Language: A Semiotic Approach to Literature and Art*, ed. L. S. Roudiez, trans. A. Jardine, T. Gora and L. S. Roudiez. New York: Columbia University Press.

Kristeva, Julia (1982) *Powers of Horror: An Essay on Abjection*, trans. L. S. Roudiez. New York: Columbia University Press.

Kristeva, Julia (2004) From 'The subject in process', in E. Scheer (ed.), *Antonin Artaud: A Critical Reader*. London and New York: Routledge, pp. 116–24.

Kruks, Sonia (2010) 'Simone de Beauvoir: Engaging Discrepant Materialisms', in D. Coole and S. Frost (eds), *New Materialisms: Ontology, Agency, and Politics*. Durham: Duke University Press, pp. 258–80.

LaCapra, Dominick (1978) *A Preface to Sartre*. Ithaca: Cornell University Press.

Lacassagne, Alexandre (1886) 'Péderastie', *Dictionnaire encyclopédique des sciences médicales*, 2nd series. Paris: Masson Asselin, 22, pp. 239–59 <https://gallica.bnf.fr/ark:/12148/bpt6k31264m/f259.item.r=P%C3%A9derastie> (last accessed 12 August 2019).

Latour, Bruno (2010) 'An Attempt at a Compositionist Manifesto' <http://www.bruno-latour.fr/sites/default/files/120-NLH-finalpdf.pdf> (last accessed 20 September 2017).

Laqueur, Thomas W. (1992) 'Sexual Desire and the Market Economy during the Industrial Revolution', in C. Domna (ed.), *Discourses of Sexuality: From Aristotle to AIDS*. Ann Arbor: University of Michigan Press, pp. 185–215.

Lebovic, Nitzan (2013) *The Philosophy of Life and Death: Ludwig Klages and the Rise of a Nazi Biopolitics*. New York: Palgrave Macmillan.

Lehmann, Hans-Thies (1999) *Postdramatisches Theater: Essay*. Frankfurt am Main: Verlag der Autoren.

Lehmann, Hans-Thies (2013) *Tragödie und dramatisches Theater*. Berlin: Alexander Verlag.

Lehmann, Hans-Thies (2016) *Tragedy and Dramatic Theatre*. Abingdon: Routledge.

Lettow, Susanne (2017) 'Turning the Turn', *Thesis Eleven*, 140 (1): 106–21.

Lévi-Strauss, Claude (1969) *The Elementary Structures of Kinship*. Boston: Beacon Press.

Levi, Neil and Michael Rothberg (eds) (2003) *The Holocaust: Theoretical Readings*. New Brunswick, NJ: Rutgers University Press.

Lévy, Bernard-Henri (2000) *Le siècle de Sartre: enquête philosophique*. Paris: B. Grasset.

Lockwood, Alan (2008) 'Acts of Cruelty', *Brooklyn Rail*, 6 February <https://brooklynrail.org/2008/02/theater/acts-of-cruelty> (last accessed 10 July 2018).

Lough, Richard (2015) 'Court Rules Orangutan Held in Argentina Zoo is "Non-Human Person" and Can Be Freed' <http://www.reuters.com/> (last accessed 6 January 2015).

Lukács, György (1981) [1952] *The Destruction of Reason*, trans. P. Palmer. Atlantic Highlands, NJ: Humanities Press.

Lunning, Frenchy (2016) 'Allure and Abjection', in K. Behar (ed.), *Object-Oriented Feminism*. Minneapolis: University of Minnesota Press, pp. 82–105.

Lyons, Charles (1968) *Bertolt Brecht: The Despair and the Polemic*. Carbondale: Southern Illinois University Press.

MacCannell, Juliet Flower (1991) *The Regime of the Brother: After the Patriarchy*. London: Routledge.

Manser, Anthony (1962) *Sartre: A Philosophical Study*. London: University of London Athlone Press.

Marhoefer, Laurie (2011) 'Degeneration, Sexual Freedom, and the Politics of the Weimar Republic, 1918–1933', *German Studies Review*, 34 (3): 529–49 <https://www.jstor.org/stable/41303797> (last accessed 14 August 2018).

Marx, Karl and Friedrich Engels (1932) *Das Kommunistische Manifest*. Berlin: Internationaler Arbeiterverlag; *The Communist Manifesto*, ed. F. L. Bender. New York: Norton, 1988.

Massumi, Brian (2002) *Parables for the Virtual: Movement, Affect, Sensation*. Durham, NC: Duke University Press.

Massumi, Brian (2010) 'The Future Birth of the Affective Fact: The Political Ontology of Threat', in M. Gregg and G. J. Seigworth (eds), *Affect Reader*, pp. 52–70.

Massumi, Brian (2015a) 'The Supernormal Animal', in R. Grusin (ed.), *The Nonhuman Turn*. Minneapolis: University of Minnesota Press, pp. 1–17.

Massumi, Brian (2015b) *Politics of Affect*. Cambridge: Polity.

Mbembe, Achille (2013) 'Necropolitics', in T. Campbell and A. Sitze (eds), *Biopolitics: A Reader*. Durham, NC: Duke University Press, pp.161–92.

McCall, Dorothy (1967) *The Theatre of Jean-Paul Sartre*. New York: Columbia University Press.

McLaren, Angus (1997) *The Trials of Masculinity: Policing Sexual Boundaries, 1870–1930*. Chicago: University of Chicago Press.

Mehlmann, Sabine (1998), 'Das vergeschlechtlichte Individuum – Thesen zur historischen Genese des Konzepts männlicher Geschlechtsidentität', in H. Bublitz (ed.), *Das Geschlecht der Moderne: Genealogie und Archäologie der Geschlechterdifferenz*. Frankfurt: Campus, pp. 95–118.

Meillassoux, Quentin (2008) [2006] *After Finitude: An Essay on the Necessity of Contingency*, trans. R. Brassier. New York: Continuum.

Meißner, Hanna (2016) 'New Material Feminisms and Historical Materialism: A Diffractive Reading of Two (Ostensibly) Unrelated Perspectives', in V. Pitts-Taylor (ed. and intro.), *Mattering: Feminism, Science, and Materialism*. New York: New York University Press, pp. 43–57.

Merleau-Ponty, Maurice (1968) *The Visible and the Invisible*, trans. A. Lingis, Evanston: Northwestern University Press.

Miller, Elaine (2004) 'Vegetable Genius: Plant Metamorphosis as a Figure for Thinking and Relating to the Natural World in Post-Kantian German Thought', in B. V. Foltz and R. Frodemann (eds), *Rethinking Nature: Essays in Environmental Philosophy*. Albany: SUNY Press, pp. 114–34.

Mitchell, Juliet (2001) *Mad Men and Medusas: Reclaiming Hysteria*. New York: Basic Books.

Mitscherlich, Alexander (1963) *Auf dem Weg zur vaterlosen Gesellschaft: Ideen zur Sozialpsychologie*, München: Piper, 1963; *Society Without the Father: A Contribution to Social Psychology*, trans. E. Mosbacher. New York: Harper Perennial, 1993.

Mitscherlich, Alexander and Margarete Mitscherlich (1967) *Die Unfähigkeit zu trauern: Grundlagen kollektiven Verhaltens*. München: Piper; *The Inability to Mourn: Principles of Collective Behavior*, preface by R. J. Lifton, trans. B. R. Placzek. New York: Grove, 1975.

Mitscherlich, Margarete (1987) 'Antisemitismus – eine Männerkrankheit?', in M. Mitscherlich, *Die friedfertige Frau: Eine psychoanalytische Untersuchung zur Aggression der Geschlechter*. Frankfurt am Main: Gutenberg.

Modiano, Patrick (1968) *La Place de l'Etoile*. Paris: Gallimard.

Montvalon, Jean-Baptiste de (1997) 'Pour Lionel Jospin, la "France" n'est pas coupable de Vichy', *Le Monde*, Edition international, Sélection hebdomadaire, 1 Novembre, p. 8.

Morton, Timothy (2010) 'Guest Column: Queer Ecology', *PMLA*, 125 (2): 273–82.

Morton, Timothy (2012a) 'An Object-Oriented Defense of Poetry', *New Literary History*, 43 (2): 205–24.

Morton, Timothy (2012b) 'They Are Here', in R. Grusin (ed.), *The Nonhuman Turn*. Minneapolis: University of Minnesota Press, pp. 167–92; see also <https://vimeo.com/41887863> (last accessed 16 May 2017).

Morton, Timothy (2013) *Hyperobjects: Philosophy and Ecology after the End of the World*. Minneapolis: University of Minnesota Press.

Morton, Timothy (2016) 'All Objects Are Deviant', in K. Behar (ed.), *Object-Oriented Feminism*. Minneapolis: University of Minnesota Press, pp. 64–81.

Mosse, George L. (1966) *Nazi Culture: Intellectual, Cultural, and Social Life in the Third Reich*. New York: Grosset & Dunlap.

Mosse, George (1978a) *Nazism: A Historical and Comparative Analysis of National Socialism*, an interview with M. A. Ledeen. New Brunswick, NJ: Transaction.

Mosse, George (1978b), *Toward the Final Solution: A History of European Racism*. New York: Harper & Row.

Mosse, George (1985) *Nationalism and Sexuality: Respectability and Abnormal Sexuality in Modern Europe*. New York: Fertig.

Mosse, George L. (1996) *The Image of Man: The Creation of Modern Masculinity*. New York: Oxford University Press.

Murphy, Jay (2015) 'The Artaud Effect' <htttp://ctheory.net/ctheory_wp/the-artaud-effect> (last accessed 21 December 2016).

Mussolini, Benito (1932) *Mussolinis Gespräche mit Emil Ludwig*. Berlin: Zsolnay.

Nealon, Jeffrey T. (2016) *Plant Theory: Biopower and Vegetable Life*. Stanford: Stanford University Press.

Neimanis, Astrida (2017) 'Nature Represents Itself: Bibliophilia in a Changing Climate', in V. Kirby (ed.), *What If Culture Was Nature All Along?* Edinburgh: Edinburgh University Press, pp. 179–98.

Nietzsche, Friedrich Wilhelm (1967) *The Will to Power*, trans. Walter Kaufman and R. J. Hollingdale. New York: Random House.

Nietzsche, Friedrich Wilhelm (1980) *Kritische Studienausgabe der sämtlichen Werke in 15 Bänden*, ed. G. Colli and M. Montinari. München: Gruyter.

Nixon, Kari and Lorenzo Servitje (eds) (2016) *Endemic: Essays in Contagion Theory*. London: Palgrave Macmillan.

Nordau, Max (1895) *Degeneration*. New York: D. Appleton.

Nussbaum, Martha C. (2006) *Frontiers of Justice: Disability, Nationality, Species Membership*. Cambridge, MA: Harvard University Press.

Nye, Robert (1982) 'Degeneration and the Medical Model of Cultural Crisis in the French Belle Epoque', in S. Drescher, D. Sabean and A. Sharlin (eds), *Political Symbolism in Modern Europe: Essays in Honor of George L. Mosse*. New Brunswick, NJ and London: Transaction Books, pp. 19–41.

Nye, Robert (1984) *Crime, Madness and Politics in Modern France: The Medical Concept of National Decline*. Princeton: Princeton University Press.

Nye, Robert (1994) 'Sexuality, Sex Difference and the Cult of Modern Love in the French Third Republic', *Reflections/Reflexions Historiques*, 20 (1): 57–76.

Olrik, Hilde (1986–7) 'La théorie de l'imprégnation', *Nineteenth-Century French Studies*, 15 (1–2): 128–40.

Orlie, Melissa A. (2010) 'Impersonal Matter', in D. Coole and S. Frost (eds), *New Materialisms: Ontology, Agency, and Politics*. Durham, NC: Duke University Press, pp. 116–36.

Oxley, Rebecca (2017) 'Pregnant Men: Paternal Postnatal Depression and a Culture of Hormones', in V. Kirby, *What If Culture Was Nature All Along?* Edinburgh: Edinburgh University Press, pp. 90–109.

Paxton, Robert (1999) 'The Trial of Maurice Papon', *New York Review of Books*, 46 (20): 32.

Paxton, Robert (2014) 'When France Went Dreadfully Wrong', *New York Review of Books*, 61 (13): 60, 62.

Peukert, Detlev J. K. (1989) *The Weimar Republic: The Crisis of Classical Modernity*, trans. Richard Deveson. New York: Hill & Wang.

Pitts-Taylor, Victoria (ed. and intro.) (2016) *Mattering: Feminism, Science, and Materialism*. New York: New York University Press.

Pocock, J. G. A. (1985) *Virtue, Commerce and History*. Cambridge: Cambridge University Press.

Podd, Rachel (2018), Review of 'C. Lynteris and N. H. A. Evans (eds), *Histories of Post-Mortem Contagion: Infectious Corpses and Contested Burials*', H-Sci-Med-Tech, H-Net Reviews, April, at <http://www.h-net.org/reviews/showrev.php?id=51410> (last accessed 26 March 2020).

Povinelli, Elizabeth A. (2016) 'The World Is Flat and Other Super Weird Ideas', in K. Behar (ed.), *Object-Oriented Feminism*. Minneapolis: University of Minnesota Press, pp. 107–19.

Protevi, John (2017) Review of 'S. Ellenzweig and John H. Zammito (eds), *The New Politics of Materialism: History, Philosophy, Science*. London and New York: Routledge' , in *Notre Dame Philosophical Reviews*, 12: 01, at <https://ndpr.nd.edu/news/the-new-politics-of-materialism-history-philosophy-science/> (last accessed 26 March 2020).

Pucciani, Oreste (1985) 'Sartre, Ontology, and the Other', in W. M. Calder et al. (eds), *Hypatia: Essays in Classics, Comparative Literature and Philosophy Presented to Hazel E. Barnes on Her Seventieth Birthday*. Boulder: Colorado Association University Press, pp. 151–67.

Rabinbach, Anson (1982) 'The Body Without Fatigue: A Nineteenth-Century Utopia', in S. Drescher, D. Sabean and A. Sharlin (eds), *Political Symbolism in Modern Europe: Essays in Honor of George L. Mosse*. New Brunswick, NJ and London: Transaction Books, pp. 42–62.

Rentzou, Efthymia (2016) 'Animal', in E. Hayot and R. Walkowitz, *A New Vocabulary for Global Modernism*. New York: Columbia University Press, pp. 29–42.

Rimbaud, Arthur (1963) *Oeuvres complètes*, eds R. de Renéville and J. Mouquet. Paris: Gallimard.

Roberts, Celia (2007) *Messengers of Sex: Hormones, Biomedicine and Feminism*. Cambridge: Cambridge University Press.

Robertson, Ritchie (2004) 'Scandinavian Modernism and the Battle of the Sexes: Kafka, Strindberg and *The Castle*', *Rutgers German Studies*, The Spring 2003 Rodig Maxwell Lecture, Occasional Papers Series, p. 1.

Rosenbaum, Heidi (1982) *Formen der Familie: Untersuchungen zum Zusammenhang von Familienverhältnissen, Sozialstruktur und sozialem Wandel in der deutschen Gesellschaft des 19. Jahrhunderts*. Frankfurt am Main: Suhrkamp.

Roussetzki, Rémy (2000) 'Theater of Anxiety in Shelley's The Cenci and Musset's Lorenzaccio', *Criticism*, 42 (1): 31–57.

Rousso, Henry (1987) *Le Syndrôme de Vichy*. Paris: Seuil.

Rousso, Henry (1998) *La Hantise du passé*. Paris: Textuel.

Rovelli, Carlo (2016) *Seven Brief Lessons on Physics*. New York: Riverhead Books.

Roy, Matthew M. (2001) *August Strindberg's Perversions: On the Science, Sin and Scandal of Homosexuality in August Strindberg's Works*. Dissertation, University of Washington.

Rubin, Gayle (1975) 'The Traffic in Women: Notes on the "Political Economy" of Sex', in R. Reiter (ed.), *Toward an Anthropology of Women*. New York: Monthly Review Press, pp. 157–210 <https://genderstudies-groupdu.files.wordpress.com/2014/08/the-rraffic-in-women.pdf> (last accessed 11 September 2019).

Rupprecht, Caroline (2006) *Subject to Delusions: Narcissism, Modernism, Gender*. Evanston: Northwestern University Press.

Russett, Cynthia Eagle (1989) *Sexual Science: The Victorian Construction of Womanhood*. Cambridge, MA: Harvard University Press.

Santner, Eric L. (1996) *My Own Private Germany: Daniel Paul Schreber's Secret History of Modernity*. Princeton: Princeton University Press.

Santner, Eric L. (2001) *On the Psychotheology of Everyday Life: Reflections on Freud and Rosenzweig*. Chicago: University of Chicago Press.

Santner, Eric L. (2006) *On Creaturely Life*. Chicago: University of Chicago Press.

Santner, Eric L. (2011) *The Royal Remains: The People's Two Bodies and the Endgames of Sovereignty*. Chicago: University of Chicago Press.

Santner, Eric (2016) *The Weight of All Flesh*. New York: Oxford University Press.

Sartre, Jean-Paul (1938) *La Nausée*. Paris: Gallimard.

Sartre, Jean-Paul (1943) *L'Etre et le néant: Essai d'ontologie phénoménologique*. Paris: Gallimard.

Sartre, Jean-Paul (1945) *Les Chemins de la liberté II: Le Sursis*. Paris: Gallimard.

Sartre, Jean-Paul (1947) *Les Mouches*, in J.-P. Sartre, *Huis clos suivi de Les Mouches*. Paris: Gallimard, pp. 95–245.

Sartre, Jean-Paul (1949a) 'Qu'est-ce qu'un collaborateur?' in *Situations III*. Paris: Gallimard, pp. 43–61.

Sartre, Jean-Paul (1949b) 'Paris sous l'Occupation', in J.-P. Sartre, *Situations III*. Paris: Gallimard, pp.15–42.

Sartre, Jean-Paul (1960a) *Critique de la raison dialectique*, tome I, Paris: Gallimard.

Sartre, Jean-Paul (1960b) *Les Séquestrés d'Altona: Pièce en cinq actes*. Paris: Gallimard.

Sartre, Jean-Paul (1964a) *Les Mots*, Paris: Gallimard; (1964) *The Words*, trans. B. Frechtman. New York: Braziller.

Sartre, Jean-Paul (1964b) *Nausea*, trans. L. Alexander. New York: New Directions.

Sartre, Jean-Paul (1968) 'The Humanism of Existentialism', *Essays in Existentialism*, ed. W. Baskin. New York: Citadel (first published in 1946 as 'Existentialism Is a Humanism').

Sartre, Jean-Paul (1970) [1946] *L'Existentialisme est un humanisme*. Paris: Nagel.

Sartre, Jean-Paul (1976a) [1948] *Anti-Semite and Jew*, trans. George J. Becker. New York: Schocken Books.

Sartre, Jean-Paul (1976b) *Sartre on Theater*, eds M. Contat and M. Rybalka, trans. F. Jellinek. New York: Pantheon.

Sartre, Jean-Paul (1976c) *Critique of Dialectical Reason*, trans. A. Sheridan-Smith, vol. 1. London: New Left Books.

Sartre, Jean-Paul (1989) *The Flies, No Exit and Three Other Plays*. New York: Vintage, pp. 1–124.

Sartre, Jean-Paul (1992) [1956] *Being and Nothingness: A Phenomenological Essay on Ontology*, trans. and intro. H. E. Barnes. New York: Washington Square Press.

Sartre, Jean-Paul (2000) 'Beyond Bourgeois Theatre', *Brecht Sourcebook*, eds C. Martin and H. Bial. London: Routledge, pp. 50–7.

Scarry, Elaine (1985) *The Body in Pain: The Making and Unmaking of the World*. New York: Oxford University Press.

Scheer, Edward (ed.) (2004) *Antonin Artaud: A Critical Reader*. London and New York: Routledge.

Scheffler, Karl (1908) *Die Frau und die Kunst*. Berlin: Verlag Julius Bard, at <https://archive.org/details/diefrauunddiekun00sche/page/n5/mode/2up> (last accessed 21 March 2020).

Schnurbein, Stefanie von (2001) *Krisen der Männlichkeit: Schreiben und Geschlechterdiskurs in skandinavischen Romanen seit 1890*, Göttingen: Wallstein.

Sedgwick, Eve Kosofsky (1985) *Between Men: English Literature and Male Homosocial Desire*. New York: Columbia University Press.

Sengoopta, Chandak (2000) *Otto Weininger: Sex, Science, and Self in Imperial Vienna*. Chicago: University of Chicago Press.

Serres, Michel (2007) *The Parasite*. Minneapolis: University of Minnesota Press.

Shaviro, Steven (2015) 'Consequences of Panpsychism', in R. Grusin (ed.), *The Nonhuman Turn*. Minneapolis: University of Minnesota Press, pp. 19–44.

Sheldon, Rebekah (2015) 'Form/Matter/Chora: Object-Oriented Ontology and Feminist New Materialism', in R. Grusin (ed.), *The Nonhuman Turn*. Minneapolis: University of Minnesota Press, pp. 193–222.

Shelley, Percy Bysshe (1909) *The Cenci*. Boston: Heath.

Simmel, Georg (1918) *Lebensanschauung: Vier metaphysische Kapitel*. Berlin: Duncker & Humblot.

Smith, Andrew (2004) *Victorian Demons: Medicine, Masculinity and the Gothic at the Fin de Siècle*. Manchester: Manchester University Press.

Smith, John H. (1989) 'Abulia: Sexuality and Diseases of the Will in the Late Nineteenth Century', *Genders*, 6: 102–24.

Smith, Matthew Wilson (2018) *The Nervous Stage: Nineteenth-Century Neuroscience and the Birth of Modern Theater*. New York: Oxford University Press.

Sokol, Walter (ed.) (1963) *Anthology of German Expressionist Drama: A Prelude to the Absurd*. Ithaca: Cornell University Press.

Solomon-Godeau, Abigail (1997) *Male Trouble: A Crisis in Representation*. New York: Thames & Hudson.

Sontag, Susan (1999) [1976] 'Introduction', in A. Artaud, *Selected Writings*, trans. H. Weaver, ed. S. Sontag. Los Angeles: University of California Press, pp. xvii–lix <https://www.worldcat.org/title/antonin-artaud-selected-writings/oclc/18134493/viewport> (last accessed 16 August 2019).

Speir, Ronald (1989) 'Baal', in S. Mews, *Critical Essays on Bertolt Brecht*. Boston: Hall, pp. 19–30.

Spengler, Oswald (1926) *The Decline of the West: Form and Actuality*, trans. C. F. Atkinson. New York: Alfred A. Knopf.

Spinoza, Benedict de (1994) *A Spinoza Reader: The Ethics and Other Works*, ed. and trans. E. M. Curley. Princeton: Princeton University Press.

Spreen, Constance (2003) 'Resisting the Plague: The French Reactionary Right and Artaud's Theatre of Cruelty', *Modern Language Quarterly*, 64 (1): 71–96.

Stanton, Domna C. (ed.) (1992) *Discourses of Sexuality: From Aristotle to AIDS*. Ann Arbor: University of Michigan Press.

Stekel, Wilhelm (1923) *Der Fetischismus. Dargestellt für Ärzte und Kriminologen*. Berlin and Vien: Urban & Schwarzenberg.

Stendhal (1926) [1831] *The Red and the Black*, trans. C. K. Scott Moncrieff. New York: Modern Library.

Stenport, Anna Westerstahl (ed.) (2012) *The International Strindberg: New Critical Essays*. Evanston: Northwestern University Press.

Stern, Daniel N. (1985) *The Interpersonal World of the Infant*. New York: Basic Books.

Stewart, Balfour (1881) *The Conservation of Energy*. New York: D. Appleton.

Strindberg, August (1955a) 'Author's Foreword', *Six Plays of Strindberg*, trans. E. Sprigge. Garden City, NY: Doubleday, pp. 61–73.

Strindberg, August (1955b) *The Father*, in A. Strindberg, *Six Plays of Strindberg*, trans. E. Sprigge. Garden City, NY: Doubleday, pp. 1–57.

Strindberg, August (1960a) *Creditors: A Tragi-Comedy*, in A. Strindberg, *Five Plays of Strindberg*, trans. Elizabeth Sprigge. Garden City, NY: Anchor, pp. 1–52.

Strindberg, August (1960b) *The Dance of Death: A Drama in Two Parts. Five Plays of Strindberg*, trans. Elizabeth Sprigge. Garden City, NY: Anchor, pp. 121–235.

Strindberg, August (1970) *Pre-Inferno Plays*, trans. and intro. Walter Johnson. New York: Norton.

Szondi, Peter (1965) *Theorie des modernen Dramas (1880–1950)*. Frankfurt am Main: Suhrkamp.

Tabbert-Jones, Gudrun (1984) *Die Funktion der liedhaften Einlage in den frühen Stücken Brechts: Baal, Trommeln in der Nacht, Im Dickicht der Städte, Eduard II. von England und Mann ist Mann*. Frankfurt am Main: Peter Lang.

Taylor, Gary (2000) *Castration: An Abbreviated History of Western Manhood*. New York and London: Routledge.

Theatre Artaud/Berlin (1986–1991) <https://www.youtube.com/watch?v=oHlQNITjt9w> (last accessed 7 July 2018).

Theweleit, Klaus (1980) *Männerphantasien*, 2 vols. Hamburg: Rowohlt.

Theweleit, Klaus (1987) *Male Fantasies, Vol. 1: Women Floods Bodies History*, trans. S. Conway, foreword by B. Ehrenreich. Minneapolis: University of Minnesota Press.

Theweleit, Klaus (1989) *Male Fantasies, Vol. 2: Male Bodies: Psychoanalyzing the White Terror*, foreword by A. Rabinbach and J. Benjamin. Minneapolis: University of Minnesota Press.

Thibault, Ghislain (2016) 'Needles and Bullets: Media Theory, Medicine, and Propaganda, 1910–1940', in K. Nixon and L. Servitje (eds), *Endemic: Essays in Contagion Theory*. London: Palgrave Macmillan, pp. 67–92.

Thomas, Downing and Steven Ungar (1999) 'Between *L'Irréparable* and *l'Irrepérable* Subject to the Past', *STCL*, 23 (1): 3–9.

Tickner, Lisa (1992), 'Men's Work? Masculinity, Anxiety, and the Male Body on the Line', *Differences*, 4 (3): 1–37.

Triumph des Willens, film, dir. Leni Riefenstahl, Reichsparteitagfilm der L.R. Studio-Film, Berlin, 1934/35.

Türk, Johannes (2011) *Die Immunität der Literatur*. Frankfurt am Main: S. Fischer.

Vanoye, Francis (2004) 'Cinemas of cruelty?' in E. Scheer (ed.), *Antonin Artaud: A Critical Reader*. London and New York: Routledge, pp. 178–83.

Vertommen, Sigrid (2016) 'Female Bodily (Re)Productivity in the Stem Cell Economy: A Cross-Materialist Feminist Approach', in V. Pitts-Taylor (ed. and intro.), *Mattering: Feminism, Science, and Materialism*. New York: New York University Press, pp. 204–23.

Virno, Paolo (2013) 'An Equivocal Concept: Biopolitics', from *A Grammar of the Multitude*, trans. Isabella Bertoletti, J. Cascaito and A. Casson, in T. Campbell and A. Sitze (eds), *Biopolitics: A Reader*. Durham, NC: Duke University Press, pp. 269–73.

Vogl, Joseph (2015) *Der Souveränitätseffekt*. Zürich: diaphanes.

Vork, Robert (2013) 'Things That No One Can Say: The Unspeakable Act in Artaud's *Les Cenci*, *Modern Drama*, 56 (3): 306–26.

Waal, Frans de (2006) *Primates and Philosophers*. Princeton: Princeton University Press.

Ward, Lester F. (1907) [1903] *Pure Sociology: A Treatise on the Origin and Spontaneous Development of Society*. New York: Macmillan.

Weininger, Otto (1980) [1903] *Geschlecht und Charakter: Eine prinzipielle Untersuchung*. München: Matthes & Seitz, 1980; *Sex and Character: An Investigation of Fundamental Principles*, trans. L. Löb, eds D. Steuer and L. Marcus. Bloomington: Indiana University Press, 2005.

Wiedmer, Caroline (1999) *The Claims of Memory: Representations of the Holocaust in Contemporary Germany and France*. Ithaca. NY: Cornell University Press.

Williams, Alex (2017) 'Prozac Nation Is Now the United States of Xanax', *New York Times*, 10 June <https://www.nytimes.com/2017/06/10/style/anxiety-is-the-new-depression-xanax.html> (last accessed 13 February 2018).

Wilson, Elizabeth A. (2008) 'Organic Empathy: Feminism, Psychopharmaceuticals, and the Embodiment of Depression', in S. Alaimo and S. Hekman (eds), *Material Feminisms*. Bloomington: Indiana University Press, pp. 373–99.

Wolfe, Cary (2003) *Animal Rites: American Culture, the Discourse of Species, and Posthumanist Theory*. Chicago: University of Chicago Press.

Wolfe, Cary (2007) 'Bring the Noise: *The Parasite* and the Multiple Genealogies of Posthumanism', intro. to M. Serres, *The Parasite*, new edn. University of Minnesota Press, pp. xi–xxviii.

Wolfe, Cary (2010) *What Is Posthumanism?* Minneapolis: University of Minnesota Press.

Wolfe, Cary (2013) *Before the Law: Humans and Other Animals in a Biopolitical Frame*. Chicago and London: University of Chicago Press.

Wolfe, Cary (2014) ' "A New Schema of Politicization": Thinking Humans, Animals, and Biopolitics with Foucault', in J. D. Faubion (ed.), *Foucault Now: Current Perspectives in Foucault Studies*. Cambridge: Polity.

Woo, Yunjin La-mei (2016) 'Infecting Humanness: A Critique of the Autonomous Self in Contagion', in K. Nixon and L. Servitje (eds), *Endemic: Essays
in Contagion Theory*. London: Palgrave Macmillan, pp. 191–218.

Wright, Elizabeth (1989) *Postmodern Brecht: A Re-Presentation*. London:
Routledge.

Yampolsky, Mikhail (2004) From 'Voice Devoured: Artaud and Borges on
Dubbing', in E. Scheer (ed.), *Antonin Artaud: A Critical Reader*. London
and New York: Routledge, pp. 169–77.

Yuran, Noam (2014) *What Money Wants: An Economy of Desire*. Stanford:
Stanford University Press.

Zaretsky, Adam (2016) 'OOPS: Object-Oriented Psychopathia Sexualis', in K.
Behar, *Object-Oriented Feminism*. Minneapolis: University of Minnesota
Press, pp. 145–80.

Žižek, Slavoj (2004a) 'From Politics to Biopolitics . . . and Back', *South
Atlantic Quarterly*, 103 (2–3): 501–21.

Žižek, Slavoj (2004b) *Organs without Bodies: On Deleuze and Consequences*.
New York: Routledge.

Žižek, Slavoj (2008) *Enjoy your Symptom! Jacques Lacan in Hollywood and
Out*. London: Routledge.

Index

EU representative:
Easy Access System Europe
Mustamäe tee 50, 10621 Tallinn, Estonia
Gpsr.requests@easproject.com

www.ingramcontent.com/pod-product-compliance
Lightning Source LLC
Chambersburg PA
CBHW080549270326
41929CB00019B/3241

9 781474 467445